Human Rights in Latin America

1964–1980

A Selective Annotated Bibliography

Compiled and Edited by the Hispanic Division

LIBRARY OF CONGRESS   WASHINGTON   1983

*This bibliography was compiled in cooperation with the
Latin American Studies Association and
under the auspices of the Ford Foundation
and the Organization of American States.*

Library of Congress Cataloging in Publication Data

Main entry under title:

Human rights in Latin America, 1964–1980.

    Includes index.
    Supt. of Docs. no.: LC 1.12/2:L 34/2/964–80
    1. Civil rights—Latin America—Bibliography.
2. Political rights—Latin America—Bibliography.
I. Library of Congress. Hispanic Division.
Z7164.L6H85   1983   [JC599.L3]   016.3234′098   82–600339
ISBN 0-8444-0415-2

For sale by the Superintendent of Documents, U.S. Government Printing Office, Washington, D.C. 20402

Contents

Preface

It was concern over violations of human rights that led the first colonists to people the territory known today as the United States of America. From the same concern came much of the impetus for the American Revolution, the guarantees set forth in the Constitution of the new nation, and the Bill of Rights. Thus, a concern for "human rights" is no new issue; it has been with us since before the emergence of the Republic. The fact that, in recent years, human rights have become a more conscious component of foreign policy only underscores the way that they permeate and have permeated our civilization. Human rights have not been and cannot be either a single party or a bipartisan issue; they are an issue built into the very marrow of the American experience.

The bibliography that we present here is, as all bibliographies must be, a selective one. The time period it covers is short— from approximately 1964 to 1980—and the countries covered are those of only one part of one hemisphere. The format of materials included is that deriving only from books, significant pamphlets, and journals; newspaper articles, because of their unwieldy character and large numbers, have been excluded purposely. Yet, even with these limitations, we believe that the bibliography provides convincing testimony of real concern emerging at many levels over the need for greater recognition and protection of human rights throughout Latin America. The questions raised in the testimony go beyond the discrete political events of one country or another; they are questions that can plague any complex society.

Rather than create the items to which it refers, a bibliography merely reflects them. Many of the items in this compilation are polemical in character and popular rather than scholarly in approach. Far more are critical of rightist than leftist regimes. Yet, these are simply characteristics of recent human rights literature. Most of this literature is produced to appeal to the layman rather than the scholar and could be classified, generally, as a literature of protest and opposition. Since most Latin American countries are governed by regimes of the political right, much of the literature has, therefore, a leftist cast. Those countries with strict control over all published work tend to be represented by fewer items than those with less control, as attested by the plethora of internally produced items for Chile and Brazil and the relative absence of such items for Cuba and Uruguay.

Many individuals were involved in the production of this work. Most compilation was done by representatives or part-time employees of the Latin American Studies Association, and most editing by staff associated with the Library of Congress. Patricia Weiss Fagen was the person who first conceived of the project and who obtained initial financing for the Latin American Studies Association from the Ford Foundation. Fabiola Letelier, María Elena Arana, María Emma McMurtry, Virginia Russ, and Patricia Weiss Fagen compiled the bulk of the original entries. Fabiola Letelier and Georgette Magassy Dorn then arranged for a supplementary grant to the Latin American Studies Association from the Organization of American States. Georgette Magassy Dorn, Constance Crowder Carter, Anne L. Ross, and William E. Carter edited the entries and the annotations, and María Emma McMurtry, Inge Harman, and Anne L. Ross copy edited the entire manuscript. Thus the bibliography is the product of many hours of dedicated labor on the part of ten persons.

Special thanks are due to Michael Seyfrit for steering this publication through the computer printing stage. Without his assistance this project would have been delayed greatly.

In publishing this work, the Hispanic Divison of the Library of Congress neither endorses nor condemns any of the multiple views set forth in the publications. It does implicitly recognize, however, that the issue of human rights is, and will remain for the indefinite future, a major one for Latin America. To understand that part of our hemisphere without reference to the question of human rights is to understand it only partially. Views such as those expressed in much of this literature are not only part of intellectual discourse in Latin America today; they are at the core of such discourse. The rhetoric with which they are presented may and will change from year to year. The ferment they reflect, however, will probably be with us for many decades to come. It is in the interest of helping us understand that ferment that we present this work.

William E. Carter
Chief
Hispanic Division

Introduction

Since the late 1960s attention to human rights problems in Latin America has grown measurably as an increasing number of authoritarian governments have restricted or entirely closed the political, legal, and social institutions which normally advocate individual and collective citizens' rights. This in turn, has led to the growth and creation of numerous national and international bodies dedicated to protecting basic rights and to a renewed interest in publications related to human rights.

An earlier florescence of writing about human rights occurred in the post-World War II period. Then, a number of important institutions either turned to, or were established to address, the issue of human rights. Thus, the Charter of the United Nations referred specifically to human rights. Following the charter's adoption, that organization approved and attempted to implement a series of human rights guarantees. The documents legitimizing these efforts represented a synthesis of very divergent ideological assumptions and priorities among the many members making up the United Nations. Thus, the first years of attempted implementation were marred by recurring debates about such matters as individual versus collective rights, political liberties versus economic needs, and national sovereignty versus international responsibility.

Until the late 1960s writing about human rights in the Western Hemisphere largely reflected a Western liberal perspective and was concerned with assessments of the constitutional protections and legal procedures for protecting rights. Most was couched in legal terms and written primarily for lawyers. There was, to be sure, a substantial body of literature about social justice, ethics, authoritarian rule, and popular struggles for greater equality and political power. However, these issues were not considered to be within the purview of "human rights" until the 1970s.

Many of the bibliographic references in this volume have been drawn from international law, theology, political theory, philosophy, economics, political science, history, and literature. More numerous than the contributions from such academic disciplines, however, are the documents and descriptions of human rights violations and the accounts of active daily struggles to promote human rights under repressive conditions. This bibliography is not comprehensive in the areas of international jurisprudence or philosophy as related to human rights, even though it does contain basic works of this nature that are believed to have contributed to U.S. and Latin American conceptualizations. In addition, since Latin American nations are members of the United Nations, and since many have ratified the basic rights covenants, the bibliography also contains works that define the operation of the United Nations human rights mechanisms.

With regard to general works, this bibliography is necessarily selective rather than comprehensive, since our main efforts have gone into gathering references that bear directly on the situation facing Latin America today. However, when general works dealing with the theory or philosophy of human rights have been produced by Latin Americans or have depended heavily on Latin American examples, we have included them.

With the exception of general legal and philosophical works, few of the entries in this bibliography are the product of "disinterested scholarship." Many are first-hand descriptions of torture and mistreatment which are intended to win support and mobilize opposition, or at least to move readers to concern and action.

In addition to this type of writing, there are many reports issued by national and international human rights organizations and government agencies to inform officials and influence government policies and international resolutions. Other entries represent the efforts of private ad hoc groups to influence national and international political decisions.

Although drawn from every country and all sectors of society, the numbers of references in this bibliography do not correlate with the numbers of human rights violations to be found in any given country or social sector. In the first place, like any body of literature, reports of issues and human rights violations are biased in favor of populations that can read and write. In the second place, in some countries basic rights are so massively ignored or violated that it is difficult for those within the country even to report the violations. Where this situation is severe, where institutions such as schools, trade unions, churches, and professional associations have been purged and subjected to constant government vigilance, it is difficult for human rights organizations to function openly or independently of the government, and risky for human rights advocates to publish material relating their concerns.

Indeed, if one were to plot a country-by-country count of titles on or about human rights and/or political comment or criticism couched in the language of universal human rights, one would discover that domestic writings related to human rights are most likely to be found in a climate of political control that limits but does not altogether silence criticism. An example of such a climate would be a country where, in spite of rather tight government restrictions and repeated abuses, institutional umbrellas remain that can protect human rights activities: a church opposed to government practices, strongly rooted in the community, and supported in its opposition by the hierarchy; a press sufficiently independent to be able to report information that the government would prefer not be made public and offer a forum for some opponents of the government; and professional associations and academic and intellectual centers that are financially solvent and not directly controlled by military or government officials.

In view of the diversity of material directly and indirectly advocating, promoting, describing, or condemning one or another human rights position or issue, it is difficult for bibliographers to arrive at consistent guidelines for works to be included or excluded. Except for excluding newspaper articles and manifestos, the compilers of this volume decided to avoid imposing rigid inclusion-exclusion criteria. First, we assumed that virtually all the written material emanating from groups and organizations whose sole or principal concern was human rights was, by definition, within scope. Second, we sought descriptions, debates, and discussions regarding the presence or absence of "rights" in Latin America. Third, we included accounts and analyses of forms of repression—judicial, political, economic, social, and cultural —affecting a whole people or some segment of society, reports of the forms of resistance and opposition adopted by individuals and groups demanding specific rights, and calls for commitment, concern, and involvement of people on behalf of human rights both broadly and narrowly defined.

A major portion of entries concerning these topics are the published reports from four international organizations—two intergovernmental: the United Nations Human Rights Commission and the Inter-American Commission on Human Rights; and two private: Amnesty International and the International Commission of Jurists. A smaller number come from the International League for Human Rights and from European- or Latin American-based private human rights groups. One or more of these entities has sent fact-finding missions to almost every Latin American country. The United Nations investigations and reports are the broadest in scope, covering the whole range of rights in the two covenants. The reports of the Inter-American Commission on Human Rights are more limited in scope and cover mainly political rights, violations of the rights of the person, and judicial and political abuses. Amnesty International's focus on political prisoners has led it to concentrate on torture, cruel and degrading punishment, "disappeared" persons, executions, politically motivated arrests, and denials of rights occurring as a result of states of siege and emergency and military and paramilitary oppression. Amnesty also provides general country analyses concerning the plight of groups that are vulnerable to persecution from government authorities. The International Commission of Jurists concentrates its reporting on the deterioration of constitutional guarantees and legal protections, the uses and abuses of states of siege, and the legitimacy of and justification for government decrees limiting the normal range of rights. Both Amnesty International and the International Commission of Jurists are especially concerned with the conduct of political trials, and with sentencing procedures.

The United States government has also contributed a large number of reports and evaluations regarding human rights in Latin America. Congressional hearings, especially those of the Subcommittee on International Organizations of the House International Relations Committee, are among the richest sources of human rights material. These combine expert testimony from Latin Americans and concerned North American country specialists with expositions of State Department positions regarding specific human rights allegations.

One of the largest bodies of literature in this bibliography comes from Catholic and Protestant Church-supported programs and centers inside and outside Latin America. Church-supported publications provide information similar to that of Amnesty International and other private human rights groups on matters such as torture, the absence of habeas corpus procedures, and disappeared prisoners.

Among the nonreligious groups and organizations located outside given countries but writing about human rights issues inside those countries, there are four separate but overlapping categories. First, there are several independent research centers, the publications of which cover a broad range of poltical issues, including human rights, particularly human rights and foreign policy. Second, there are hundreds of "solidarity groups" that produce newsletters and reports intended to raise public awareness about situations in particular nations. Third, there is a large body of writing from exile groups, who often represent a formal political party or political orientation in their home countries. Fourth, human rights themes account for an increasingly large portion of publications emanating from university departments with a Latin American focus, as well as from scholarly and political centers concerned with Latin America. Fifth, certain professional organizations with strong collateral ties to Latin America document human rights violations which affect their professional counterparts. All five of these types of associations and activities may be found in several European countries and in those few Latin American countries not under military rule.

Probably the most interesting and historically significant references in this bibliography come from Latin America itself, and are written by those living under military rule. In form as well as content, they provide a window on the political realities in the Southern Hemisphere and a barometer of changing conditions.

Lawyers and lawyers' associations are particularly important for human rights activities. Throughout Latin America, some lawyers have been working within the framework of broadly gauged human rights organizations, more often than not with a religious affiliation. The consequent merging of legal concerns for political rights and constitutional guarantees with theological concerns for social justice and community action gives human rights writing in Latin America its special cast. Reports and analyses from human rights groups in Latin America often combine both of these perspectives.

In the United States the theme of human rights has attained stature and permanence both as an area of intellectual inquiry and as a moral imperative in human relations. This will probably continue for many years to come, and the moral, legal, philosophical, and political components of the theme will be debated and analyzed time and again, and from constantly changing points of view.

The bibliography presented here is far from complete; purposeful exclusions have been made, some important items have undoubtedly escaped our survey, and relevant material continues to appear daily. In spite of such shortcomings, we believe that the varied and extensive coverage presented here will be of long-standing use to all those interested in basic human rights issues, as well as to all who wish to understand the dynamics of Latin America in the latter part of the twentieth century.

Patricia Weiss Fagen
San Jose State University
San Jose, California

Human Rights—General

1

Abranches, Dunshee C. A. de. *Proteção internacional dos direitos humanos.* Rio de Janeiro, Livraria Freitas Bastos, 1964. *159 p.*

Studies the concepts of rights and obligations which appear in U.N. and O.A.S. human rights declarations.

2

Agudelo Ramírez, Luis E. *Derechos humanos; información básica.* Bogotá, Asociación Colombiana Pro Derechos Humanos, 1978. *[16] p.*

Pamphlet by the director of the Colombian Association for Human Rights, outlining international and regional human rights organizations for the general public.

3

Agudelo Ramírez, Luis E. *Derechos humanos, revolución inconclusa.* Bogotá, Asociación Colombiana Pro Derechos Humanos, 1979. *152 p.*

Compares European, Mexican, and Soviet declarations and constitutions, as well as human rights resolutions by the U.N. and by regional groups. Discusses Third World participation in human rights advocacy. Notes increasing awareness of human rights violations in Latin America.

4

Alcalá-Zamora y Castillo, Niceto. *Estudios procesales.* Madrid, Editorial Tecnos [1975]. *779 p. (Biblioteca Tecnos de estudios jurídicos)*

Presents a general plan to standardize Hispanic-American and European arbitration procedures for settling international grievances. Contains brief but useful references to cooperative efforts among Latin American countries to establish uniform procedures for human rights cases.

5

Alzamora Valdés, Mario. *Los derechos humanos y su protección.* Lima, JUS, 1977. *267 p.*

Not available for annotation.

6

American Center of PEN. *PEN freedom to write: global report.* New York, American Center of PEN, 1977. *1 v.*

Lists 606 cases of repression in 55 countries, focusing on writers, editors, and journalists. Periodic revisions of the report will be published.

7

American Society of International Law. *Proceedings of the American Society of International Law at its meeting; 70th.* Washington, 1976. *228 p.*

Topics treated include the development and enforcement of guidelines for multinational enterprise, refugees, population, and the frontiers of international law.

8

Arzobispado de Santiago, Chile. Vicaría de la Solidaridad. *Derechos humanos; declaraciones, pactos y convenios internacionales.* Santiago, 1978. *150 p. (Estudios, no. 2)*

A selection of international human rights documents, including the text of historical documents such as the Magna Carta and the first amendments of the U.S. Constitution, United Nations documents and those of other international organizations.

9

Arzobispado de Santiago, Chile. Vicaría de la Solidaridad. *Simposio internacional, la iglesia catedral recibe al mundo. Solidaridad, nov. 1978: 1-12.*

Papers presented at a symposium devoted to the discussion of human rights in contemporary society. Participants included Chileans holding differing ideological views.

10

Arzobispado de Santiago, Chile. Vicaría de la Solidaridad, Comité Patrocinador en el Año de los Derechos Humanos, eds. *Todo hombre tiene derecho a ser persona; concursos: afiches, literarios, pintura infantil.* Santiago, 1978. *172 p.*

Defends man's rights to direct his own life through such diverse media as the short story, poetry, essays, posters, and children's drawings.

11

Assembly for Human Rights. *Montreal statement of the Assembly for Human Rights: March 22-27, 1968. New York [1968?]* *17 p.*

Group of private individuals expresses concern about worldwide human rights in 1968, the year proclaimed by the U.N. as the International Year for Human Rights. Examines discrimination, apartheid, slavery, refugees, civil and political rights, and economic and social rights.

12

Association Internationale de Droit Penal. *United Nations resolutions relating to torture. Revue internationale de droit penal, no. 3 and 4, 1977, Appendix B: 212-243.*

Examines legal aspects of efforts to end torture. Details the effects of torture on victims and cites relevant international law.

13

Azuara Pérez, Leandro. *Fundamentación filosófica de las garantías individuales. Universidad Autónoma de México. Revista de la Facultad de Derecho, v. 27, jul./dic. 1977: 465-498.*

Philosophical analysis of human rights based on the writings of Rousseau, Hobbes, Locke, Spencer and Popper, pointing out their relevance to contemporary societies.

14

Barbagelata, Aníbal Luis. *Derechos fundamentales. Montevideo, Fundación de Cultura Universitaria, 1973. 164 p.*

Not available for annotation.

15

Barnet, Richard J. *No room in the lifeboats. Washington, World Peacemakers [1978?] 10 p. (World peace paper, no. 3)*

Discusses the adverse effects of scarcity of resources on democratic values. By way of remedy, suggests that such values be reaffirmed.

16

Baxter, R. R. *Humanitarian law or humanitarian politics? The 1974 Diplomatic Conference on Humanitarian Law. Harvard international law journal, v. 16, winter 1975: 1-26.*

Suggests the subordination of national to international interests in order to achieve agreements on human rights, because unity of purpose is necessary for enforcement.

17

Berger, Peter L. *Are human rights universal? Commentary, v. 64, Sept. 1977: 60-63.*

Examines the possibility of formulating universal standards of basic human rights.

18

Bianchi Gundián, Manuel. *La paz y los derechos humanos. Santiago, Editorial Andrés Bello, 1969. 92 p.*

Contains a general discussion of human rights.

19

Bilder, Richard B. *Commentary: rethinking international human rights; some basic questions. Wisconsin law review, no. 1, 1969: 171-217.*

Assesses human rights accomplishments over a twenty-five year period. Accompanied by a discussion of the definition, scope, and causes of human rights violations.

20

Boren, Theo C. van. *Partners in the promotion of human rights. Netherlands international law review, v. 24, special issue, 1977: 55-71.*

Argues that international human rights law, rather than being pre-eminently the domain of government, is the collective responsibility of all organs of society, and especially of individuals and non-governmental organizations.

21

Bosseiyt, Marc. *La distinction juridique entre les droit civils et politiques et les droits économiques, sociaux et culturels. Revue des droits de l'homme, v. 8, no. 4, 1975: 783-820.*

Analyzes distinctions between basic civil and political rights and economic, social, and cultural rights.

22

Britto Mello Boson, Gerson de. Internacionalização dos direitos do homen. *São Paulo, Brazil, Sugestões Lírias, 1972. 134 p.*

Analyzes human rights agreements, enforcement efforts, and the questions of international legal and governmental responsibilities.

23

Buergenthal, Thomas. *Human rights, international law, and the Helsinki Accord. Montclair, N.J., Universe Books, 1977. 203 p.*

General discussion of the human rights issue within the context of the Helsinki Accord.

24

Camargo, Pedro Pablo. *Problemática mundial de los derechos humanos. Bogota, Universidad La Gran Colombia, 1974. 376 p. (Fondo Rotatorio de la Gran Colombia, Serie A, no. 4)*

Comprehensive review of individual rights according to national and international law. Analyzes past and present constitutions in diverse political systems, including those of socialist countries. The study provides a comparative framework for the evaluation of U.N. and regional organizations' protection of human rights. Includes bibliographies.

25

Candelas, Jacinto. *Los derechos humanos. Madrid, Editorial Ayuso, 1976. 113 p.*

Considers the role of Christian practices within the context of the human rights movement, labor conditions, and human rights in the Third World. Also includes the Universal Declaration of Human Rights.

26

Carbonell de Masy, Rafael. *Protección nacional y protección internacional de los derechos humanos. Acción, (Asuncion), v. 33, junio 1977: 6-8.*

Discusses national and international human rights protection as defined in the Universal Declaration of Human Rights. Sets forth duties for governmental and other organizations.

27

Carrillo Salcedo, Juan Antonio. *El derecho al desarrollo como derecho de la persona humana. Revista española de derecho internacional, v. 25, no. 1-4, 1972: 119-125.*

Asserts that socio-economic development is a basic human right.

28

Castillo Velasco, Jaime. *El derecho a vivir en la patria. Arzobispado de Santiago. Vicaría de la Solidaridad. Cuaderno jurídico, no. 4, nov. 1977: 91-119.*

Examines the right of individuals to live in their own country and enjoy basic liberties.

29

Castro, Juventino V. *Lecciones de garantías y amparo. Mexico, Editorial Porrúa, 1974. 595 p.*

Defines and analyzes constitutional provisions concerning human rights in international law. Includes bibliography.

30

Christol, Carl Quimby. *Law and human rights. Geneva, World Peace Through Law Center [1968]. 30 p. ([World Peace Through Law Center] Pamphlet series, no. 11)*

Prepared for World Law Day - Human Rights, September 16, 1968. Includes bibliography.

31

Chukunta, N. K. Onuoha. *Human rights and the brain drain. International migration, v. 15, no. 4, 1977: 281-287.*

Points to the contradiction expressed by members of international human rights groups when they condemn the brain drain but also uphold the right to emigrate as an international human right.

32

Claude, Richard P. *Reliable information: the threshold problem for human rights research. Human rights, v. 6, winter 1977: 169-187.*

Examines the study of human rights and finds that it is largely an unexplored field. Contains a bibliography organized by country.

33

Claude, Richard P. *The western tradition of human rights in comparative perspective. Comparative juridical review, v. 14, 1977: 3-66.*

Attempt is made to apply sociological and legal methods to the study of human rights in liberal democracies.

34

Comisión Evangélica Latinoamericana de Educación Cristiana. *El Derecho a una vida digna. Derechos humanos, agosto 1978: 1-36. (Serie cuadernos, no. 2)*

A discussion of fundamental human, economic, social and political rights, and the struggle to preserve these rights.

35

Comisión Evangélica Latinoamericana de Educación Cristiana. *Evangelio y derechos humanos. Lima, CELADEC, Centro de Documentación y Editorial, 1978. 19 p. (Serie G, no. 6)*

Discussion of the universality of human rights.

36

Conference on Strategies for Strengthening the Implementation of Human Rights, Bellagio, Italy, 1979. *Report of the Conference on Strategies for Strengthening the Implementation of Human Rights: the role of the national and international NGO's. [New York] International League for Human Rights, Federation Internationale des Droits de l'Homme, 1979. 1 v. (various pagings)*

Report of a conference, the goals of which were the development of strategies for joint action by domestic and international human rights institutions and the establishment of domestic human rights networks. Discusses the need for a systematic gathering of information and for improved cooperation among non-governmental organizations. Provides recommendations for action.

37

Corporación Integral para el Desarrollo Cultural y Social (CODECAL). *Los derechos humanos, ¡ como hacerlos realidad! Bogota, CODECAL, 1979. 146 p.*

List of basic human rights of individuals and organizations. Includes suggestions about their protection.

38

Corporación Integral para el Desarrollo Cultural y Social (CODECAL). *Los derechos humanos; elementos para una reflexión. Bogota, Colombia, 1979. 189 p.*

Contains the principal works presented at the first Colombian Symposium on Human Rights, held under the auspices of UNESCO in November of 1976.

39

Corporación Integral para el Desarrollo Cultural y Social. *Derechos humanos, material de reflexión cristiana ecuménica. Bogota, Colombia, Gráficas Gramcolor, 1979. 150 p.*

Contains articles presented at a symposium on human rights sponsored by UNESCO in Bogotá in 1976. The papers deal with the increasing involvement of church groups with questions relating to human rights. The publication of this volume was supported by the Inter-American Foundation.

40

Corzo Sinobas, José María. *Declaraciones de carácter internacional sobre "derechos humanos" en el siglo XX. Caceres, Spain, 1975. 88 p.*

A compilation of human rights texts including the International, U.S., and Universal Declarations of Human Rights, as well as policy statements of the Catholic Church.

41

Cranston, Maurice William. *Human rights today.* London, Ampersand Books, 1962. 126 p.

Brief introduction to the philosophic underpinnings of human rights declarations and to the problems of their enforcement.

42

Cranston, Maurice William. *What are human rights?* New York, Taplinger Co., 1973. 170 p.

A volume of political philosophy about the importance and the nature of the Universal Declaration of Human Rights. Discusses the difference between universal rights and rights codified in laws of nations.

43

Cuadra Moreno, Héctor. *La proyección internacional de los derechos humanos. Mexico, UNAM, Instituto de Investigaciones Jurídicas, 1970. 308 p. (Serie B)*

Discusses human rights and related problems such as racial discrimination. Includes relevant U.N. and O.A.S. judicial international instruments.

44

Da Fonseca, Glenda. *How to file complaints of human rights violations; a practical guide to inter-governmental procedures. Geneva, World Council of Churches, 1975. 152 p.*

Guide to filing human rights complaints in international organizations. Includes proper procedures for the U.N., the International Labor Organization, and the European and Inter-American Commissions on Human Rights.

45

Derechos humanos; declaraciones, pactos y convenios internacionales. *Santiago de Chile, Arzobispado de Santiago, Vicaría de la Solidaridad, 1978. 150 p. (Estudios, 1978)*

The second of two issues on human rights containing the major human rights documents from international and regional associations of nations from the Middle Ages to the present. Includes a section (III) on the Americas.

46

Los derechos humanos: declaraciones y convenios internacionales. *Con un estudio preliminar de Antonio Truyol. Nueva ed. Madrid, Editorial Tecnos, 1977. 187 p.*

A compendium of human rights declarations and international conventions. Truyol's epilogue is entitled: "Los derechos humanos, diez años después."

47

Derechos humanos y derechos de los estados. *Tegucigalpa, Consejo Asesor de la Jefatura de Estado, 1977. 38 p.*

Includes the Universal Declaration of Human Rights, the American Convention on Human Rights, the Declaration of the Rights of the Child, and the Charter on the Economic Duties and Rights of the States.

48

Dinstein, Yoram. *Collective human rights of peoples and minorities. International comparative law quarterly, v. 25, Jan. 1976: 102-120.*

Treatment of collective human rights as outlined in international law. Discusses the right to physical preservation, the right to self-determination, and the right to utilize natural resources.

49

Direito, Carlos Alberto Menezes. *O estado moderno e a proteção dos direitos do homem. Rio de Janeiro, Livraria Freitas Bastos, 1968. 245 p.*

This textbook traces the theories of the rights of man and the development of the modern state in the context of international and regional pacts protecting those rights.

50

Direitos humanos. *Rio de Janeiro, Tempo e Presença Editora, 1976. 40 p. (CEI suplemento, 15)*

Highlights the theological and biblical bases for the human rights struggle.

51

Dolan, Jo Ann, and Maria Laetitia van den Assum. *Torture and the 5th U.N. Congress on crime prevention. International Commission of Jurists. Review, no. 14, June 1975: 55-64.*

Analysis of torture and law enforcement agencies throughout the world. Includes reactions by Amnesty International and the U.N. Sub-Committee on Prevention of Discrimination and Protection of Minorities.

52

Domínguez, Jorge, Richard Falk, Nigel Rodley, and Ben Whitaker. *Human rights and international relations. New York, McGraw-Hill, 1977. 160 p.*

Discusses the concept of human rights in the international context. Includes incisive articles on world order and the rights of minority groups.

53

Les droits de l'homme en Amérique Latine: human rights in Latin America. *World Council of Churches. Commission of the churches on international affairs public statements newsletter, no. 1, 1976: 18-19.*

Trilingual (French, English and German) issue containing position statements of the World Council of Churches.

54

Eide, Asbjørn. *Human rights in the world society: the commitments, the reality, the future. Pine Plains, N.Y., Earl M. Coleman, 1980. 300 p.*

Overview of the human rights system, differentiating between the real and the ideal. Includes analysis of the strengths and weaknesses of institutions that defend human rights and of efforts on the part of individual states to incorporate human rights into foreign policy.

55

Emerson, Rupert. *The fate of human rights in the Third World. World politics, v. 27, Jan. 1975: 201-226.*

Suggests that the basic human rights issue is not of imposing alien values or setting up standards by which others should be judged, but of attempting to discern how the Third World perceives the dignity of man.

56

Fagen, Patricia Weiss. *The links between human rights and basic needs. Background (Center for International Policy), spring 1978: 1-11.*

Review of the current debate on human rights and discussion of the role the U.S. and international development and funding institutions should play. Questions giving aid to repressive regimes.

57

Falk, Richard. *Militarization and human rights in the Third World. Bulletin of peace proposals (Oslo), v. 8, no. 3, 1977: 220-232. (Special issue: Human Rights)*

Examines "escalating repression in the capitalist portion of the Third World" with emphasis on socio-economic factors. Author claims that the Third World is being fundamentally shaped by a crisis in capital formation that pervades all but the richest countries.

58

Ferrari, Leo C. *Human rights in a changing world; the problem of preserving human values in the upheavals caused by science and technology. Fredericton, New Brunswick, Canada, Department of Labour, New Brunswick Human Rights Commission, 1975. 112 p.*

Explores the need to redefine human rights to reflect changes in basic values.

59

Finn, James. *A friendly disagreement about human rights. Worldview, v. 20, July-Aug. 1977: 4-8.*

Debate on the need for restraint or risk in the pursuit of human rights.

60

Forsythe, David P. *The 1974 Diplomatic Conference on Humanitarian Law: some observations. American journal of international law, v. 69, Jan. 1975: 77-91.*

Analyzes the central issues of the 1974 Diplomatic Conference on the Reaffirmation and Development of International Humanitarian Law.

61

Forsythe, David P. *Political prisoners: the law and politics of protection. Vanderbilt journal of transnational law, v. 9, spring 1976: 295-322.*

Questions the adequacy of international legal procedures with regard to the handling of political prisoners.

62

Forum sobre derechos humanos. *El Foro, v. 53, no. 3, 1966: 7-20.*

General discussion of human rights and listing of standards protecting such rights.

63

Foundation for Legal Aid in Chile. *The protection of human rights and the impact of emergency situations under international law; the Chilean case. [n.p.] Foundation for Legal Aid in Chile [1975?]*

Explores the relationship between declared states of emergency and the violation of human rights.

64

Fraenkel, Jack R., ed. *The struggle for human rights; a question of values. New York, Random House, 1975. 71 p.*

Examines the effectiveness of the Universal Declaration of Human Rights.

65

Franco Filho, Georgenor de Sousa. *A proteção internacional aos direitos humanos; pequenas observações, Belem, Brazil, 1975. 79 p.*

Brief review of theory and legal instruments for protecting human rights. A chapter is devoted to human rights in Brazil and the special constitutional guarantees available for the protection of basic rights.

66

Frowein, Jochen A. *The guarantees afforded by the institutional machinery of the Convention [on Human Rights].* In International Colloquy about the European Convention on Human Rights, 3d, Brussels, 1970. *Privacy and human rights; reports and communications presented at the third international colloquy about the European Convention on Human Rights, organized by the Belgian Universities and the Council of Europe, with the support of the Belgian government, Brussels, 30 September-3 October 1970. Edited by A.H. Robertson. Manchester, Great Britain, Manchester University Press [1973] p. 284-304.*

Discusses legal protection of the individual as defined by the convention.

67

Fruchterman, Richard L. *Asylum: theory and practice.* U.S. Judge Advocate's General Department (Navy). *JAG journal, v. 26, spring 1972: 169-180.*

Defines commonly misunderstood types of asylum and refuge, pointing out U.S. pronouncements and practice.

68

Galey, Margaret E. *New aspects of the international protection of human rights. Muscatine, Iowa, Stanley Foundation, 1977. 40 p.*

At head of title: Twenty-fifth report of the Commission to Study the Organization of Peace.

Contains 72 recommendations concerning the implementation of human rights at the international level. Among the rights discussed are religious freedom, freedom from torture, and freedom from terrorism.

69

García Bauer, Carlos. *Teoría de los derechos humanos. Revista de la asociación Guatemalteca de derecho internacional, v. 2, no. 1, 1971: 7-34.*

Suggests that a systematization and intensification in the juridical study of human rights will result in a greater respect for those rights.

70

García Ramírez, Sergio. *Los derechos humanos y el derecho penal. Mexico, Secretaría de Educación Pública, 1976. 205 p. (Sepsetentas, 254)*

Historical analysis of the human rights provisions in international law. Includes bibliographic references.

71

García-Velutini, Oscar. *Sobre derechos personales y la dignidad humana. Caracas, Editorial Sucre, 1980. 200 p.*

Discusses abortion as a violation of the basic rights of those unborn. The author is a Venezuelan legal scholar.

72

Garibaldi, Oscar M. *General limitations on human rights: the principle of legality. Harvard international law journal, v. 17, summer 1976: 503-557.*

Focuses on references to national law in the Universal Declaration and Human Rights Covenants that permit limitations on human rights.

73

Garretón, Manuel Antonio. *En torno a la problemática actual de los derechos humanos; derechos humanos y crisis social. Derechos humanos; estudios. Santiago, Arzobispado de Santiago, Vicaría de la Solidaridad, v. 1, mayo 1978: 11-20.*

Succinct analysis of the concept of the protection of human rights and the value of that concept for society. Focuses on human rights as a system of values acquired during a historical period.

74

Gastil, Raymond D. *The comparative survey of freedom. Freedom at issue, v. 7, Jan./Feb. 1977: 5-17.*

Country by country survey of the status of civil and political freedom in the world. Includes map.

75

Gotesky, Rubin, and Ervin Laszlo, eds. *Human dignity; this century and the next: and interdisciplinary inquiry into human rights, technology, war, and the ideal society. New York, Gordon and Breach, Science Publishers, 1970. 380 p. (Current topics of contemporary thought, v. 5)*

Useful collection of papers by philosophy professors. Presents theses on the universal definition of human rights and on the relationship of human rights to technology and war.

76

Gramatica, Filippo. *L'aspetto penale del diritto internazionale umanitario. I diritto dell'uomo como base del diritto internazionale umanitario. Les droits de l'homme, base du droit international humanitaire. Human rights as the basis of international humanitarian law. Atti...Actes...Proceedings... Luzano, Bellinzona, Grassi, 1971: 223-231. (Proceedings of International Conference on Humanitarian Law, San Remo, Italy, 1970)*

Discusses human rights as correlates of international humanitarian law.

77

Grisez, Germain G. *The right to be educated; philosophical reflections. In Drinan, Robert, ed. The right to be educated. Washington, Corpus Books, 1968. p. 52-74.*

Relates the right to education to the right to religious freedom. Argues for a pure merit system of educational opportunity.

78

Gross, Leo. *International law aspects of the freedom of information and the right to communicate. In Philip C. Horton, ed. The Third World and press freedom. New York, Praeger, 1978. 253 p. (Praeger special studies)*

Advocates an international bill of rights that will include the right to obtain information.

79

Haas, Ernst B. *Human rights and international action: the case of freedom of association. Stanford, Calif., Stanford University Press, 1970. 184 p. illus.*

Case study of the International Labor Organization from 1950 to 1968, focusing on the role of this organization in the protection of human rights and in international integration.

80

Haksar, Urmila. *Minority protection and International bill of human rights. Bombay, India, Allied Publishers, 1974. 181 p.*

Argues that minority status derives from lack of dominance rather than from lack of numbers.

Discusses changes in minority protection since adoption of the Universal Declaration of Human Rights.

81

Herrera, Felipe. *L'ordre social international et les droits de l'homme. International Commission of Jurists. Journal, v. 9, no. 1, June 1968: 16-21.*

Argues that the Universal Declaration of Human Rights deals with economic, social, and cultural as well as with civil and political rights, and makes an appeal for greater compliance.

82

Herrera Gutiérrez, José Celestino. *La protección internacional de los derechos del hombre; filosofía y realizaciones. Mexico, Universidad Nacional Autónoma de México, Facultad de Derecho, 1965. 147 p.*

Thesis on the antecedents to the Universal Declaration of Human Rights and on its principal consequences in the area of international public rights. Includes an overview of the San Francisco Charter, the external history of the Universal Declaration of Human Rights, and repercussions of that Declaration.

83

Hervada Xiberta, Francisco Javier, and José M. Zumaquero. *Textos internacionales de derechos humanos. Pamplona, Spain, Ediciones Universidad de Navarra, 1978. 1012 p.*

Extensive annotated survey of juridical texts pertaining to human rights; international in coverage and including both historical and contemporary documents.

84

Holmes, John W. *Everything has its season--and that adds to complexity: morality, realism, and foreign affairs. International perspectives, Sept./Oct. 1977: 20-25.*

Argues that morality and foreign policy are matters that have no permanent solution but must be reassessed constantly.

85

Hübner Gallo, Jorge Iván. *Panorama de los derechos humanos. [Santiago de Chile] Editorial Andrés Bello [1973] 271 p.*

History of human rights and organizations protecting them. Includes basic human rights documents and a chapter on Marxism and human rights.

86

Human rights. *Oslo, Universitetsforlaget, 1977. 288 p. illus., maps. (Bulletin of peace proposals, v. 8, no. 3, 1977)*

Special issue by the International Peace Research Institute that gathers together articles on the United Nations, militarization, economic development, education and the Third World and suggests topics for future research.

87

[Human rights]. *Texas international law journal, v. 12, spring/summer 1977: 129-330.*

Collection of articles by prominent authorities on legal aspects of human rights charters, organizations, and implementation.

88

Human rights organizations and periodicals directory. *Berkeley, Calif., Meiklejohn Civil Liberties Institute, 1975. 97 p.*

Revised version of 1973 edition with over 175 new entries. Lists organizations and periodicals dedicated to the expression and protection of human rights, emphasizing those that provide information or assistance on legal questions and/or engage in litigation.

89

The human rights to individual freedom. *A symposium on World Habeas Corpus. Edited by Luis Kutner, foreword by Arthur J. Goldberg. Coral Gables, Fla., University of Miami Press, 1970. 249 p.*

Good general introduction to the comparative history of procedures used to protect the individual. Includes bibliography.

90

Humphrey, John P. *Report of the Rapporteur. In The International Law Association. 53d Conference, Buenos Aires, 1968. Report. London, The International Law Association, 1969: 437-458.*

Part of a report by the International Committee on Human Rights of the International Law Association, focusing on human rights enforcement procedures, the need for objective reporting by governments, and the need for an effective international court of human rights.

91

Inter-American Society of Psychology. *Resolution on psychological practice and human rights. Chicago, Inter-American Society of Psychology, De Paul University, 1977. 2 p.*

Condemns the infringement of human rights by psychology and psychologists.

92

International Colloquy about the European Convention on Human Rights, 3d, Brussels, 1970. *Privacy and human rights; reports and communications presented at the third international colloquy about the European convention on human rights, organized by the Belgian Universities and the Council of Europe, with the support of the Belgian government, Brussels, 30 September-3 October 1970. Edited by A. H. Robertson. Manchester, University Press [1973]. 457 p.*

Not available for annotation.

93

International Commission of Jurists. *Racial problems in the public service. Geneva, 1965. 199 p.*

At head of title: Report of the British Guiana Commission of Inquiry constituted by the International Commission of Jurists.

Examines discrimination in employment by the civil service of Guyana.

94

International Conference on Humanitarian Law, San Remo, Italy, 1970. *Human rights as the basis of international humanitarian law. Proceedings. Lugano, Bellinzona, Grassi [1971]. 385 p.*

Contains papers presented at the conference as well as the text of the discussions. Includes the topics of human rights and armed conflict, individual rights, protection of political exiles, and the dynamics of human rights. Appendixes follow, consisting of major international human rights documents and resolutions, and press commentaries. In English, French and Italian.

95

International Observance of World Law Day--Human Rights, Geneva, 1968. *The international observance: World Law Day—Human Rights 1968; [proceedings]. Geneva, World Peace Through Law Center [1969]. 51 p. ([World Peace Through Law Center] Pamphlet series, no. 12)*

Not available for annotation.

96

International Symposium on Human Rights [Santiago, 1979?]. *The Charter of Santiago, Chile. Santiago, Arzobispado de Santiago [1979?] [5] p.*

A signed declaration asserting the basic human rights to which all are entitled.

97

International treaties, declarations and other acts concerning sex-based discrimination and the rights of women in international law. *Dobbs Ferry, N.Y., Oceana Publications, 1978. 5 v.*

Volume 1 is entitled Sex-based discrimination and is authored by Rita Falk Taubenfeld and Howard J. Taubenfeld. Four more loose leaf volumes to be published.

98

An introduction to the study of human rights. *Based on a series of lectures delivered at King's College, London in the autumn of 1970. Introduction by Sir Francis Vallat. London, Europa Publications [1972] 127 p.*

General discussion of human rights with emphasis on the principles of self-determination and non-discrimination. Includes bibliography.

99

[Iorns, John, and Doug McNeill, comp.] Against torture. *[Wellington], New Zealand, Committee for the Campaign Against Torture, 1973. 32 p.*

Pamphlet compiled from material supplied by Amnesty International. Includes addresses, essays, lectures, and a bibliography.

100

Ireland, Patricia. *International advancement and protection of human rights for women. Lawyer of the Americas, v. 10, spring 1978: 87-98.*

Discusses "the need for and the theoretical and practical problems involved in the international advancement and protection of human rights in general and human rights for women in particular."

101

Jaramillo Arbeláez, Delio. *Derecho internacional humanitario. Bogotá, Universidad Santo Tomás de Aquino, Oficina de Publicaciones, 1976-1977. 3 v.*

Three part review of international humanitarian law, its declarations and texts.

102

Jaramillo Arbeláez, Delio. *Derecho internacional humanitario: convenios de Ginebra. Bogotá, Universidad Santo Tomás de Aquino, 1976. 2 v. (various pagings)*

General study of the Geneva Conventions. Includes appendix listing the principal human rights juridical documents.

103

Joyce, James Avery. *The new politics of human rights. London, Macmillan Press, 1978. 305 p.*

Examines the politicization of human rights and the shift in the basis of foreign policy from that of security considerations to that of human rights. Includes short section on Chile under the junta.

104

Juvigny, Pierre. *Modern scientific and technical developments and their consequences on the protection of the right to respect for a person's private and family life, his home and communications. In International Colloquy about the European Convention on Human Rights, 3d, Brussels, 1970. Privacy and human rights; reports and communications presented at the third international colloquy about the European convention on human rights, organized by the Belgian universities and the Council of Europe, with the support of the Belgian government, Brussels, 30 September - 3 October 1970. Edited by Arthur Henry Robertson. Manchester, United Kingdom, University Press, 1973. p. 129-138.*

Analyzes violations of privacy through recording techniques, data processing and collection, and centralization of information.

105

Kamenka, Eugene, and Alice Erh-Soon Tay, eds. *Human rights. New York, St. Martin's Press, 1978. 148 p.*

The development of the idea of human rights, the internal complexities of that idea, and its place in the world today as seen by a group of professionals.

106

Klare, Michael T. *The scourge of modern militarism. Worldview, July/Aug. 1978: 37-41*

Examines the impact of militarism both in the junta-dominated societies of the Third World and in the industrialized countries.

107

Komite Europa - Latijns Amerika. *Latijns Amerika in de grup het buitenlands Kapitaal. Heverlee, Belgium, Verspreidingscentrum A. Hernatif, 1975. 52 p. illus.*

Contains documentation presented at the Russell Tribunal concerning dependency and U.S. economic penetration. Includes material on human rights violations in Uruguay, Brazil, Bolivia, Chile, and Argentina.

108

Kutner, Luis. *Constructive notice: a proposal to end international terrorism. New York law forum, v. 19, fall 1973: 325-350.*

Outlines the major aspects of international law as it relates to terrorism. Considers the accountability of heads of state for crimes against humanity.

109

Kutner, Luis. *Due process of rebellion. Valparaiso University law review, v. 4, fall 1972: 1-86.*

Focuses upon the international protection of the rights of both active and passive participants in revolutionary action. Examines the origins and effect of conventional international law concerning rebellion, discusses the establishment of international tribunals and the Writ of Habeas Corpus, and considers internal causes and characteristics of revolution.

110

Kutner, Luis. *World habeas corpus, human rights and world community. De Paul law review, v. 17, fall 1967: 3-37.*

Explores the relevance for human rights of the concept of world habeas corpus. Traces the historical development of the concept.

111

Kutner, Luis. *World habeas corpus, human rights and the world community. In World Conference on World Peace Through the Rule of Law, 3d, Geneva, 1967. World peace through law; the Geneva World Conference. Geneva, World Peace Through Law Center, 1969. p. 430-438.*

Deplores the ease of securing military commitments. Argues that strengthening habeas corpus protections will lead to greater observance of basic rights.

112

Lador-Lederer, J. Josef. *International Group Protection: aims and methods in human rights. Leyden, Netherlands, Sijthoff, 1968. 481 p.*

Examines the question of group protection through authority.

113

Lauterpacht, Elihu. *Some concepts of human rights. Howard law journal, v. 11, no. 2, spring 1965: 264-274.*

Discusses the relationship between customary international law and human rights.

114

Lee, L. T. *Law, human rights and population: a strategy for action. Virginia journal of international law, v. 12, 1972: 309-25.*

Explores the relationship between population growth and changing concepts of human rights.

115

Lillich, Richard, and Frank Newman, eds. *International human rights: problems of law and policy. New York, McGraw-Hill, 1977.*

Discusses questions such as terrorism and human rights procedures at the regional and U.N. levels.

116

Lima, Alceu Amoroso. *Os direitos do homem e o homem sem direitos. Rio de Janeiro, Livraria Francisco Alves Editora, 1974. 170 p.*

Expository treatment of the 1948 Declaration of the Rights of Man by a prominent Brazilian intellectual.

117

Litrento, Oliveiros Lessa. *O problema internacional da jurisdição doméstica: o homem. Rio de Janeiro, Freitas Bastos, 1966. 132 p.*

Discusses the role of individuals and states within institutionalized international systems. Special attention is given to conflicts arising from the concept of state sovereignty on the one hand and the international protection of human rights on the other.

118

Litrento, Oliveiros Lessa. *O problema internacional dos direitos humanos. Rio de Janeiro, Editora Río, 1973. 149 p.*

General treatment covering subjects such as the rights of man, the rights of the state, and institutionalized international society.

119

Lopez-Rey, Manuel. *Crime and human rights. Federal probation, v. 42, Mar. 1978: 10-15.*

Questions whether many violations of human rights should not be considered criminal acts.

120

Lyons, David. *Human rights and the general welfare. Philosophy and public affairs, v. 6, no. 2, winter 1977: 113-129.*

Examines the relationship between human rights and the general welfare since the time of John Stuart Mill.

121

McDougal, Myres, and H. Lasswell. *Human rights and world public order: human rights in comprehensive context. Northwestern University law review, v. 72, May/June 1977: 227-307*

Argues that certain rights transcend cultural, religious, and philosophical systems.

122

McGregor, Ian. *Human rights. London, Batsford, 1975. 96 p.*

Introduction to concepts contained in the Universal Declaration of Human Rights. Gives special attention to rights of minorities, freedom of the press, freedom of religion, and apartheid.

123

Macpherson, C. B. *Human rights as property rights. Dissent, v. 24, winter 1977: 72-77.*

Maintains that the full concession of human rights demands a broad concept of property.

124

Marmorstein, Victoria E. *World Bank power to consider human rights factors in loan decisions. The Journal of international law and economics, v. 13, no. 1, 1978: 113-136.*

Calls for the incorporation of human rights considerations in the loan decisions of the World Bank.

125

Martín Guidi, J. *La protección de los derechos humanos con libertad y autoridad. Colegio de Abogados de la Plata. Revista, no. 9, 1966: 217-240.*

Argues for the protection of human rights and

states that this should be considered a national priority.

126

Mayo, Bernard. *What are human rights? In D. D. Raphael, ed. Political theory and the rights of man. Bloomington, Indiana University Press, 1967. p. 68-80.*

Claims that human rights, natural rights, and inalienable rights are interchangeable. Examines the relationship between rights and duties.

127

The meaning of human rights and the problems they pose. *Ecumenical review, v. 27, Apr. 1975: 139-146.*

At head of title: A substantial part of a paper prepared by the U.N. Working Group of the G.D.R. Regional Committee of the Christian Peace Conference, for the consultation on human rights, held by the C.C.I.A. at St. Pölten, Austria, in October 1974.

Defines the substance of human rights in socialist and capitalist societies.

128

Melden, Abraham Irving, ed. *Human rights. Belmont, Calif., Wadsworth Publications, 1970. 152 p.*

Series of essays dealing with matters such as the nature of civil government, the fallacies of anarchy, natural rights, racial discrimination, justice, and punishment.

129

Milne, Alan John Mitchell. *Freedom and rights. London, Allen and Unwin, 1968. 376 p.*

Review of the concept of human rights in the writings of philosophers.

130

Montealegre Klenner, Hernán. *La seguridad del estado y los derechos humanos. Santiago, Academia de Humanismo Cristiano, 1979. 789 p.*

Analysis of the legal tools available to the state for the maintenance of public order. Reviews international law and laws enacted by particular Latin American countries.

131
Moskowitz, Moses. *International concern with human rights. Dobbs Ferry, N.Y., Oceana Publications, 1975. 239 p.*

Human rights activist examines gap between the legal code governing human rights and actual protection of such rights.

132
Moskowitz, Moses. *The politics and dynamics of human rights. Dobbs Ferry, N.Y., Oceana Publications, 1968. 283 p.*

Analyzes the political and legal problems involved in the active promotion of human rights.

133
Moulian, Tomás. *Una perspectiva de los derechos humanos. Derechos humanos; estudios. Santiago, Vicaría de la Solidaridad, v. 1, mayo 1978: 21-30.*

Deft analysis of the concept of human rights from the perspectives of the liberal state and the socialist and Marxist state. Refutes the idea that the liberal concept of human rights is coterminous with a bourgeois state.

134
Movimiento Ecuménico por los Derechos Humanos. *Documento de fundación. 2d ed., Buenos Aires, 1976. 24 p.*

Results of three ecumenical assemblies. Included are several Vatican documents and Movimiento Ecuménico declarations.

135
Mujica Rodriguez, Rafael. *Los derechos humanos reconocidos. Lecciones y ensayos (Buenos Aires), no. 25, 1962/1963: 187-214.*

Focuses on generally recognized human rights and instruments available for enforcement.

136
Nash, June, and Helen I. Safa, eds. *Sex and class in Latin America. New York, Praeger, 1976. 330 p. (Praeger special studies in international politics and government)*

Collection of readings on women in Latin America. Topics covered include sexual subordination, women in productive roles, and political mobilization of women.

137
Nelson, Jack L., and Vera M. Green, eds. *International human rights: contemporary issues. Pine Plains, N.Y., Earl M. Coleman, 1980. 300 p.*

Discusses the nature, definiton, deficiencies, and practices of human rights in a variety of settings, including Chile and Bolivia.

138
Newman, Frank C. *The International Bill of Human Rights: does it exist? In Antonio Cassese, ed. Current problems of international law: essays on U.N. law and on the law of armed conflict. Milan, Italy, A. Giuffrè, 1975. p. 107-116. (Pubblicazioni della Facoltà di giuresprudenza della Università de Pisa, no. 60) ([Pubblicazioni] Istituto di diritto internazionale D. Anzilotti, no. 5)*

Discusses the desirability of enacting strong international standards for the protection of human rights. Includes bibliographic references.

139
Nobel Symposium, 7th, Oslo, 1967. *International protection of human rights; proceedings. Edited by Asbjörn Eide and August Schon. New York, Interscience Publishers [1968] 300 p.*

International in orientation, these papers address theoretical and practical problems of human rights.

140
Obieta, Joseph A., ed. *El derecho internacional de la persona humana. Bilbao, Spain, Mensajero [1974] 582 p.*

Sponsored by the Instituto de Derechos del Hombre y de los Grupos Humanos; lists international agreements, accords, and other instruments on human rights currently in force.

141
O'Donnell, Daniel. *States of exception. International Commission of Jurists. Review, no. 24, Dec. 1978: 52-60.*

Examines "states of exception" as governmental tactics undermining the protection of human rights.

142

Okolie, Charles. *International law perspectives of developing countries: the relationship of law and economic development to basic human rights. New York, Nok Publishers, 1975.*

Discusses the often conflicting issues of economic development, human rights, and law.

143

Palacios, C. P. *Protección internacional de los derechos humanos. Revista de derecho (Quito), no. 15, 1968: 63-77.*

Not available for annotation.

144

Paskins, Barrie. *What's wrong with torture? British journal of international studies, v. 2, July 1976: 138-148.*

Defines torture and questions accepted moral positions on the matter.

145

Peces-Barba Martínez, Gregorio. *Textos básicos sobre derechos humanos. Con la colaboración de Liborio Hierro Sánchez-Pescador. Madrid, Universidad Complutense, Facultad de Derecho, 1973. 459 p.*

Collection of historical texts on human rights, arranged chronologically.

146

Peidro Pastor, I. *Aspectos filosóficos jurídicos y de los pactos internacionales sobre derechos humanos. Anuario de derecho (Panama City), no. 9, 1970/71: 67-79.*

Not available for annotation.

147

Pérez, Carlos Andrés. *Human rights and the world economic order. Current world leaders; speeches and reports, v. 6, Dec. 1977: 10-14.*

President Pérez of Venezuela spoke on June 28, 1977, about the need for a new international economic structure to ensure universal political and civil rights.

148

Pérez Pérez, Alberto. *Medidas internacionales de protección de los derechos humanos. Anuario uruguayo de derecho internacional, v. 2, 1963: 275-316.*

Author analyzes the structure of jurisdictions contained in various pacts, treaties and conventions which may be used to enforce sanctions against violators of human rights.

149

Peris Gómez, Manuel. *Juez, estado, y derechos humanos. Valencia, España, Fernando Torres, 1976. 350 p. (Interdisciplinar 2, no. 36)*

Emphasizes the importance of an easily understood juridical system that enforces compliance to rights provided by law. The three parts treat the role of the judge, the power of the state and the concept of human rights.

150

Petit-Pierre, Max. *A contemporary look at the International Committee of the Red Cross. International review of the Red Cross, no. 119, Feb. 1971: 63-81.*

Lists the Red Cross principles, discusses the activities and limitations of the ICRC, and describes the ICRC organization and purpose within the context of the humanitarian tradition.

151

Pollis, Adamantia, and Peter Schwab, eds. *Human rights: cultural and ideological perspectives. New York, Praeger, 1979. 165 p.*

Collection of articles which compare and account for the differing cultural perspectives on human rights. Includes a bibliography by John T. Wright, and an examination of political rights in Latin America by C. Neale Ronning.

152

Polson, Terry Ellen. *The rights of working women: an international perspective. Virginia journal of international law, v. 14, no. 4, summer 1974: 729-746.*

Documents the struggle for equal employment opportunity by women throughout the world and appeals for closer adherence to existing laws.

153

The prevention and suppression of torture. *Pau, France, Association Internationale de Droit Pénal, 1977. 310 p. (Revue internationale de droit pénal, v. 48, no. 3/4, 1977)*

"Numéro spécial consacré aux travaux du Comité Internationale des Experts sur la Torture réuni á l'Institut Supérieur de Sciences Criminelles, Syracuse (Sicile) Italie, 16-18 Décembre 1977."

Listing of provisions in national constitutions and the U.N. Charter concerning the prevention of torture. Includes legal analysis.

154

Pronk, J. P. *Human rights and development aid. International Commission of Jurists. Review, no. 18, June 1977: 33-39.*

Argues that development aid should be more responsive to the rights of individuals than to the interests of states. Refers briefly to Latin America.

155

The push for human rights. *Newsweek, June 20, 1977: 46-61.*

A special report which looks at some of the most notorious abuses of human rights around the world.

156

Quadri, Ricardo Pedro. *La Conferencia Internacional de Derechos Humanos de Teheran; sus objectivos y conclusiones. [Buenos Aires] Ministerio de Relaciones Exteriores y Culto, Comité Argentino para la celebración del Año Internacional de Derechos Humanos, 1968. 13 p.*

Analysis of the objectives and resolutions of the Teheran Conference. Discusses present advances, problem areas, and goals of human rights.

157

Quadri, Ricardo Pedro. *Elementos para la interpretación de los pactos internacionales de derechos humanos. Buenos Aires, Ministerio de Relaciones Exteriores y Culto, 1968. 121 p.*

Juridical and historical exegesis of international pacts relating to human rights by the Argentine delegation to the U.N. Includes annexes and bibliography.

158

Quadri, Ricardo Pedro. *La intervención por razones humanitarias en el derecho internacional. [Buenos Aires] Zeta Duplicator, 1971. 50 p.*

Historical overview of the intervention, in defense of human rights, by one country or group of countries into the affairs of other countries.

159

Quadri, Ricardo Pedro. *The status of the doctrine of humanitarian intervention in the light of the present state of international law. [Buenos Aires] Zeta Duplicator, 1971.*

Questions whether armed intervention in defense of human rights is justified.

160

Ramcharan, B. G., ed. *Human rights: thirty years after the Universal Declaration; commemorative volume on the occasion of the thirtieth anniversary of the Universal Declaration of Human Rights. The Hague, Boston, M. Nijhoff, distribution, Kluwer Boston, 1979. 274 p.*

"Published under the auspices of the International Forum on Human Rights."

International lawyers review current human rights practices and suggest improvements.

161

Ramella, P. A. *Los pactos sobre derechos humanos. Revista jurídica argentina la ley, v. 143, 1971: 1042-1051.*

Not available for annotation.

162

Raphael, David Daiches. *The liberal Western tradition of human rights. International social science journal (Paris), v. 18, no. 1, 1966: 22-30.*

Argues that Western liberalism's concern for civil and political rights broadened during the 18th century to include certain social and economic guarantees.

163
Raphael, David Daiches, ed. *Political theory and the rights of man.* London, Macmillan, 1967. *151 p.*

Essays by U.S. and British professors, contrasting the human rights concepts of classical political theory with those contained in the Universal Declaration of 1948.

164
Rávago Bustamante, Enrique de. *Las atribuciones del gobierno y las situaciones de urgencia. Advocatus, v.3, enero/abr.* 1964: 13-21.

Maintains that declared states of emergency have detrimental effects on the democratic process, and questions their value and legality.

165
Richards, Jason. *Two for global freedoms. Maryknoll, v.71, Nov.* 1977: 26-29.

U.S. Congressmen Koch and Fraser speak out in favor of the protection of human rights.

166
Robertson, Arthur Henry. *Human rights in the world, being an account of the United Nations covenants on human rights, the European Convention, the American Convention, the Permanent Arab Commission, the proposed African Commission and recent developments affecting humanitarian law. New York, Humanities Press,* 1972. *280 p.*

Analyzes U.N. and other international covenants designed to protect human rights. Includes bibliographic references.

167
Robertson, Arthur Henry. *The international protection of human rights. Nottingham, United Kingdom, University of Nottingham,* 1970. *21 p.*

Montague Burton international relations lecture, 1969-70, focusing on civil rights and international law.

168
Robertson, Arthur Henry. *Work paper on human rights. In World Peace Through Law. The Geneva World Conference [1967]. Geneva, World Peace Through Law Center,* 1969. *p. 404-418.*

Head of Council of Europe's Directorate of Human Rights cites landmark achievements over the previous twenty years at both worldwide and regional levels. Included is a discussion of progress made in developing the Inter-American Convention on Human Rights.

169
Rodriguez, Atahualpa. *Academic repression in the Third World. Brighton, United Kingdom, Institute of Development Studies, University of Sussex,* 1977. *26 p.*

General treatment of the causes and nature of academic repression in the Third World, accompanied by a call for action.

170
Rolz-Bennett, José. *Human rights, 1945-1970. [New York] United Nations [1970]. 11 p. (U.N. Office of Public Information. [Publication] OPI/407)*

Review of the major achievements of the U.N. in the field of human rights. Included are the Universal Declaration, the Covenants, and recommendations concerning self-determination, racial discrimination, the right to life, slavery, servitude, prostitution, forced labor, statelessness, refugees, the status of women, the rights of children, and the handling of war crimes.

171
Ronning, C. Neale. *Human rights and humanitarian laws in the Western Hemisphere. Social research, v.38, summer* 1971: 320-336.

Summary of the last two decades of inter-American activity in the human rights field. Recommends the establishment of norms to prevent and control civil conflict.

172
Rossilion, C. *I.L.O. examination of human rights situations; new procedures for special surveys on discrimination. International Commission of Jurists. Review, no. 12, 1974:* 40-49.

Examines International Labor Organization traditions of technical investigations and impartial examinations and describes a new system of "special surveys" intended to address the question of discrimination in employment.

173

Rozo Acuña, Eduardo, and Hugo Riveros Perilla. *Trayectoria de los derechos humanos. Bogota, Universidad Externado de Colombia, 1973. 2 v.*

At bottom of title: En conmemoración del vigésimo quinto aniversario de la Declaración Universal de los Derechos Humanos de las Naciones Unidas.

Volume 1 presents historical overview of classic human rights documents, such as the bill of rights of England and of the U.S. Volume 2 discusses human rights provisos in the constitutions of the nations of Latin America, Africa, Eastern Europe, and in statements and documents of international organizations.

174

Ruthven, Malise. *Torture, the grand conspiracy. London, Weidenfeld and Nicholson, 1978. 342 p.*

Historical overview of the use of torture throughout the world, including Latin America.

175

Said, Abdul Aziz, ed. *Human rights and world order. New Brunswick, N.J., Transaction Books, 1978. 170 p.*

Articles by outstanding U.S. scholars treating human rights from a variety of perspectives. Among issues covered are international terrorism and the role of human rights in U.S. foreign policy.

176

Sakharov, Andrei. *Peace, progress and human rights. Index on censorship, v. 5, summer 1976: 3-9.*

Text of a Nobel lecture presented in 1975, arguing that peace, progress and human rights are indissolubly linked.

177

Sánchez, Walter, ed. *Derechos humanos y relaciones internacionales. Obra editada con el auspicio de la Comisión Interamericana de Derechos Humanos y la Fundación Konrad Adenauer. Santiago, Chile, Talleres Gráficos Corporación, 1979. 240 p.*

Presents papers on transcultural views of human rights, terrorism versus national security, human rights and international politics, the improvement of the U.N. machinery in upholding human rights, and human rights in the Third World.

178

Sarosdy, Randall L. *Jurisdiction following illegal extraterritorial seizure; international human rights obligations as an alternative to constitutional stalemate. Texas law review, v. 54, Nov. 1976: 1439-1470.*

Analyzes the due process issue and recent developments in international human rights legislation.

179

Scoble, Harry M., and Laurie S. Wiseberg. *Human rights NGO's: notes towards comparative analysis. Droits de l'homme: human rights journal (Paris), v. 9, no. 4, 1976: 611-644.*

The co-directors of Human Rights Internet discuss the framework and effectiveness of the leading non-governmental human rights institutions, such as Amnesty International, the International Commission of Jurists, the League for the Rights of Man, and the International Committee of the Red Cross.

180

Shue, Henry. *Torture. Philosophy and public affairs, v. 7, fall 1977: 124-143.*

Condemnation of torture, accompanied by the argument that it is widespread and growing.

181

Snyder, Richard C., Charles F. Herman, and Harold D. Lasswell. *A global monitoring system: appraising the effects of government on human dignity. International studies quarterly, v. 20, June 1976: 221-260.*

Theoretical proposition set forth for discussion at a meeting of the International Studies Association that political scientists appraise governments' policies and practices throughout the world in order to assess the extent to which governments affect human dignity, as defined in part by the Universal Declaration of Human Rights.

182

Sohn, Louis B., and Margaret Galey. *New aspects of the international protection of human rights. 25th report of the Commission to Study the Organization of Peace.* New York, Stanley Foundation, 1976. 40 p.

Issues discussed here include the international protection of women's rights, the rights of indigenous peoples, and a renewed interest in protecting religious freedom.

183

Sohn, Louis B., and Thomas Buergenthal, eds. *Basic documents on international protection of human rights.* Indianapolis, Bobbs-Merrill, 1973. 244 p.

Intended as a companion volume to the editors' International protection of human rights, this is a separate reference work for basic human rights texts.

184

Sohn, Louis B., and Thomas Buergenthal, eds. *International protection of human rights.* Indianapolis, Bobbs-Merrill, 1973. 1402 p.

Extensive volume, written for lawyers, that presents a comprehensive introduction to human rights protection under international law. Included are essays and case studies dealing with the status of individuals under international law, the protection of the rights of aliens, humanitarian intervention, and the United Nations and European Conventions. A basic reference work.

185

Sovetov, A. *The human rights myth and anti-communism. International affairs,* v. 6, June 1978: 12-21.

Article in a Soviet journal, published in Moscow, which asserts that social systems differ in their guarantees of human rights and that communism is a system that protects human rights.

186

Soysal, Mumtaz. *Indivisible and universal: reflections on peace and human rights. Matchbox,* winter 1978: 1-3.

Statement of appreciation by the vice chairman of Amnesty International's executive committee for the Nobel Peace Prize Committee's recognition of Amnesty's work.

187

Suckow, Samuel. *Conference on humanitarian law, phase II. International Commission of Jurists. Review,* no. 14, June 1975: 42-54.

Progress report on the second session of the Diplomatic Conference on the Reaffirmation and Development of International Humanitarian Law. Discusses seating national governments and committee decisions on wars and weapons.

188

Suckow, Samuel. *Conference on international humanitarian law: concluded. International Commission of Jurists. Review,* no. 19, Dec. 1977: 46-62.

Last of four articles emanating from the Conference. Reports on draft protocols for the protection of victims of international conflict.

189

Suckow, Samuel. *Development of international humanitarian law: a case study. International Commission of Jurists. Review,* no. 12, June 1974: 50-57.

First of four articles on the Diplomatic Conference on the Reaffirmation and Development of International Humanitarian Law Applicable in Armed Conflict. Discusses recent attempts to redefine the Geneva Convention's treatment of sick and wounded members of armed forces so as to include those injured in guerrilla style wars.

190

Suckow, Samuel. *Humanitarian Law Conference. International Commission of Jurists. Review,* no. 16, June 1976: 51-60.

Progress report on the Third Session of the Diplomatic Conference on the Reaffirmation and Development of International Humanitarian Law. Deals with the question of armed conflict.

191

Summer Conference on International Law, 5th, Cornell University, 1964. *Human rights: protection of the individual under international law; proceedings.* South Hackensack, N.J., F. B. Rothman, 1970. 286 p.

Contains papers presented at the conference dealing with international legal protection of human rights. Includes bibliographic references.

192

Tiwari, S. C. *Forms of international organization action for the protection of human rights; pt. 1.* Indian yearbook of international affairs, v. 13, 1964: 28-58.

Cogent description of the mechanisms established by the U.N., the Council of Europe, and the O.A.S. to implement human rights charters.

193

La torture. *Unité des chrétiens; revue trimestrielle de formation et d'information eccuméniques,* no. 25, jan. 1977: whole issue.

Deals with the position of Christian churches regarding torture.

194

Toward a humanitarian diplomacy: a primer for policy. *Tom J. Farer, ed.* New York, New York University Press, 1980. 229 p.

General treatment of the subject of human rights, with special focus on the relationship between human rights and U.S. foreign policy. A major book on the subject.

195

Truyol y Serra, Antonio. *Los derechos humanos; declaraciones y convenios internacionales.* 2d ed. Madrid, Editorial Tecnos, 1977. 187 p.

Valuable collection of human rights voting records on rights declarations from the U.N.

General Assembly. Includes notes and a bibliography.

196

Tuttle, James C., ed. *International human rights; law and practice. The roles of the United Nations, the private sector, the government, and their lawyers.* Chicago, American Bar Association, 1978. 205 p.

General appraisal of the human rights situation by outstanding personalities such as Donald M. Fraser, Patricia Derian, Hubert H. Humphrey, and Theo C. van Boven. A collection of papers prepared for the American Bar Association's first national institute on the topic of international human rights law.

197

Unione Giuristi Cattolici Italiani. *Diritti fondamentali dell'uomo. Relazioni del XXVII Convegno nazionale di studio,* Roma, 6-8 dicembre 1976. [Milan] Editrice Guiffrè e Institia, 1977. 123 p. (Quaderni di Institia, no. 27)

Discussion of the human rights provisions of international law. Includes bibliographic references.

198

Valencia Rodríguez, Luis. *¿Que régimen jurídico internacional concedería el máximo valor y la máxima protección a los derechos humanos?* Quito, Editorial Casa de la Cultura Ecuatoriana, 1972. 28 p.

Not available for annotation.

199

Van Dyke, Vernon. *Human rights without distinction as to language.* International studies quarterly, v. 20, Mar. 1976: 3-38.

Examines language policies of international organizations, national governments, and education in light of the U.N. provision that there not be discrimination by language.

200

Van Dyke, Vernon. *The individual, the state, and ethnic communities in political theory.* World politics, v. 24, Apr. 1977: 343-369.

Appeals for inclusion of group rights within the international framework of human rights.

201

Varela Feijóo, J. *La protección de los derechos humanos*, Barcelona, Spain, Editorial Hispano Europea, 1972. *373 p.*

Not available for annotation.

202

Vasak, Karel. *National, regional and universal institutions for the promotion and protection of human rights. Droits de l'homme: human rights, v. 1, no. 2, 1968: 165-179.*

Comparative analysis of the scope and functions of existing institutions for the protection of human rights. Includes those sponsored by individual countries, those of countries grouped by geographic region, and those of universal orientation, such as the U.N.

203

Vasak, Karel. *Regionalization of the international protection of human rights and fundamental freedoms. In World Peace Through Law. The Washington World Conference [1965]. St. Paul, Minnesota. West Publishing Company, 1967. p. 356-362.*

Speech by administrator of Council of Europe's Directorate of Human Rights at Second World Conference. Supports regional over U.N. protection of human rights.

204

Veil, Simone. *Human rights, ideologies, and population policies. Population and development review, v. 4, June 1978: 313-321.*

Questions whether states are justified in adopting population policies, and explores implications of various means of implementation.

205

Wiener, Hesh. *The age of information: computers raise as many questions as they answer. Centerpiece. Special Features. New York, The New York Times Syndication Sales Corporation, 1978. 20 p.*

Discusses how modern computers can be used by repressive regimes to violate human rights.

206

Wiener, Hesh. *Why police states love the computer. Business and society review, no. 22, summer 1977: 38-43.*

Explores the relationship between repression and computers. Argues that those who sell and service computers share responsibility for the uses to which they are put.

207

William, Douglas. *Human rights, economic development and aid to the Third World: an analysis and proposal for action. ODI; Overseas Development Institute review, no. 1, 1978: 14-37.*

Considers the relationship of human rights to economic development and explores basic concepts found in the Universal Declaration of Human Rights.

208

Wiseberg, Laurie, and Harry Scoble. *The International League for Human Rights: the strategy of a human rights NGO. Georgia journal of international comparative law, v. 7, summer 1977: 289-313.*

Case study of the International League for Human Rights, the oldest political interest group devoted to the protection of human rights.

209

Woito, Robert. *Human rights and war. Chicago, World Without War Publications, 1977. 8 p.*

Discusses the relationship between human rights and war and explores the ways in which human rights principles are formed and applied.

210

Woito, Robert, ed. *International human rights kit. Chicago, World Without War Publications, 1977. 196 p.*

An introduction to the issue of human rights, including questions and answers; the texts of the U.S. and Soviet Bill of Rights, the Universal Declaration of Human Rights, and the two International Covenants; opposing viewpoints; analysis of the Third World; table of human rights assessment procedures; and suggestions for effective action.

211

World Conference on World Peace Through the Rule of Law, 2d, Washington, 1965. *Building law rules and legal institutions for peace; declaration of faith, global work program, resolutions, adopted unanimously by the Second World Peace Through Law Conference, September 18, 1965, Washington, D.C. Geneva, World Peace Through Law Center, 1965. 23 p.*

Not available for annotation.

212

World Conference on World Peace Through the Rule of Law. 3d, Geneva, 1967. *Geneva World Conference on World Peace Through Law and World Assembly of Judges; program. Geneva [1967]. 88 p. illus.*

Conference program that contains statement of purpose, agenda (including human rights as a topic), and listing of participants.

213

World Congress on Philosophy of Law and Social Philosophy, St. Louis, 1975. *Equality and freedom, international and comparative jurisprudence: papers of the World Congress on Philosophy of Law and Social Philosophy, St. Louis, 24-29 August, 1975. Edited by authorization of Internationale Vereinigung für Rechts- and Sozialphilosophie (IVR) by Gray Dorsey. Dobbs Ferry, N.Y., Oceana Publications [1977]. 8 v.*

Legal scholars and sociologists present papers defending freedom from destructive or intrusive acts by governments or groups of persons. Emphasis is on safeguarding freedom from oppression, the free development of science and learning, and new legal institutions.

214

World Council of Churches. *How to file complaints of human rights violations: a practical guide to inter-governmental procedures. Geneva, 1975. 152 p.*

Step by step guide for filing of human rights complaints. Includes analysis of the responsibilities of various U.N. dependencies charged with different aspects of the human rights question.

215

World Peace Through Law Center. *International legal protection for human rights: the handbook for National Law Day, August 21, 1977. 75 p.*

Not available for annotation.

216

World Peace Through Law Center. *International Refugee Law Day, Geneva, 1976. 40 p.*

Discusses international action with regard to refugees and the treatment of the refugee question in the 1951 Convention and the 1967 Protocol. Proclaims July 28, 1976, as the 25th anniversary of the Convention Relating to the Status of Refugees.

217

World Peace Through Law Center. *World Law Day, Sept. 16, 1968; sponsored by the World Peace Through Law Center, in cooperation with International Year for Human Rights. Geneva, 1968. 43 p. illus., ports.*

Not available for annotation.

218

World Peace Through Law Center. Committee on the International Legal Protection of Refugees. *Towards the second quarter century of refugee law; report. Washington, World Peace Through Law Center, 1976.*

Examines refugee law that has been developed during the last 25 years by the international community.

219

Yale Task Force on Population Ethics. *Moral claims, human rights, and population policies. Theological studies, v. 35, Mar. 1974: 83-113.*

For the field of human rights and population control, compares traditional U.S., Marxist, and Catholic policies with those of the U.N.

Human Rights in Latin America

220

Aguilar León, Luis. *Estrategia marxista en relación con los derechos humanos en América Latina. [Caracas] Instituto de Formación Demócrata Cristiana IFEDEC, 1978. 30 p.*

A historian examines Marxist interpretations of human rights and points out essential differences from what the Marxists perceive as "bourgeois" views of human rights. Summarizes Soviet human rights strategies in Latin America.

221

Alba, Victor, et al. *Human rights and the liberation of man in the Americas. Notre Dame, Ind., University of Notre Dame Press, 1970. 278 p.*

Includes papers presented at the Sixth Annual Conference of the Catholic Inter-American Cooperation Program (CICOP), New York, January 24-25, 1969. Includes bibliographical references.

222

Alcalay, Milos. *Solidaridad y derechos humanos. Caracas, Centro de Información, Documentación, y Análisis Latino-americanos [1977]. (Centro de Información, Documentación, y Análisis Latinoamericanos, no. 79)*

Brings together newspaper articles written between 1976 and 1978 that discuss the relationship between human rights and the Catholic Church, international organizations, and international politics.

223

Alzamora Valdez, Mario. *Los derechos de libertad y de los derechos sociales en las constituciones americanas. Instituto de Derecho Comparado. Boletín, v. 14, no. 15, 1965: 68-90.*

Discusses provisions safeguarding human rights in the constitutions of the countries of the Americas.

224

América Latina: ¿Una literature exiliada? Nueva sociedad (San Jose), Costa Rica, no. 35, marzo/abril 1978: 1-189. *Consideration, by distinguished Latin American writers, of the consequences of censorship, persecution, repression, and torture as experienced either by them or by their professional colleagues.*

225

American Society of International Law. *Proceedings of its meeting. 72d; 1978. Washington, 1978. 376 p.*

Includes section on human rights in Latin America.

226

Arraiz, Rafael Clemente. *Contenido y defensa de los derechos humanos en el sistema interamericano. Academia de Ciencias Políticas y Sociales (Caracas). Boletín, v. 36, oct./dic. 1977: 117-127.*

Speech on the Venezuelan Constitution's human rights provisions, their application, and their place in the changed political context of the Americas in the 1970s. Considers human rights protection in the hemisphere.
Historical approach to the problem of assessing costs and benefits of modernizing armed forces in the Third World. Warns that the acceptance of more complex technology by Asian, African, and Latin American countries may increase their dependence on former colonial powers and on the Soviets. Points out that arms may be used internally rather than against external threats.

227

Asbjørn, Eide. *The transfer of arms to Third World countries and their international uses. International social science journal, v. 28, no. 2, 1976: 307-325.*

228

Barreiro, Julio. *In defense of human rights. The Ecumenical review, v. 27, Apr. 1975: 104-110.*

Examination of human rights violations throughout the world. Includes sections on Latin America.

229

Bayón, Damián, ed. *El artista latinoamericano y su identidad.* Caracas, Monte Avila Editores, 1977. *150 p.* illus., plates. *(Col. estudios)*

Record of proceedings of a symposium held in Austin, Texas, in 1975. Among the topics discussed were freedom of speech and freedom of the press in the Latin American political context. Includes bibliographies.

230

Beltrán, Virgilio Rafael, ed. *El papel político y social de las fuerzas armadas en América Latina; ensayos.* Caracas, Monte Avila Editores, 1970. *350 p.*

Collection of sociological studies on the role of the military in the twentieth-century politics of Latin America, especially in Brazil, Peru, Argentina, Uruguay, and Cuba.

231

Bianchi Gundián, Manuel. *La paz y los derechos humanos.* Santiago de Chile, Editorial Andrés Bello, 1969. *92 p.*

Essay and speeches by the president of the Inter-American Commission on Human Rights concerning the development of human rights organizations and charters in Latin America. Emphasizes the commission's work from 1960 to 1968.

232

Borosage, Robert, and Christine Macy. *The C.I.A.'s covert operations versus human rights.* Washington, Center for National Security Studies, 1978. *23 p.*

Pamphlet strongly critical of the C.I.A.'s effect on human rights problems throughout the world. Includes Latin America. The work is being revised currently.

233

Bouchaud, Joseph. *El fuego: de feu qui nous vient d'Amérique Latine.* Paris, Éditions Ouvrières, 1973. *109 p.* (Col. a pleine vie)

This French publication discusses the activist role of the Catholic Church in Latin America on behalf of social justice.

234

Brownlie, Ian, ed. *Basic documents on human rights.* Oxford, Great Britain, Clarendon Press, 1971. *531 p.*

A valuable handbook on international human rights sources. Contains useful comparisons of laws, declarations, and conventions from states in Europe, Asia, and Latin America. Includes U.N. initiatives and considers the influence of trade and development on human rights.

235

Buergenthal, Thomas. *International and regional human rights law and institutions: some examples of their interactions.* Texas international law journal, v. 12, spring/summer 1977: 321-330.

Article on the relationships between the U.N. and regional organizations, such as the Inter-American Commission on Human Rights.

236

Buergenthal, Thomas. *The revised O.A.S. Charter and the protection of human rights.* American journal of international law, v. 69, 1975: 828-836.

Analyzes the transformation of the inter-American system for the protection of human rights, resulting from O.A.S. Charter revisions. Traces the development of the O.A.S. Charter.

237

Building a better thumbscrew. *New scientist (London), v. 59, July 19, 1973: 139-141.*

Anonymous investigation of torture in Latin America and the Far East includes assertions about the role of the U.S. Agency for International Development and the International Police Academy.

238

Cabranes, José A. *Human rights and non-intervention in the inter-American system.* Michigan law review, v. 65, Apr. 1967: 1147-1182.

Survey of the O.A.S. change from indifference to concern for human rights, as evidenced by its establishment of the Inter-American Commission on Human Rights.

239

Cabranes, José A. *The protection of human rights by the Organization of American States. American journal of international law, v. 62, Oct. 1968: 889-909.*

Details the efforts of the O.A.S. on behalf of human rights and discusses the international and domestic priorities that must exist in order to insure enforcement of these rights at an international level.

240

Camargo, Pedro Pablo. *La protección jurídica de los derechos humanos y de la democracia en América; los derechos humanos y el derecho internacional. Mexico, Editorial Excelsior, 1960. 481 p.*

General study of the fundamental rights of man from a philosophical and historical viewpoint. Includes discussions on the role of the U.N. and the development of international protection of human rights.

241

Camargo, Pedro Pablo. *Proyecto de Convención Interamericana sobre Protección de Derechos Humanos; contraproyecto. Mexico, Agencia Mexicana de Noticias, 1969. 79 p.*

Text and discussion of a proposal prepared for the Specialized Inter-American Conference on Human Rights, 1969, San José, Costa Rica, suggesting the creation of a new Commission of Human Rights to replace the existing O.A.S. commission.

242

Carmona, Fernando. *Subdesarrollo y negación de los derechos humanos. Universidades, v. 12, enero/marzo 1972: 46-60.*

Discusses the effects of capitalism and economic dependency on human rights efforts in Latin America.

243

Castillo Velasco, Jaime. *Violación de derechos humanos en America latina. [Caracas] Instituto de Formación Democrática Cristiana [1978] 24 p.*

Classifies Latin American dictatorships into several categories, such as personalista or caudil-
lista, hereditary, or socialist. Discusses violations of human rights from a theoretical as well as a practical point of view.

244

Center for International Policy. *Human rights and the U.S. foreign assistance program. Washington, 1978. 61 p. illus.*

Summary of violations of human rights in Argentina, Brazil, Chile, and Nicaragua prepared to counteract the U.S. State Department's annual human rights report used by Congress to allocate foreign aid.

245

Chagnon, Jacquelyn, and Roger Rumpf, eds. *If you want peace ...defend life. 10th Annual World Period of Peace. [s.l., s.n.] 1976. 24 p.*

Articles address the issues of human rights and foreign policy, the technology of torture, and give case studies of Argentina and other countries. Presents an action guide and list of resources.

246

Chomsky, Noam, and Edward Herman. *Why American business supports Third World fascism. Business and society review, no. 23, fall 1977: 13-21.*

Argues that private U.S. economic penetration in selected Latin American, Asian, and Middle Eastern countries contributes to human rights abuses and militarization.

247

Claude, Richard P., ed. *Comparative human rights. Baltimore, Johns Hopkins University Press, 1976. 410 p.*

Contributions by social scientists and lawyers about Latin American and Anglo-American human rights. Includes particularly useful discussion by William Devall on practical obstacles and conceptual problems of current social science research. Includes bibliographic references.

248

Claudius, Thomas, and Franz Stepan. *Amnesty International; Portrait einer Organisation. Munich, Vienna, Oldenbourg Verlag, 1978. 326 p.*

Detailed description of Amnesty International, during the years 1961 to 1975, with brief references to its Latin American offices. Includes bibliographic references and index.

249

Clutterbuck, Richard L. *Guerrillas and terrorists*. London, Farber and Farber, 1977. *125 p.*

Exposition of past and present guerrilla movements and terrorism, particularly in Southeast Asia, Northern Ireland, the Middle East, Cuba, Chile, and Guatemala. Designed to increase awareness of the public and the media to the goals and methods of this kind of war. Includes bibliography.

250

Collier, David, ed. *The new authoritarianism in Latin America*. Princeton, N.J., Princeton University Press, 1979. *1 v. (various pagings)*

At head of title: Sponsored by the Joint Committee on Latin American Studies of the Social Science Research Council and the American Council of Learned Societies.

Collected essays by U.S. and Latin American social scientists comparing and contrasting economic, social, and political policies of new authoritarian regimes. Includes bibliographic references.

251

Colonnese, Louis M., ed. *Human rights and the liberation of man in the Americas*. Notre Dame, Ind., University of Notre Dame Press, 1970. *278 p.*

Includes several chapters on human rights in Latin America in the 1960s, by such authors as Helder Câmara, Victor Alba, Robert J. Alexander, Juan Luis Segundo, and Jorge Mejía. The chapters were originally presented as papers at the 6th Annual Catholic Inter- American Cooperation Program (CICOP) Conference in New York in 1976.

252

Comblin, Joseph. *A ideologia da segurança nacional: o poder militar na América Latina*. Rio de Janeiro, Civilização Brasileira, 1978. *251 p.*

Examines militarism and the national security doctrine in Latin America. Includes chapters on the concept of national security in Latin America, with case studies of Brazil, Peru, Chile, Argentina, Uruguay, Ecuador, and Bolivia.

253

Comisión Evangélica Latino Americana de Educación Cristiana (CELADEC). *Derechos humanos: derechos de mi pueblo?* Lima, 1978. *27 p.*

Depicts in comic book format the current state of human rights in Latin America. Published in commemoration of the 30th anniversary of the Universal Declaration of the U. N. Includes bibliographies.

254

Comisión Evangélica Latinoamericana de Educación Cristiana and Centro Nacional de Comunicación Social. *El Salvador*. Mexico, 1979. *63 p.* (CENCO, *América Latina derechos humanos*)

Includes a report on human rights violations in El Salvador and maintains that there has been religious persecution in that country. Also contains short articles on Guatemala, Colombia, Ecuador, Chile, and Mexico.

255

Crahan, Margaret E., ed. *Human rights and basic needs in the Americas*. Washington, Woodstock Theological Center, Georgetown University, 1981. *1 v.*

Major work dealing with the similarities and differences in the human rights approaches of dominant normative traditions in the hemisphere and with the impact of national and international economic factors and national security objectives on human rights observance. Also considers strategies and achievements of secular and religious nongovernmental organizations working for the promotion of human rights.

256

Demas, William G. *Human rights in the Caribbean. Trinidad and Tobago review, v. 2, Feb. 1978: 5, 19-20.*

Seminar on human rights and their promotion in the Caribbean, sponsored by the International

Commission of Jurists and the Organization of Commonwealth Caribbean Bar Associations. Suggests ways to resolve conflicting goals of stimulating economic development and protecting civil and political rights.

257

DePassalacqua, John L. A. *Regional institutions assuring the development of fundamental liberties: the American hemisphere. The Catholic lawyer, v. 20, summer 1975: 202-212.*

Discusses treaties and organizations supporting guarantees of fundamental freedoms.

258

Los derechos de la mujer trabajadora; carta adoptada por el Undécimo Congreso Mundial de la CIOSL, México, 1975. *Nueva sociedad, no. 22, 1976: 156.*

Not available for annotation.

259

Derian, Patricia M. *Human rights in Latin America. Washington, U.S. Department of State, Bureau of Public Affairs, 1979. 3 p. (Current policy, no. 68)*

The Assistant Secretary for Human Rights and Humanitarian Affairs briefly describes U.S. human rights policy and reviews the present human rights situation in Argentina, Cuba, Nicaragua, El Salvador, Guatemala, Uruguay, and other American nations. Speech given at Florida International University, Miami, May 18, 1979.

260

Díaz, Gladys, ed. *Report on the subject of human rights. New York, Office for Political Prisoners and Human Rights in Chile, 1978. 19 p. (Chile report, 1978)*

Report from a former political prisoner on human rights as they relate to free speech, unionization, health, education and missing persons.

261

Duchacek, Ivo D. *Rights and liberties in the world today; constitutional promise and reality. Santa Barbara, Calif., ABC-Clio, 1973. 269 p. illus.*

Comparative study of political, economic, and social rights and freedoms expressed in national constitutions. Includes Latin America.

262

Duff, Ernest A., and John F. McCamant. *Violence and repression in Latin America: a quantitative and historical analysis. New York, The Free Press, 1976. 322 p.*

Quantitative analysis of repression and violence by Latin American governments in the 1950's and 1960's. Correlates indicators of several variables: suspension of constitutional rights, arrests, exiles and executions, restrictions of political parties, and censorship of media. Includes bibliography.

263

Eldridge, Joseph. *Política de derechos humanos para América Latina; papel del Congreso. Centro de Investigaciones y Docencia Económicas (Mexico), sem. 2, no. 4, 1978: 275.*

Discusses the role of the U.S. Congress relating to the protection of human rights in Latin America.

264

Farer, Tom J. *Human rights and the anti-Marxist crusade: never the twain shall meet. Notre Dame, Ind., University of Notre Dame, Center for Civil Rights, 1977. 25 p.*

Examines the threat to U.S. strategic interests that is posed by the continued U.S. support of right wing governments.

265

Fearn, Colleen Fahey. *Status of women: the United Nations and Mexico. California western international law journal, v. 8, winter 1978: 93-129.*

General examination of discrimination against women. Includes discussion of "machismo" and the impact of unwritten cultural laws on the status of women in Mexico.

266

Festschrift für Karl Loewenstein; aus Anlass seines achtzigsten Geburtstages. *Hrsg. von Henry Steele Commager [et al.] Tübingen, German Federal Republic, Mohr, 1971. 516 p. port.*

Essays written in honor of Karl Loewenstein, an international lawyer and humanist, that discuss human rights in Latin America in the context of international law and the North American influence. Also considered are the writ of habeas corpus, the protection of rights and freedoms through law within Latin American juridical systems, and the writ of mandamus and injunctions as safeguards to further the observance of basic rights.

267

Fix-Zamudio, Héctor. *Constitución y proceso civil en latinoamérica. Mexico, UNAM, Instituto de Investigaciones Jurídicas, 1974. 125 p. (Serie B, Estudios comparativos-UNAM, Instituto de Investigaciones Jurídicas. Derecho latinoamericano, no. 5)*

Discusses civil procedure and civil rights in Latin America. Includes an extensive bibliography.

268

Fix-Zamudio, Héctor. *Influencia del derecho angloamericano en la protección procesal de los derechos humanos en América Latina. In Festschrift für Karl Loewenstein; aus Anlass seines achtzigsten Geburtstages. Tübingen, German Federal Republic, Mohr, 1971. p. 485-508.*

Traces the origins of habeas corpus in England and the U.S., noting implications for Latin American constitutional law.

269

Fix-Zamudio, Héctor. *Procédures garantissant la jouissance des libertés individuelles en Amérique Latine. International Commission of Jurists. Journal, v. 9, déc. 1968: 65-105.*

Discusses individual liberties and juridical control over their constitutional protection in Latin America and internationally.

270

Fontaine, Pierre-Michel. *Les projets de Convention Interaméricaine des Droits de l'Homme: analyse juridique et considerations politiques. Revue belge de droit international, v. 5, no. 1, 1969: 146-174.*

Describes and analyzes the legal protection of human rights according to the Inter-American Convention on Human Rights.

271

Foro Internacional sobre la Vigencia de los Derechos Humanos en América Latina, Montevideo, 1971. *Foro internacional sobre la vigencia de los derechos humanos en América Latina. [Montevideo] Universidad de la República, Departamento de Publicaciones [1972]. 197 p. (Col. Historia y cultura, no. 22)*

Addresses delivered at a forum of university professors, lawyers, and representatives of labor unions. Discussions of enforcement of human rights sanctions and of current conditions in Uruguay, the Dominican Republic, and Argentina. Summaries in English and French.

272

Fournier, Fernando. *The inter-American human rights system. DePaul law review, v. 21, winter 1971: 376-396.*

Review of guarantees of individual constitutional rights in the San José Pact of 1969.

273

Fox, Donald T. *Doctrinal development in the Americas; from non-intervention to collective support for human rights. New York University journal of international law and politics, v. 1, 1968: 44-60.*

Holds that the implementation of the positive ideals of human rights and representative democracy are consistently expressed in inter-American treaties. Maintains that most Latin American societies are sufficiently advanced to demand humane treatment and their governments sufficiently influenced by international public opinion to recognize the seriousness of O.A.S. recommendations.

274

Fox, Donald T. *The protection of human rights in the Americas. The Columbia journal of transnational law, v. 7, no. 2, 1968: 222-234.*

Discusses the slowness of the O.A.S. in providing a means for the promotion of human rights in the Americas. Analyzes the formation of the O.A.S.'s Inter-American Commission on Human Rights and its activities since 1960.

275

Galeano, Eduardo. *Cemetery of words. Trans. William Rowe. Index on censorship, v. 7, March/Apr. 1978: 3-5.*

Literary comment on intellectual repression in the Southern Cone region of Latin America.

276

Galeano, Eduardo. *Defensa de la palabra; literatura y sociedad en America Latina. Nueva sociedad (San Jose, Costa Rica), no. 33, nov./dic. 1977: 17-24.*

Discusses the linguistic and literary dilemma of Latin America, where illiteracy is high, political promises often hollow, and censorship common.

277

Galeano, Eduardo. *In defense of the word. Trans. William Rowe. Index on censorship, v. 6, July/Aug. 1977: 15-20.*

A distinguished Uruguayan writer, now in exile, comments on repressive measures taken against writers in Latin America.

278

Galeano, Eduardo. *Sobre verdugos, sordomudos, enterrados y desterrados. Nueva sociedad (San Jose, Costa Rica), no. 35, marzo/abr. 1978: 36-47.*

Subjects covered include dictatorship, repression, exile, and the responsibilities of intellectuals.

279

García Bauer, Carlos. *Los derechos humanos, preocupación universal. Guatemala, Universidad de San Carlos, 1960. 532 p.*

Discussion of the compatibility of the Quito Convention on Human Rights with doctrines of non-intervention and national sovereignty.

280

García Bauer, Carlos. *Protection of human rights in America. In International Institute of Human Rights. René Cassin amicorum discipulorumque liber. Problèmes de protection internationale des droits de l'homme. Paris, Editions A. Pédone, 1969. p. 75-88.*

Briefly traces the history of fundamental human rights laws and declarations in the U.S. and Latin America, the U.N., and the O.A.S. Covers political, civil, economic, social, and cultural rights.

281

García Fernández, Andrés. *Los derechos humanos: reflexiones, vivencias, denuncias. Buenos Aires, 1973. 107 p.*

Includes thirty brief radio broadcasts on human rights issues and the text of the Universal Declaration of Human Rights.

282

García Rendón, Godofredo. *La protección de los derechos humanos en el plano universal. Revista de jurisprudencia peruana, v. 24, agosto 1966: 1000-1012.*

International survey taken in 1966 concerning the protection of human rights and the need for people to achieve political and economic self-determination. Includes many Latin American countries.

283

Gastil, Raymond D. *Freedom in the world; political rights and civil liberties, 1978. New York, Freedom House, 1978. 335 p. illus.*

Comparative global survey of freedom. Part I includes tables that rate each country on a seven-point scale according to the degree of political and civil freedom it allows. Part II summarizes the state of these freedoms on a country-by-country basis. All the Latin American countries, with few exceptions, are included.

284

Glaser, Kurt, and Stefan T. Possony. *Victims of politics: the state of human rights. New York, Columbia University Press, 1979. 614 p. illus.*

Analyzes, from various standpoints, how political ideologies affect human rights. Includes chapters on racism and political repression in Latin America.

285

Goldman, Robert K. *The protection of human rights in the Americas: past, present and future. New York, New York*

University, Center for International Studies, 1972. 52 p. (Policy papers, v. 5, no. 2)

Reviews the historical origins of the development of human rights programs in the Americas, regional agreements, and U.S. policy relating to human rights. Provides a description of the Inter-American Commission of Human Rights.

286

González Machado, Tristán. *Los derechos humanos y la represión en América Latina. Cristianismo y sociedad, v. 12, no. 40/41, 1974: 93-109.*

Examination of repression of advocates of social change in Latin America.

287

Green, James Frederick. *Non-governmental organizations. Society, v. 15, Nov./Dec. 1977: 65-70.*

Addresses the need for non-governmental organizations to work for the protection of human rights.

288

Guzmán Carrasco, Marco Antonio. *No intervención y protección internacional de los derechos humanos. Quito, Editorial Universitaria, 1963. 414 p.*

Describes various instruments designed to protect human rights, such as the U.N. Charter and international covenants as well as American agreements since 1948. Reviews the principles of non-intervention and self-determination as they apply to Latin America.

289

Haas, Ernst B. *Human rights and international action; the case of freedom of association. Stanford, Calif., Stanford University Press, 1970. 184 p.*

Functionalist test of the possibility of effective protection of human rights through international organizations based on cases about freedom of association brought before the International Labor Organization between 1963 and 1968. Includes Latin American countries.

290

Hammerskjöld Forum, 12th, New York, Dec. 12, 1967. *International protection of human rights; background paper and proceedings. John Carey, author of the working paper, editor of the proceedings. Dobbs Ferry, N.Y., Published for the Association of the Bar of the City of New York by Oceana Publications, 1968. 116 p. (Oceana book, no. 20-12)*

Cogent introduction to and discussion of U.N. human rights functions. Includes brief bibliographies on the Central American Convention on Human Rights and on the Inter-American Commission on Human Rights. Includes bibliographic references.

291

Henderson, James D. *Another aspect of the violencia. [Unpublished] A paper presented to the 26th Annual Meeting of the Southeastern Council on Latin American Studies, Tampa, Fla., April 20, 1979. 29 p.*

Traces the history and political aspects of the decades long violencia in Colombia, the civil war that stretched from the late 1950's into the early 1960's during which tens of thousands of campesinos were killed. The paper appears in the 1980 Southeastern Council of Latin American Studies Annals.

292

Hennelly, Alfred and John Langan, eds. *Human rights in the Americas: the struggle for consensus. [Washington, Woodstock Theological Center, 1981]. 1 v.*

Papers selected by two Jesuit fellows of the Woodstock Theological Center, dealing with the efforts to achieve a consensus of strategies among secular and religious organizations defending human rights in the hemisphere.

293

Hernández, U. F. *Protection of the individual against the trade unions: Latin America. In International Symposium on Comparative Law, 10th, 1973. Proceedings. [Ottawa] Canadian and Foreign Law Research Centre. 1970: 262-281.*

Compares Latin American labor codes and constitutional provisions protecting workers in order to assess their conformity with Article 20 of the Universal Declaration of Human Rights, which prohibits obligatory membership in any association.

294

Human rights. *Fribourg, Switzerland, Pax Romana, 1976. 39 p. illus. (Convergence, no. 3/4, 1976)*

Editorials from the Catholic apostolic student movement in defense of its advocacy of human rights. Reports on inquiries conducted by Catholic lawyers in Paraguay, Argentina, and Brazil in 1975.

295

Human rights. *In International Law Association. Report of the fifty-fourth conference held at The Hague, August 23rd to August 29th, 1970. [London] 1971. p. 596-662.*

Lists laws protecting human rights in the Americas.

296

Human rights. *In International Law Association. Report of the fifty-fifth conference held at The Hague, August 21st to August 26th, 1972. [London] 1974. p. 539-624.*

Contains general laws with references to Latin America.

297

Human rights and the aid banks: MacNamara steps into the fray. *Inter dependent, v. 4, Oct. 1977: 4.*

Brief news item in a U.N. monthly about the president of the World Bank's opposition to legislation restricting foreign aid to countries which violate human rights.

298

Inter-American Bar Foundation. *The legal protection of human rights in the Western Hemisphere. Washington, 1978. 118 p.*

Provides introduction to basic human rights concepts and the role of the defense lawyer in the Americas as well as to changing U.S. policy objectives. Authored by Latin American lawyers and by U.S. policy experts. Appendixes include declarations of rights for the Americas, and a summary of human rights provisions in all American constitutions.

299

Inter-American Specialized Conference on Human Rights, San José, Costa Rica, 1969. *Final act. Washington, General Secretariat of the Organization of American States, 1970. 18 p. facsims. (Organization of American States. Official records. OEA/Ser. C/VI.18.1)*

Recommends a study by the Inter-American Commission on Human Rights concerning the violation of political rights in Latin America. Includes comments by the representatives of Argentina, El Salvador, and Mexico.

300

International Commission of Jurists. *The Central American Draft Convention on Human Rights and the Central American Court. In its Journal, no. 6, 1965: 129-135.*

Not available for annotation.

301

International Commission of Jurists. *Human rights in the world: Latin America; expulsion, the right to return, passports. In its Review, June 1975: 3-8.*

Commission reports on the increased number of politically motivated expulsions that violate international laws, the American Convention on Human Rights, and the Universal Declaration of Human Rights.

302

International Commission of Jurists. *Human rights in the world: the rule of law in South America. In its Review, Dec. 1973: 11-17.*

Situation report by the Commission's editorial staff assessing South America's human rights record for 1973. Criticizes new military regimes in Chile and Uruguay and notes abuses in Argentina and Brazil. Praises Colombian and Costa Rican ratification of the Inter-American Convention on Human Rights.

303

International Commission of Jurists. *Latin America: integration, the guerrilla movement, and human rights. In its Bulletin, no. 32, Dec. 1967: 26-35.*

Editorial comment on the need to recognize economic rights as human rights and to work toward economic integration in Latin America as a means of preventing guerrilla and governmental violence.

304

International Confederation of Free Trade Unions. *Les droits humains et syndicaux: 11e Congrès mondial de la C.I.S.L., Ciudad de México, D.F., 17-25 Octobre 1975. Bruxelles, Confédération Internationale des Syndicats Libres, 1976. 52 p.*

Addresses relating to civil rights, union rights, and rights of association at the 11th World Congress of the Confederation of Free Trade Unions. Includes comments by the Secretary General of Mexico's Confederation of Labor.

305

International League for Human Rights. *Annual review, International League for Human Rights. 1976-77. [New York] 1977. 22 p.*

Continues: International League for the Rights of Man. Annual report.

Organization's report on its handling of human rights complaints and on the work of its oversight commissions in Latin America and elsewhere.

306

International League for the Rights of Man. *Annual report. [New York] 1972 +*

Continued by: International League for the Rights of Man. Annual review, International League for the Rights of Man

Annual report for its membership covering human rights conditions throughout the world. Includes Latin America. Appendix lists the League's recent publications.

307

International League for the Rights of Man. *Annual review, International League for the Rights of Man. 1974-75. [New York] 1975. 42 p.*

Continues: International League for the Rights of Man. Annual report.

Organization's report on its protests against arbitrary imprisonment throughout the world, urging U.N. action. Section on the Americas, reprints of U.S. newspaper articles on human rights, and list of League affiliates.

308

Jiménez de Aréchaga, Eduardo. *International protection of freedom in the Americas. In Rio, Angel del, ed. Responsible freedom in the Americas. New York, Greenwood Press, 1968. p. 399-410.*

Describes the lack of freedom in the Americas, as well as the obstacles to its full development. Includes a discussion of the efforts of international organizations to promote freedom.

309

Johnson, Kenneth F., and María Mercedes Fuentes. *Política de poder; participación política en América Latina. Buenos Aires, Ediciones IDELA, 1973. 269 p.*

Analyzes the freedom of political participation in each Latin American country. Includes bibliographic references.

310

Joshi, K. C. *American Convention on Human Rights. International journal of legal research, v. 7, 1972: 39-46.*

Deals with the Inter-American Commission on Human Rights, its organization, functions, and procedures, as well as the Inter-American Court of Human Rights and its jurisdiction.

311

Jutkowitz, Joel M. *Ideology, values, and public freedom: an essay assaying the historical context. In Morris J. Blachman, and Ronald G. Hellman, eds. Terms of conflict: ideology in Latin American politics. Philadelphia, Institute for the Study of Human Issues, 1977. p. 237-247.*

Reviews the trend toward militarism in Latin America and the factors most responsible for it. Essay was presented during 1973 to 1974 at a seminar series sponsored by the Center for Inter-American Relations.

312

Klare, Michael, and Nancy Stein. *Secret U.S. bomb school exposed: police terrorism in Latin America. NACLA's Latin America & empire report, v. 8, Jan. 1974: 19-23.*

Attempts to document U.S. counterinsurgency programs in Latin America and the growth in U.S. weapons exports to the Third World. Includes graphs and footnotes.

313

Kutner, Luis. *World habeas corpus, human rights, and the world community. In World Conference on World Peace Through the Rule of Law, 3d, Geneva, 1967. World peace through law; the Geneva World Conference. Geneva, World Peace Through Law Center, 1969: 430-438.*

Argues that strengthening the enforcement of habeas corpus protections will strengthen respect for basic rights.

314

LeBlanc, Lawrence J. *Economic, social, and cultural rights and the inter-American system. Journal of inter-American studies and world affairs, v. 19, Feb. 1977: 61-82.*

Examines the formation of the two principal inter-American human rights instruments--the American Declaration of the Rights and Duties of Man and the American Convention on Human Rights--and asserts that they fail to establish duties of states in the field of economic and social rights.

315

LeBlanc, Lawrence J. *The Inter-American Commission on Human Rights. Revue des droits de l'homme. Human rights journal, v. 9, no. 4, 1976: 645-655.*

Covers the Inter-American Commission on Human Rights and its negotiations with the Brazilian government, as well as solutions to specific cases concerned primarily with the rule of exhausting domestic legal remedies.

316

Loescher, Gil, and Ann Loescher. *Human rights; a global crisis. New York, E. P. Dutton, 1978. 130 p. illus.*

Study of the application of the U.N.'s 1948 Universal Declaration of Human Rights. Illus-

trates restrictions on freedoms in several countries, including Brazil. Includes brief histories of the U.N.'s and Amnesty International's efforts on behalf of human rights and a copy of the U.N. Declaration.

317

Loveman, Brian, and Thomas M. Davies, Jr., eds. *The politics of antipolitics: the military in Latin America. Lincoln, University of Nebraska Press, 1978. 309 p.*

Historical studies of the internal organization and policy-making functions of the military in various Latin American countries with summaries of recent political and military developments in Argentina, Bolivia, Brazil, Chile, and Peru. Refers briefly to torture and the repression of civil rights.

318

Luard, David Evan Trant, ed. *The International protection of human rights. New York, Praeger [1967]. 384 p.*

Collection of articles on the basic international and European human rights organizations and charters, as well as on the protection of the press and trade unions. Provides references to inter-American associations and activities. Includes bibliographies.

319

Martins, D. H. *Suspensión de garantías o estado de sitio ante el derecho constitucional e internacional de los estados Americanos. Revista de la Facultad de Derecho y Ciencias Sociales (Montevideo), v. 17, abr./dic. 1966: 453*

Not available for annotation.

320

Maryknoll Project for Justice and Peace. *La lucha: contemporary issues in Latin America; an action-resource packet. New York, Orbis Books and Friendship Press [1972?]*

Includes articles, folders, a booklet, film lists, and other material dealing with political, economic, social, cultural, and religious aspects of Latin America and its relations with the U.S. Supplements issued twice yearly.

321

Mendonça, Otavio. *O advogado e os direitos do homem. Revista brasileira de cultura*, v. 6, no. 20, abr./jun. 1974: 81-94.

Scholarly paper discussing human rights, delivered at the opening of the Conferencia Nacional da Ordem dos Advogados do Brasil, the fifth national conference of the Brazilian lawyers' association.

322

Morales Avilés, Ricardo. *Sobre la militancia revolucionaria de los intelectuales. Thesis; nueva revista de filosofía y letras*, v. 1, jul. 1979: 63-69.

Statement by a Nicaraguan poet who died in jail. Sets forth the duty of the "intelectual comprometido" of fighting for the destruction of capitalism in order to bring about a "superior society."

323

Moreno, Francisco José, and Barbara Mitrani, eds. *Conflict and violence in Latin American politics; a book of readings. New York, Crowell [1971] 452 p. (Latin American politics and government collections)*

Book of representative readings dealing with the nature and character of instability in Latin America. Many of the articles focus on patterns of violence within political systems.

324

Moreno Rodríguez, R. *Los derechos humanos reconocidos. Lecciones y ensayos (Buenos Aires)*, no. 25, 1963: 187-214.

Not available for annotation.

325

Nadel, Laurie, and Hesh Wiener. *Government: would you sell a computer to Hitler? Computer decisions*, v. 9, Feb. 1977: 22-26.

Journalist's account of the use of computers by Latin American dictatorships and their police forces to repress human rights.

326

Neira, Hugo. *Guerra total contra las élites en América Latina. Estudios centroamericanos (Universidad Centroamericana, José Simeón Cañas)*, v. 32, abr./mayo 1977: 297-308.

Analyzes the significance of the exile of many of Latin America's intellectuals, militarization of the universities, press censorship, and the arrest and torture of political opponents.

327

North American Congress on Latin America. *U.S. strategies for Central America. [New York] 1973. 39 p. illus. (NACLA's Latin America & empire report, v. 7, May/June 1973)*

Overview of social conditions in Central America. Includes a negative assessment of the impact of U.S. private investments there.

328

Orfila, Alejandro. *Human rights: a historical moment for the Americas. Hispania*, v. 62, Mar. 1979: 134-135.

The secretary general of the O.A.S. urges acceptance of the American Convention on Human Rights by member countries of his organization.

329

Orfila, Alejandro. *Human rights in the Americas. Worldview*, v. 20, Oct. 1977: 25-27, 35.

The secretary general of the O.A.S. advocates the establishment of an inter-American counterpart to the European Court of Human Rights.

330

Orfila, Alejandro. *In defense of human rights. The Americas in the 1980's: an agenda for the decade ahead. Washington, University Press of America, 1980. p. 125-139.*

The secretary general of the O.A.S. describes the efforts of his organization to promote the observance of human rights in Latin America. Focus is primarily on the work of the Inter-American Commission on Human Rights.

331

Orrega Vicuña, Claudio. *Basic human rights and political development: 15 years of experience in Latin America. Presented* at a colloquium, Woodrow Wilson International Center for Scholars, Smithsonian Institution, Washington, January 15, 1981. [Washington, 1981]. 67 p. [mimeo].

Political analysis of human rights issues in Latin America from 1965 to 1980, placing them in the context of basic continent wide trends.

332
Ortiz Colindres, Enrique. El derecho de asilo. Tegucigalpa, Editorial Nuevo Continente, 1971. 371 p.

Outlines the historical evolution of the right to asylum and how this right can be safeguarded in the world, with special emphasis on Latin America.

333
Ortúzar, Ximena. Represión y tortura en el Cono Sur. [Fotografías, Francisco Orduña y SIGLA] Mexico, Extemporáneos, 1977. 102 p. illus. (Col. Latinoamérica. Serie Testimonio, no. 1)

Collection of anonymous personal accounts of torture in Chile, Uruguay, and Argentina; prison conditions in Paraguay; and the Brazilian military's suppression of the government's political opponents.

334
O'Shaughnessy, Hugh. What future for the Amerindians of South America? London, Minority Rights Group [1973]. [32] p. illus., maps. (Minority Rights Group. Report, no. 15)

Prefaced by articles from the Universal Declaration of Human Rights, this report summarizes the dilemma of Amazon Basin dwellers and urges that indigenous peoples be protected from annihilation.

335
Pérez, Carlos Andrés. Human rights and the world economic order. Current world leaders; speeches and reports, v. 6, Dec. 1977: 10-14.

Speech given by President Pérez of Venezuela on June 28, 1977, addressing the need for a new international economic structure to ensure universal political and civil rights.

336
Pérez, R. Derecho y libertad en la sociedad actual. Caracas, Universidad Simón Bolívar, 1971. 70 p.

Discusses specific safeguards to protect basic rights in democratic societies with special emphasis on Venezuela.

337
Poesía del toque de queda. Poems at curfew. Introd. Robert Pring-Mill. [New York, Index on Censorship, 1977?]. 36 p.

Poems dealing with censorship. Read for the evening of Spanish-American poetry at the Poetry Society of London, October 27, 1977.

338
Portales, Carlos, and Augusto Varas. América del Sur: armamentismo y derechos humanos. APSI: actualidad internacional, v. 3, nov. 17/30, 1978: 1, 9.

Article on the benefits for economy and society when nations, such as Argentina and Chile, sign arms limitations agreements.

339
Pring-Mill, Robert, trans. Poems at curfew. Index on censorship, v. 7, no. 1, Jan./Feb. 1978: 43-51.

English translation of Latin American poems dealing with censorship, accompanied by an introduction in which the political mission of contemporary Latin American literature is discussed.

340
Quadri, Ricardo Pedro. Elementos para la interpretación de los pactos internacionales de derechos humanos. Buenos Aires, Ministerio de Relaciones Exteriores y Culto, 1968. 121 p.

Juridical and historical exegesis of international pacts relating to human rights by the Argentine delegation to the U.N. Includes appendixes and bibliography.

341
Rama, Angel. La riesgosa navegación del escritor exiliado. Nueva sociedad (San Jose, Costa Rica), no. 35, marzo/abr. 1978: 5-15.

Explores the effects of cultural repression on intellectual activity and suggests that writers oppose such repression politically.

342

Reagan's election: its meaning for U.S.-Latin American policy. *Update, v. 5, Nov./Dec. 1980: 1-2.*

Expresses concern over future U.S.-Latin American policy especially in the area of upholding the observance of human rights in the hemisphere.

343

Rips, Geoff. *Elections in Latin America: legitimizing the dictatorships. USLA reporter, v. 8, no. 1, 1978: 6-7, 15.*

Analyzes the shift toward democracy by the military regimes in Latin America. Examines the countries individually, indicating the background of future leaders.

344

Russell Tribunal II on Repression in Brazil, Chile, and Latin America, 2d, Rome and Brussels, 1974-1975. *Brasile, violazione dei diritti dell'uomo, a cura di Linda Bimbi. Milano, Feltrinelli, 1975. 319 p.*

Presents addresses and legal papers from the 1974-1975 meeting of the Russell Tribunal, including an exposition by Dutch theologian Jan Rutgers on the Catholic Church and the military in Brazil. Includes several statements on "Torture and the Strategy of Terror."

345

Russell Tribunal on Repression in Brazil, Chile, and Latin America, 2d, Rome and Brussels, 1974-1975. *Found guilty: the verdict of the Russell Tribunal session in Brussels. Nottingham, Great Britain, Bertrand Russell Peace Foundation for the Spokesman [1976]. [38] p. (Spokesman pamphlet, no. 51)*

Explanation of the standard of judgement in the U.N.'s Charter used to determine the validity of facts in human rights cases against Brazil, Chile, Uruguay, and Bolivia. Suggests that international, rather than national laws protect human rights.

346

Russell Tribunal on Repression in Brazil, Chile, and Latin America, 2d. *Repression in Latin America. Nottingham, United Kingdom, Bertrand Russell Peace Foundation for Spokesman Books, 1975. [166] p.*

Evidence, charges, and verdicts against Brazil, Chile, Uruguay, and Bolivia for human rights violations.

347

Sandifer, Durward V. *Human rights in the inter-American system. Howard law journal, v. 11, spring 1965: 508-526.*

Reviews the history of human rights in the Americas, emphasizing the importance of the rule of law. Considers the present achievements and failures of the inter-American system. Presented at the Symposium of the Uniform Commercial Code at Howard University School of Law on April 10 to 11, 1964.

348

Sandifer, Durward V., and L. Ronald Scheman. *The foundations of freedom; the interrelationship between democracy and human rights. New York, Praeger, 1966. 139 p.*

Book defines human rights and attempts to demonstrate that democratic government is practical and necessary in order to ensure fundamental human rights. Examples drawn from Latin America and the U.S.

349

Schilling, Paulo R. *Los militares: instrumento de opresión o factor de liberación? Cristianismo y sociedad, no. 2/3, 1974: 61-93.*

Theoretical and structural study of the military and its political role in Latin America.

350

Schwelb, Egon. *Civil and political rights: the international measures of implementation. American journal of international law, v. 62, Oct. 1968: 827-868.*

Describes the practical means available to settle human rights grievances through international and regional institutions, such as the U.N. and the Council of Europe. The author discusses reporting, fact-finding and conciliation procedures. Refers briefly to suggestions from several Latin American countries.

351

Seymour, James D. *Indices of political imprisonment. Universal human rights, v. 1, Jan./Mar. 1979: 99-103.*

Provides data based on figures from Amnesty International on the number of political prisoners and "prisoners of conscience" in most nations. Uruguay, Cuba, and Argentina emerge as the Latin American countries with the greatest number of political prisoners, while Venezuela accounts for the least.

352

Sheahan, John. *Market-oriented economic policies and political repression in Latin America. Williamstown, Mass., Williams College, Center for Development Economics, 1973. 40 p. (Research memorandum, no. 70).*

Observes that political repression has increased in those Latin American countries that have emphasized maximum efficiency in their economic policies. States the need to take into account a country's capacity for change when formulating national economic goals.

353

Spiro, Elizabeth Peterson. *Linking human rights and international aid. Worldview, v. 21, May 1978: 29-30.*

Suggests that the U.S. Congress establish a short list of gross violations of human rights which must be considered before international financial institutions decide to lend money. Mentions the cases of Argentina and Brazil.

354

Stavenhagen, Rodolfo. *The future of Latin America: between underdevelopment and revolution. Latin American perspectives, v. 1, spring 1974: 124-148.*

Reviews past and present cases of military repression in Latin America and evaluates alternative solutions to the existing structural problems.

355

`Swepston, Lee. *Latin American approaches to the "Indian problem." International labour review, v. 117, Jan./Apr. 1978: 179-196.*

Examines the issues that were presented at the Convention on Indigenous and Tribal Populations that was sponsored by the International Labor Organization. Among the issues discussed are administrative systems, land ownership, labor problems, citizenship, and legal status.

356

Symposium on Inter-ethnic Conflict in South America, Bridgetown, Barbados, 1971. *La situación del indígena en América del Sur: aportes al estudio de la fricción inter-étnica en los indios no-andinos. Geneva, World Council of Churches, 1972. 453 p. (Publications of the Department of Ethnology, University of Berne, no. 3)*

"Organized by the Ethnology Department of the University of Berne."

Collection of papers by social anthropologists about the relationship of government policies to the decimaton of indigenous American groups in Venezuela, Colombia, Ecuador, Peru, Bolivia, Paraguay, Argentina, Brazil, and the Guianas.

357

Thomas, Ann Van Wyman, and A. J. Thomas. *The Inter-American Commission on Human Rights. Southwestern law journal, v. 20, June 1966: 282-309.*

Discusses the function and powers of the Inter-American Commission on Human Rights; analyzes the Commission's activities during the 1965 Dominican Republic crisis; and compares the Inter-American Commission with the European Commission.

358

Trigo, Ciro Félix, and Roberto Pérez Paton. *Derechos humanos: I. Estructura y análisis. II. Protección en el orden internacional, [por] Ciro Félix Trigo. Amparo jurisdiccional de los derechos y libertades constitucionales, [por] Roberto Pérez Paton. La Paz, Editorial U.M.S.A., 1960. 87 p. (Universidad Mayor de San Andrés, Publicaciones de la Facultad de Derecho y C. P., Cuaderno no. 23)*

Gives text of the American Convention on Human Rights, an introduction to its history, and theoretical discussions of "amparo" and human rights. Includes bibliography.

359

Uribe Vargas, Diego. *Los derechos humanos y el sistema inter-americano. Madrid, Ediciones Cultura Hispánica, 1972. 359 p. (Col. de Monografías jurídicas)*

At head of title: Centro de Estudios Jurídicos Hispano-americanos.

Colombian law professor explains Latin American ideological stands on individual human rights, national sovereignty, and international laws and courts. Concludes with studies of the rights of man in the Americas and Latin American nations' opinions about the possibility of establishing a Pan American court of justice for human rights cases. Includes bibliography.

360

Valdivia Portugal, Alberto, ed. *Las libertades sindicales y los derechos humanos en la perspectiva del sindicalismo libre y democrático. [n.p.], Costa Rica, Confederación Costarricense de Trabajadores Democráticos, 1979. 1 v. (unpaged)*

At head of title: CCTD (Confederación Costarricense de Trabajadores Democráticos), CTCA (Confederación de Trabajadores de Centroamérica), and ORIT (Organización Regional Interamericana del Trabajo)

Consists of a brief introduction to the pacts in the texts of Convenios nos. 87, 98, and 135 that sanction trade union rights, and a discussion of the pacts of the International Labor Organization (ILO). Includes remarks by Thomas Buergenthal.

361

Van Dyke, Vernon. *Human rights and the rights of groups. American journal of political science, v. 18, Nov. 1974: 725-741.*

Article calls attention to the problem of group rights, the protection of which has been overlooked by political philosophers and by international organizations.

362

Van Dyke, Vernon. *One man, one vote, and majority rule as human rights. Revue des droits de l'homme (Paris), v. 6, Sept. 1973: 447-466.*

Compares special qualifications for voting rights, and the resulting restrictions, in Africa and Latin America.

363

Weissbrodt, David. *The role of international nongovernmental organizations in the implementation of human rights. Texas international law journal, v. 12, spring/summer 1977: 293-320.*

Survey of non-governmental organizations, such as Amnesty International, which observe and advise the U.N. and the O.A.S. on human rights matters. Examples are drawn from Chile, Brazil, and Uruguay.

364

Wiarda, Howard J, *Democracy and human rights in Latin America: toward a new conceptualization. Orbis, v. 22, spring 1978: 137-160.*

Deals with the issues of human rights and U.S. relations with authoritarian regimes of Latin America and raises questions about the universality and relevancy of human rights in different societies.

365

Women in Dialogue. *Inter-American meeting. Translation coordinated by Ruth Fitzpatrick. Notre Dame, Ind., Catholic Committee on Urban Ministry, 1979. 129 p.*

"Translations of Seminar Sessions held 'outside the walls' during CELAM III, Third Conference of Latin American Bishops."

These sessions, which were held to insure that the Catholic feminist voice be heard at the Conference, covered such issues as women and liberation, domestic workers, the family, poverty, and birth control, with special emphasis on Latin America. Includes their conclusions.

366

World Conference on World Peace Through the Rule of Law. *World Peace Through Law; [Papers presented] 1st + 1963 + St. Paul, Minn., West Pub. Co.*

Presents papers on human rights problems. Continued by its World Law Review.

367

World Conference on World Peace Through the Rule of Law, Athens, 1963. *World peace Through law; the Athens World Conference. St. Paul, Minn., West Pub. Co., 1964. 874 p.*

Record of addresses and working sessions from the first world conference. In working session IV, the creation of an Inter-American Court of Justice is advocated by a Cuban exile, and a Costa Rican recommends the establishment of regional courts for specialized purposes such as the protection of human rights.

368

World Council of Peace. *For national independence, sovereignty and development in Latin America; WPC Bureau meeting, Panama, October 15-18, 1974. Helsinki, Information Centre of the World Peace Council, 1974. 55 p.*

Includes a resolution against fascism in Latin America, a declaration on the Southern Cone countries, and proposals for the World Peace Council program of action for Latin America.

369

World Health Organization. *Health aspects of human rights; with special reference to developments in biology and medicine. Geneva, 1976. 48 p.*

Study designed to support the 23rd World Health Assembly's resolution reaffirming the right to health as a human right. Comments on birth control, human experimentation, medical records, and compulsory health protection.

370

Zaragoza, Juan de Miguel. *Los derechos del hombre en las sociedades dualistas hispanoamericanas. Información jurídica (Madrid), enero/marzo 1971: 7-39.*

Analysis of political, economic, and social factors that affect the protection of legal human rights in Latin America.

Argentina

371

Aja Espil, Jorge. *Cuadro comparativo de la Declaración Universal de Derechos Humanos y la Constitución Argentina. [Buenos Aires], Ministerio de Educación y Justicia, Comisión Argentina para la UNESCO, 1963. 14 p.*

Compares human rights provision in the Universal Declaration of Human Rights with those of the Argentine Constitution.

372

American Federation of Labor-Congress of Industrial Organizations. *Torture in Argentina. Free trade union news, v. 33, Nov. 1978: 1-4.*

Provides a personal account of an Argentine's abduction, interrogation, and torture by the security forces of his country.

373

American Friends Service Committee. *Everyone can save a life: a resource and action update on Argentina. Philadelphia, Pa., American Friends Service Committee, Peace Education Division, Human Rights Desk, 1977. 1 v. (unpaged)*

Packet designed to provide both background and current information on the economic, political, and human rights situation in Argentina. Includes recommendations.

374

Amnesty International. *Evidence of torture: studies of the Amnesty International Danish Medical Group. London, Amnesty International Publications, 1977. 39 p. illus.*

Analyzes the adverse medical effects of torture. Includes case studies from Argentina, Chile, and Uruguay.

375

Amnesty International. *Report of an Amnesty International mission to Argentina, November 6-15, 1976. London, Amnesty International Publications, 1977. 92 p.*

Assesses the status of human rights in Argentina since the military coup of 1976. Reveals evidence of torture, political executions, jailings, and disappearances. Includes the names of 489 disappeared individuals.

376

Argentina: genocidio y resistencia. *Bilbao, Spain, Zero; Madrid, Distribuidor Exclusivo ZYX, 1977. 63 p. illus. (América Latina, no. 1. Cuadernos Aesla)*

Examines the economic insecurity and the institutionalized repression that have gripped Argentina since the coup of 1976. Attributes the upsurge in violence to the drop in real wages.

377

Argentina: the war goes on. *North American Congress on Latin America. NACLA's Latin America & empire report, v. 11, Jan. 1977: 3-24.*

Economic and political analysis of the 1976 coup in Argentina. Discusses the repressive policies of the military regime.

378

Argentina: under the gun; a political, economic and theological overview. *Infor act bulletin, June 1978: 1-18.*

Provides information concerning the repression of civil liberties in present day Argentina.

379

Argentine Commission for Human Rights. Washington Information Bureau. *Human rights, democratic liberties and U.S.-Argentine relations. Washington, 1977. [31] p.*

Legal and political analysis of violations of human rights in Argentina. Includes references.

380

Argentine Information and Solidarity Committee. *Repression of the Argentine Church. New York, 1976. 6 p.*

Press conference held in Montreal, Canada, on June 23, 1976, by the Rev. Antonio Reiser, an Argentine political refugee. Examines the effects of repression on the poor and on Catholic Church activists who work on their behalf.

381

Argentine Information Service Center. *Argentina today; a dossier on repression and the violation of human rights.* 2d ed. [s.l.] 1977. [34] p.

Describes the effects of governmental repression on Argentine society. Includes documentation.

382

Argentine Information Service Center. *Repression in Argentina: the right of option.* [s.l.] 1976. 13 p.

Examines the civil rights of Argentines arrested without charges during the state of siege. Includes decrees enacted by the military junta to cancel temporarily civil and political rights.

383

Argentine Information Service Center. *22 [i.e. Twenty-two] disappeared children. Argentina outreach,* v. 3, June/July 1978: 14-15.

Lists the names of 22 missing young persons. Pleads with international human rights organizations to work on their behalf.

384

Argentine Support Movement. *Argentina: 1976; repression and resistance.* London, 1976. [15] p.

Examines the military coup in Argentina and the popular opposition to it. Includes appendixes.

385

Argentine Support Movement. *Argentina: the trade union struggle.* London, 1976. 1 v. (various pagings)

Resolutions of the British Trade Union Conference decry the repression of trade unionists in Argentina. Lists governmental mechanisms designed to control the labor movements and unions.

386

Asamblea Permanente por los Derechos Humanos. *Acta de fundación; temas de seminario; estatutos.* Buenos Aires [1977] 7 p.

Includes the Assembly's Declaration of Principles as well as information on its operating rules and the human rights seminars it sponsored in 1976.

387

Asamblea Permanente por los Derechos Humanos. *Declaración pública.* Buenos Aires, 1978. 1 p.

Reaffirms the Assembly's commitment to the promotion of human rights and the eradication of terrorism.

388

Asamblea Permanente por los Derechos Humanos. *2 [i.e. Dos] años de lucha por los derechos humanos.* Buenos Aires, 1977. 11 p. illus.

Provides a brief chronology of events from 1975 to 1977 pertaining to human rights in Argentina.

389

Asamblea Permanente por los Derechos Humanos. *Letter, 1978 Sept. 7, Buenos Aires, to Teniente General Jorge Rafael Videla, Buenos Aires.* [3] leaves.

Open letter to the President of Argentina pleading for an end to repression. Requests that charges against 4,000 political prisoners be resolved.

390

Asamblea Permanente por los Derechos Humanos. *1978 [i.e. Mil novecientos setenta y ocho]; asegurar la paz y salvaguardar la vida.* Buenos Aires, 1977. 22 p. illus.

"Sesión plenaria del Consejo de Presidencia de la APDH."

Reports on the activities of the Assembly during 1977. Calls for an investigation into the matter of missing persons.

391

Asamblea Permanente por los Derechos Humanos. *¿Por que el Profesor Alfredo Bravo sigue detenido?* Buenos Aires, 1978. 8 p.

Discusses the efforts to secure the freedom of Alfredo Bravo, an Argentine professor who has been held without charges since September, 1977.

392

Asamblea Permanente por los Derechos Humanos. *Presentación colectiva elevada al Excelentísimo Sr. Presidente de la Nación Teniente General Don Jorge Rafael Videla, para determinar la situación de personas desaparecidas. Buenos Aires, 1977. 12 p.*

Petition delivered on August 9, 1977, concerning the disappearance of detained individuals.

393

Astrada, Etelvina. *Poesía política y combativa argentina. Madrid, Zero ZYX, 1978. 285 p. (Col. Guernica, no. 15)*

Contains poems by 40 Latin American writers; some poems were written by well-known authors such as Julio Cortázar, Enrique Lihn, and Juan Gelman, others by lesser known writers. Many of the poems deal with the imprisonment of writers and with exile, while others deal with anti-Americanism.

394

Berg, Gracia. *Human rights sanctions as leverage: Argentina, a case study. Journal of legislation, v. 7, 1980: 93-112.*

Discusses some of the factors that are relevant to the effectiveness of the human rights sanctions as leverage in countries not dependent on United States aid. Reviews current legislation in Argentina and provides background for study of its effectiveness.

395

Brewin, Andrew, Louis Duclos, and David MacDonald. *One gigantic prison: the report of the fact-finding mission to Chile, Argentina, and Uruguay. Toronto, Inter-Church Committee on Chile, 1976. 69 p.*

Report of the Inter-Church Committee's mission to South America in October, 1976, to investigate human rights violations in Argentina, Chile, and Uruguay.

396

Caistor, Nick. *Cleansing the teaching area. Index on censorship, v. 7, May/June 1978: 18-23.*

Maintains that education has deteriorated in Argentina since the military coup of March, 1976.

397

Carter's "human rights" means Videla/Pinochet. *Workers' vanguard, Sept. 9, 1977: 1, 11.*

Evaluation of President Carter's human rights policy toward Chile by the Marxist working-class weekly of the Spartacist League of the United States.

398

Catholic Institute for International Relations. *Death and violence in Argentina. London, 1976. 11 p.*

Priests' report on violence and threats of violence against church people in Argentina. Lists those arrested, missing, freed, deported, and exiled.

399

Centre Argentin d'Information et de Solidarité. *Prisons argentines. Paris, 1976. 17 p.*

Letters and testimonies of political prisoners describing torture and illegal detentions. Call for the Argentine people and the international community to work toward their release.

400

Chacra, A. *Los derechos humanos en la Argentina. Buenos Aires, Cooperadora de Derecho y Ciencias Sociales, 1964. 112 p.*

Compares the articles outlined in the United Nations Declaration of Human Rights with the provisions pertaining to civil and political rights guaranteed in the Argentine Constitution.

401

Comisión Argentina por los Derechos Humanos. *Argentina: los crímenes de la dictadura; octubre 1976-febrero 1977. Mexico, 1977. 80 p.*

Reports on violations of human rights by the Argentine government between 1976 and 1977. Includes clippings, official declarations, denunciations, and testimony describing arrests, disapperances, and torture.

402

Comisión Argentina por los Derechos Humanos. *Argentina: proceso al genocidio. Madrid, E. Querejeta, 1977. 328 p.*

Makes allegations concerning the repression in Argentina after the military takeover by General Videla.

403

Comisión Argentina por los Derechos Humanos. *Documentos, crónicas e información acerca de la situación represiva en la República Argentina, a partir del golpe militar del 24 de marzo de 1976. Paris, 1976. 1 v. (unpaged)*

Significant, well-documented contributions to the literature on human rights in Argentina. Discusses governmental repression and the illegality of human rights violations. Provides information concerning prison conditions, involuntary detentions, kidnappings, and political executions since the 1976 coup.

404

Comisión Argentina por los Derechos Humanos. *El régimen argentino y la doctrina de la seguridad nacional. Boletín CADHU, Nov./Dec. 1977: 3.*

Analyzes the military regime's suppression of civil and political liberties.

405

Comisión Argentina por los Derechos Humanos. *Testimonios de la represión en Argentina. Mexico, 1977. [42] p.*

Summarizes the Commission's three 1976 reports concerning the violation of human rights in Argentina. Provides evidence as to their continued occurrence.

406

Comisión Argentina por los Derechos Humanos. *Villa Devoto: una "carcel modelo" de la dictadura militar. Boletín CADHU, no. 5, Sept./Oct. 1978: 6-7.*

Describes the Villa Devoto prison in Buenos Aires and the status of its female inmates.

407

Committee for the Defense of Human Rights in Argentina. *Argentina '76: a dossier on political repression and the violation of human rights. Ontario, Canada, 1977. 15 p.*

Discusses the Argentine military regime and the response of the Catholic Church to it. Includes testimony on repression.

408

Cortázar, Julio. *El lector y el escritor. Denuncia, v. 4, set. 1978: 10.*

Contains remarks made by Julio Cortázar in 1978 at the P.E.N. Club in Stockholm, Sweden. Denounces the political isolation of the Southern Cone nations of Latin America.

409

Dana Montaño, Salvador M. *Las garantías de los derechos en el derecho público provincial argentino. Cordoba, Argentina, Universidad de Córdoba, 1963. 242 p.*

Examines the guarantees of fundamental freedoms outlined in the constitutions of the provinces of Argentina. Includes a comparative analysis of the writ of amparo.

410

Dowie, Mark. *Terror 3: the General and the children. Mother Jones, July 1978: 37-48.*

Account of the human rights violations endured by members of an Argentine family.

411

Drinan, Robert F. *Religious and political repression in Argentina. Commonweal, Feb. 18, 1977: 103-104.*

Reports on Congressman Drinan's visit to Argentina on behalf of Amnesty International. Suggests the suspension of U.S. aid in response to the human rights abuses of the Videla regime.

412

Foro de Buenos Aires por la Vigencia de los Derechos Humanos. *Proceso a la explotación y a la represión en la Argentina. Buenos Aires, 1973. 222 p.*

Decries the human rights violations of the military regime in Argentina. Describes working conditions, the detention of political prisoners, and torture.

413

Foro por el Respeto de los Derechos Humanos en Argentina. *Un año después del golpe; situación del movimiento obrero en Argentina. Paris, 1977. 38 p.*

Reports on the resistance movement in Argentina one year after the coup. Analyzes laws harmful to labor relations, negotiations, and strikes.

414

Fuentes, Abel. *Argentine: entre la terreur et l'espérance; temoignage écrit dans un camp de concentration. Paris, CIMADE-Information, 1977. 28 p.*

Discusses the torture of political prisoners in Argentina. Translated from Spanish.

415

Galeano, Eduardo. *Cemetery of words. Index on censorship, v. 7, Mar./Apr. 1978: 3-5.*

Literary commentary on the repression of intellectuals in the Southern Cone region of Latin America.

416

García F., Patricio, ed. *Prontuario: técnica del interrogatorio, la represión, y el asesinato. Exclusivo. Santiago, Editora N. Quimantu, División de Publicaciones Educativas, 1973. 96 p. (Documentos especiales)*

Journalistic profile of torturers and tortured in Argentina. Includes descriptions of interrogation techniques, prison conditions, and interviews with survivors and psychiatrists.

417

González, Marian Baxter. *Nobel peace award ruffles Argentine regime. Latinamerica press, v. 12, Oct. 30, 1980: 1-2, 8.*

Adolfo Pérez Esquivel, Director of Servicio Paz y Justicia de América Latina, was awarded the Nobel Peace Prize in 1980. A pacifist Christian human rights activist, Pérez Esquivel accepted the award on behalf of "the poor of Latin America, the peasants and workers, and all those who strive for a more just and human society."

418

Graham-Yool, Andrew. *Letter from Argentina. Index on censorship, v. 2, summer 1973: 43-45.*

Reviews censorship in Argentina from 1967 to 1973. Maintains that censorship affects all aspects of national life.

419

Graham-Yool, Andrew. *The press in Argentina, 1973-1978. London, Writers and Scholars Educational Trust, 1978. 171 p.*

Chronology of events since 1973 concerning the suppression of the press by the Argentine military regime. Among the topics discussed are press censorship and the violation of the human rights of journalists.

420

Inter-Church Committee on Human Rights in Latin America. *Argentina: two years of military rule. Toronto, Ontario, 1978. 23 p.*

Documents both human rights violations in Argentina and the Canadian efforts to curb these abuses.

421

International Commission of Jurists. *Argentina. In its Review, June 1976: 1-4.*

Portrays the activities of the Argentine military in 1976. Includes an overview of the regime's economic, judicial, and legislative policies.

422

International Commission of Jurists. *Argentina: subjection of the judiciary. In its Bulletin, Sept. 1968: 13-17.*

Discussion of the executive reorganization of the judiciary in the Province of Santa Fe, Argentina, and of the opposition to it by the press and various legal associations.

423

International Commission of Jurists. *Human rights in the world: plight of defense lawyers in Argentina. In its Review, June 1975: 1-3.*

Summarizes a report which examines the repression encountered by Argentine lawyers in their defense of clients accused of political crimes. The report was prepared by Heleno Claudio Fragoso of the I.C.J. mission to Argentina in March, 1975.

424

International Commission of Jurists. *Report of mission to Argentina, March, 1975. [Geneva?, 1976?] 20 p.*

Heleno Claudio Fragoso, a Brazilian criminal attorney, examines the repression of defense attorneys by the Argentine military government.

425

International Commission of Jurists. Centre for the Independence of Judges and Lawyers. *Attacks on the independence of judges and lawyers in Argentina. International Commission of Jurists bulletin, v. 1, Feb. 1978: whole issue.*

Reports on the intimidation of lawyers and judges in political trials. Includes abstracts of cases and lists of missing or detained lawyers.

426

International League for Human Rights. *Report of a mission to Argentina; 18-25 January 1978. [New York, 1978?] 19 p.*

Investigation by a fact-finding mission of prominent French and North American jurists. Evaluates the human rights situation in Argentina and looks into reports of missing French citizens there.

427

Jitrik, Noé. *Escritores argentinos: dependencia o libertad. Buenos Aires, Ediciones del Candil, 1967. 129 p.*

Examines the political role of the writer and the critic.

428

Jitrik, Noé. *Primeros tanteos: literatura y exilio. Nueva sociedad (Costa Rica), no. 35, marzo/abr. 1978: 48-55.*

Prominent literary critic portrays the situation of the Argentine writer under past and present regimes. Analyzes the consequences of literary exile.

429

Joint Working Group for Refugees from Chile in Britain. *Political prisoners and refugees in the Southern Cone of Latin America. [London] 1977. 25 p.*

Reviews the Joint Working Group's assistance program. Attempts to determine achievable goals.

430

Jordan, David C. *Argentina's military commonwealth. Current history, v. 76, Feb. 1979: 66-69, 89-90.*

Examination of current domestic politics and foreign affairs in Argentina. Discusses both the weakening of American-Argentine ties since World War II and the strain that President Carter's human rights policy has caused between the two countries.

431

Kinzer, Stephen. *Argentina in agony: how a nation can destroy itself while pretending everything is normal. New republic, Dec. 23/30, 1978: 17-21.*

Examines political turmoil and violations of human rights in Argentina between 1976 and 1978.

432

Kovadloff, Jacob. *Press suppression in Argentina: the Timerman case. USA today, v. 108, Sept. 1979: 30-32.*

Describes both the confiscation of the newspaper, La Opinión by the Argentine government and the 30-month detention of its publisher, Jacobo Timerman.

433

Lafue-Veron, Madeleine. *Human rights in Argentina after the March 24th military coup. New York, Argentine Information Service Center, 1976. 25 p.*

Report prepared on behalf of the International Movement of Catholic Jurists detailing events that preceded the military coup. Summarizes current legislation suppressive of political activity and provides testimony on the arrests and kidnappings of trade unionists, farm workers, priests, and professionals.

434

Lernoux, Penny. *Military repression angers Argentine Catholic Church.* New York, Alicia Patterson Foundation, 1977. 10 p.

Historical analysis of the Catholic Church's defense of human rights in Argentina.

435

Levenstein, Harvey. *Scandal, anti-Semitism rocks regime.* In these times, v. 1, June 1/7, 1977: 11.

Comments on both the upsurge of anti-Semitism among the military in Argentina and the threat that anti-Semitism poses to the stability of the Videla government.

436

Levy, Daniel. *Higher education policy in authoritarian regimes: comparative perspectives on the Chilean case.* New Haven, Conn., Yale Higher Education Research Group Working Paper, 1980. 60 p.

The military reorganization of and policies toward Chilean universities, outlined and compared to those of Argentina and Brazil.

437

Maurer, Harry. *Anti-Semitism in Argentina.* Nation, Feb. 12, 1977: 170-173.

Discusses the repression of Argentine Jews after the coup of 1976.

438

Moras Mom, Jorge R., and Laura T. A. Damianovich. *Delitos contra la libertad.* Buenos Aires, Ediar Sociedad Anónima Editora; Comercial, Industrial y Financiera, 1972. 308 p.

Theoretical work that suggests legal remedies for governmental suppression of freedom in Argentina.

439

National Academy of Sciences. *National Academy of Sciences Committee on Human Rights: results of a visit to Argentina and Uruguay.* Washington, 1978. 16 p.

Three person task force report on the effects of the repression of the Argentine scientific community by the military regime. Describes the task force's efforts to secure the release of a mathematician and his wife who were imprisoned in Uruguay.

440

North American Congress on Latin America. *Argentina in the hour of the furnaces.* New York, 1975. 105 p.

Ideological review of political events that followed the victory of the Peronist Justicialist Liberation Front in 1973. Includes chronologies and reproductions of previous articles.

441

Norton, Bruce. *Terrorism in Argentina: U.S. strategy for the Southern Cone.* CALA newsletter, v. 6, Nov. 1977: whole issue.

Portrays the worsening state of civil and political rights in Argentina.

442

Organization of American States. Inter-American Commission for Human Rights. *Informe sobre la situación de los derechos humanos en Argentina.* Washington, 1980. 289 p. (O.A.S. [Official records] OEA/Ser.L/V/II.49, doc. 19)

Report of human rights violations in Argentina from 1975 to 1979 drawn from interviews held by representatives of the Commission with former political prisoners and their relatives in the fall of 1979. Includes specific recommendations.

443

Pellegrini, Vicente. *Los derechos humanos en el presente contexto socio-político de Argentina.* Centro de Investigaciones y Acción Social. Revista, v. 25, Dec. 1976: 11-41.

Examines the violation of human rights in Argentina. Discusses the reaction of the Catholic Church to this violence.

444

Pevzner, Sam. *Anti-Semitism in Argentina. Jewish currents*, Dec. 1976: 4-7.

Describes the upsurge of anti-Semitism in Argentina. Makes an appeal for prompt action to remedy the situation.

445

Pike, David Wingate. *Human rights: the conscience of the individual. Latin American yearly review (France)*, v. 3, 1975: 4-ll.

Portrays the state of human rights in the Southern Cone, Panama, and Cuba with background summaries concerning U.S. human rights policy and the activities of the Catholic Church.

446

Primakc, Joel. *Human rights in the Southern Cone. Bulletin of the atomic scientists*, v. 37, Feb. 1981: 24-29.

Claims that repression in Uruguay and Argentina has had disastrous effects on education and science.

447

Rama Sindical del Movimiento Peronista Montonero. *Represión y resistencia. Buenos Aires*, 1977. 15 p.

Analyzes the adverse effects of the military regime on the Argentine labor movement. Includes a list of more than 500 active union members who have been kidnapped or murdered.

448

Rips, Geoff. *The structure of repression in Argentina. USLA reporter*, v. 8, no. 1, 1978: 8-9.

Examines the institutionalization of repression in Argentina. Provides statistics on political prisoners.

449

Roberts, Thomas E. *The Writ of Amparo: a remedy to protect constitutional rights in Argentina. Ohio State law journal*, v. 31, fall 1970: 831-851.

Historical analysis of the provisions in the Argentine Constitution that protect a citizen's rights against the decrees of a dictatorial government. Discusses the writ of amparo and compares the Argentine, Brazilian, and Mexican constitutional provisions relating to this writ.

450

Rodríguez, Abelardia, and Héctor Schmuler. *El papel político-ideológico de los medios de comunicación; el caso de la crisis argentina de 1975. Caracas, Instituto Latinoamericano de Investigaciones Sociales*, 1977. 105 p. (*Serie materiales de trabajo, no. 8*)

Well documented analysis of the impact of the mass media in Argentina. Describes the position of the media during both the July 9, 1975, political crisis and the subsequent coup. Includes a useful summary.

451

Rodríguez Larreta, Enrique. *Kidnapped in Buenos Aires. Index on censorship*, v. 6, July/Aug. 1977: 22-29.

Account of a Uruguayan journalist's search for his missing son in Argentina.

452

Sierra, Gerónimo de. *Migrantes uruguayos hacia la Argentina. Mexico, Instituto de Investigaciones Sociales*, 1977. 31 p.

"Documento preparado para la VI reunión del Grupo de Trabajo sobre Migraciones Internas de la Comisión de Población y Desarrollo de CLASCO."

Not available for annotation.

453

Sofer, Eugene F. *A new terror grips Argentina. Present tense*, v. 5, no. 1, 1977: 19-25.

Describes anti-Semitism in Argentina and comments on the effects of this violence upon the Jewish citizenry.

454

Soler, Sebastián, and Eduardo H. Marquardt. *Deprivation of personal freedom in Argentine law. International Commission of Jurists. Review*, v. 3, no. 2, 1961: 16-38.

Study of the conditions in Argentine law under which an individual can be denied his rights.

455

Symposium on Inter-ethnic Conflict in South America, Bridgetown, Barbados, 1971. *La situación del indígena en América del Sur: aportes al estudio de la fricción inter-étnica en los Indios no-andinos. Geneva, World Council of Churches, 1972. 453 p. (Publications of the Dept. of Ethnology, Univ. of Berne, no. 3)*

This collection of papers by social anthropologists examines governmental policies that lead to the eradication of indigenous populations in Latin America.

456

Terror, Argentine style. *Matchbox, winter 1977: 1-2.*

Unsigned article depicting the violence perpetrated against intellectuals in Argentina by the Videla government despite that government's pledge to uphold human rights.

457

Timerman, Jacobo. *Prisoner without a name, cell without a number. Translated by Toby Talbot. New York, Alfred A. Knopf, 1981. 164 p.*

The former editor of the Buenos Aires newspaper, La Opinión, describes his arrest by a military faction in 1977 and his repeated interrogations and torture, and addresses the question of anti-Semitism. After the Supreme Court ruled that he was being held without cause, he was moved into house arrest until his final release in 1979.

458

Torrens, Nissa. *Time of silence. Index on censorship, v. 7, May/June 1978: 24-28.*

Examines the suppression of human rights as a consequence of political dissent in Argentina.

459

Torturas. *Cuadernos de marcha, Dec. 1970: whole issue.*

Examines torture in Argentina, Brazil, and Uruguay. Reproduces the "black book" of torture.

460

U.N. Commission on Human Rights. *Further promotion and encouragement of human rights and fundamental freedoms, including the question of the programme and methods of work of the Commission. New York, 1978. 17 p. (U.N. [Document] E/CN. 4/1273/Add. 1)*

At head of title: Economic and Social Council. Agenda item 11 of the provisional agenda.

Report prepared by the Secretary General pursuant to Decision 4 (XXXIII) of the Commission on Human Rights. Summarizes the main points concerning the coexistence of public and confidential procedures for dealing with the violations of human rights mentioned during the 33d session. Includes comments and observations by Argentina.

461

U.N. General Assembly. *Los derechos humanos en la Argentina; la Declaración Universal de Derechos Humanos de las Naciones Unidas; la Constitución nacional y las veintidos constituciones provinciales. Buenos Aires, Cooperadora de Derecho y Ciencias Sociales [1964] [123] p.*

At head of title: Amado Chacra, ed.

Compares the rights guaranteed in the Universal Declaration of Human Rights with the provisions outlined in the National Constizution of Argentina. The study was sponsored by the Asociación Argentina.

462

Wade, Nicholas. *Repression in Argentina: scientists caught up in tide of terror. Science, v. 194, Dec. 24, 1976: 1397-1399.*

Reports on the dismissal and arrest of Argentine scientists by officials of the Videla government. Discusses efforts to secure their release.

463

Walsh, Rodolfo. *Witness in difficult times. Index on censorship, v. 6, Sept./Oct. 1977: 3-7.*

Open letter by an Argentine writer denouncing the repression of civil rights in his country. The author was kidnapped the day after his letter was released to the public and has not been seen since.

464

Wheaton, Phillip. *Plan Mercurio; round-up for political exiles. Counter spy, v. 28, Dec. 1976: 29-33.*

The co-director of the Ecumenical Program for Inter-American Communication and Action discusses both the decline of democratic governments in the Southern Cone region of Latin America and the extermination of foreign political exiles in Argentina.

465

World University Service. United Kingdom Council. *Chile, Argentina, Uruguay: an outline of conditions in 1977. London, 1977. 21 p.*

Examines the erosion of basic human rights in the Southern Cone. Discusses the international efforts to aid Argentine, Chilean, and Uruguayan refugees, the role of the Catholic Church in Chile, and the repression of the press in Argentina. Gives recommendations and includes bibliography.

466

Youth of the Intransigent Party. *For peace, democracy, social justice and national liberation. Buenos Aires, 1978. 9 p.*

Describes the deterioration of living conditions in Argentina. Comments on the repression practiced by the military regime and requests the support of the international community to help terminate it.

Bolivia

467

Albó, Javier. *Achacachi; rebeldes pero conservadores.* In *Actes des XLIIe Congrès International des Americanistes, v. 3. Paris, 1976. 32 p.* (Published as an extract)

Deals with the struggles for land and rights of Bolivian Indians.

468

Asamblea Permanente de Derechos Humanos de Bolivia. *Declaración Universal de Derechos Humanos.* La Paz, 1978. 1 v. (unpaged)

Discusses human rights violations in Bolivia. Written in commemoration of the 30th anniversary of the Universal Declaration of Human Rights.

469

Asamblea Permanente de Derechos Humanos de Bolivia. *Estudio sobre el valor adquisitivo del salario de los mineros. La Paz, 1978. 26 p.*

Examines the economic conditions of Bolivian miners. Includes tables and appendix.

470

Asamblea Permanente de Derechos Humanos de Bolivia. *El fascismo en Bolivia; la Declaración de los Derechos Humanos y la represión en Bolivia. La Paz, 1977. 19 p.*

Examines government repression of human rights in Bolivia.

471

Asamblea Permanente de Derechos Humanos de Bolivia. *El golpe militar del 17 de julio de 1980 en Bolivia. [La Paz, 1980]. 18 p.*

Succinct description of the sequence of the July 1980 coup which toppled President Lydia Gueiler. Describes the taking of political prisoners, the suppression of labor organizations, and the muzzling of the media. States that from the outset torture was used to subdue political prisoners.

472

Asamblea Permanente de Derechos Humanos de Bolivia. *La huelga de hambre. La Paz, 1978. 285 p.*

Reports on the 28 day hunger strike in support of the Assembly of Human Rights in Bolivia. Includes tables and photographs.

473

Asamblea Permanente de Derechos Humanos de Bolivia. *La iglesia de Bolivia:¿compromiso o traición? Ensayo de análisis histórico. La Paz, 1978. 153 p.*

Analyzes the role of the Catholic Church in Bolivia since Vatican II.

474

Asamblea Permanente de Derechos Humanos de Bolivia. *Informe de actividades y resúmen histórico del primer año de existencia de la Asamblea, noviembre 1976-diciembre 1977. La Paz, 1977. 6 p.*

Brief account of the activities of the Asamblea Permanente de Derechos Humanos during its first year of existence.

475

Asamblea Permanente de Derechos Humanos de Bolivia. *El proceso electoral; resumen de las normas prácticas que deben observarse en las elecciones. La Paz, 1978. 15 p.*

Explains, in laymen's terms, the electoral law of Bolivia.

476

Asamblea Permanente de Derechos Humanos de Bolivia. *Protesta popular y represión. Coripata, Bolivia, 1978. 37 p.*

Describes both the repression of civil and political rights in Bolivia and the protests such repression elicits.

477

Asamblea Permanente de Derechos Humanos de Bolivia. *Reflexión cristiana sobre la Declaración Universal de los Derechos Humanos. La Paz, 1977. 46 p.*

Religious interpretation of the Universal Declaration of Human Rights and how it applies to Bolivia.

478

Basso, Lelio, ed. *Atti della prima sessione del Tribunale Russell II. Venice, Italy, Marsilio Editore, 1975. 376 p.*

Charges and testimony from the Bertrand Russell Tribunal on human rights violations in Chile, Uruguay, and Bolivia.

479

Bolivia: 1971-76; pueblo, estado, iglesia; testimonios de cristianos. *Lima, Centro de Estudios y Publicaciones, 1976. 191 p. illus. (CEP, no. 16)*

Report, containing letters signed by Bolivian Catholic clergymen, that protests the loss of traditional religious freedoms and civil rights under the military regime of Hugo Banzer.

480

Centro de Información y Documentación Boliviano. *Los derechos y el campesino. La Paz, 1978. 11 p. (Los campesinos opinan, no. 3)*

Discusses the peasants' role in the Bolivian social structure and the injustices to which they are often subjected.

481

Centro de Información y Documentación Boliviano. *El nuevo rol de la mujer campesina. La Paz, 1978. 12 p. (Los campesinos opinan, no. 1)*

Describes the adverse living conditions and the discrimination faced by peasant women of the Bolivian altiplano.

482

Comisión Episcopal Boliviana. Secretariado General. *Hablan los obispos; orientando sobre constitucionalización del país y próximas elecciones. La Paz, Impresiones Impacto, 1978. 13 p.*

Guidelines on the electoral process presented by the bishops of Bolivia in response to the increasing repression of political rights in their country.

483

Fernández Viscarra, David. *Conservación del orden y garantías constitucionales. La Paz, 1968. 46 p.*

Abstracts of a Bolivian government hearing in which the Socialist Party charges that the government has violated the constitutional rights of many citizens. Includes the government's reply.

484

Font, Carlos. *El movimiento estudiantil lucha y se reorganiza en Bolivia. Organización Continental Latinoamericana de Estudiantes, v. 12, no. 5, 1978: 22-26.*

Reports on the Bolivian student movement since the Banzer takeover in 1971.

485

Joint Working Group for Refugees from Chile in Britain. *Political prisoners and refugees in the Southern Cone of Latin America. [London] 1977. 25 p.*

Reviews the Joint Working Group's assistance program. Attempts to determine achievable goals.

486

Lewis, Norman. *Eastern Bolivia: the white promised land. Copenhagen, International Group for Indigenous Affairs, Secretariat 1978. 27 p.*

Describes the threat to indigenous peoples implicit in a plan to colonize Eastern Bolivia with white South Africans and Rhodesians.

487

Lora, Guillermo. *The Thesis of Pulacayo. NACLA's Latin America & empire report. v. 8, Feb. 1974: 19-23.*

Reproduces the statements made by Guillermo Lora, a young leader of the Revolutionary Labor Party, in a NACLA interview of 1972. Includes the text of his Thesis of Pulacayo, a work presented at the First Extraordinary Congress in the Pulacayo Mine, on November 8, 1946.

488

Malloy, James. *Bolivia: the uncompleted revolution. Pittsburgh, University of Pittsburgh Press, 1970. 396 p.*

Provides a good current history of Bolivian economic and social change before and after the 1952 revolution.

489

The military coup and human rights in Bolivia. *Clamor, Año 2, Sept. 1980: 1-24.*

Discusses events leading up to the coup, methods used during the first days of the takeover, the massacre at Caracoles, and the treatment of prisoners. Also treats the Catholic Church's response to the coup and protests lodged by the Catholic archbishop and bishops denouncing rights violations.

490

Morales Dávila, Manuel. *Los derechos humanos en Bolivia, 1971- 1977. Lima, Confederación Nacional de Profesionales de Bolivia, 1978. 183 p.*

Reviews the efforts of the President of the Bolivian National Professional Association to denounce human rights violations by the government of General Banzer. Advocates the establishment of legal mechanisms to hear such complaints.

491

National Union of Mineworkers. *Trade union and human rights in Chile and Bolivia: report of the National Union of Mineworkers delegation. London, NUM, 1977. 23 p.*

Briefly reports on the delegation's findings concerning the violation of human rights in both Chile and Bolivia during 1976.

492

Quiroga Santa Cruz, Marcelo. *Los derechos de los bolivianos también son derechos humanos; intervención de Marcelo Quiroga Santa Cruz ante el Senado de los Estados Unidos. Socialismo y participación, no. 3, mayo 1978: 120-126.*

Statements concerning human rights in Bolivia presented before the U.S. Senate by a Bolivian

statesman who later was killed during the July 1980 military takeover of the Lydia Gueiler government.

493

Sánchez, Fernanda. *Bolivian military junta attempts to legalize violence. Latinamerica press, v. 12, Nov. 13, 1980: 5-6.*

Discusses the law of state security promulgated in October of 1980 by the Bolivian military regime which took power earlier in the year. Political observers report that from July through October 1980 the junta was responsible for the death, arrest, torture, disappearance, and exile of broad sectors of the population but that pressures from the Catholic Church and international human rights organizations have brought about the release of some prisoners.

494

Sandoval, Godofredo, and Javier Albó. *Ojje pa encima de todo: historia de un centro de residentes ex-campesinos en La Paz. La Paz, Centro de Investigación y Promoción del Campesinado, 1978. 1 v. (various pagings) (Cuaderno, no. 16)*

Not available for annotation.

495

Washington Office on Latin America. *Bolivia; a background paper on violations of human rights, 1971-77. Washington, 1977. 5 p.*

Examines the repression of human rights in Bolivia during the six years of the Banzer regime.

496

Washington Office on Latin America. *Bolivia: García Meza regime encounters increasing difficulties. Update, v. 5, Oct. 1980: 3, 5.*

Decries atrocities by the Bolivian junta which came to power two months before. Reports that General García Meza has succeeded in crushing resistance, but not in restoring normalcy.

Brazil

497

Alarcón, Rodrigo. *Brasil, represión y tortura*. Santiago de Chile, 1971. *180 p.*

General discussion of terror under the early phase of the military government in Brazil in the late 1960's.

498

Alencar, Tito de. *Brazil: government by torture*. Look, v. 34, July 14, 1970: 70-71.

Personal account by a Catholic seminarian of his ordeal under the Brazilian system of justice.

499

Alves, Marcio Moreira. *Brazil: what terror is like*. Nation, v. 212, Mar. 15, 1971: 337-341.

Analyzes the military regime's efforts to gain political control of the Brazilian people.

500

Alves, Marcio Moreira. *El despertar de la revolución brasileña*. Mexico, Editorial Diógenes, 1972. *256 p.*

Testimony by an exiled Brazilian concerning the military government's use of torture to obtain information from political prisoners.

501

Alves, Marcio Moreira. *Torturas e torturados*. Prefácio de Alceu Amoroso Lima. Rio de Janeiro [Emprèsa Jornalística PN] 1966. *235 p.*

Discusses the torture of prisoners in contemporary Brazil. Includes interviews.

502

American Committee for Information on Brazil. *Terror in Brazil; a dossier*. New York, 1970. *16 p.*

Contains personal and eyewitness accounts of torture and repression in Brazil. Provides a chronology of political events from 1964 to 1970. Includes legal documents.

503

American Friends of Brazil. *Brazilian information bulletin*. Berkeley, Calif., 1974. *19 p. illus.*

This issue contains articles on political prisoners in Brazil and the military coup in Chile, as well as on maltreatment of Indians in Brazil.

504

American Society of International Law. *Economic development and human rights: Brazil, Chile, and Cuba*. In *Proceedings of the American Society of International Law at its 67th annual meeting, Washington, D.C., 1973. p. 198-227.*

Panelists from North American and Chilean universities assess the performance of governments in Cuba, Brazil, and Chile with regard to economic development and human rights.

505

Amnesty International. *Report of allegations of torture in Brazil*. 3d ed. London, Amnesty International Publications, 1976. *104 p.*

Analyzes the relationship between military repression and rapid economic development in Brazil. Originally published in 1972.

506

Arns, Paulo Evaristo. *Em defesa dos direitos humanos: encontro com o repórter*. Rio de Janeiro, Editora Brasília, 1978. *223 p.*

Presents the position of the Catholic Church in Brazil concerning human rights.

507

Barnet, Richard. *Letter from Rio*. Harper's magazine, v. 245, Sept. 20, 1972: 16, 19-20, 22.

Provides an overview of both economic development and repressive social control in Brazil from 1964 to 1972.

508

Betto, Frei. *Cartas da prisão*. 4. ed. Rio de Janeiro, Civilização Brasileira, 1978. *232 p.*

Letters by a Dominican friar who was imprisoned for aiding the escape of individuals implicated in the post-1964 student movements against the military regime. Describes prison conditions and the systematic violation of human rights in Brazil.

509

Bezerra, Gregório. *Memórias; segunda parte, 1946-1969.* Rio de Janeiro, Editôra Civilização Brasileira, 1979. 255 p.

Memoirs by a member of the Brazilian Communist Party that reflect on the institutionalization of torture by the Brazilian military. Includes an account of the author's arrest and torture after the 1964 coup.

510

Bicudo, Hélio Pereira. *O direito e a justiça no Brasil: uma análise crítica de cem anos.* São Paulo, Brazil, Edicões Simbolo, 1978. 240 p.

Provides a useful introduction to changes in Brazilian law since 1930. Does not distinguish between human rights and other rights that are outlined in the Brazilian legal codes.

511

Bicudo, Hélio Pereira. *Meu depoimento sobre o esquadrão da morte.* 6. ed., rev. e aumentada. São Paulo, Brazil, Pontifícia Comissão de Justiça e Paz de São Paulo, 1977. 307 p.

Not available for annotation.

512

Biocca, Ettore. *Strategia del terrore: il modelo brasiliano.* Lungomare Nazario Sauro, Bari, Italy, De Donato editore SpA, 1974. 251 p. illus. (Atti, no. 36)

Examines governmental repression in Brazil up to 1974. Includes a chapter on death squads.

513

Boal, Augusto. *Milagre no Brasil.* Rio de Janeiro, Civilização Brasileira, 1979. 291 p.

Describes the 1971 abduction, imprisonment, and torture of a Brazilian theater director accused of subversion.

514

Boechat Rodrigues, Leda. *Direito e política: os direitos humanos no Brasil e nos Estados Unidos.* Pôrto Alegre, Brazil, Associação dos Juízes do Rio Grande do Sul, 1977. 227 p. (Col. Ajuris, no. 8)

Studies and contrasts the legal and political aspects of human rights in Brazil and the United States. Includes an essay reviewing William O. Douglas' positions on human rights questions.

515

Braga, Teodomiro, and Paulo Barbosa. *Meu filho Alexandre Vannucchi; depoimento de Egle Vannucchi Leme e José de Oliveira Leme.* São Paulo, Brazil, Edição S. A., 1978. 24 p.

Articles, letters, and poems recount the torture and murder of a student leader by Brazil's secret police.

516

Brazil: report on torture (Motion picture). *Made by Saul Landau.* Washington, Institute for Policy Studies, 1971. 30 min. sd. color. 16 mm.

Portrays the torture of political prisoners in Brazil. Reenacts the personal experiences of the exiled actors.

517

Broucker, José de. *Dom Hélder Câmara: the violence of a peacemaker.* Translated from the French by Herma Briffault. Maryknoll, N.Y., Orbis Books, 1970. 154 p. illus.

Discusses, in the context of various interviews, Dom Hélder Câmara's views on both political action and social justice. Gives an account of his struggle against the supression of civil rights by the Brazilian military authorities.

518

Bruneau, Thomas C. *The political transformation of the Brazilian Catholic Church.* London, Cambridge University Press, 1974. 240 p.

Examines the politicization, beginning in the 1960's, of the Catholic Church in Brazil. Includes a selected bibliography.

519

Carl, Beverly May. *Erosion of constitutional rights of political offenders in Brazil. Virginia journal of international law, v. 12, Mar. 1972: 157-191.*

Analyzes the stern measures that were taken by the Brazilian government in 1971 against individuals who opposed its views and plans.

520

Carreira, Evandro. *A idéia-força dos direitos humanos; discurso pronunciado no Senado Federal, no dia 15 de março de 1977. Brasília [1977?] 23 p.*

Text of a speech delivered on the floor of the Brazilian Senate, analyzing the impact of the concept of protecting human rights.

521

Casaldáliga, Pedro. *Yo creo en la justicia y en la esperanza. Bilbao, Spain, Editorial Española Desclée de Brouwer, 1975. 200 p. (Col. El credo que ha dado sentido a mi vida, no. 9)*

Protests against inhuman working conditions in rural Brazil. Written as a diary of confessions by a Brazilian bishop.

522

Cayuela, José. *¿Hélder Câmara [sic], Brasil: un Vietnam católico? Santiago de Chile, Editorial Pomaire, 1969. 280 p.*

Provides a biographical account of Dom Hélder Câmara, with an emphasis on his ideological radicalization and dedication to non-violence. Discusses harsh social conditions in Brazil's northeast.

523

Celso Uchôa Cavalcante, Pedro, and Jovelino Ramos. *De muitos caminhos. São Paulo, Brazil, Editôra e Livraria Livramento, 1978. 371 p. (Memorias de exílio; Brasil 1964-197?, no. 1)*

Personal accounts of Brazilian exiles and refugees who suffered human rights abuses under Brazil's military government. Includes the case of Tito de Alencar Lima, who died under torture in jail.

524

Chaves Neto, João Ribeiro. *Patética. Rio de Janeiro, Civilização Brasileira, 1978. 99 p.*

Play based on the torture-induced death of journalist Vladimir Herzog. It was denied the first prize voted to it by the National Theater Service in the 1977 Playwrights Competition, and was subsequently confiscated by the government.

525

Christian social witness in repressive societies and United States responsibility. *New York, United Presbyterian Church, U.S.A., Unit on Church and Society, 1974. 47 p.*

Background policy paper and recommendations adopted by the 186th General Assembly (1974) of the United Presbyterian Church, U.S.A. Includes reports on Brazil and Chile.

526

Christo, Carlos Alberto Libanio. *Against principalities and powers: letters from a Brazilian jail. Translated by John Drury. 2d ed. Maryknoll, N.Y., Orbis Books, 1977. 241 p.*

Translation of Dai sotterranei della storia. Letters of a Dominican priest who was held prisoner for four years by the antiterrorist division of Brazil's special police services. Provide a glimpse of the Brazilian prison system and its political prisoners.

527

Ciclo de debates do Teatro Casa Grande. *Rio de Janeiro, Editora Inubia, 1976. 238 p.*

At the Teatro Casa Grande in Rio de Janeiro in 1975, intellectuals, artists, and other critics spoke out about censorship in Brazil and the loss of national identity.

528

Coelho, Edmundo Campos. *Em busca de identidade: o exército e a política na sociedade brasileira. Rio de Janeiro, Forense- Universitária, 1976. 207 p. (Col. Brasil-análise e crítica)*

Examines the development and organization of the Brazilian military. Seeks to explain the identity crisis that the military experienced because of its national security role after 1964.

529

Comité de Solidaridad con los Pueblos Latinoamericanos. *Testimonios de lucha; Chile, Brasil, [y] Uruguay. In its Boletín, no. 2, 1974: whole issue.*

Presents an account of the activities of popular resistance movements in Brazil and Uruguay. Describes U.S. involvement in Brazil and Chile. Includes a transcript of Allende's last words.

530

Conselho Indigenista Missionário-CIMI. *Y-juca pirana: o índio: aquele que deve morrer; documento de urgência de bispos e missionários. Brasília, 1973. 31 p.*

Calls attention to the violation of the human rights of indigenous populations in Brazil. Written on the occasion of the 25th anniversary of the Universal Declaration of Human Rights.

531

Cooperation in Documentation and Communication. *Bibliographical notes for understanding the Brazilian model: political repression & economic expansion. [Edited by Mary Riesch and Harry Strharsky] Washington, CoDoC International Secretariat, 1974. [78] p. (Its Common catalogue, no. 2)*

Lists Brazilian documents on both politics and economics. Comprises one volume of a series devoted to Third World issues.

532

Dassin, Joan R. *A report on human rights in Brazil: a report as of March, 1979. Universal human rights, v. 1, July/Sept. 1979: 35-49.*

States that Brazilians have regained many civil and political rights in recent years. Brazil has also become a temporary shelter for many political refugees for countries from the Southern Cone. A reversal of the liberalization process seems unlikely.

533

Davis, Shelton H. *Victims of the miracle; development and the Indians of Brazil. London, Cambridge University Press, 1977. 205 p. maps.*

Analyzes the impact of rapid economic development in Brazil. Focuses on the policies of the government toward the indigenous populations. Discusses the ecological and sociological effects of the Polamazonia Program. Includes documentation.

534

Davis, Shelton H., and Robert O. Mathews. *The geological imperative; anthropology and development in the Amazon Basin of South America. Cambridge, Mass., Anthropology Resource Center, 1976. 103 p. illus.*

Analyzes the national and international resource policies that uproot the Indian populations of the Amazon Basin. Discusses the role of multinational corporations in that region. Includes essays on both the Yanomamö and eastern Peru.

535

Declaração Universal dos Direitos Humanos. *Brasília, Ministério da Justiça, 1978. 33p.*

Contains a Portuguese translation of the Universal Declaration of Human Rights. Includes brief descriptions of each of the provisions that are outlined in the Declaration.

536

Della Cava, Ralph. *Catholicism and society in twentieth century Brazil. Latin American research review, v. 9, no. 2, 1976: 7-50.*

Focuses on the pastoral role of the Brazilian Catholic Church, particularly its concern for the poor and its defense of human rights.

537

Della Cava, Ralph. *Democratic stirrings. Journal of current social issues, v. 16, summer 1978: 22-28.*

Describes new developments in Brazil pointing towards greater freedom of expression and the role of the churches in securing such rights.

538

Della Cava, Ralph. *Election in Brazil: up from farce, mandate for civilian rule. Commonweal, v. 106, Jan. 1979: 5-6.*

Brief analysis of new political developments in Brazil.

539

Della Cava, Ralph. *Fontes para o estudo de catolicismo e sociedade no Brasil. Religião e sociedade, no. 5, jun. 1980: 211-240.*

The first of three contributions which consist of a selective inventory of sources for the study of the Catholic Church and society in Brazil for the period from 1964 to 1978.

540

¿Desaparecidos? Dosie da repressão. *Istoé, v. 2, set. 1978: 24-32.*

Documents the search of Brazilian families for missing relatives. Discusses the alleged suicides, car accidents, and shootouts involving individuals who are detained for political crimes.

541

Dias, José Carlos, and Arnaldo Malheiros Filho. *Contra a censura prévia. São Paulo, Brazil, Dias e Malheiros Advogados S/C, 1977. 80 p.*

Contains legal documentation on the censorship case in which the Catholic weekly newspaper, O São Paulo, sought a constitutional guarantee to end government review of copy before printing.

542

Direitos humanos. *O São Paulo, v. 22, jul. 8-14, 1978: whole issue.*

Special human rights issue of the Archdiocese of São Paulo weekly, containing articles by well-known Brazilians such as Cardenal Arns and Dalmo de Abreu, an attorney.

543

Encontro Nacional das Entidades de Anistia; os presos, os mortos, os desaparecidos. *Rio de Janeiro, Comitê Brasileiro pela Anistia, 1979. 141 p.*

Document prepared for the National Meeting of Groups for Amnesty held in Rio de Janeiro on June 15, 1979. Includes lists of political prisoners and of deaths under the military regime since 1964, as well as missing political prisoners. Accounts are partial and incomplete.

544

End of the miracle; Geisel and repression. *Brazilian information bulletin, no. 14, summer 1974: 1-19.*

Criticizes the violations of human rights in Brazil. Comments on the adverse effects of rapid economic development in that country.

545

Exigencias cristãs de uma ordem política. *2a. ed. [São Paulo] Edições Paulinas, 1977. 22 p. (Documentos da CNBB, no. 10)*

"Documento aprovado pela XV Assembléia Geral da CNBB, Itaici, 8 a 17 de fevereiro de 1977."

Examination of Christian ethics by Brazilian Catholic bishops. Discusses both the rights and duties of the state and individual freedom and security.

546

Faoro, Raymundo. *Direitos humanos no Brasil. Rio de Janeiro, Orden dos Advogados do Brasil, Conselho Federal, 1978. 7 p.*

Stresses the importance of human rights in a democracy.

547

Fon, Antonio Carlos. *Tortura; a história da repressão política no Brasil. São Paulo, Brazil, Global Editôra e Distribuidora, 1979. 79 p.*

Describes the systematic torture employed by the Brazilian police in the interrogation of political prisoners. Includes an account of the author's own imprisonment.

548

Freire, Marcos. *Nação oprimida. Rio de Janeiro, Paz e Terra, 1977. 188 p.*

An important opposition figure from Brazil's northeast recounts the years of repression and censorship in Congress, the universities, trade unions, and the press. Criticizes the official economic policies, and explains the goals of the opposition.

549

Garcia, Basileu. *Outline of provisional or procedural imprisonment in Brazil. International Commission of Jurists. Journal, v. 3, winter 1961: 39-51.*

Analyzes the conditions of provisional imprisonment as defined in Brazilian law.

550

Grimaldi, Darcy. *Liberdade com restrições. Pôrto Alegre, Brazil, Livraria do Globo, 1976. 95 p.*

Discusses fundamental rights. Concludes that the right to food, shelter, and education should not be restricted to the elite. Written by a prisoner in a Brazilian jail.

551

Guimarães, Ulysses. *Rompendo o cerco. Rio de Janeiro, Paz e Terra, 1978. 188 p. (Col. Documentos da democracia brasileira, v. 2)*

Not available for annotation.

552

Halliday, Fred. *Brazil: the underside of the miracle. Ramparts, v. 12, Apr. 1974: 14-18, 20.*

Examines the adverse effects of the Brazilian economic miracle. Reveals both the existence of torture and the suppression of political opponents.

553

Heaphey, James J. *The Brazilian Congress and human rights. Albany, University of New York at Albany, Comparative Development Studies Center [1976?] 60 p.*

Analyzes the interest the Brazilian Congress has shown in human rights.

554

International Commission of Jurists. *Brazil. In its Review, Apr./June 1971: 5-8.*

Describes the failed attempts to eliminate torture and repression during the presidency of General Garrastazu Medici.

555

International Commission of Jurists. *Brazil. In its Review, June 1976: 5-7.*

Provides an update on the political situation in Brazil. Discusses both torture and press censorship.

556

International Commission of Jurists. *The extermination of Indians in Brazil. In its Bulletin, Sept. 1968: 18-24.*

Examines reports of March 1978, concerning the genocide of Amazonians and other Amerindians in the interior of Brazil.

557

International Commission of Jurists. *Human rights in the world: Brazil. In its Review, June 1972: 4.*

Examines allegations that were presented by the International Commission of Jurists before the Inter-American Commission on Human Rights of the O.A.S. The first allegation describes the torture and mistreatment of political prisoners. The second allegation discusses the arrest and detention of three well-known jurists.

558

International Commission of Jurists. *Human rights in the world: Brazil. In its Review, Dec. 1974: 4-8.*

Reports on human rights violations during the first nine months of the Geisel regime. Lists the resolutions of the 1974 National Conference of the Brazilian Bar Association.

559

Joint Working Group for Refugees from Chile in Britain. *Political prisoners and refugees in the Southern Cone of Latin America. [London] 1977. 25 p.*

Review of an international program to assist political prisoners and refugees from Argentina, Bolivia, Brazil, and Chile.

560

Jordão, Fernando Pacheco. *Dossier Herzog: prisão, tortura e morte no Brasil. São Paulo, Brazil, Global Editôra e Distribuidora, 1979. 223 p.*

Describes Vladimir Herzog's torture and death while being interrogated by security agents of the military regime. Discusses civilian opposition to the systematic violation of human rights by the Brazilian government.

561
Klein, Lucia and Marcus Figueiredo. *Legitimidade e coação no Brasil pos-64.* Rio de Janeiro, Forense-Universitaria, 1978. 202 p.

In separate sections, the two authors, both social scientists, analyze the impact and the nature of authoritarian rule in Brazilian society.

562
Langguth, A. J. *Hidden terrors.* New York, Pantheon Books, 1978. 339 p.

Former New York Times reporter maintains that the encouragement U.S. government advisors gave to the Brazilian military regime set in motion military takeovers in Argentina, Chile, and Uruguay. The case of Dan Mitrione, a U.S. policy advisor for Uruguay who was kidnapped and later murdered, is also discussed.

563
Levine, Robert M. *Brazil's definition of democracy.* Current history, v. 70, Feb. 1979: 70-73, 83.

Asserts that Brazil is poised for accelerated political change after the November, 1978, elections whether, on the one hand, the military reacts harshly to its opposition, or, on the other, it makes concessions for greater political freedom.

564
Levy, Daniel. *Higher education policy in authoritarian regimes: comparative perspectives on the Chilean case.* New Haven, Conn., Yale Higher Education Research Group Working Paper, 1980. 60 p.

The military reorganization of and policies toward Chilean universities, outlined and compared to those of Argentina and Brazil.

565
Machado, Cristina Pinheiro. *Os exilados; 5 mil brasileiros á espera da anistia.* São Paulo, Brazil, Editôra Alfa-Omega, 1979. 129 p.

Reports on the experiences of Brazilian exiles. Discusses both the 1964 government in exile and the silence of the 1970's.

566
Machado, José Antonio Pinheiro. *Opinião vs. censura: momentos de luta d um jornal pela liberdade.* Pôrto Alegre, Brazil, L&PM Editores, 1978. 163 p.

Reports on the impact of pre-publication censorship in Brazil. Documents the conflict between the government and the opposition weekly, Opinião, from 1972 to 1977. Discusses the imprisonment of the weekly's personnel as well as the court case.

567
Martins, Roberto Ribeiro. *Liberdade para os brasileiros; anistia ontem e hoje.* Com a colaboração de Paulo Ribeiro Martins e Luís Antônio Palmeira. Rio de Janeiro, Civilização Brasileira, 1978. 198 p. (Col. Retratos do Brasil, v. 115)

Analyzes the Brazilian interpretation and application of the legal concept of amnesty after 1964.

568
Mendonça, Otávio. *O advogado e os direitos do homem.* Revista brasileira de cultura, v. 6, abr./jun. 1974: 81-94.

"Discurso na instalação da V Conferencia Nacional da Ordem dos Advogados do Brasil."

Traces the development of human rights theory. Outlines the human rights provisions in the Brazilian Constitution of 1824.

569
Os militares em busca de saídas. *Veja*, no. 468, agto. 24, 1977: 28-34.

Not available for annotation.

570
Minority Rights Group. *The position of blacks in Brazilian society.* [London, 1974?] 22 p. (Report-Minority Rights Group, no. 7)

Not available for annotation.

571

Moisés, José Alvaro, et al. *Contradições urbanas e movimentos sociais.* Rio de Janeiro, Paz e Terra, 1977. 86 p. illus., port. (Centro de Estudos de Cultura Contemporânea. Co-edições CEDEC/Paz e Terra, v. l)

Not available for annotation.

572

Morris, Fred B. *In the presence of mine enemies. Harper's magazine,* v. 251, Oct. 1975: 57-60, 63-66, 70.

Author's account of torture during his imprisonment in Brazil for political crimes.

573

Morris, Fred B. *In the valley of the shadow. The other side,* v. 12, July/Aug. 1976: 22-30.

Provides a first hand account of the torture of political prisoners in Brazil.

574

Morris, Fred B. *Sustained by faith under Brazilian torture. Christian century,* v. 92, Jan. 22, 1975: 56-60.

Testimony from a U.S. citizen concerning his interrogation and torture during detention as a political prisoner in Brazil.

575

Moura, Clóvis. *Diário da guerrilha do Araguaia. São Paulo,* Brazil Editôra Alfa-Omega, 1979. 80 p.

Documents the armed struggle against the military regime in the Araguaia forests of the Xambioá-Marabá region of southern Pará, Brazil, between 1972 and 1974. Written by the directors of the guerrilla forces of Araguaia, the document is one of the first published accounts of the insurrection.

576

Moura, Ernesto de. *Political kidnappings in Brazil. Third world,* v. 1, May 1979: 47-48.

Reports on the abduction of two Uruguayans and their children from exile in Brazil. Speculates on the effects of the publicity surrounding the case.

577

Mulligan, Joseph E. *The United States and Brazil: an interview with Dom Hélder Câmara. America,* v. 141, Oct. 13, 1979: 192-194.

Criticizes the actions of multinational corporations that lead to the displacement of Brazilian peasants from their lands. Comments adversely on the military regime's efforts to destroy trade unionism.

578

National Conference of Brazilian Bishops. *Comunicação pastoral ao povo de Deus.* São Paulo, Brazil, Edições Paulinas, 1976. 22 p.

Pastoral letter written in response to both the assassination of two priests and the kidnapping of a bishop.

579

National Conference of Brazilian Bishops, Rio de Janeiro, 1976. *Violence in Brazil. Origins,* v. 6, Mar. 3, 1977: 588-594.

"Translation by the U.S. Catholic Conference Office of International Justice and Peace...and Latinamerica Press."

Text of the Rio de Janeiro resolution of October, 1976, condemning the Brazilian military for its abrogation of human rights.

580

Nóbrega, Vandick Londres da. *1964 (i.e. Mil novecentos e sessenta e quatro): segurança e defensa do Brasil.* Rio de Janeiro, Livraria Freitas Bastos, 1977. 597 p., 39 leaves of plates, illus.

"149 conclusões em portugues, frances, ingles e alemão a partir da página 293."

Analyzes the military's role in Brazil. Refers to the U.S. human rights policy and to the Brazilian government's reaction to that policy. Includes summaries of conclusions in French, English, and German.

581

Oliveira, Eliézer Rizzo de. *As forças armadas: política e ideologia no Brasil, 1964-1969.* Petrópolis, Brazil, Vozes, 1976. 133 p. (Col. Sociologia brasileira, v. 6)

Examines the doctrine of national security in Brazil since 1964. Includes a discussion on the training of the military.

582

Oliveira Costa, Albertina, et al., eds. *Memorias do exilio, das mulheres.* Rio de Janeiro, Paz e Terra, 1980. 1 v.

Several women tell their stories of life in exile. The book explores themes of politics, feminism, and human rights.

583

Page, Joseph A. *The little priest who stands up to Brazil's generals. New York times magazine,* May 23, 1971: 26-27, 80-82, 84.

Describes the political opposition of Dom Hélder Câmara, Archbishop of Recife, to the military regime.

584

Pinto, Paulo Broussard de Souza. *E hora de mudar. Pôrto Alegre, Brazil, L&PM Editôres,* 1977. 120 p.

Senator from Rio Grande do Sul argues for a more democratic civilian government.

585

Pinto, Paulo Broussard de Souza. *Oposição. Pôrto Alegre, Brazil, L&PM Editôres,* 1975. 200 p.

Discusses civil rights issues in Brazil.

586

Puech, Luíz Roberto de Rezende. *Na vivência do direito social. São Paulo, Brazil, Editora Resenha Universitária,* 1975. 281 p.

Examines trade unionism in Brazil citing specific court cases. Discusses international human rights in last chapter.

587

Quigley, Thomas. *Brazil: new generals vs. renewal bishops. Christianity and crisis,* v. 34, Apr. 1, 1974: 61-64.

Describes the Catholic Church's opposition to the Brazilian military's disregard for human rights,

the emergence of a more active role for the bishops, and the shift in attitudes among church activists.

588

Repression of the Church in Brazil: reflection on a situation of oppression (1968-1978). *Rio de Janeiro, Centro Ecumênico de Documentação e Informação,* 1978. 1 v. *(various pagings)*

Documents anti-Catholic tactics, of the Brazilian military regime, including the raid on the headquarters of the National Conference of Bishops. The dossier was assembled at the request of Cardinal Arns of São Paulo and Bishop Balduino of Goiás and was prepared by CEDI, an ecumenical research service.

589

Rodrigues, Lêda Boechat. *Direito e política: os direitos humanos no Brasil e nos Estados Unidos. Pôrto Alegre, Brazil, Associação dos Juízes do Rio Grande do Sul,* 1977. 227 p. *(Coleção Ajurio, 8)*

Studies and contrasts the legal and political aspects of human rights in Brazil and the United States. Includes an essay reviewing William O. Douglas' positions on human rights questions.

590

Ross, Timothy. *Information control in Brazil. Index on censorship,* v. 1, autumn/winter 1972: 129-148.

Examines the basis for a series of repressive decrees issued by the Brazilian regime, concerning matters of culture and communication.

591

Russell Tribunal II on Repression in Brazil, Chile, and Latin America, 2d, Rome and Brussels, 1974-1975. *Brasile, violazione dei diritti dell'uomo, a cura di Linda Bimbi. Milan, Italy, Feltrinelli,* 1975. 319 p.

Contains addresses and legal papers from the Tribunal's 1974-1975 meeting. Includes an exposition by Jan Rutgers concerning the relationship between the Catholic Church and the military in Brazil. Contains statements on torture.

592

Sanders, Thomas G. *Decompression in Brazil. Hanover, N.H., American Universities Field Staff, 1975. 11 p. (East Coast South America series, v. 19, no. 1)*

Analyzes the military's plan to restore democratic procedures in Brazil. Examines policy changes during the 1974 to 1976 period. Concludes that real improvements have taken place.

593

Sanders, Thomas G. *Human rights and political process in Brazil. Hanover, N.H., American Universities Field Staff, 1980. 11 p. (American Universities Field Staff, Reports, 1980/11, South America)*

In 1974 the Brazilian government noticeably lessened restrictions on political activity and a process of "decompression" and democratization began, with a vastly improved situation regarding human rights.

594

Schilling, Paulo R. *Brasil, seis años de dictadura: torturas; texto y selección de documentos. Cuadernos de marcha, no. 37, mayo 1970: 1-79.*

Discusses militarism in Brazil, the permanent counterrevolution, and cooperation between the police and the military.

595

Schilling, Paulo R. *El militarismo brasileño, segunda parte. Cristianismo y sociedad, v. 12, no. 42, 1974: 64-96.*

Not available for annotation.

596

Shankman, Paul. *The denouement of the South American Indians. Journal of ethnic studies, v. 7, fall 1979: 87-94.*

Reviews books that discuss the destruction of native American culture in Brazil and Paraguay.

597

Simon, Pedro. *MDB: uma opção democrática. Pôrto Alegre, Brazil, L&PM Editôres, 1976. 277 p. (Col. Política, v. 2)*

Not available for annotation.

598

Statement of solidarity on human rights: Chile and Brazil. *Washington, United States Catholic Conference, 1974. 1 v. (unpaged)*

Discusses human rights violations in both Brazil and Chile.

599

Symposium on Inter-ethnic Conflict in South America, Bridgetown, Barbados, 1971. *La situación del indígena en América del Sur: aportes al estudio de la fricción inter-étnica en los Indios no-andinos. Geneva, World Council of Churches, 1972. 453 p. (Publications of the Dept. of Ethnology, University of Berne, no. 3)*

Collection of papers by social anthropologists that examines the relationship between government policies and the decimation of indigenous populations in Latin America.

600

Tortura in Brasile. *Florence, Italy, Cultura Editrice [1972?], 82 p.*

At head of title: Libro bianco.

Describes torture methods in Brazil and presents the case histories of individuals who claim that they were tortured. Includes a listing of alleged torturers.

601

Torturas. *Cuadernos de marcha, no. 44, dic. 1970: 1-80.*

Examines torture in Argentina, Brazil, and Uruguay. Includes the "black book" of torture.

602

Troyano, Annez Andraus. *Estado e sindicalismo. São Paulo, Brazil, Edições Simbolo, 1978. 184 p. illus. (Col. Ensaio e memória, no. 12)*

Not available for annotation.

603

Tyson, Brady. *Economic growth and human rights in Brazil: the first nine years of military tutelage. American journal of international law, v. 67, Nov. 1973: 208-213.*

Comments on the effects of nine years of military rule on the status of human rights and economic development in Brazil. Discusses torture, censorship, income distribution, and educational patterns.

604

U.N. Commission on Human Rights. *Periodic reports on human rights: reports on civil and political rights, including the right of self-determination and the right to independence, for the period July 1968-June 1971. New York, United Nations, 1972. 32 p. (U.N. [Document] E/CN. 4/1098)*

At head of title: Economic and Social Council. Twenty-ninth session.

Received from governments under the Economic and Social Council Resolution 1074 C(XXXIX) 1. Includes the reports submitted by Barbados and Brazil.

605

U.S. Library of Congress. Foreign Affairs and National Defense Division. *The status of human rights in selected countries and the U.S. response. Prepared for the Subcommittee on International Organizations of the Committee on International Relations, U.S. House of Representatives by the Foreign Affairs and National Defense Division, Congressional Research Service, Library of Congress, [Barbara Branaman...et al.] Washington, U.S. Govt. Print. Off., 1977. 79 p.*

At head of title: 95th Congress, 1st session. Committee print.

Includes an updated summary of the status of human rights in Brazil, Paraguay, Peru, and Uruguay.

606

Valle, Luis del. *El Cardenal Arns de São Paulo: la injusticia, escándalo de un continente cristiano. Proceso (Mexico), enero 15, 1979: 14-17.*

Reports on a speech by Cardinal Arns that addresses the human rights needs of the poor.

607

La violence militaire au Brésil. *Traduit du portugais. Paris, François Maspero, 1971. 174 p. (Col. Cahiers libres, no. 215/216)*

At head of title: Pau de arara.

Ideological analysis of the use of torture by the Brazilian military regime.

608

Washington Office on Latin America. *Brazil: societal consequences of 15 years of military rule. Update Latin America, Feb./Mar. 1979: 1-2, 6.*

Analyzes the effects of the military regime's disregard for human rights in Brazil. Provides examples of the government's encroachment on the civil and political rights of citizens, including censorship, the prosecution of dissenters, and the manipulation of statistics.

609

Wipfler, William L. *Repression and terror: the price of "progress" in Brazil. Christianity and crisis, v. 30, Mar. 16, 1970: 44-48.*

Briefly examines the Brazilian military government's increasing abridgement of the political rights of its citizens at a time of expanding U.S. government and business involvement in that country.

Caribbean (English-speaking)

610

Cross, Malcolm. *The East Indians of Guyana and Trinidad.* *[London] Minority Rights Group [1972] 28 p. illus., tables (Minority Rights Group. Report, no. 13)*

Briefly surveys East Indian race relations in the Caribbean. Alludes to the effects of immigration, employment, and voting patterns on current racial tensions.

611

Demas, William G. *Human rights in the Caribbean.* *Trinidad and Tobago review, v. 2, Feb. 1978: 5, 19-20.*

Examines the conflict between economic development and human rights in the Caribbean region.

612

International Commission of Jurists. *Guyana. In its Review, Dec. 1978: 5-8.*

Discusses the government's "referendum to abolish referenda" of July 20, 1978, and the criticisms that were raised against it by the Guyana Council of Churches, various professional groups, and the political opposition.

613

International Commission of Jurists, eds. *Human rights and development: human rights and their promotion in the Caribbean. Bridgetown, Barbados, Cedar Press, 1978. 208 p.*

Report of a 1977 international seminar, cosponsored by the Organization of Commonwealth Caribbean Bar Associations, that focuses on the promotion of civil, cultural, economic, and political rights in the Caribbean. Includes seminar documents and international human rights instruments.

614

International Commission of Jurists. *Human rights in the world: Guyana. In its Review, June 1974: 7-12.*

Reports on racial discrimination against East Indians in Guyana.

615

International Commission of Jurists. *St. Kitts-Nevis-Anguilla. In its Bulletin, Mar. 1968: 26-30.*

Describes the detainment of individuals under the emergency regulations that were established in St. Kitts. Discusses the application of the rule of law.

616

Lacey, Terry. *Violence and politics in Jamaica, 1960-70: Internal security in a developing country. Totowa, N.J., F. Cass, 1977. 184 p.*

Focuses on the internal security problems in Jamaica during that nation's period of transition from colonialism to independence.

617

Latin American round table, a forum for hemispheric affairs. *[Human rights in Grenada] Washington, Transnational Institute, Institute for Policy Studies [1977?] [47] leaves.*

Presents case histories of human rights violations in Grenada from 1973 to 1977. Contains a personal account by Senator Maurice Bishop.

618

Mahant, H. E. *The strange fate of a liberal democracy: political opposition and civil liberties in Guyana. Round table, Jan. 1977: 77-89.*

Characterizes Guyana's political orientation as being neither democratic nor authoritarian. Bases these observations on the extent to which the government intervenes in the economy and uses repressive political and civil measures.

619

Phillip, K. G. *Due process of law in the Trinidad and Tobago Constitution. Journal of the Indian Law Institute, v. 15, July/Sept. 1973: 415-419.*

Not available for annotation.

620

Ramphal, S. S. *Safeguarding human rights; the Guyana contribution: United Nations Human Rights Seminar on the Effective Realization of Civil and Political Rights at the National Level, Kingston, Jamaica, April-May, 1967.* Georgetown, *Printed by the Govt. Printery for the Ministry of External Affairs [1967] 55 p. illus. (U.N. [Document] ST/TAO/HR/29 [text] 33)*

Surveys the status of human rights in Guyana based on reports from a seminar on civil and political rights. Discusses both the protection of Amerindians and law enforcement in times of national emergency.

621

U.N. Commission on Human Rights. *Further promotion and encouragement of human rights and fundamental freedoms, including the question of the programme and methods of work of the Commission. New York, United Nations, 1978. 1 p. (U.N. [Document] E/CN. 4/1273/Add. 3)*

At head of title: Economic and Social Council. Thirty-fourth session, agenda item 11.

Report, prepared by the Secretary General, pursuant to Decision 4 (XXXIII) of the Commission on Human Rights. Includes the comments and observations submitted by Barbados.

622

U.N. Commission on Human Rights. *Periodic reports on human rights: reports on civil and political rights, including the right of self- determination and the right to independence, for the period July 1968-June 1971. New York, United Nations, 1972. 32 p. (U.N. [Document] E/CN. 4/1098)*

At head of title: Economic and Social Council. Twenty-ninth session.

Reports submitted by Barbados and Brazil in conformance with Resolution 1074 C(XXXIX) of the Economic and Social Council.

623

U.N. Commission on Human Rights. *Periodic reports on human rights: reports on civil and political rights, including the right of self- determination and the right to independence, for the period July 1968-June 1971. New York, United Nations, 1972. 4 p. (U.N. [Document] E/CN. 4/1098/Add. 17)*

At head of title: Economic and Social Council. Twenty-ninth session.

Report submitted by Jamaica in conformance with Resolution 1074 C(XXXIX) of the Economic and Social Council.

624

U.N. Commission on Human Rights. *Periodic reports on human rights: reports on civil and political rights, including the right of self- determination and the right to independence, for the period July 1968-June 1971. New York, United Nations, 1973. 17 p. (U.N. [Document] E/CN. 4/1098/Add. 20)*

At head of title: Economic and Social Council.

Reports submitted by Guatemala, Trinidad and Tobago in conformance with Resolution 1074 C(XXXIX) of the Economic and Social Council.

625

U.N. Commission on Human Rights. *Periodic reports on human rights: reports on economic, social, and cultural rights, for the period July 1969-June 1973. New York, United Nations, 1974. 30 p. (U.N. [Document] E/CN. 4/1155/ Add. l)*

At head of title: Economic and Social Council. Thirty-first session.

Reports submitted by Barbados and Costa Rica in conformance with Resolution 1074 C(XXXIX) of the Economic and Social Council.

626

U.N. Commission on Human Rights. *Periodic reports on human rights: reports on economic, social, and cultural rights, for the period July 1969-June 1973. New York, United Nations, 1974. 33 p. (U.N. [Document] E/CN. 4/1155/ Add. 2)*

At head of title: Economic and Social Council. Thirty-first session.

Report submitted by Jamaica in conformance with Resolution 1074 C(XXXIX) of the Economic and Social Council.

627

U.N. Secretary General. *Human rights questions. Allegations regarding infringements of trade union rights; note.*

New York, United Nations, 1976. 3 p. (U.N. [Document] E/5765)

At head of title: Economic and Social Council. Sixtieth session, agenda item 7.

Reply, dated Feb. 5, 1976, of the Bahamian government to the allegations made against it by the Bahamas Engineering and General Union concerning the repression of trade union rights.

628

Wachtel, Howard, and Michael Moffitt. *De-railing development: the International Monetary Fund in Jamaica. Washington, Institute for Policy Studies, 1978. 20 p.*

Analyzes the influence of the International Monetary Fund on the economic and social policies of the Jamaican government. Charges that the IMF's conservative policies do not take into account human rights considerations.

Chile

629

La Academia de Humanismo Cristiano. *Derechos humanos: inquietud y esperanza. Análisis, v. 1, jun. 1978: 1-40.*

Provides an overview of the human rights movement in Chile. Includes a description of the activities of the Vicaría de la Solidaridad of the Archdiocese of Santiago.

630

Alexander, Robert J. *Chile a year after the military coup. Freedom at issue, Nov./Dec. 1974: 4-6, 15-19.*

Discusses the reasons for the military takeover in Chile. Examines the country's economic problems.

631

American Society of International Law. *Economic development and human rights: Brazil, Chile, and Cuba. In Proceedings of the American Society of International Law at its 67th annual meeting, Washington, D.C., 1973. p. 198-227.*

Panelists from North American and Chilean universities assess the performance of governments in Cuba, Brazil, and Chile with regard to economic development and human rights.

632

Amnesty International. *Chile: un informe de Amnistía International. London, Amnesty International Publications, 1974. 88 p. illus., map.*

Provides undocumented information on Chile after the military coup. Includes chapters on political prisoners, executions, torture, and refugees.

633

Amnesty International. *Disappeared prisoners in Chile. London, Amnesty International Publications, 1977. 128 p.*

Urges the military regime to publish information on the whereabouts of 1,500 individuals who were arrested by the Chilean secret police. Documents disappearances that occurred during 1977.

634

Amnesty International. *Evidence of torture: studies of the Amnesty International Danish Medical Group. London, Amnesty International Publications, 1977. 39 p. illus.*

Reports on the medical effects of torture. Includes case studies from Argentina, Chile, and Uruguay.

635

Andreas, Carol. *Nothing is as it should be; a North American feminist tells of her life in Chile before and after the golpe militar. Cambridge, Mass., Schenkman Pub. Co., 1976. 147 p.*

Describes the status of human rights in Chile before and after the 1973 coup. Includes observations on the women's movement.

636

Año internacional de la celebración de los derechos humanos en Chile. *Santiago, Editorial Andrés Bello, 1969. 179 p.*

Contains a collection of lectures that were given during the presidency of Eduardo Frei. The lectures cover human rights, the Chilean Constitution, and the Inter-American Court of Justice.

637

Arzobispado de Santiago. Vicaría de la Solidaridad. *Aporte...para la preparación de "Puebla." Santiago, 1978. [34] leaves.*

Describes the legal services that the Vicaría offers to political prisoners in Chile.

638

Arzobispado de Santiago. Vicaría de la Solidaridad. *Informe sobre 384 casos de personas desaparecidas. Santiago, 1976. 5 v.*

Consists of a brief that was presented to the Chilean Supreme Court on August 20, 1976, by the Vicaría on behalf of 384 detained or disappeared Chileans. Cites the more common characteristics of each arrest. Volume 5 contains additional cases.

639

Arzobispado de Santiago. Vicaría de la Solidaridad. *El poder judicial y el recurso de amparo. Cuadernos jurídicos, no. 3, oct. 1977: 6-40.*

Examines the concept of habeas corpus and the Chilean judiciary. Provides evidence of human rights violations.

640

Arzobispado de Santiago. Vicaría de la Solidaridad. *Presentación a la Corte Suprema realizada el 3 de noviembre por los Vicarios Episcopales del Cardenal Arzobispado de Santiago en favor de 651 personas detenidas/desaparecidas. Separata de la Solidaridad, nov. 1978: whole issue.*

Not available for annotation.

641

Arzobispado de Santiago. Vicaría de la Solidaridad. *Presentación al Presidente de la Corte Suprema; marzo 1976. Santiago, Arzobispado de Santiago, Vicaría de la Solidaridad, Unidad de Comunicaciones, 1976. 181 p. illus.*

Brief, presented before the Supreme Court, that discusses the legal protection of human rights in Chile. Includes the decision of the Court on the case.

642

Arzobispado de Santiago. Vicaría de la Solidaridad. *Presentación con motivo de la inaguración del año judicial; marzo 1978. Santiago, 1978. [82] p.*

Reports on the system of military justice that was established in 1977. Discusses the effect of the system on the human rights protections that are outlined in the Chilean Constitution. Analyzes the writ of amparo.

643

Arzobispado de Santiago. Vicaría de la Solidaridad. *Segundo año de labor; enero 1978. Santiago, 1978. 172 p. illus.*

Annual report that describes the legal, social, and spiritual assistance provided by the Vicaría to political prisoners and their families during 1977.

644

Arzobispado de Santiago. *Vicaría de la Solidaridad. Seguridad nacional y régimen militar. Santiago, Chile, 1977. 71 p.*

Discusses national security and human rights issues under Chile's military government.

645

Axelsson, Sun, Birgitta Leander, and Raul Silva, eds. *Evidence on the terror in Chile. Translated [from the Swedish] by Brian McBeth. London, Merlin Press, 1974. 139 p.*

Examines the repression of civil and political rights in Chile after the military coup of 1973. Contains anonymous statements.

646

Basso, Lelio, ed. *Atti della prima sessione del Tribunale Russell II. Venice, Italy, Marsilio Editore, 1975. 376 p.*

Charges and testimony from the Bertrand Russell Tribunal on human rights violations in Chile, Uruguay, and Bolivia.

647

Bizzarro, Salvatore. *Chile under the jackboot. Current history, v. 70, Feb. 1976: 57-60,81-83.*

Discusses the authoritarian rule of the Chilean military junta.

648

Bravo, Gabriela. *La lucha por el reconocimiento de los presos desaparecidos en Chile. OCLAE, (Organización Continental Latino-Americana de Estudiantes), v. 21, abr. 1978: 39-47.*

Testimony given before the Commission of Human Rights in Geneva that describes the situation of detained or disappeared individuals in Chile. Presented by the wife of a political prisoner.

649

Breslin, Patrick. *Interventions. Garden City, N.Y., Doubleday, 1980. 263 p.*

Novel set in Santiago, Chile, in the wake of the military coup of 1973. Deals with the disappearance, imprisonment, and torture of people and mentions the role of the U.S. in the situation.

650

Brewin, Andrew, Louis Duclos, and David MacDonald. *One gigantic prison: the report of the fact-finding mission to Chile, Argentina, and Uruguay.* Toronto, Inter-Church Committee on Chile, 1976. 69 p.

Reports on the Inter-Church Committee's mission to South America in October, 1976, to investigate human rights violations in Argentina, Chile, and Uruguay.

651

Byron Chaikin, Rosalind. *Labor and human rights: a Chilean chronicle.* AFL-CIO free trade union news, v. 33, Nov. 1978: 6-8.

Asserts that the Pinochet regime continues to persecute trade unionists. Written by the wife of an AFL-CIO vice-president who accompanied her husband on a visit to Chile.

652

Cárdenas, Juan Pablo, et al. *La universidad de los disidentes: paz, guerra, y derechos humanos. Análisis,* nov./dic. 1978: whole issue.

Examines the effect the military junta has had on both university life and politics in Chile. Comments on the suppression of human rights.

653

La carrera docente. *Mensaje,* v. 27, nov. 1978: 673-752.

Editorial that questions the Chilean government's explanation of the 1976 assassination of Orlando Letelier.

654

Carter's "human rights" means Videla/Pinochet. *Worker's vanguard,* Sept. 9, 1977: 1, 11.

Evaluates President Carter's human rights policy toward Chile. Written by the Spartacist League of the United States.

655

Carvajal Barrios, Leonardo. *Definición del olvido.* La Habana, Casa de las Américas, 1975. 119 p.

Consists of a collection of short stories set in post-Allende Chile. Many of the stories depict the living conditions of political prisoners.

656

Cassese, Antonio. *Foreign economic assistance and respect for civil and political rights: Chile - a case study.* Texas international law journal, v. 14, spring 1979: 251-263.

Assesses the effect of human rights policy on decisions to provide foreign economic assistance to Chile.

657

Cassidy, Sheila. *Audacity to believe.* London, Collins, 1977. 333 p.

English physician gives an account of her imprisonment and torture in Chile. Describes prison conditions.

658

Cassidy, Sheila. *Tortured in Chile.* Index on censorship, v. 5, summer 1976: 67-73.

Author's account of the torture she underwent after she was arrested for treating a wounded Chilean revolutionary.

659

Centro de Estudios y Documentación Chile América. *[A cinco años del golpe militar] Chile-América, set./oct. 1978:* whole issue.

Describes the status of human rights in Chile during the five years after the military overthrow of President Allende. Includes commentary on both the Supreme Court and the assassination of Orlando Letelier.

660

Chicago Commission of Inquiry into the Status of Human Rights in Chile. *Report.* Santiago, 1974. [98] leaves.

Contains interviews and documents pertaining to the status of human rights in Chile after the military coup of 1973.

661

Chicago Commission of Inquiry into the Status of Human Rights in Chile. *Terror in Chile. New York review of books, v. 21, May 30, 1974: 38-41.*

Contains part 1 of the Chicago Commission's inquiry as well as a report by Amnesty International.

662

Chile and the British labour movement. *London, Chile Solidarity Campaign, 1976. 1 v. (various pagings)*

Booklet that examines the lack of human rights and the repression of trade unions in Chile.

663

Chile: blood on the peaceful road. *Latin American perspectives, v. 1, summer 1974: whole issue.*

Special issue that examines political events in Chile after 1970. Articles discuss imperialism, dependency, and political repression. Of particular interest is Jorge Nef's article concerning the impact of the military coup on human rights.

664

Chile Committee for Human Rights. *The Catholic Church and the military dictatorship. Its Newsletter, v. 1, Apr. 1976: whole issue.*

Analyzes the Catholic Church's influence on the military government in Chile. Includes a chronology of church-state confrontations.

665

Chile Committee for Human Rights. *Chile's secret prisoners. London, 1977. 40 p.*

Examines the efforts by Chilean families to ascertain the status of their missing relatives. Describes the assistance that the relatives received from Catholic Church groups. Includes discussions on both the military and the secret police.

666

Chile Committee for Human Rights. *DINA: the transformation of horror into normality. Its Newsletter, v. 2, Sept. 1977: whole issue.*

Criticizes the activities of the Chilean secret police.

667

Chile Committee for Human Rights. *Fury and sorrow: the disappeared in Chile. Its Newsletter, v. 2, May 1977: whole issue.*

Examines the status of detained or disappeared persons in Chile.

668

Chile Committee for Human Rights. *Goodbye my country...I'm leaving but I take you with me. Its Newsletter, v. 3, Jan. 1978: whole issue.*

Analyzes the impact of the military takeover in 1973 on the Chilean press.

669

Chile Informative. *Collected documents for Canadian inquiry into human rights in Chile; special edition. Toronto, 1977. 36 p.*

Inquiry into human rights violations in Chile. Lists basic rights which ought to be protected in a democracy.

670

Christian Democratic World Union. *Study of reported violations of human rights in Chile, with particular reference to torture and other cruel, inhuman, or degrading treatment or punishment. [New York, United Nations] 1975. 1 v. (various pagings) (U.N. [Document] E/CN. 4/1166/ Add. 13)*

At head of title: Economic and Social Council.

Not available for annotation.

671

Christian social witness in repressive societies and United States responsibility. *New York, United Presbyterian Church, U.S.A., Unit on Church and Society, 1974. 47 p.*

Contains the policy statement and recommendations that were adopted by the 186th General Assembly of the United Presbyterian Church, U.S.A. Includes reports on Brazil and Chile.

672

Cid, Francisco Javier, ed. *El humanismo de Fernando Vives.* Santiago, *Instituto Chileno de Estudios Humanísticos* [1976] 132 p.

Examines the philosophy of Vives Solar, an active member of the Chilean Christian movement. Provides a discussion of his position on human rights.

673

Comisión Chilena de Derechos Humanos. *Acta Constitutiva.* Santiago, 1978.[2] p.

Outlines the objectives in the constitution of the newly founded Chilean Human Rights Commission. Identifies the human rights that are guaranteed in the U.N. Charter and in the charters of other international organizations of which Chile is a member. Includes the text of the U.N. Universal Declaration of Human Rights.

674

Comité de Defensa de los Derechos Humanos de Chile. *Chile: violación de los derechos humanos. Its Informe, feb. 1979: whole issue.*

Provides information on detained or disappeared prisoners. Discusses arbitrary detentions and other human rights violations.

675

Comité de Defensa de los Derechos Humanos de Chile. *Chile: violación de los derechos humanos. Its Informe, abr. 1979: whole issue.*

Summarizes recent changes in the handling of terrorists. Discusses the cases of detained or disappeared persons. Includes a list of their names.

676

Comité de Defensa de los Derechos Humanos de Chile. *[Human rights violations in Chile] Informativo CODEH, abr. 5, 1979: whole issue.*

Reports on the status of political prisoners in Chile. Provides the names of persons whose human rights were allegedly violated during May, 1979.

677

Comité de Defensa de los Derechos Sindicales. *[Report of union involvement in demonstrations] Informativo Codes, v. 1, no. 5, 1979: whole issue.*

Describes the police attacks on peaceful demonstrators during May, 1979. The discussion focuses on union members who participated in the demonstrations.

678

Comité de Prisioneros Políticos y Desaparecidos. *[Treatment of political prisoners in Chile] Boletín chileno, set. 1977: whole issue.*

Editorializes against the Chilean military government's treatment of political prisoners. Includes a newspaper article by an exiled Chilean attorney.

679

Comité de Solidaridad con los Pueblos Latinoamericanos. *Testimonios de lucha; Chile, Brasil [y] Uruguay. Its Bolitín, no. 2, 1974: whole issue.*

Presents an account of the activities of the popular resistance movements in Brazil and Uruguay. Describes U.S. involvement in Brazil and Chile. Includes a transcript of Allende's last words.

680

Comité Inter-Mouvements Auprès des Evacués. Bureau de Defense des Droits de l'Homme. Section Amerique Latine. *L'appareil répressif et le prisonnier politique; le cas du Chile.* Paris, *CIMADE-Information,* 1977. 41 p. (Dossiers de CIMADE-Information, no. l)

Discusses torture techniques and the psychological effects of imprisonment.

681

Comité Inter-Mouvements Auprès des Evacués. Bureau de Defense des Droits de l'Homme. Section

Amerique Latine. *Temoignages: disparitions, tortures, prisons au Chili: 4 ex-prisonniers parlent. Paris, CIMADE-Information, 1976. 14 p.*

Describes the suppression of civil and political rights by the Chilean military junta. Written by exiled relatives of political prisoners.

682

Comité Permanente de la Conferencia Episcopal Chilena. *Chile: nuestra convivencia nacional. Nueva sociedad, no. 30, marzo 1977: 1-156.*

Discusses the human rights situation in Chile in the mid 1970's.

683

Congress of Catholic Lawyers. *Human rights. Convergence, no. 3/4, 1976: whole issue.*

Contains recommendations concerning the elimination of torture in Latin America.

684

Cooperation in Documentation and Communication. *Bibliographical notes for understanding the military coup in Chile. [Edited by Mary Riesch and Harry Strharsky] Washington, CoDoC International Secretariat, 1974. 96 p. (Its Common catalogue, no. 1)*

Drawn from the publications of the member organizations of CoDoC in Latin America and the United States.

685

Coordinating Committee of Mapuches Living in Exile. *The tragedy of the Mapuches. London, 1979. 4 p.*

Reviews the history of the Mapuches. Contains a statement that the exiled Mapuches approved of during their January, 1978, conference in London.

686

Corvalán, Luís. *Words from prison. Helsinki, World Peace Council [1975?]21 p.*

Contains the letters that Luis Corvalán wrote to his family while he was imprisoned in Dawson

Island. Also contains the testimony that he gave to the Inter-American Comission on Human Rights in 1974. Corvalán, a secretary of the Communist Party of Chile, was awarded the 1973-74 Lenin Peace Prize.

687

De Maio, Ernest. *What is happening to our union brothers and sisters in Chile. Labor today, Feb. 1974: 6-7.*

Author's account of the Chilean military junta's repression of civil and political rights. Written by the vice-president of the United Electrical Workers, U.S.A.

688

Derechos humanos. *Santiago, Arzobispado de Santiago, Vicaría de la Solidaridad, 1978. 114 p. (Estudios, no. 1)*

Provides a historical review of the promotion of human rights in Chile.

689

Derechos humanos: inquietud y esperanza. *Análisis, v. 1, jun. 1978: whole issue.*

Examines the Catholic Church's promotion of human rights in Chile. Discusses both the Universal Declaration of Human Rights and the military junta's economic policies.

690

Los detenidos desaparecidos: tragedia nacional. *Mensaje, jun. 1978: 357-361.*

Editorial that asks the military regime for clarification concerning the fate of detained persons in Chile who have disappeared.

691

Dinges, John. *Chile's Murder, Inc.: U.S. investigators working on the Letelier murder case have discovered an international assassination campaign by the Chilean regime. Inquiry, Jan. 822, 1979: 18-21.*

Reports on the U.S. government's investigation into the murder of Orlando Letelier. Suggests that the Chilean secret police and other Latin American anti-communist activists were involved in this and other assassinations.

692

Dinges, John. *What Townley can't tell: Chile's global hitmen. Nation,* v. 228, June 2, 1979: 617, 633-636.

Charges that the U.S. government was involved in efforts to conceal the military junta's alleged international terrorist activities.

693

¿Donde están? v. 1. *Santiago, Arzobispado de Santiago, Vicaría de la Solidaridad [1978] 251 p. illus.*

Contains the case histories of 54 disappeared Chileans. Includes a summary of the facts and findings in each case. Written by religious leaders without the cooperation of the military authorities.

694

Dorfman, Ariel. *Culture et résistance au Chili. Geneva, Institut d'Action Culturelle, 1977. 43 p. illus. (Document IDAC, no. 15)*

At head of title: Rever, anticiper, préparer un monde différent.

Examines the repressive tactics of the military junta in Chile. Written by an exiled Chilean writer.

695

Elgueta, Bernardo, et al. *Five years of military government in Chile (1973-1978). Pine Plains, N.Y., Earl M. Coleman, 1980. 300 p.*

Reports on events in Chile between 1973 and 1978. Written by individuals who oppose the Pinochet regime.

696

EPICA Task Force. *Highlights from Chile's religious revolution, 1968-1973. Washington, 1973. 32 p.*

Chronicles the major events during the presidency of Salvador Allende.

697

Foxley, Ana María. *Reportaje especial: el derecho a ser persona. Hoy (Chile), nov. 22/28, 1978: 7-11.*

Notes briefly the promotion of human rights in Chile. Includes a report on a children's art competition and interviews with religious leaders concerning their activities on behalf of human rights.

698

Foxley, Ana María. *El simposio por dentro: buscando la respuesta. Hoy (Chile), nov. 29/dic. 5, 1978: 11-15.*

Examines the role of the Catholic Church as a defender of human rights in Chile. Describes the military junta's opposition to the Church.

699

Frenz, Helmut. *Human rights: a Christian viewpoint. Christianity and crisis,* v. 36, June 21, 1976: 146-151.

Contains portions of a speech written by a Lutheran bishop who was expelled from Chile by the military junta. Discusses the Christian commitment to the promotion of human rights.

700

Fyra latinamerikanska militärdiktaturer. *Stockholm, Amnesty International, Svenska Sektionen, 1974. 2 v. in one.*

Examines violations of human rights in Latin America. Volume 1 deals with Brazil and Chile and volume 2 treats Bolivia and Uruguay. Both volumes list the names of intellectuals who have been jailed or exiled.

701

González, Alejandro. *Panorama de los derechos humanos y su situación en Chile. Derechos humanos, estudios. Santiago, Arzobispado de Santiago, Vicaría de la Solidaridad, v. 1, mayo 1978: 31-68.*

A lawyer for the Vicaría de la Solidaridad expounds specific basic human rights, such as the right to personal integrity, freedom, security, asylum, due process, and free association.

702

Hauser, Thomas. *The execution of Charles Horman: an American sacrifice. New York, Harcourt Brace Jovanovich, 1978. 255 p.*

Describes the disappearance and death of a U.S. citizen in Chile during the military coup of 1973. Does not provide documentation.

703

Illanes Benitez, Oswaldo. *The Supreme Court of Chile. International Commission of Jurists. Review, v. 7, winter 1966: 269-277.*

Not available for annotation.

704

Indigenous Minorities Research Council. *El proyecto de la nueva ley indígena que auspicia la Junta Militar chilena apunta hacia nuestra pronta extinción como minoría étnica nacional de Chile. Boletín informativo Mapuche, marzo 1979: 1-5.*

Examines the newly enacted law concerning indigenous populations in Chile. Focuses on the poverty of the Mapuches.

705

Institute for Policy Studies. *Orlando Letelier and Ronni Karpen Moffit. Washington, 1978. 94 p. illus.*

Discusses the assassinations of the former Chilean ambassador and his assistant. Contains articles, poems, prayers, and speeches that were written in their honor.

706

International Commission of Enquiry into the Crimes of the Military Junta in Chile. *Documents. New times, Apr. 1974: 26-31.*

Documents both the violation of human rights in Chile and the alleged conspiracy of the military junta against the citizenry.

707

International Commission of Enquiry into the Crimes of the Military Junta in Chile, ed. *First session of the International Commission of Enquiry into the Crimes of the Military Junta in Chile, Dipoli, Finland, March 21-24, 1974; documents. Helsinki, Secretariat [1974]47 p.*

Contains the minutes of the Commission's opening session, including its membership roster,

bylaws, and an address by President Allende's widow. Appeals to physicians and lawyers to promote human rights.

708

International Commission of Enquiry into the Crimes of the Military Junta in Chile. *Terror and violence as an institutionalized system in Chile. Helsinki, Kirjapaino Kursüvi Oy, 1977. 28 p.*

Report adopted by the Commission at a meeting of the Secretariat held in Europa House, Luxembourg, on September 25, 1977. Contains sections on violations of international and Chilean law. Lacks supporting documentation.

709

International Commission of Enquiry into the Crimes of the Military Junta in Chile. *Two years of military dictatorship in Chile; Stockholm, House of Parliament, September 6th-7th, 1975. [Helsinki] The Commission, 1975. 42 p.*

Denounces the human rights violations of the Chilean military junta. Examines the detention of Luís Corvalán and appeals for the release of Ezequiel Ponce, Carlos Lorca, and Ricardo Lagos. Includes a list of junta members.

710

International Commission of Enquiry into the Crimes of the Military Junta in Chile. Juridical Sub-Commission. *The crimes of the Chilean military junta in the light of Chilean law and international law. [Helsinki] Juridical Subcommission of the International Commission of Enquiry into the Crimes of the Military Junta in Chile [1974?] 43 p.*

Brief East German statement that challenges the legitimacy and competence of the Chilean military government and courts to prosecute political opponents. Includes no supporting evidence.

711

International Commission of Enquiry into the Crimes of the Military Junta in Chile. Juridical Sub-Commission. *Meeting; documents. Berlin, German Democratic Republic, 1977. 41 p.*

Provides the documents of the February 6, 1977, meeting of the Commission in East Germany. Discusses both missing persons and human rights violations in Chile.

712

International Commission of Jurists. *Arrests and detentions and freedom of information in Chile, September 1976; a supplement to the report of the International Commission of Jurists mission to Chile, April 1974. Geneva [1977] 32 p.*

Analyzes Chilean decrees enacted after 1972 which pertain to arrest, detention, and freedom of speech. Provides information on legal irregularities and disappeared detainees.

713

International Commission of Jurists. *Chile; the system of military justice. In its Review, Dec. 1975: 1-4.*

Contains the October, 1975, report of the U.N. Commission on Human Rights. Discusses recommendations that were made by the Human Rights Commission of the O.A.S. and the International Commission of Jurists concerning human rights violations in Chile.

714

International Commission of Jurists. *Human rights in the world: Chile and Uruguay: contrasts and comparisons. In its Review, June 1974: 5-7.*

Editorial requesting that the Chilean military government abide by the International Covenant on Civil and Political Rights, a document that was ratified in 1972 by the Allende government.

715

International Commission of Jurists. *The legal system in Chile. In its Review, Dec. 1974: 45-59.*

Provides extracts from a report of an April, 1974, ICJ mission, the purpose of which was to investigate the status of human rights and the rule of law in Chile.

716

International Commission of Jurists. *Report of mission to Chile. Geneva, 1974. 1 v. (various pagings)*

Examines the effects of military rule on the Chilean Constitution. Gives special attention to justice for political prisoners and to civil rights during states of siege.

717

International Confederation of Free Trade Unions. *Les droits humains et syndicaux: 11e Congrès mondial de la C.I.S.L., Ciudad de México, D.F., 17-25 octobre 1975. Brussels, Rue Montagne aux Herbes Potagères, 1976. 52 p.*

Contains statements by representatives of national and international labor unions concerning government repression of union activity. Includes a declaration by the CISL regarding the human rights situation in Chile. Also includes a list of countries that have ratified human rights agreements.

718

International Trade Union Committee for Solidarity with the Workers and People of Chile. *What the DINA and Pinochet deny; the truth about the missing prisoners in Chile: their faces, their lives, their testimonies. [Prague] 1977. 59 p. illus.*

Cover title: We accuse fascism.

Provides the names and photographs of Chileans who were allegedly arrested and of whom the military government claims to have no arrest record.

719

Joint Working Group for Refugees from Chile in Britain. *Political prisoners and refugees in the Southern Cone of Latin America. [London] 1977. 25 p.*

Review of an international program to assist political prisoners in and refugees from Argentina, Bolivia, Brazil, and Chile.

720

Landau, Saul. *They educated the crows: an Institute report on the Letelier-Moffitt murders. Washington, Transnational Institute, 1978. 44 p.*

Reviews the Institute's investigation of the assassinations of Orlando Letelier and Ronni Moffitt. Discusses the alleged cover up.

721

Latin American Working Group. *Worlds apart: economic relations and human rights; Canada-Chile. Its Letter, v. 5, May/June 1978: whole issue.*

Describes the support given to the Pinochet regime by Canadian private and government sectors.

722

Lauterpacht, Elihu, and John G. Collier, eds. *Individual rights and the state in foreign affairs: an international compendium. New York, Praeger, 1977. 743 p. (Praeger special studies)*

Provides country-by-country analyses of individual rights at the national and international levels. Chile and Mexico are among the countries assessed.

723

Lawner, Miguel. *¡Venceremos! Dos años en los campos de concentración de Chile; two years in Chilean concentration camps; 2 år i Chiles kz-lejre.Arhus, Husets Forlag /S.O.L., 1976. [80] p. illus. (Serien for oversat litteratur, 10)*

Cover title: 2 år i Chiles kz-lejre.

Provides sketches of the lives of political prisoners in one of the camps of the military junta in Chile. Written in Danish, English, and Spanish.

724

Lefranc Walker, Carlos. *El asesinato de Orlando Letelier. Denuncia, v. 4, no. 36, 1978: 9.*

Reports on the investigation of the murder of Orlando Letelier. Discusses the possible involvement of the Pinochet government.

725

Leigh Guzmán, Gustavo. *La junta de gobierno frente a la juricidad y los derechos humanos. Discurso pronunciado por el General Leigh el 29 de Abril de 1974 en la Universidad Católica de Chile. [Santiago] Editora Nacional Gabriela Mistral [1977?] 30 p.*

Examines both the legitimacy of the Chilean military junta and its lack of respect for human rights. Includes a general discussion of military justice during wartime.

726

Lernoux, Penny. *Chile will never be the same. Nation, v. 218, Mar. 16, 1974: 328-332.*

Analyzes the abuse of the human and civil rights of Chileans following the 1973 coup.

727

Letelier, Isabel, and Michael Moffitt. *Human rights, economic aid, and private banks: the case of Chile. Washington, Institute for Policy Studies, 1978. 16 p.*

Documents the increase in private bank loans to the Chilean military junta after the overthrow of Salvador Allende in 1973.

728

Letelier, Orlando. *Chile: economic freedom and political repression. Washington [Institute for Policy Studies] 1976. 17 p.*

"A joint publication by Race & Class, the Transnational Institute and Spokesman Pamphlets."

Examines the economic policies of the military regime in Chile and the effect of these policies on political repression.

729

Levy, Daniel. *Higher education policy in authoritarian regimes: comparative perspectives on the Chilean case. New Haven, Conn., Yale Higher Education Research Group Working Paper, 1980. 60 p.*

The military reorganization of and policies toward Chilean universities, outlined and compared to those of Argentina and Brazil.

730

List of demands of the Chilean people for an end to repression against the workers and people to achieve basic respect for human rights in Chile. *Chilean resistance courier, July 1978: 66-75.*

Provides a list of political, economic, and educational demands for reform.

731

Lonquen: una primera respuesta. *Santiago, Arzobispado de Santiago, Vicaría de la Solidaridad, 1979. [6?] p. illus. (Solidaridad, v. 65, primera quincena, marzo 1979)*

Describes cases of persons who have disappeared.

732

MacEóin, Gary, ed. *Chile: terror by computer. Commonweal, v. 100, July 26, 1974: 399-402.*

Describes the systematic repression of the political opposition in Chile.

733

MacEóin, Gary. *Chile: under military rule. New York, IDOC North America, 1977. 153 p.*

Dossier of documents and analyses listing human rights violations.

734

Marinello, Juan. *Denuncia de las violaciones de los derechos humanos por la Junta Militar de Chile en la educación, la ciencia y la cultura. La Habana, Comité Central del Partido Comunista de Cuba, Departamento de Orientación Revolucionaria, 1976. 30 p.*

Contains a speech delivered to UNESCO's Executive Council on September 16, 1975, that denounces the Chilean military junta.

735

Meyers, Barbara. *Chile: human rights in recess. LADOC, v. 7, Sept./Oct. 1976: 35-39.*

Discusses repression, torture, and censorship in Chile. Describes the Catholic Church's defense of human rights.

736

Morales de Tohá, Moy. *Human rights in Chile today. Washington, Institute for Policy Studies, 1976. 11 leaves.*

Cover title: Latin American round table, a forum for hemispheric affairs.

Examines the violation of human rights in Chile after the military coup in 1973. Asserts that the Pinochet regime does not have the support of the majority of Chileans. Written by the wife of the Minister of Defense under Allende.

737

Morales Echevers de Tohá, Raquel. *Chili: témoignage sur la mort de mon mari. Croissance des jeunes nations, v. 149/150, July/Aug. 1974: 13-14.*

Describes the jailing and murder of President Allende's Minister of the Interior by agents of the military junta. Written by the Minister's widow.

738

Moreno Laval, Jaime. *Derechos humanos: visto y oído en Chile. Hoy, v. 2, dic. 6/12, 1978: 15-17.*

Criticizes the actions of both the Chilean government and the Ad Hoc Committee on the Situation of Human Rights in Chile during the Committee's investigation in that country.

739

Moreno Laval, Jaime. *Gobierno: tempestad exterior. Hoy, v. 2, nov. 29/dic. 5, 1978: 7.*

Reports on the findings of the Ad Hoc Committee on the Situation of Human Rights in Chile. Maintains that violations of human rights continue.

740

Nací al mundo pa'cantar. *Santiago, Arzobispado de Santiago, Vicaría de la Solidaridad, 1978. [37] p. illus.*

Provides a collection of poems and photographs, the aim of which is to promote human rights in Chile. Written anonymously.

741

Nallet, Thérèse. *Chili: une réfugiée témoigne. Croissance des jeunes nations. v. 144, fev. 1974: 72-79.*

Contains an interview with a young Chilean woman exiled in France whose husband was imprisoned, tortued, and executed by agents of the military junta.

742

Nef, Jorge. *The politics of repression: the social pathology of the Chilean military. Latin American perspectives, v. 1, summer 1974: 58-77.*

Analyzes the impact of the military coup on democratic institutions in Chile.

743

Non-Intervention in Chile. *Behind the human rights rhetoric. Chile newsletter, v. 4, Apr./May 1977: whole issue.*

Examines the status of human rights in Chile and Argentina.

744

Non-Intervention in Chile. *[Chilean union activity] Chile action bulletin, Dec./Jan. 1979: whole issue.*

Analyzes Chilean labor union activity. Includes a discussion of the Sandinistas in Nicaragua.

745

Nueva ley indígena: ¿el fin de un pueblo? *Solidaridad, abr. 1979: 12-15.*

Expresses the concern of the Catholic Church for the welfare of the Mapuches in light of the passage of the Law on Indigenous Matters. Includes the opinions of several anthropologists.

746

¿Un nuevo engaño del gobierno de los comandantes en jefe? Sustitución en Chile de la DINA por la Central Nacional de Informaciones. *Nueva sociedad, nov./dic. 1977: 177-181.*

Comments on the efforts of the military junta to reorganize the Chilean secret police.

747

Organization of American States. Inter-American Commission on Human Rights. *Informe sobre la situación de los derechos humanos en Chile; resultado de la observación "in loco" practicada en la República de Chile del 22 de julio al 2 de agosto de 1974. Washington, Organization of American States, General Secretariat, 1974. 175 p. (Organization of American States. Official records. OEA/Ser. L/V/II.34 doc. 21)*

"Aprobado por la Comisión en la 424a sesión, celebrada el 24 de octubre de 1974."

Reports on the findings of the Commission concerning the status of human rights in Chile immediately after the military coup in 1973. Provides a review of political developments during that time.

748

Organization of American States. Inter-American Commission on Human Rights. *Observations by the government of Chile on the "Report on the status of human rights in Chile". Washington, Organization of American States, General Secretariat, 1975. 83 p. (Organization of American States. Official records. OEA/Ser. P/AG/doc. 500/75)*

Contains the Chilean government's reply to the July 22/August 2, 1974, report of the Inter-American Commission on Human Rights.

749

Organization of American States. Inter-American Commission on Human Rights. *Second report on the situation of human rights in Chile. Washington, Organization of American States, General Secretariat, 1976. 191 p. (Organization of American States. Official records. OEA/Ser. L/V/II.37 doc. 19 corr. 1)*

"Approved by the Commission at its 469th meeting, March 12, 1976".

Continues the Commission's evaluation of the status of human rights in Chile. Recommends that the repressive practices of the Chilean government be modified.

750

Organization of American States. Inter-American Commission on Human Rights. *Third report on the situation of human rights in Chile. Washington, Organization of American States, General Secretariat, 1977. 92 p. (Organization of American States. Official records. OEA/Ser.L/V/II.40 doc. 10)*

Reports on the Commission's findings concerning the human rights policies of the military junta in Chile. Notes that violations continue.

751

Orrego Vicuña, Claudio. *Un deber de conciencia para los chilenos. Santiago, 1979. [18] p.*

Unpublished paper that reflects on the moral, political, and national security implications of the assassination of Orlando Letelier. Discusses the legal responsibilities of the Chilean military junta.

752

Precht Bañados, Cristián. *Los derechos humanos en Chile: una experiencia solidaria. Separata solidaridad, dic. 1978: whole issue.*

Special issue that discusses the involvement of the Catholic Church in the promotion of human rights in Chile.

753

The present situation of human rights in Chile. *[New York] United Nations, General Assembly, 1975. 74 p. (U.N. [Document] A/C.3/639)*

Cover title: Protection of human rights in Chile. Comparison of the human rights situations before and during the Pinochet regime. Aims to discredit international criticism of the military government.

754

Puebla: esperanza y compromiso. *Solidaridad, v. 64, primera quincena, feb. 1979: whole issue.*

Examines the application in Chile of the recommendations that were formulated by the Catholic Bishop's Conference in Puebla, Mexico.

755

Quiero la unidad y la paz: 40 años de sacerdocio. *Solidaridad, v. 47, primera quincena, jul. 1978: whole issue.*

Provides a report on the Catholic Church's promotion of human rights in Chile. Includes editorial remarks.

756

Quigley, Thomas E. *Chile: the repression continues. Christianity and crisis, v. 35, Aug. 18, 1975: 192-195.*

Discusses totalitarian control of Chile by the military junta.

757

Rogers, William D., and F. J. McNeil. *U.S. discusses human rights items in O.A.S. General Assembly. U.S. Department of State. Department of State bulletin, June 23, 1975: 879-883.*

Statements in praise of the Chile report of the Inter-American Commission on Human Rights. Includes the U.N. General Assembly's vote of thanks.

758

Romero, Vicente. *Chile: terror y miseria. Madrid, Ediciones Mayler, 1977. 215 p. illus.*

Spanish journalist's account of his detention and interrogation by the secret police in Chile. The author was expelled from the country by the military authorities.

759

Ronning, C. Neale. *National priorities and political rights in Spanish America. In Pollis, Adamantia, and Peter Schwab, eds. Human rights; cultural and ideological perspectives. New York, Praeger, 1979. p. 101-114.*

Review of human rights policies in Latin America, with emphasis on the policies of Chile, Cuba, Mexico, and Venezuela. Examines the reasons why the human rights goals set by these nations have not been attained.

760

Ryskind, Allan B. *Should Chile be treated as a pariah? Human events, Dec. 18, 1976: 10-14, 19.*

Criticizes journalistic allegations that the military junta is a terrorist regime.

761

Sanders, Michael. *Book burning and brutality. Index on censorship, v. 3, spring 1974: 7-16.*

Discusses the impact of the military coup on the lives of Chilean intellectuals. Written by a former detainee.

762

Sanders, Thomas Griffin. *Military government in Chile. [New York] American Universities Field Staff, 1975. 2 v. (West Coast South America series, v. 22, no. 1-2) (Field staff reports)*

Examines the effect of the military takeover in Chile.

763

Schoultz, Lars. *Human rights and United States policy toward Latin America. New Scholar, v. 7, nov. 1/2, 1979: 87-104.*

Praises recent changes in U.S. human rights policy in Latin America. Discusses current human rights violations in Chile in the context of the militarism of the 1970's.

764

Sierra, Malú. *Cardenal Silva Henríquez: el derecho a hablar. Hoy, v. 2, dic. 6/12, 1978: 18-23.*

Examines, in an interview with the Cardinal, the Catholic Church's attitude toward the military junta in Chile.

765

Silva Henríquez, Raúl. *El boletín de la vicaría presta su voz a quienes no pueden hacerse oir. Separata solidaridad, oct. 1977: whole issue.*

Cardinal of Santiago, Chile, discusses the role that religious activists play in Chilean politics.

766

Silva Henríquez, Raúl. *Por una Iglesia corresponsable y solidaria del mundo. Santiago, Arzobispado de Santiago, Vicaría de la Solidaridad, 1977. [19] p. illus. (Formación, no. 9)*

A comic book, written by the Cardinal of Santiago, Chile, that advocates Christian action to protect human rights.

767

Söderman, Jacob. *The disappearance of arrested persons in Chile. Helsinki, 1976. 26 p.*

Advocates the prompt release of political prisoners in Chile. Written by a member of the Finnish Parliament.

768

Solidarität mit den politischen Gefangenen in Chile. *Rettet das leben von Luis Vitale. Frankfurt, German Federal Republic. Gruppe Internationale Marxisten [1973?] 32 p. (Rote heft der GIM, no. 2)*

East German communist pleads for the release of a Marxist theoretician who was imprisoned in Chile.

769

Statement of solidarity on human rights: Chile and Brazil. *Washington, United States Catholic Conference, 1974. 1 v. (unpaged)*

Discusses human rights violations in both Brazil and Chile.

770

Stern, Laurence. *To die in Santiago. Potomac (Washington post), Jan. 20, 1974: 6-10, 14, 16, 28.*

Author's account of his experiences in Chile on the eve of military coup.

771

Stiphout, G. P. van. *Disappearance of persons: responsibility under international law. The Netherlands, Foundation of Legal Aid in Chile, 1978. 55 p.*

Reviews the treatment of Chilean political prisoners in light of the standards that are outlined in both international and Chilean law.

772

Styron, Rose. *Torture in Chile. New republic, v. 174, Mar. 20, 1976: 15-17.*

Describes human rights violations in Chile.

773

Szulc, Tad. *A very quiet horror. Playboy, v. 24, Feb. 1977: 107-108, 114, 182, 184-186.*

Orlando Letelier discusses his torture during imprisonment for political crimes in Chile.

774

Todo hombre tiene derecho a ser persona. *Concursos: afiches, literario, pintura infantil. Santiago, Arzobispado de Santiago, Vicaria de la Solidaridad, 1978. 172 p. col. plates.*

"Chile en el Año de los Derechos Humanos: 1978."

Anthology of prize-winning stories, posters, essays, and children's art and poetry in commemoration of the Year of Human Rights in Chile.

775

Twin Cities Resistance Committee. *The Letelier-Moffitt murders. Pan y agua, v. 1, winter 1979: 5-6.*

Accuses the Chilean and U.S. governments of involvement in the assassinations of Orlando Letelier and Ronni Moffit. Does not consider these governments' investigations to be adequate.

776

Tyndale, Wendy. *Chile under the military regime. London, Chile Committee for Human Rights, 1975. 38 p.*

Summarizes the reports of the Chile Committee for Human Rights. These reports examine the suppression of civil and political rights in post-Allende Chile.

777

U.N. Ad Hoc Working Group on the Situation of Human Rights in Chile. *Report of the Economic and Social Council: protection of human rights in Chile. New York, United Nations, 1977. 347 p. (U.N. [Document] A/32/227)*

At head of title: General Assembly. Thirty-second session, agenda item 12.

Covers both U.N. relations with the government of Chile and constitutional and legal questions about freedom and repression. Letters, reports, and government decrees are appended.

778

U.N. Ad Hoc Working Group on the Situation of Human Rights in Chile. *Report of the Economic and Social Council; protection of human rights in Chile. [New York] 1978. 1 v. (various pagings) (U.N. [Document] A/33/331)*

At head of title: United Nations General Assembly.

Not available for annotation.

779

U.N. Commission on Human Rights. *Rights of persons belonging to national, ethnic, religious, and linguistic minorities; comments received from governments pursuant to Commission Resolution 14 A (XXXIV). New York, United Nations, 1978. 21 p. (U.N.[Document] E/CN.4/1298)*

At head of title: Economic and Social Council. Thirty-fifth session, item 23 of the provisional agenda.

Includes the reply submitted by the government of Chile.

780

U.N. Commission on Human Rights. *Study of reported violations of human rights in Chile, with particular reference to torture and other cruel, inhuman, or degrading treatment or punishment. New York, United Nations, 1975. 23 p. (U.N. [Document] E/CN.4/1166/Add. 8)*

At head of title: Economic and Social Council. Thirty-first session, item 7 of the provisional agenda.

Reports on violations of the human rights of physicians and trade unionists in Chile. Includes letters from the World Federation of Trade Unions. Lists torturers in the junta and trade unionists who were killed. Written in compliance with Resolution 8(XXVII) of the Sub-Commission on the Prevention of Discrimination and Protection of Minorities and General Assembly Resolution 3219(XXXIX).

781

U.N. Commission on Human Rights. *Study of reported violations of human rights in Chile, with particular reference to torture and other cruel, inhuman, or degrading treatment or punishment.New York, United Nations, 1975. 3 p. (U.N. [Document] E/CN.4/1177)*

At head of title: Economic and Social Council. Thirty-first session, agenda item 7.

Letter from the Russian representative on the Commission on Human Rights to the Director of the Division of Human Rights.

782

U.N. Commission on Human Rights. *Study of reported violations of human rights in Chile, with particular reference to torture and other cruel, inhuman, or degrading treatment or punishment. New York, United Nations, 1976. 7 p. (U.N. [Document] E/CN.4/1166/Add. 14)*

At head of title: Economic and Social Council.

Emphasizes the violations of civil liberties and the torture of political prisoners in Chile.

783

U.N. Commission on Human Rights. *Study of reported violations of human rights in Chile, with particular reference to torture and other cruel, inhuman, or degrading treatment or punishment. New York, United Nations, 1976. [97] p. (U.N. [Document] E/CN.4/ 1188)*

At head of title: Economic and Social Council.

Expanded report on violations of civil liberties and torture of political prisoners in Chile.

784

U.N. Commission on Human Rights. *Study of reported violations of human rights in Chile, with particular reference to torture and other cruel, inhuman, or degrading treatment or punishment. New York, United Nations, 1978. 75 p. (U.N. [Document] E/CN.4/1266)*

At head of title: Economic and Social Council.

Provides a wide-ranging examination of human rights issues in Chile. Discusses, among other issues, constitutional freedoms, national security, torture, and economic and social rights.

785

U.N. Commission on Human Rights. *Study of reported violations of human rights in Chile, with particular reference to torture and other cruel, inhuman, or degrading treatment or punishment; note by the Secretariat. New York, United Nations, 1978. 77 p. (U.N. [Document] E/CN.4/1290)*

At head of title: Economic and Social Council. Thirty-fourth session, agenda item 5.

Contains the observations of the government of Chile on the report by the Ad Hoc Working Group on the Situation of Human Rights in Chile (E/CN.4/1266).

786

U.N. Commission on Human Rights. *Study of reported violations of human rights in Chile, with particular reference to torture and other cruel, inhuman, or degrading treatment or punishment; supplementary information submitted by the World Federation of Trade Unions. [New York] United Nations, 1975. 17 p. (U.N. [Document] E/CN.4/1166/Add. 10)*

At head of title: Economic and Social Council. Thirty-first session, agenda item 7.

Consists of a letter from the Chilean Labor Federation to the Chairman of the thirty-first session of the Commission on Human Rights. Discusses violations of human rights by the military junta from 1973 to 1975.

787

U.N. Economic and Social Council. *Protection of human rights in Chile. New York, United Nations, 1976. 229 p. (U.N. [Document] A/31/253)*

At head of title: General Assembly.

Treats of civil liberties, imprisonment, torture, and the exile of political dissidents.

788

U.N. Economic and Social Council. *Protection of human rights in Chile: [documents submitted by] the Permanent Representative of Chile to the United Nations. New York, United Nations, 1976. 47 p. (U.N. [Document] A/C.3/31/4)*

At head of title: General Assembly.

Discusses civil liberties, political prisoners, and torture in Chile.

789

U.N. *Economic and Social Council. Protection of human rights in Chile: letter dated 17 Oct. from the Permanent Representative of Chile to the United Nations addressed to the Secretary General. [New York] United Nations, 1975. [4] p. (U.N. [Document] A/10303)*

At head of title: General Assembly. Thirtieth session, agenda item 12.

Statement annexed to the progress report of the Ad Hoc Working Group on the Situation of Human Rights in Chile (A/10285).

790

U.N. Economic and Social Council. *Protection of human rights in Chile: report. New York, United Nations, 1975. 132 p. (U.N. [Document] A/1-285)*

At head of title: General Assembly.

Review of civil liberties in Chile.

791

U.N. Economic and Social Council. *Study of reported violations of human rights in Chile, with particular reference to torture and other cruel, inhuman, or degrading treatment or punishment: memorandum from the Permanent Representative of Chile to the United Nations Office in Geneva. New York, United Nations, 1975. 6 p. (U.N. [Document] E/CN.4/ 117/Add. 1)*

Letter of February 20, 1975, to the Director of the Division of Human Rights. Access to this document is restricted.

792

U.N. General Assembly. *General debate. Letter dated 29 Oct. 1976 from the Permanent Representative of Chile to the United Nations addressed to the Secretary General. [New York] United Nations, 1976. 3 p. (U.N. [Document] A/31/300)*

Consists of a response by Cardinal Raúl Silva Henríquez to the Chilean Ambassador at the Vatican. Discusses the U.N. plenary session of October 14, 1976.

793

U.N. Secretary General. *Protection of human rights in Chile; letter dated 17 October 1975 from the Permanent Representative of Chile to the United Nations. Report of the Economic and Social Council. [New York] United Nations, 1975. 2 p. (U.N. [Document] A/10303)*

At head of title: General Assembly. Thirtieth session, agenda item 12.

Letter to the Secretary General in which Vice Admiral Ismael Huerta refutes the allegations made by the Ad Hoc Working Group on the Situation of Human Rights in Chile.

794

U.N. Secretary General. *Protection of human rights in Chile; letter dated 24 October 1975 from the Permanent Representative of Chile to the United Nations. Report of the Economic and Social Council. [New York] United Nations, 1975. 74 p. (U.N. [Document] A/C.3/639)*

At head of title: General Assembly. Third Committee. Thirtieth session, agenda item 12.

Cover title: The present situation of human rights in Chile.

Denies that the human rights of Chileans are being suppressed.

795

U.N. Secretary General. *Protection of human rights in Chile; report. Report of the Economic and Social Council. (U.N. [Document] A/10295)*

At head of title: General Assembly. Thirtieth session, agenda item 12.
Report of U.N. activity in Chile as authorized by paragraph no. 5 of General Assembly Resolution 3219.

796

U.N. Secretary General. *Protection of human rights in Chile; report. Report of the Economic and Social Council. [New York] United Nations, 1977. 22 p. (U.N. [Document] A/32/234)*

At head of title: General Assembly. Thirty-second session, agenda item 12.

Nineteen governments and international organizations describe their efforts to promote human rights in Chile.

797

U.N. Special Rapporteur on the Situation of Human Rights in Chile. *Protection of human rights in Chile. New York, United Nations, 1979. 5 p. (U.N. [Document] A/RES/33/175)*

At head of title: Adopted at the 90th plenary meeting, 20 December 1978.

Consists of a resolution that discusses Antonio Cassese's study (E/CN.4/Sub.2/412, v. 1-4).

798

U.N. Sub-Commission on Prevention of Discrimination and Protection of Minorities. *Report of the Sub-Commission on its thirtieth session.Geneva, 15 August-2 September 1977. 50 p. (U.N. [Document] E/CN.4/1261)*

At head of title: Economic and Social Council. Commission on Human Rights.

Continues the study that was prepared by Antonio Cassese, (U.N. [Document] E/CN.4/Sub.2/412, v. 1-4).

799

U.N. Sub-Commission on Prevention of Discrimination and Protection of Minorities. *Report of the Sub-Commission on its thirty-first session. New York, United Nations, 1978. [86] p. (U.N. [Document] E/CN.4/1296, E/CN.4/Sub.2/417)*

At head of title: Economic and Social Council. Commission on Human Rights.

Examines the status of human rights in Chile.

800

U.N. Sub-Commission on Prevention of Discrimination and Protection of Minorities. *Study of the impact of foreign economic aid and assistance on respect for human rights in Chile. New York, United Nations, 1978. 4 v. tables. (U.N. [Document] E/CN.4/Sub.2/412)*

At head of title: Economic and Social Council. Commission on Human Rights. Thirty-first session, item 13 of the provisional agenda.

Analyzes the effect of the economic policies of the Pinochet regime. Discusses foreign economic assistance to Chile.

801

U.N. Third Committee. *Report of the Economic and Social Council: protection of human rights in Chile. [New York] United Nations, 1976. 85 p. (U.N. [Document] A/C.3/31/6)*

At head of title: General Assembly. Thirty-first session, agenda item 12.

Contains the reply of the Chilean Government to the report of the Ad Hoc Working Group on the Situation of Human Rights in Chile (U.N.

[Document] A/32/227). Discusses the state of siege, the concept of national security, the defense of political prisoners, the judicial system, the status of women, and the repression of cultural, economic, and social rights.

802

U.N. Third Committee. *Report of the Economic and Social Council: protection of human rights in Chile; addendum. [New York] United Nations, 1976. 180 p. tables. (U.N. [Document] A/C.3/31/6/Add. 1)*

At head of title: General Assembly. Thirty-first session, agenda item 12.

Continuation of the response by the government of Chile to the report of the Ad Hoc Working Group on the Situation of Human Rights in Chile (U.N. [Document] A/32/227). Refutes allegations made against the Dirección Nacional de Inteligencia (DINA). Discusses decisions of the Chilean Supreme Court. Includes Constitutional Acts No. 1, 2, 3, and 4 as well as an address by General Augusto Pinochet.

803

U.N. Third Committee. *Report of the Economic and Social Council: protection of human rights in Chile; documents submitted by the permanent representative of Chile to the United Nations. [New York] United Nations, 1976. 47 p. (U.N. [Document] A/C.3/31/4)*

At head of title: General Assembly. Thirty-first session, agenda item 12.

Continues the series of comments by the Chilean government on the report of the Ad Hoc Working Group on the Situation of Human Rights in Chile (U.N. [Document] A/32/227).

804

U.N. Third Committee. *Report of the Economic and Social Council: protection of human rights in Chile; letter dated 30 September 1976 from the Permanent Representative of Chile...addressed to the Secretary General. [New York] United Nations, 1976. 3 p. (U.N. [Document] A/C.3/31/5)*

At head of title: General Assembly. Thirty-first session, agenda item 12.

Public declaration by the Supreme Court of

Chile in response to Human Rights in Chile (U.N. [Document] A/32/227).

805

U.N. Third Committee. *Report of the Economic and Social Council: protection of human rights in Chile; letter dated 19 November 1976 from the Permanent Representative of Chile to the United Nations addressed to the Secretary General. [New York] United Nations, 1976. 2 p. (U.N. [Document] A/C.3/31/12)*

At head of title: General Assembly. Thirty-first session, agenda item 12.

Declaration of the Auxiliary Bishops of Santiago that stresses the need to release persons who were detained during the state of siege.

806

U.N. Third Committee. *Report of the Economic and Social Council: protection of human rights in Chile; letter dated 30 November 1976 from the Acting Permanent Representative of the Union of Soviet Socialist Republics to the United Nations addressed to the Secretary General. [New York] United Nations, 1976. [3] p. (U.N. [Document] A/C.3/31/13)*

At head of title: General Assembly. Thirty-first session, agenda item 12.

Discusses the release of Chilean political prisoners.

807

U.N. Third Committee. *Report of the Economic and Social Council: protection of human rights in Chile; letter dated 3 December 1976 from the Permanent Representative of Chile to the United Nation s... to the Secretary General. [New York] United Nations, 1976. 3 p. (U.N. [Document] A/C.3/31/14)*

At head of title: General Assembly. Thirty-first session, agenda item 12.

Provides the response of the Chilean Government to the Soviet Union's delegation's request for the release of political prisoners.

808

U.N. Third Committee. *Report of the Economic and Social Council: letter dated 17 November 1978 from the Permanent Representative of Chile...addressed to the Secretary General.*

[New York] United Nations, 1978. 77 p. tables. (U.N. [Document] A/C.3/33/7)

At head of title: General Assembly. Thirty-third session, agenda item 12.

Contains the critical response of the Chilean government to the U.N. study (E/CN.4/Sub.2/412, v. 1-4). Denies that the United Nations has the right to conduct such a study.

809

Valdés, Hernán. *Tejas Verdes: diario de un campo de concentración en Chile. 2a. ed. Barcelona, Spain, Editorial Laia, 1978. 225 p. (Laia B)*

Describes life in a Chilean prison camp after the military coup of 1973.

810

Varas, Florenica and Claudio Orrego. *El caso Letelier. Santiago, Chile, Ediciones Aconcagua, 1980. 160 p. illus. (Colección Lautaro)*

A journalist and a sociologist present all the available facts and describe the circumstances and events of the assassination of Orlando Letelier in Washington, D.C. in 1976. The book is based on evidence gathered by the police, the F.B.I., interviews with survivors, and people associated with Letelier. Also includes the legal proceedings against the persons involved in the assassination.

811

Vázquez, Francisco. *El derecho humano de libertad personal en Chile; análisis jurídico de las nuevas disposiciones del gobierno militar. Caracas, Instituto Latino-Americano de Investigaciones Sociales, Fundación Friedrich Ebert, 1976. 292 p. (Serie materiales de trabajo, no. 6)*

Analyzes the military government's repression of the legal rights of Chileans. Includes a discussion of the institutional mechanisms that were once available to protect these rights.

812

Vázquez Carrizosa, Alfredo. *Ante la tragedia de Chile: el derecho de asilo y los derechos humanos. Bogotá, Editorial Colombia Nueva [1974?] 67 p.*

Reports on efforts to aid the Chileans who sought asylum in the Colombian Embassy during the military coup of 1973.

813

Villegas, Sergio. *Chile - el estadio; los crímenes de la junta militar. Buenos Aires, Editorial Cartago, 1974. 157 p.*

Provides an eyewitness account of detentions in Chile's National Stadium. Describes the last hours of the Allende government.

814

Violación por parte de la junta chilena de los principios establecidos de la Declaración Universal de los Derechos Humanos en el terreno de la juventud: violation by the Chilean military junta of the principles established in the Universal Declaration of Human Rights in the area of youth. *Reggio, Nell'Emilia, Italy, Technostampa [1975?]110 p.*

Reports on human rights abuses allegedly committed by the military junta in Chile. Gives personal accounts of torture and lists names of individuals who were tortured.

815

Winn, Peter. *The economic consequences of the Chilean counterrevolution: an interim assessment. Latin American perspectives, v. 1, summer 1974: 92-105.*

Condemns the military regime's policies toward democratic political institutions, trade unions, and the economy.

816

Women's Campaign for Chile. *Political prisoners in the women's section of "Tres Alamos" concentration camp. London, Women's Campaign for Chile, Chile Committee for Human Rights, 1976. 31 p.*

Contains the testimony of prisoners who spent 15 months in Tres Alamos.

817

Zorin, V. *The U.N. and human rights; the 34th session of the U.N. Commission on Human Rights. International affairs, v. 6, June 1978: 89-96.*

Comments on the annual meeting of the U.N. Commission on Human Rights in Geneva, February to March 1978. Notes widespread and flagrant violations of human rights in Israeli-occupied territories, South Africa, and Chile.

Colombia

818

Barrientos Restrepo, Samuel. *The idea of habeas corpus in Colombia. In The human rights to individual freedom. Coral Gables, Fla., University of Miami Press, 1970. p. 51-55.*

Describes the protection of individual liberties in Colombian law and advocates the enactment of international habeas corpus procedures according to the U.N. Charter and the Universal Declaration of Human Rights.

819

Bayer, Tulio. *Gancho ciego: 365 noches y una misa en la Cárcel Modelo de Bogotá. Medellin, Colombia, Ediciones Hombre Nuevo [1978] 217 p.*

Guerrilla provides an account of his imprisonment in Bogotá during 1962.

820

Camargo, Pedro Pablo. *La dictadura constitucional y la suspensión de derechos humanos, con un breve comentario sobre la justicia penal militar en Colombia. Bogota, Universidad la Gran Colombia, 1975. 82 p. (Serie A, Textos-Universidad la Gran Colombia, no. 5)*

Examines the suspension of constitutional human rights guarantees during states of siege.

821

Camargo, Pedro Pablo. *El régimen concordatario colombiano. Bogota, Sociedad Colombiana de Abogados, 1974. 54 p.*

Criticizes as unconstitutional the proposed revision of the 1887 Colombia-Vatican Concordat. The author considers both versions of the document to be detrimental to the protection of civil rights.

822

Camargo, Pedro Pablo. *Right to judicial protection: "amparo" and other Latin American remedies for the protection of human rights. Lawyer of the Americas, v. 3, June 1971: 191-230.*

Considers judicial procedures to protect civil rights in several Latin American countries. Treats Colombia and Mexico at length.

823

Colombian National Association of Peasants. *Colombia: repression of Indian peasants. LADOC, v. 5, Apr. 1975: 19-20.*

Denounces the torture, arbitrary abduction, and incarceration of indigenous people in Colombia who organize agrarian leagues.

824

Foro Nacional por los Derechos Humanos en Colombia. *Documentos; testimonios. Bogota, Fondo Editorial Suramérica, Sindicato de Trabajadores del Instituto de Crédito Territorial, Seccional Cundinamarca, 1979. 349 p. (Col. Política)*

Provides documents from the 1979 Bogotá meeting of the Foro. Criticizes repression by the military and the use of torture during states of siege.

825

López Mejía, Carlos Arturo. *Actividad de policía y libertad. Bogotá [s.n.] 1970. [65] p.*

Thesis presented at the Universidad Javeriana in Bogotá. Argues for the respect of civil rights by the police.

826

Melguizo, Gerardo. *L'internement administratif et la détention préventive en Colombie. International Commission of Jurists. Revue, v. 3, no. 2, 1961: 63-68.*

Outlines rarely invoked provisions in the Colombian Constitution that suspend civil and political rights during states of siege. Discusses proposed congressional changes to the provisions.

827

Organización Colombiana Pro Defensa de los Derechos Humanos. *La violación de los derechos humanos en Colombia: el problema indígena, la justicia militar o de excepción, el trato a los presos políticos, el Concordato. Bogota, Ediciones Libro Abierto, 1974. 49 p.*

At head of title: Pedro Pablo Camargo (asesor de derechos humanos), Angelina de Coral (presidenta).

Consists of a report submitted by the Colombian human rights organization to the Inter-American Commission on Human Rights.

828

Rights violations key complaint. *U.S. Foreign Broadcast Information Service. Daily report: Latin America, v. 6, no. 043, 1980: Fl.*

Statement by the head of the rebel 19 April Movement to the effect that the principal goal in the seizure of the Dominican Embassy was to attract attention to political repression in Colombia.

829

Sanín Greiffenstein, Jaime. *La defensa judicial de la Constitución. Bogotá, Librería Editorial Temis, 1979. 1 v. (unpaged)*

Analysis of the rule of law and its application in Colombia, by the former dean of the University of Medellín law school.

830

Simposio Colombiano sobre Derechos Humanos, lst, Bogotá, 1976. *Primer Simposio Colombiano sobre Derechos Humanos. Bogota, CODECAL, 1976. 54 leaves.*

Report on a symposium sponsored by UNESCO. Outlines human rights goals in government, law, education, and politics. Analyzes the human rights policy of the Catholic Church in Colombia.

831

Symposium on Inter-ethnic Conflict in South America, Bridgetown, Barbados, 1971. *La situación del indígena en América del Sur: aportes al estudio de la fricción inter-étnica en los Indios no andinos. Geneva, World Council of Churches, 1972. 453 p. (Publications of the Dept. of Ethnology, Univ. of Berne, no.3)*

"Organized by the Ethnology Department of the University of Berne."

Collection of papers by social anthropologists dealing with the relationship of government policies to the extermination of indigenous American groups in Venezuela, Colombia, Ecuador, Peru, Bolivia, Paraguay, Argentina, Brazil and the Guianas.

832

Triana, Francisco Yezid. *Derechos humanos y garantías sindicales. Bogotá, Gráficas Pazgo, 1978. 223 p. ports.*

Provides a general introduction to international labor law. Discusses Colombia's ratification of the International Labor Organization Covenants 87 and 98 as well as the Colombian government's resistance to their enforcement. Suggests reform measures.

833

Umaña Luna, Eduardo. *Los derechos humanos en Colombia: ¿transformación o revolución? Bogota, Ediciones Crítica Jurídica, 1974. 451 p.*

Considers current human rights practices in Colombia in light of the standards set by the provisions outlined in the Universal Declaration of Human Rights.

834

Uribe Vargas, Diego, ed. *El defensor de los derechos humanos: un proyecto de ombudsman para Colombia. [s.l., s.n.] 1977. 103 p.*

Advocates the creation of the office of ombudsman for the defense of human rights in Colombia. Recommends its enactment into law.

Costa Rica

835

Brenes Córdoba, Alberto. *Tratado de las personas. Notas y comentarios de Eladio Vargas. San Jose, Editorial Costa Rica, 1974. 308 p. (Col. Escuela libre de derecho)*

Textbook that describes the legal rights and obligations of persons individually and as family members in Costa Rica. Written by a noted jurist and professor. Includes a bibliography.

836

Carazo Odio, Rodrigo. *Discurso pronunciado por el Presidente de Costa Rica Lic. Rodrigo Carazo ante la XXXIII Asamblea General de las Naciones Unidas. New York [s.n.] 1978. [21] p.*

Speech presented by President Carazo before the U.N. General Assembly. Analyzes the human rights policy of Costa Rica.

837

Hernández, Rubén, and Gerardo Trejos. *La tutela de los derechos humanos. San Jose, Editorial Juricentro, 1977. 160 p. (Col. Escuela libre de derecho)*

Definition, classification, and explication of civil rights as a component of the Costa Rican Constitution.

838

Ortiz Martín, Gonzalo. *Análisis de los articulados de la Declaración Universal de los Derechos Humanos emitida por la Asamblea de las Naciones Unidas y correspondientes de la Constitución Política de Costa Rica. Revista de ciencias jurídicas (Costa Rica), mayo 1964: 59-88.*

Compares the human rights provisions that are outlined in the Costa Rican Constitution with the provisions that are included in the Universal Declaration of Human Rights.

839

U.N. Commission on Human Rights. *Periodic reports on human rights: reports on economic, social and cultural rights, for the period July 1969-June 1973. New York, United Nations, 1974. 30 p. (U.N. [Document] E/CN.4/1155/Add. 1)*

At head of title: Economic and Social Council. Thirty-first session.

Provides reports submitted by the governments of Barbados and Costa Rica in compliance with Economic and Social Council Resolution 1074 C(XXXIX).

Cuba

840

Alonso Avila, Antonio. *Violación de los derechos humanos por la legislación comunista de Castro. Miami, La Voz de Cuba, 1962. 72 p.*

Summarizes Cuban legislation enacted since 1959 which is considered to be in conflict with international declarations of human rights and with pre-1959 Cuban constitutional provisions.

841

American Society of International Law. *Economic development and human rights: Brazil, Chile, and Cuba. In its American journal of international law, v. 67, Nov. 1973: 198-227. (Its Proceedings of the 67th annual meeting, Washington, D.C., 1973)*

Scholars from North American and Chilean universities assess the performance of governments in Cuba, Brazil, and Chile with regard to economic development and human rights.

842

Amnesty International. International Secretariat. *Memorandum submitted to the government of the Republic of Cuba by Mr. Thomas Hammarberg, chairperson of the International Executive Committee, and Mr. Roger Plant of the International Secretariat of Amnesty International. London, 1978. 8 p.*

Memorandum, presented to the Cuban government, which describes a brief visit to Cuba in 1977 by Amnesty International representatives. Discusses the status of political prisoners in that country.

843

Band, Richard B. *Havana knows: Castro's assassins strike again. American opinion, v. 17, June 1974: 23-25, 27-30.*

Comments on the condition of political prisoners in Cuba.

844

Calzón, Frank. *Castro's Gulag; the politics of terror. Washington, Council for Inter-American Security, 1979. 52 p.*

Reviews the situation of political prisoners in Cuba. Cites individual cases of torture. Information was gathered from interviews with former political prisoners.

845

Casal, Lourdes, ed. *El caso Padilla: literatura y revolución en Cuba. Introd., selección, notas, guía y bibliografía por Lourdes Casal. Miami, Ediciones Universal, 1972. 141 p.*

Collection of documents related to the controversy over freedom of literary expression within the revolution which was triggered by the arrest of the poet, Heberto Padilla. Included are declarations, articles, and interviews with the poet himself.

846

Castro and freedom of religion in Cuba. *LADOC, v. 8, Mar./Apr. 1978: 1-ll.*

Reports on a meeting between Fidel Castro and members of the Jamaican clergy to discuss the status of civil liberties and religious freedom in Cuba.

847

Clark, Juan M., José I. Lasaga, and Rose S. Reque. *The 1980 Mariel exodus: an assessment and prospect. A special report. Washington, Council for Inter-American Security, 1981. 21 p.*

Analyzes the chain of events which led around 124,000 people to leave Cuba for the United States. Also focuses on the overall U.S. policy concerning the resettlement of the refugees.

848

Crahan, Margaret. *Religious freedom in Cuba. Cuba review: church, theology, and revolution, v. 5, Sept. 1975: 22-27.*

Excerpts of congressional testimony by a North American historian on religious freedom and human rights in Cuba. Suggests that the present religious crisis, though coterminous with the revolutionary regime, is not the result of government repression.

849

Cuadra, Angel. *Poemas en correspondencia (desde prisión): a correspondence of poems (from jail)*. Translated by Donald D. Walsh. Washington, Solar [1978?] 69 p.

Bilingual edition of recent poems by a young Cuban poet who has been in prison since 1967. Briefly freed in 1976, he was re-incarcerated in 1977 in a remote location in Cuba.

850

Cuba: revolution and the intellectual; the strange case of Heberto Padilla. *Index on censorship, v 1, summer 1972: 65-88, 101-134.*

Contains a collection of articles that describes the imprisonment and subsequent house arrest of the Cuban poet Heberto Padilla. Suggests possible international repercussions if the poet is not freed.

851

Domínguez, Jorge I. *Cuba: order and revolution*. Cambridge, Mass., Belknap Press of Harvard University, 1978. 683 p.

Important scholarly work on Cuba that briefly mentions the curtailment of academic freedom, intellectual expression, and other civil rights in Cuba.

852

Domínguez, Jorge I., and others. *Enhancing global human rights*. New York, Council on Foreign Relations, McGraw-Hill, 1979. 270 p.

Analyzes the impact of human rights issues on international relations and examines how non- and inter-governmental organizations assess human rights violations. Discusses Cuba and Mexico specifically. Makes recommendations.

853

Edwards, Jorge. *Persona non grata: an envoy in Castro's Cuba*. Translated from the Spanish by Colin Harding. 2d ed. London, Bodley Head, 1977. 275 p.

Personal account about censorship and the curtailment of freedom of expression in Cuba by a Chilean writer and diplomat. Depicts the harrowing conflict between the state and creative writers such as Heberto Padilla and Guillermo Cabrera Infante.

854

Fagen, Patricia Weiss. *Toward detente with Cuba: issues and obstacles*. Washington, Center for International Policy, 1977. 19 p.

Examines major issues in U.S.-Cuban relations, including the matter of human rights violations in Cuba.

855

Fiallo, Amalio. *Seminario sobre derechos humanos: el presidio político en Cuba*. [Santiago de Chile] Instituto de Formación Demócrata Cristiana, 1977. 39 p.

"Capítulo de su libro en proceso de edición: Cuba; una revolución reaccionaria."

Parts of an unpublished book on Cuba. Includes excerpts from the Inter-American Commission on Human Rights report of 1978. Describes mistreatment of dissidents in Cuba.

856

Fite, Clifton Edgar. *In Castro's clutches*. Foreword by W. A. Criswell. Chicago, Moody Press, 1969. 158 p.

Record of efforts to free the author's son, a Baptist missionary arrested and jailed in Cuba for alleged espionage between 1965 and 1968.

857

From the prisons of Cuba--a cry for help! *Dissent, v. 17, May/June 1970: 208-211.*

Appeal sent in December, 1969, to the U.N. Commission on Human Rights by 47 political prisoners in Cuba.

858

Grant, Frances. *What of Cuba and human rights? Freedom at issue, Nov./Dec. 1977: 9-11.*

Describes human rights violations in Cuba. Maintains that these injustices should be remedied before the U.S. resumes diplomatic relations with Cuba.

859

Hageman, Alice, and Philip E. Wheaton, eds. *Religion in Cuba today: a new church in a new society.* New York, Association Press, 1971. 317 p.

Essays, interviews and letters collected to illustrate cooperation of church and state in Cuba.

860

International Commission of Jurists. *Cuba and the rule of law.* Geneva, 1962. 267 p.

Report critical of human rights violations in Cuba from 1960 to 1962. Concludes that Cuba does not uphold the rule of law.

861

Jacqueney, Theodore. *Castro's political prisoners: a report from Cuba.* AFL-CIO free trade union news, v. 32, May 1977: 1-2, 7, 10.

Describes plight of Cuban political prisoners. Discusses some well-known cases and the general situation of women prisoners.

862

Jacqueney, Theodore. *The yellow uniforms of Cuba.* Worldview, v. 20, Jan./Feb. 1977: 4-10.

Presents interviews with former political prisoners and with the families and friends of those in prison.

863

McColm, R. Bruce. *Revolution's end.* The American spectator, v. 13, May 1980: 7-10.

Interview with Carlos Franqui, an early supporter of Castro, now a critic of the Cuban revolution. Describes prisons and the use of torture. Mentions systematic restrictions of internal movement in Cuba.

864

Mederos, Elena. *Human rights and Cuban law.* Worldview, v. 22, Nov. 1979: 42-44.

Maintains that in many cases human rights violations are legal under Cuban law. Concludes that the law itself is in violation of human rights.

865

Mesa-Lago, Carmelo. *Cuba in the 1970's; pragmatism and institutionalization.* Albuquerque, University of New Mexico Press, 1974. 179 p.

Scholarly review of Cuba in the 1970's. Of special interest are the analyses of state manipulation of intellectuals through hiring and firing practices and of increased Soviet influence on methods of social control.

866

Organization of American States. Inter-American Commission on Human Rights. *Report on the situation regarding human rights in Cuba.* Washington, Organization of American States, General Secretariat, 1962. 9 p. (Organization of American States. Official records. OEA/Ser. L/V/II.4 doc. 30)

First in a series of reports on human rights violations in Cuba. Original in Spanish.

867

Organization of American States. Inter-American Commission on Human Rights. *Report on the situation of political prisoners and their relatives in Cuba.* Washington, Organization of American States, General Secretariat, 1963. 64 p. (Organization of American States. Official records. OEA/Ser. L/V/II.7 doc. 4)

Continuation of series on human rights in Cuba. Original in Spanish.

868

Organization of American States. Inter-American Commission on Human Rights. *Report on the situation of human rights in Cuba.* Washington, Organization of American States, General Secretariat, 1967. 33 p. (Organization of American States. Official records. OEA/Ser. L/V/ II.17 doc. 4 rev. 1)

Continuation of series on human rights in Cuba. Original in Spanish.

869

Organization of American States. Inter-American Commission on Human Rights. *Second report on the situation of political prisoners and their relatives in Cuba. Washington, Organization of American States, General Secretariat, 1970. 45 p. (Organization of American States. Official records. OEA/Ser. L/V/II.23 doc. 6 rev. 1)*

At bottom of title: Approved by the Commission at its third meeting held on April 8, 1970.

Discusses the right to life, due process, and freedom from arbitrary arrest. Concludes with specific recommendations for eliminating human rights violations in Cuba.

870

Organization of American States. Inter-American Commission on Human Rights. *Fifth report on the situation of human rights in Cuba. Washington, Organization of American States, General Secretariat, 1976. 94 p. (Organization of American States. Official records. OEA/Ser. 6 CP/INF.872/76)*

At bottom of title: Approved by the Commission at its 471st meeting held on May 25, 1976.

Continuation of series on human rights in Cuba. Assesses the rights of political prisoners in Cuba. Appendixes list prisoners and Commission resolutions concerning some of them.

871

Organization of American States. Inter-American Commission on Human Rights. *Sixth report on the situation of political prisoners in Cuba. Washington, Organization of American States, General Secretariat, 1979. 39 p. (Organization of American States. Official records. OEA/Ser. L/V/II.48 doc. 7)*

Continuation of the Commission's reports on the situation of political prisoners in Cuba. Examines the Cuban legal system as it relates to the right to freedom and to imprisonment for political reasons. Discusses prison conditions, individual cases brought to the attention of the Commission, and the recent release of 3,600 political prisoners.

872

Otero, J. F. *The overflow in Cuban jails. AFL-CIO free trade union news, v. 33, July 1978: 4-5, 11.*

Denounces the world's tendency to ignore the numerous political and trade union prisoners in Cuban jails. Describes prison conditions and lists prominent leaders who are being detained.

873

Padilla, Heberto. *Poesía y política; poemas escogidos de Heberto Padilla: poetry and politics; selected poems of Heberto Padilla. Translated by Frank Calzón, et al. [Madrid, Playor, 1974] 136 p. (Georgetown University Cuban series)*

Poems by a major Cuban poet, some referring to human rights.

874

Peerman, Dean. *Cuba: no room for naysayers? Christian century, v. 94, Sept. 28, 1977: 845-849.*

Summarizes Castro's position on human rights: "For those within the revolution, complete freedom; for those against the revolution, no freedom."

875

Portell-Vilá, Herminio. *Cuba; the new dominant caste. In Veenhoven, Willem A., ed. Case studies on human rights and fundamental freedoms; a world survey. v. 3. The Hague, Martinus Nijhoff, 1976. p. 369-395.*

States that Cuba today curbs freedom of expression by jailing Protestant and Catholic clergy.

876

Raab, Enrique. *Cuba: vida cotidiana y revolución. Buenos Aires, Ediciones de la Flor, 1974. 84 p. plates.*

Impressions of an Argentine admirer of Cuba's revolution during his one-month visit in 1974. As a journalist, he faults the government for the Cuban press's lack of information and drabness.

877

Ripoll, Carlos. *Dissent in Cuba. New York times book review, Nov. 11, 1979: 11-12, 31.*

Report about individual Cuban writers and intellectuals imprisoned or exiled. Summarizes Cuban government efforts to suppress dissident intellectuals.

878

Sauvage, Leo. *A victim of Castro; the case of Huber Matos. The new leader, v. 60, Mar. 28, 1977: 4-6.*

Discusses the role of Huber Matos in the Cuban Revolution and his subsequent imprisonment by the Castro government.

879

Thomas, Hugh. *Points of the compass: Castro plus 20; Cuba's martial apotheosis. Encounter, v. 51, no. 4, 1978: 112-120.*

Assessment of 20 years of Castro's government. Alludes to Cuba's refusal to comply with Amnesty International's requests for information about 40,000 political prisoners.

880

U.N. Commission on Human Rights. *Implementation of the International Convention on the Suppression and Punishment of the Crime of Apartheid; reports submitted by States Parties under Article VII of the Convention. Addendum. New York, United Nations, 1978. 11 p. (U.N. [Document] E/CN.4/1277/Add. 8)*

At head of title: Economic and Social Council. Thirty-fourth session.

Report on Cuba.

881

U.S. Congress. House. Committee on International Relations. *Subcommittee on International Trade and Commerce. U.S. trade embargo of Cuba. Hearings...94th Congress, 1st session, on H.R. 6382... Washington, U.S. Govt. Print. Off., 1976. 653 p.*

Report of hearings held between May 8 and September 23, 1975, presenting various views on the U.S. trade embargo of Cuba. Includes ample documentation.

882

Valladares, Armando F. *Boniato Prison: tale of a massacre. Worldview, v. 20, Oct. 1977: 11-15.*

From a collection of poems entitled From My Wheelchair smuggled out of a Cuban prison. Includes an interview with the poet's wife and a letter from Valladares to Amnesty International.

883

Wulf, Lucien de. *Un cura en Cuba roja. Lima [s.n.] 1971. 32 p.*

Account by a Belgian priest of religious persecution in Cuba. Cites abuses of human rights, such as imprisonment without due process of law.

Dominican Republic

884

Bianchi Gundiàn, Manuel. *Misión cumplida: la Comisión de Derechos Humanos en la República Dominicana; relatorio y documentos, 1960-1966. Santiago, Editorial Andrés Bello, 1967. [129] p.*

Summary of the Inter-American Commission on Human Rights' monitoring activities in the Dominican Republic during a period of turbulence, concluding with the general elections of 1966.

885

Clark, James A. *The church and the crisis in the Dominican Republic. Westminster, Md., Newman Press, 1967. 254 p.*

Describes church efforts to alleviate physical suffering in the Dominican Republic during the 1965 revolt.

886

Gutiérrez, Carlos María. *The Dominican Republic: rebellion and repression. Translated by Richard E. Edwards. New York, Monthly Review Press, 1972. 172 p.*

Journalist's impressions of the Dominican Republic in 1971. Analyzes the church activities in favor of civil rights. Also deals with labor unions and political parties.

887

International Commission of Jurists. *The crisis in the Dominican Republic. In its Bulletin, no. 11, Dec. 1960: 61-64.*

Discussion of the impending rupture of diplomatic relations with the Dominican Republic for its refusal to respond to the Organization of American States' condemnation of human rights violations.

888

Jonas, Susanne. *Trade union imperialism in the Dominican Republic. North American Congress on Latin America. NACLA's Latin America & empire report, v. 9, Apr. 1975: 13-30.*

Updates article published in 1965 concerning the U.S. invasion of the Dominican Republic. Suggests that the U.S. hindered local labor union organization and international labor efforts within the Dominican Republic.

889

Lillich, Richard B., et al. *Forcible self-help by states to protect human rights. Iowa law review, v. 53, 1967: 325-365.*

Evaluation of the effect of the United Nations' Charter on traditionally accepted international rights that allow countries to use force to protect their nationals serving abroad or to intervene for humanitarian reasons during times of civil disorder. One example selected is the Dominican Republic.

890

Organization of American States. *Inter-American Commission on Human Rights. Informe sobre la actuación de la Comisión Interamericana de Derechos Humanos en la República Dominicana, 1 de junio a 31 de agosto de 1965. Washington, Pan American Union, General Secretariat, 1965. 74 p. (Organization of American States. Official Records. OEA/Ser. L/V/II.13 doc. 14 rev.)*

"Aprobado en la Décima Sesión; celebrada el 15 de octubre 1965."

Activities and findings of the Commission in the Dominican Republic. Includes interviews, requests for information, and lists of imprisoned or missing persons.

891

Thomas, Ann van Wyman, and A. J. Thomas. *The Inter-American Commission on Human Rights. Southwestern law journal, v. 20, June 1966: 282-309.*

Useful exposition of the Commission's history and functions. Includes detailed account of steps taken in the Dominican Republic in 1965.

892

U.N. Economic Commission for Latin America. *República Dominicana: repercusiones de los huracanes David y Federico sobre la economía y las condiciones sociales. [New York] United Nations, 1979. 91 p. illus. (U.N. [Document] E/CEPAL/G.1098/Rev. 1)*

At head of title: Economic and Social Council.

Analysis of the effects of hurricanes David and Frederick on social and economic conditions in the Dominican Republic.

893
Wipfler, William Louis. *Power, influence and impotence: the Church as a socio-political factor in the Dominican Republic. New York, Union Theological Seminary, 1978. 490 p.*

Thesis that traces the history of the Catholic Church in the Dominican Republic, with particular reference to its involvement in politics.

Ecuador

894

Grupo de Solidaridad Ecuador. *Ecuador: democracia a tiros; la masacre de trabajadores azucareros. Quito, 1977. 9 p.*

Description of the use of force to disperse striking sugar workers in 1977.

895

Salazar, Eduardo. *Derechos del hombre. Quito, Editorial Casa de la Cultura Ecuatoriana, 1952. 175 p.*

Constitutional history of Ecuador. Discusses the Universal Declaration of Human Rights and Ecuadorean efforts to protect basic rights through legislation.

896

Symposium on Inter-ethnic Conflict in South America, Bridgetown, Barbados, 1971. *La situación del indígena en América del Sur: aportes al estudio de la fricción inter-étnica en los indios no-andinos. Geneva, World Council of Churches, 1972. 453 p. (Publications of the Department of Ethnology, University of Berne, no. 3)*

"Organized by the Ethnology Department of the University of Berne."

Collection of papers by social anthropologists about the relation of government policies to the decimation of indigenous American groups in Venezuela, Colombia, Ecuador, Peru, Bolivia, Paraguay, Argentina, Brazil and the Guianas.

El Salvador

897

Amnesty International. *El Salvador: peasants, religious leaders persecuted; El Salvador: campesinos, líderes religiosos perseguidos. New York, 1978. 12 p.*

Report on the military and on the question of the protection of human rights. Contrasts principles with practice.

898

Amnesty International. *Repression of trade unions in El Salvador. London, Amnesty International, International Secretariat, 1978. 5 p.*

Brief report on the imprisonment of trade unionists.

899

Armijo, Roberto, and Roque Dalton. *Poems from El Salvador. Index on censorship, v. 7, May/June 1978: 16-17.*

Translation of poems written by two Salvadorean poets, Roque Dalton murdered on his return from exile in Paris in 1975, and Roberto Armijo, living in exile in Paris since 1970. The translation was done by Jo Labanyi.

900

Comisión Evangélica Latinoamericana de Educación Cristiana and Centro Nacional de Comunicación Social. *El Salvador. Mexico, 1979. 63 p. (CENCO, América Latina derechos humanos)*

Includes a report on human rights violations in El Salvador, and maintains that there has been religious persecution in that country. Also contains short articles on Guatemala, Colombia, Ecuador, Chile, and Mexico.

901

Comisión Nacional de Justicia y Paz de El Salvador. *[Situación política en El Salvador]. Its Boletín, no. 2, 1977: 1-72.*

Report on the social and political situation in El Salvador, with particular reference to the plight of the Catholic Church. Includes material from the foreign and national press about human rights violations during the recent elections.

902

Comité Pro Libertad de los Presos Políticos de El Salvador. *Casos de desaparecidos. San Salvador, 1978. [17] p.*

In response to a request made to Archbishop Oscar Romero by relatives of imprisoned or missing persons, the Committee for the Liberation of Political Prisoners in El Salvador published a list identifying 99 such individuals.

903

Drinan, Robert, John J. McAward, and Thomas P. Anderson. *Human rights in El Salvador--1978; report of findings of an investigatory mission. Boston, Unitarian Universalist Service Committee, 1978. 87 p.*

Report of an inquiry conducted by U.S. Congressman Robert Drinan, John J. McAward, and Thomas P. Anderson, exposing human rights violations. Includes useful appendixes.

904

Eldridge, Joseph, and Cressida McKean. *Uncivil strife in El Salvador: landless peasants, official terror and prophetic witness. Sojourner, v. 6, July 1977: 26-28.*

Report on rights violations in rural El Salvador and on church activity on behalf of peasants.

905

Erdozaín, Plácido. *Archbishop Romero; martyr of Salvador. Translated by John McFadden. Maryknoll, N.Y., Orbis Books, 1981. 98 p.*

Traces the trajectory of the Salvadorean Archbishop from earnest and uninvolved churchman to defender of the poor and spokesman against oppression. Romero, a centrist, tried to mediate in the political turmoil engulfing his country, and spoke out against human rights violations. He was killed by an assassin while saying mass on March 24, 1980.

906

Fox, Donald T. *The Application of the November 1977 "Law of Defense and Guarantee of Public Order."* New York, International Commission of Jurists, 1978. *14 p.*

Report of a U.S. attorney who took a mission to El Salvador in July, 1978, to study the application of the above mentioned law.

907

Geyer, Georgie Anne. *From here to eternity: how a priest-congressman and the president of Georgetown University have tried to stop murder, but not necessarily revolution in tiny El Salvador. Washington post magazine, Sept. 10, 1978: 8-15.*

Describes the efforts by Revs. Timothy Healy and Robert Drinan to focus Washington's attention on the human rights violations of the Humberto Romero government in El Salvador.

908

González, José Napoleón. *El Salvador: a silenced voice. Index on censorship, v. 6, Nov./Dec. 1977: 20-23.*

Founder and former editor of La Crónica del pueblo describes his newspaper and the bribery attempts, death threats and armed attacks that preceded its closing.

909

Great Britain. Parliamentary Human Rights Group. *Human rights in El Salvador: a report of a British parliamentary delegation in December 1978. London [1979]. 70 p.*

Report of a mission to El Salvador in December 1978. Discusses British aid to El Salvador, problems facing trade unions, and human rights violations.

910

International Commission of Jurists. *Human rights in the world: El Salvador. In its Review, June 1978: 10-14.*

Report of an investigation of alleged violations of human rights in El Salvador, particularly in rural areas. Discusses portions of a new public order law that contradict major human rights declarations.

911

Los Jesuitas ante el pueblo salvadoreño. *San Salvador, Universidad Centroamericana José Simeón Cañas, 1977. 47 p.*

Jesuit pamphlet denouncing persecution of the Church in El Salvador.

912

Latin American Bureau. *Violence and fraud in El Salvador: a report on current political events in El Salvador. London, Latin American Bureau, 1977. 37 p.*

Describes government persecution of peasants, trade unionists, and students. Notes the work of the Catholic Church in the defense of human rights. Concludes with a profile of General Carlos Humberto Romero, elected president in 1977 amid allegations of fraud.

913

Mariscal, Nicolás. *Militares en El Salvador. Estudios centroamericanos, v. 33, enero/feb. 1978: 9-27.*

Analyzes political conditions in El Salvador and the role of the army in social and political spheres throughout Central America.

914

Mensaje a la clase obrera: el campesinado, y demás sectores y elementos que luchan por la liberación de los explotados y oprimidos en todos los pueblos del mundo. *San Salvador, Bloque Popular Revolucionario, 1976. 7 p.*

Urges urban and rural workers to fight actively against oppression.

915

On U.S. relations with El Salvador: the Koch-State Department correspondence. *Inter-American economic affairs, v. 30, summer 1976: 79-83.*

Congressman Edward Koch's inquiry about specific human rights violations in El Salvador and U.S. military assistance. Reprinted from the Congressional Record.

916

Organization of American States. Inter-American Commission on Human Rights. *Informe de la Subcomisión sobre la situación de los derechos humanos en las repúblicas de El Salvador y Honduras; 4 de julio al 29 de octubre de 1969. Washington, Organization of American States, General Secretariat, 1970. 176 p. (Organization of American States. Official records. OEA/Ser. L/V/II.22 doc. 13 rev. 1)*

Detailed account of the subcommittee's investigation and findings.

917

Organization of American States. Inter-American Commission on Human Rights. *Informe sobre la situación de los derechos humanos en El Salvador y Honduras. Washington, Organization of American States, General Secretariat, 1970. 12 p. (Organization of American States. Official records. OEA/Ser. L/V/II.23 doc. 9 rev.)*

"Aprobado en la novena sesión celebrada el 16 de abril de 1970."

Report on a special subcommittee's visit to El Salvador and Honduras July 4-10, 1969. Subsequently used by the Inter- American Commission on Human Rights to develop its stand on human rights conditions in those two countries.

918

Organization of American States. Inter-American Commission on Human Rights. *Report on the situation of human rights in El Salvador. Washington, Organization of American States, General Secretariat, 1979. 188 p. (Organization of American States. Official records. OEA/Ser. L/V/II.46 doc. 23 rev. 1)*

Report by a commission that responded to a Salvadorean request that its commitment to and respect for human rights be documented. Includes portions on Salvadorean human rights legislation.

919

Ortiz Pinchetti, Francisco. *El Salvador bajo el general Romero: una nación que vive en el silencio. Proceso (Mexico), enero 15, 1979: 22-24.*

Article based on Amnesty International reports, critical of the military regime in El Salvador.

920

Persecución de la iglesia en El Salvador. *San Salvador, Secretariado Social Interdiocesano, 1977. 102 p. (Colección Iglesia y derechos humanos)*

Discusses the persecution of the Catholic Church in El Salvador and those responsible for it. Contains material extracted from periodicals in 1976 and 1977.

921

Los presos políticos en El Salvador. *San Salvador, Comité de Madres y Familiares de Presos y Desaparecidos Públicos en El Salvador, 1978. 45 p.*

Surveys the situation of missing persons in El Salvador.

922

Salvador. *Ministerio de Relaciones Exteriores. Posición de El Salvador ante la Comisión Interamericana de Derechos Humanos; planteamiento y denuncia de las violaciones contra personas y bienes de salvadoreños en Honduras. [San Salvador, Imprenta Nacional, 1969] 77 p.*

"Publicaciones de la Secretaría de Información de la Presidencia de la República."

Brief exposition of the Salvadorean government's stand on human rights. In Spanish, English, French and Portuguese.

923

Ungo, Guillermo Manuel. *Visita a El Salvador de miembros de la Comisión de Derechos Humanos de la OEA y del Señor Terence Todman. Estudios centroamericanos, v. 33 enero/feb. 1978: 72-74.*

Criticizes visits to El Salvador by human rights observers.

924

Unitarian Universalist Service Committee. *Investigation in El Salvador. Boston, 1977. 5 p.*

Report on human rights violations, specifically the murder of unarmed civilians, arbitrary arrests, electoral fraud, and religious persecution.

925

United Nations. Commission on Human Rights. *Periodic report on human rights: reports on economic, social and cultural rights, for the period July 1969-June 1973. New York, United Nations, 1974. 41 p. (U.N.[Document] E/CN.4/1155)*

At head of title: Economic and Social Council. Thirty-fifth session.

Reports prepared by governments under Economic and Social Council Resolution 1074 C(XXXIX) 1. Includes the report of El Salvador.

926

Washington Office on Latin America. *Special update: El Salvador; human rights and U.S. economic policy. Washington, 1979. 15 p.*

At head of title: Latin America.

Report of a two week, in country investigation in August of 1978 based on interviews with church leaders, academics, peasants, U.S. government officials, and experts in the field of international development. Recommends U.S. policy changes.

Guatemala

927

Adams, Richard Newbold. *Crucifixion by power; essays on Guatemalan national social structure, 1944-1966. Austin, University of Texas Press [1970]. 553 p. illus., maps*

Although not a book specifically concerned with human rights, this study of Guatemala analyzes socio-political structure and development, the organization of power and the military, and the costs of growth. It is an important work to keep in mind when examining contemporary Guatemala. Includes bibliographies.

928

Aguirre Godoy, M. *Séptimo Congreso Jurídico Guatemalteco: los derechos humanos y su protección. Abogados de Guatemala. Boletín, v. 20, set./dic. 1972: 9-16.*

Brief survey of human rights resolutions by Guatemalan lawyers with an admonishment that the courts uphold the constitutional protections of human rights during states of siege.

929

Alvarado Arellano, Carlos Raúl. *Los derechos humanos en el derecho constitucional guatemalteco. Guatemala, Imprenta Graphos, 1962. 208 p.*

Thesis on human rights and Guatemalan constitutional rights from the University of San Carlos, Guatemala.

930

Amnesty International. *Situation in Guatemala. London, Amnesty International, International Secretariat, 1974. 27 p.*

Discusses political prisoners in Guatemala.

931

Amnesty International. *Guatemala. London, Amnesty International Publications, 1976. 16 p. illus.*

Describes human rights violations in Guatemala, arbitrary arrests, abductions, and other abuses. Lists actions taken by Amnesty International.

932

Amnesty International. Campaign pro abolition of torture. *Wave of political assassinations, tortures and kidnappings in Guatemala. In its Information bulletin, v. 2, Oct. 1979: 7.*

Accuses the military government of condoning the murder of over 2,000 persons in the previous 16 months.

933

Bodenheimer, Susanne Jonas. *Guatemala: the politics of violence. NACLA's Latin America & empire report, v. 6, Feb. 1972: 24-29.*

Describes human rights violations in 1971 to 1972 allegedly carried out by right wing terrorist groups, the self censorship of the Guatemalan press and radio, and the role of the American and international press.

934

Comité Pro-Justicia y Paz. *An open letter from Guatemala. Lucha: Christian response to military repression in Latin America, Jan. 1979: 2-9.*

Describes the events that followed the October 2 to 7, 1978, confrontation between citizens and the police. Suggests that Christians should fight for justice.

935

Galeano, Eduardo. *Guatemala: occupied country. Translated by Cedric Belfrage. New York, Monthly Review Press, 1969. 159 p. map.*

Depicts life among guerrillas in Guatemala and stresses their dedication to revolutionary struggle. Translation of Guatemala: país ocupado.

936

Guatemala News and Information Bureau. *Three farces of democracy. Guatemala! v. 1, June 1978: 1, 15-16.*

Account of events in Guatemala during the week of the 1978 elections. Includes a discussion of the post election violence.

937

International Commission of Jurists. *Quelques aspects de la primauté du droit en amérique latine: le rétablissement du régime constitutionnel au Guatemala. In its Bulletin, déc. 1966: 56-57.*

Commission report that condemns the suspension of constitutional and legal rights by military courts and urges future governments to restore constitutional safeguards.

938

Perera, Victor. *Guatemala: always la violencia. New York times magazine, June 13, 1971: 12-13, 50, 57, 61, 64, 71-72.*

Guatemalan novelist's account of conversations with his countrymen about human rights violations during the early months of President Arana's government.

939

Plant, Roger. *Guatemala; unnatural disaster. London, Latin American Bureau, 1978. 121 p.*

Describes Guatemala before the earthquake. Documents violations of human rights, particularly of tradesmen and peasants. Estimates that there have been 20,000 politically motivated killings during the previous ten years.

940

Plant, Roger. *Guatemala: violence and the press. Index on censorship, v. 6, Nov./Dec. 1977: 15-19.*

Describes how the press works in a country where "death squads" abduct and murder recalcitrant broadcasters and journalists.

941

Sibley, Anna Grant. *Update: twenty years of mission in Guatemala. In Report of the United Presbyterian Church in the USA; conferences on overseas missions. [s.l.] United Presbyterian Church--USA, 1978. [10] p.*

Paper presented at the Conference on Overseas Missions, St. Louis, Missouri in 1977. Describes injustices and exploitation in rural areas of Guatemala.

942

U.N. Commission on Human Rights. *Periodic reports on human rights, including the right of self-determination and the right to independence, for the period July 1968-June 1971. New York, United Nations, 1973.17 p. (U.N. [Document] E/CN.4/1098/Add. 20)*

At head of title: Economic and Social Council.

Reports from Guatemala and Trinidad and Tobago in conformance with Economic and Social Council Resolution 1074 C (**XXXIX**) 1.

943

U. N. Commission on Human Rights. *Periodic reports on human rights: reports on economic, social and cultural rights, for the period July 1969-June 1973. New York, United Nations, 1974. 1 p. (U. N. [Document] E/CN. 4/1155/Add. 22)*

At head of title: Economic and Social Council. Thirty-first session.

Report from Guatemala in conformance with Economic and Social Council Resolution 1074 C(**XXXIX**).

104

Haiti

944

Gourgue, Gérard. *Pour l'histoire, pour la vérité, et pour la justice.* Port-au-Prince, Ligue haitienne des droits humains, 1979. *[4] p. (Ligue haitienne des droits humains. Bulletin special, 1979)*

Account of a meeting of the Ligue Haitienne des Droits Humains, attended by more than 7,000 persons, that was violently disrupted by Tontons-Macoutes, the Haitian president's special police. Approximately 200 persons were wounded in the ensuing fight.

945

Haiti sous Duvalier: terrorisme d'état et visages de la résistance nationale. *[s. 1.] Organisation Extérieure du Parti Unifié des Communistes Haïtiens [1978?]. 47 leaves, illus., ports.*

Describes state terror and human rights violations in Haiti as well as the resistance to this state of affairs.

946

Heinl, Robert Debs, and Nancy Gordon Heinl. *Written in blood; the story of the Haitian people, 1942-1971.* Boston, Houghton Mifflin, 1978. 785 p. illus., plates.

General history of modern Haiti that includes references to frustrated O.A.S. and U.N. efforts on behalf of human rights. Extensive bibliography of unpublished material from U.S. government agencies and archives, as well as student theses.

947

International Commission of Jurists. *Aspectos del imperio del derecho: Haiti. In its Boletín, set. 1967: 31-36.*

Deplores Haiti's refusal to cooperate with the Commission and speaks in a general way about current allegations of government violations of the Haitian Constitution.

948

International Commission of Jurists. *La Dictadura de Duvalier en Haiti. In its Boletín, marzo 1966:1-6.*

Brief summary of human rights violations by the François Duvalier government.

949

International Commission of Jurists. *Divers aspects de la légalité: la situation en Haiti. In its Bulletin, déc. 1963: 14-20.*

Report on the background and current conditions of the François Duvalier regime. Discusses the Commission's frustrated attempts to obtain information about violations of rights by Haiti's secret police.

950

International Commission of Jurists. *Haiti's denunciation of the Inter- American Convention on Asylum. In its Bulletin, Dec. 1968: 13-18.*

Editorial comment critical of Haiti's reply to the Inter-American Commission on Human Rights' report on conditions in Haiti.

951

Organization of American States. Inter-American Commission on Human Rights. *Informe sobre la situación de los derechos humanos en Haiti. Washington, Organization of American States, General Secretariat, 1963. 50 p. (Organization of American States. Official records. OEA/Ser. L/V/II.8 doc. 5)*

"Aprobado por la Comisión Interamericana de Derechos Humanos en la Décimacuarta Sesión celebrada el 21 de octubre de 1963."

Asserts that the Haitian government rejected the Commission's request to conduct "on the spot" investigations concerning basic rights. Findings indicate that serious human rights violations exist.

952

Organization of American States. Inter-American Commission on Human Rights. *Report on the situation of human rights in Haiti. Washington, Organization of American States, General Secretariat, 1979. 81 p. (Organization of*

American States. Official records. OEA/Ser. L/V/II.46 doc. 66 rev. 1)

Report of 1978 on site observations in which Haiti's progress in the area of human rights is assessed. Examines measures to enhance the Haitian people's awareness of their civic and political rights. Findings indicate that although there has been an improvement in the status of human rights since 1971, many of the government's intentions remain to be carried out.

953
Pierre-Charles, Gérard. *El régimen de los Duvalier. América Latina: derechos humanos (Mexico), mayo 1978: 11-16.*

Denounces the Duvalier governing style. States that Haiti should still be on the O.A.S. list of human rights violators.

Honduras

Analyzes the systematic violation of human rights in Honduras after the military coup of October, 1963.

954

La barbarie hondureña y los derechos humanos: proceso de una agresión. *San Salvador, Ministerio de Defensa, Prensa y Publicidad, 1969. 11 p.*

Provides a background report concerning the 1969 Soccer War between El Salvador and Honduras. Written by the Salvadorean Ministry of Defense.

955

Derechos humanos y derechos de los estados. *Tegucigalpa, Consejo Asesor de la Jefatura de Estado, 1977. 37 p.*

Reproduces four international human rights documents that were influential in the formulation of human rights legislation in Honduras. Includes the Universal Declaration of Human Rights and the American Convention on Human Rights.

956

International Commission of Jurists. *Infringements of human rights in Honduras. In its Bulletin, Apr. 1965: 39-44.*

957

National Assembly of Religious. *Declaration of Honduran religious leaders. Lucha: Christian response to military repression in Latin America, Jan. 1979: 23-24.*

Consists of a declaration that was made at a conference of clerics during 1978 in Honduras. Repudiates the violence and repression in Nicaragua and denounces the torture of Hondurans committed to promoting human rights.

958

Organization of American States. Inter-American Commission on Human Rights. *Informe sobre la situación de los derechos humanos en El Salvador y Honduras. Washington, Organization of American States, General Secretariat, 1970. 12 p. (Organization of American States. Official records. OEA/Ser. L/V/II.23 doc. 9 rev.)*

"Aprobado en la Novena Sesión celebrada el 16 de abril de 1970."

Reports on the status of human rights in both El Salvador and Honduras. Information was gathered by a special fact finding mission in 1969.

Mexico

959

Burgoa, I. *Las garantías individuales.* 8 ed. Mexico, Editorial Porrúa, 1973. 680 p.

Comprehensive volume that discusses civil rights in Mexico.

960

Camargo, Pedro Pablo. *Claim of "amparo" in Mexico: constitutional protection of human rights. California western law review, v. 201, spring 1970: 201-217.*

Noted Colombian jurist outlines human rights guarantees in the Mexican Constitution and compares them to similar guarantees that are included in the constitutions of other Latin American countries.

961

Domínguez Fermán, Serafín. *Principios constitucionales; fundamento de la actuación de México en la O.E.A.* Mexico, Universidad Nacional Autónoma de México, 1963. 158 p.

Tesis (licenciatura en derecho) de la Universidad Nacional Autónoma de México.

Traces the historical development of Mexico's constitutional human rights protections and compares them with similar protections that are found in the O.A.S. and U.N. charters.

962

Eckstein, Susan. *Occupational inequality in urban Mexico.* In Veenhoven, Willem A., ed. *Case studies on human rights and fundamental freedoms.* The Hague, Martinus Nijhoff, 1975. p. 357-388.

Includes theoretical interpretations, a listing of occupational groupings in Mexico, and a description of occupational inequality and rights violations.

963

Goldman, Robert K., and Daniel Jacoby. *Report of the Commission of Enquiry to Mexico.* New York, International League for Human Rights, Fédération Internationale des Droits de l'Homme, Pax Romana, 1978. [48] p.

Report submitted to the International League for Human Rights, the Fédération Internationale des Droits de l'Homme, and Pax Romana. Examines charges of human rights violations in Mexican prisons.

964

González-Souza, Luís F. *La política exterior de México ante la protección internacional de los derechos humanos. Foro interna- cional, v. 18, jul./set. 1977: 108-138.*

Discusses the Mexican government's position concerning the promotion of human rights at home and abroad.

965

Growing repression in Mexico. *LADOC, v. 8, Nov./Dec. 1977: 19-22.*

Discusses the human rights violations suffered by Mexican priests and Catholic activists who work with the underprivileged. Cites documented cases.

966

Herrera Gutiérrez, José Celestino. *La protección internacional de los derechos del hombre; filosofía y realizaciones.* Mexico, 1965. 147 p.

Tesis (licenciatura en derecho) de la Universidad Nacional Autónoma de México.

Thesis analyzing civil rights in Mexico in light of provisions outlined in international law. Includes bibliography.

967

López Rosado, Felipe. *El hombre y el derecho.* 26. ed. Mexico, Editorial Porrúa, 1967. 237 p. illus., ports.

General study of Mexican law, focusing on the traditional categories of contract, property, labor, and land in the historical development of the Mexican Constitution. Includes chapter on "amparo" guarantees.

968

Lozano, José María. *Estudio del derecho constitucional patria en lo relativo a los derechos del hombre.* Mexico, Editorial Porrúa, 1972. 507 p.

Gives historical background on Mexican political institutions and an analysis of the federal power structure. Reviews the concept of sovereignty of the state and the right of individuals to defend themselves against those in authority who violate the law.

969

Mora, Juan Miguel de. *Por la gracia del Señor Presidente: México la gran mentira.* Mexico, Editores Asociados, 1975. 280 p.

Denounces torture, killings, and other human rights violations in Mexico. Supports denunciations with massive collection of press releases.

970

Nava Martínez, Consuelo Alicia. *El derecho a la vida: filosofía y realización histórica.* Mexico, 1965. 270 p.

Tesis (licenciatura en derecho) de la Universidad Nacional Autónoma de México.

General theoretical and historical treatment of human rights by a Mexican law student. Describes Mexican constitutional guarantees of rights, reproduces U.N. and U.S. declarations on human rights, and summarizes articles in the constitutions of various Latin American countries which protect basic rights.

971

Oaxaca; conflictos de clase, movilización y represión. *Mexico, Instituto de Artes del Estudio, 1978. 104 p. (Col. Cuadernos populares)*

Describes repression by force of labor unrest. Designed to educate workers and peasants.

972

Paso, Fernando del. *Martín Ennals: los desaparecidos; problema creciente en México. Proceso, agosto 7, 1978: 8-9.*

Martin Ennals, Secretary of Amnesty International, comments on his visit to Mexico to review the situation of political prisoners.

973

Paso, Fernando del. *Policía y ejército rebasan sus facultades. Proceso, agosto 7, 1978: 6-7.*

Patricia Feeney discusses illegal police and military detentions in Mexico. She mentions Amnesty International reports and refers to alleged cases of torture in Military Camp One in Mexico City.

974

Reveles, José. *Inquietud internacional: 24 parlamentarios piden a JLP que investigue desapariciones. Proceso, enero 15, 1979: 18-21.*

Report of a letter from British members of Parliament, requesting information about missing persons in Mexico who are presumed to be political prisoners.

975

Sanders, Thomas G. *Mexicans in a Mexican prison. Common ground, v. 4, winter 1978: 11-26.*

Reports on the violation of human rights of prisoners in Mexico.

976

Schwarz, Carl E. *Rights and remedies in the federal district courts of Mexico and the United States. Hastings constitutional law quarterly, v. 4, winter 1977: 67-108.*

Compares the jurisdiction, procedures, and remedies of the federal district courts in Mexico and the United States. Emphasizes the efficacy of the writ of amparo in Mexico as a broad remedy for protecting constitutional and statutory rights.

977

Stevens, Evelyn P. *Protest and response in Mexico. Cambridge, Mass., MIT Press [1974] 372 p.*

Describes the violent protests in Mexico in the 1960's and early 1970's and the response of the government to the unrest. Discusses student activism and its repression. Includes a bibliography.

978

Taylor, John. *Mexico: the guessing game. Index on censorship, v. 5, winter 1976: 34-38.*

Analyzes the forced resignation of several intellectuals from the newspaper Excelsior and the implication of this action for freedom of expression in Mexico.

979

Vásquez Muñoz, Roberto. *Veinte poemas contra el opresor y una canción esperanzada. Mexico, Chihuahua, 1973. 39 p.*

Poems that treat the violation of basic human rights in Mexico.

Nicaragua

980

Amnesty International. *The Republic of Nicaragua: an Amnesty International report, including the findings of a mission to Nicaragua May 10-15, 1976. [New York] Amnesty International Publications, 1977. 75 p.*

Discusses torture of political prisoners and the suspension of legal guarantees by military tribunals. Appendixes list political prisoners and document the use of torture.

981

Bell, Belden, ed. *Nicaragua: an ally under siege. Washington, Council on American Affairs, 1978. 158 p.*

Presents articles on human rights and Nicaragua's economic and political situation.

982

Borge, Tomás. *Desde las cárceles de la dictadura somocista habla Tomás Borge. Managua, Comité Ejecutivo Nacional Frente Estudiantil Revolucionario, 1977. 32 p.*

Personal account of prison life by a member of the Sandinista National Liberation Front (FSLN). Describes his arrest, torture, and trial before a military tribunal. Author subsequently became member of the revolutionary junta.

983

Brochman, James R. *Our man in Managua. Americas (New York), v. 136, Mar. 26, 1977: 268-269.*

"Published by the Jesuits in the U.S. and Canada."

Brief statement of concern about U.S. military and human rights policies in the Carter administration during President Somoza's state of siege in Nicaragua.

984

Capuchin Communications Office. *Terror in Nicaragua. LADOC, v. 7, May/June 1977: 6-8.*

Briefly describes types of torture used by Somoza's National Guard on rural peasants.

985

Chamorro, Claudia Lucía Cayetana. *A letter to my father. Index on censorship, v. 7, May/June 1978: 57.*

On January 10, 1978, the day Pedro Chamorro was assassinated, his daughter walked into his office at La Prensa, sat at his old manual typewriter, and wrote this letter.

986

Comisión Permanente de Derechos Humanos de Nicaragua. *Los derechos humanos en Nicaragua; segundo informe. Managua, CPDH de Nicaragua, 1978. 201 p.*

Collection of documents concerning alleged human rights abuses. Includes numerous notarized petitions for information about missing persons presumed to be detained by the Nicaraguan government.

987

Derechos humanos; Nicaragua. *Centro Regional de Informaciones Ecuménicas (Mexico), May 21, 1979: [6-14] p.*

Collection of recent press releases about the Sandinista struggle against the Somoza government.

988

Fagen, Richard R. *The Nicaraguan revolution, a personal report. Washington, D.C., Institute for Policy Studies, 1981. 36 p.*

After a brief historical introduction, the publication discusses the first eighteen months of post revolutionary Nicaragua, touching on human rights among other themes.

989

Frente Sandinista de Liberación Nacional. *Nicaragua: testimonios de torturas y violaciones de los derechos humanos. OCLAE (Organización Continental Latinoamericana de Estudiantes) v. 12, no. 3, 1978: 6-24.*

Anonymous article from the Sandinista Liberation Front; includes three personal accounts of torture under the Somoza regime.

990

Frente Sandinista de Liberación Nacional. *Nicaragua: violaciones de los derechos humanos y de las garantías ciudadanas. OCLAE (Organización Continental Latinoamericana de Estudiantes) v. 11, no. 4, 1977: 25-41. illus.*

Anonymous article listing missing persons and victims of arbitrary arrest and assassination. Published in Havana, Cuba.

991

Gannon, Francis X. *Nicaragua's agony: the Central American context. Americas, v. 31, Sept. 1979: 3-5.*

Maintains that the future of Nicaragua and all of Central America is uncertain because of the problems in efforts to foster rapid change in traditional societies.

992

Hale, Andrew. *Death in Nicaragua. Index on censorship, v. 7, May/June 1978: 56-57.*

Describes the assassination on January 10, 1978, of Pedro Chamorro, a leading newspaper publisher.

993

Harris, Robert. *Nicaragua: the censor at work. Index on censorship, v. 6, Dec. 1977: 23-30.*

Case study of censorship applied to Nicaragua's largest daily newspaper, La Prensa, in 1975 and 1976.

994

Hunt, Darryl. *Nicaragua's reign of terror. Maryknoll, Nov. 1977: 48-53.*

Maintains that the U.S. trained Nicaraguan National Guard is responsible for human rights violations.

995

International Commission of Jurists. *Human rights in the world: Nicaragua. In its Review, June 1977: 5-8.*

Commission report on mechanisms for the suppression of human rights in Nicaragua. Describes the system of military justice established during the state of siege in 1974.

996

National Assembly of Religious. *Declaration of Honduran religious leaders. Lucha: Christian response to military repression in Latin America, Jan. 1979: 23-24.*

Declaration by 460 clerics at a conference in Honduras in 1978, repudiating violence and repression in Nicaragua and denouncing the torture of Hondurans committed to the cause of human rights.

997

Nicaragua: an ally under siege. *Washington, Council on American Affairs, 1978. 148 p.*

Includes articles on the U.S. Marines in Nicaragua, the effects of U.S. Latin American policy, human rights and revolution, the Nicaraguan economy, and economic assistance to Nicaragua.

998

Nicaragua: combate de un pueblo; presencia de los cristianos. *Lima, Centro de Estudios y Publicaciones, 1978. 117 p.*

Describes church opposition to the Somoza government and concern for the protection of human rights.

999

Nicaragua: sifting through the rubble. *Latin American political report, v. 6, Oct. 13, 1978: 317-318.*

Brief reference to the O.A.S. Human Rights Commission's collection of evidence against the government.

1000

Organization of American States. Inter-American Commission on Human Rights. *Situación de los derechos* humanos en Nicaragua. [s.l.] Comisión Permanente de Derechos Humanos de Nicaragua, 1978. 81 p. (Organization of American States. Official records. OEA/Ser. L/V/II.45 doc. 16 rev. 1)

"Resultado de la observación in loco practicada del 3 al 12 de octubre de 1978."

Report of the commission sent to Nicaragua in 1978 by the O.A.S.' Inter-American Commission on Human Rights. Charges the Nicaraguan government with human rights violations. Includes correspondence, investigative procedures, and inspection agenda.

1001

U.N. Economic Commission for Latin America. *Nicaragua: repercusiones económicas de los acontecimientos políticos recientes. Nota de la Secretaría. New York, 1979. [166] p. tables. (U.N. [Document] E/CEPAL/G. 1091)*

At head of title: Economic and Social Council.

Discusses human and material costs of recent disturbances and lists the guarantees of human rights to be found in the Universal Declaration of Human Rights. Original is in Spanish.

1002

Washington Office on Latin America. *Special update: Nicaragua. Washington, 1978. 8 p.*

At head of title: Latin America.

Analyzes the roles of the U.S., the Catholic Church, Somoza, the National Guard and political dissidents within Nicaragua in 1978.

Panama

1003

Anguizola, Gustave. *Violation of human rights and civil liberties in Panama. Washington, Council for Inter-American Security, 1977. 18 p.*

Argues against a new Panama Canal treaty in view of violations of citizens' rights in Panama under the Torrijos government.

1004

Ecumenical Program for Inter-American Communication and Action (EPICA). *Panama Canal Zone; occupied territory. Washington, 1973. 52 p.*

Collection of articles relating to the Canal Zone.

1005

EPICA Task Force. *Panama; sovereignty for a land divided. Washington, 1976. 127 p.*

Argues for returning the Canal Zone to Panama to normalize the political situation. Includes bibliography.

1006

International Commission of Jurists. *Report on the events in Panama, January 9-12, 1964. Geneva [1964]. 46 p.*

"Prepared by the Investigating Committee appointed by the International Commission of Jurists."

Commission report that exonerates U.S. Canal Zone police forces of alleged human rights violations during civil disturbances. Suggests that U.S. residents of the Zone adopt a more flexible attitude.

1007

Organization of American States. Inter-American Commission on Human Rights. *Informe sobre la situación de los derechos humanos en Panamá. Washington, Organización de los Estados Americanos, Secretaría General, 1979. 122 p. (Organization of American States. Official records. OEA/Ser. L/V/II.44 doc. 38 rev. 1)*

"Aprobado por la Comisión en la 580a. sesión celebrada el 22 de junio de 1978 durante la 44a sesión."

Summary of human rights conditions in Panama. Refers to constitutional provisions and complementary provisions of the American Declaration of Human Rights. Notes relevant lawsuits and judicial decisions.

1008

Panamanian Committee for Human Rights. *v. 1. Panama, 1976. 23 p.*

First volume of a series. Anonymous accounts of executions, deportations, and arbitrary arrests in Panama between 1971 and 1976. Includes appendixes.

1009

Panamanian Committee for Human Rights. *v. 2. Panama, 1976. 37 p.*

Anonymous accounts of violations of human rights, particularly among women and labor unionists. Comments on U.S. foreign policy toward Panama. Includes appendixes.

Paraguay

Report describing the appalling situation of political prisoners in Paraguay. Also cites violations of the human rights of indigenous groups.

1010

Alexander, Robert J. *The tyranny of General Stroessner. Freedom at issue, May/June 1977: 16-18.*

Professor of political science suggests that President Stroessner may ease repression in the face of foreign criticism from groups such as the International Red Cross.

1011

Amidst persecutions and consolations; Latin American bishops discuss human rights. *LADOC, no. 15, 1977: 6-15.*

Statement issued by the entire Catholic episcopal conference on June 12, 1976, in response to increasing government repression of the Church and other groups in Paraguay.

1012

Amnesty International. *Deaths under torture and disappearances of political prisoners in Paraguay.* London, Amnesty International Publications, 1977. [18] p.

Outlines cases of political prisoners reported to have died under torture in Paraguay. Provides details concerning persons classified as "missing" but believed to be held in secret police stations and military centers.

1013

Amnesty International. *Paraguay.* [London, Amnesty International Publications] 1976. 13 p. (Amnesty International briefing, no. 4)

Report on the status of human rights in Paraguay evaluating the situation of political detainees and detailing the restrictions of academic life, the press, trade unions, and travel, as well as the repression of indigenous people and human rights activists.

1014

Amnesty International. *Prison conditions in Paraguay: conditions for political prisoners; a factual report.* London, Amnesty International Publications, 1966. 34 p.

1015

Arens, Richard, ed. *Genocide in Paraguay.* Philadelphia, Temple University Press, 1976. 224 p. illus.

Eyewitness testimony of eight scholars, with documentation, describing the systematic extermination of the Aché Indians and other indigenous groups in the interests of clearing land for industrial development.

1016

Bridges, Sydney. *Politician and farm hand: a tale of two Paraguayan prisoners. Worldview, v. 22, July/Aug. 1979: 35-39.*

Pseudonymous journalistic account of the experiences of former political prisoners in Paraguay.

1017

Cabral, Alberto. *Political murder in Paraguay. America, April 23, 1977: 376-378.*

Case history of the kidnapping, torture and murder of Joelito Filartiga, a 17 year old student, son of Dr. Joel Filartiga, a noted medical philanthropist and artist of international reputation.

1018

Galeano, Eduardo. *Cemetery of words.* Trans. William Rowe. *Index on censorship, v. 7, Mar./Apr. 1978: 3-5.*

Literary commentary on intellectual repression in the Southern Cone region of Latin America.

1019

International Commission of Jurists. *Paraguay. In its Review, Dec. 1971: 13.*

Brief comments of the 1971 fact-finding mission to Paraguay that was carried out by the International Association of Democratic Lawyers and the International Secretariat of Catholic Jurists. Based on meetings with lawyers, clerics, trade unionists, and families of political prisoners.

1020
Lernoux, Penny. *1984 revisited: welcome to Paraguay.* New York, Alicia Patterson Foundation, 1976. 12 p.

Reports on President Stroessner's repression of the Catholic Church. Asserts that church-state relations in Paraguay are the worst in Latin America.

1021
Lernoux, Penny. *Paraguay: terror and profit.* Nation, v. 223, Nov. 13, 1976: 487-493.

Describes political repression under the most durable military regime in Latin America.

1022
Levi Ruffinelli, Fernando. *Derechos humanos.* Asuncion, Talleres Gráficos Orbis, 1977. 142 p.

Lists constitutions, charters, and documents guaranteeing human rights. Analyzes the protection of civil rights in Paraguayan law.

1023
Levi Rufinelli, Fernando. *Meditaciones.* Asuncion, 1974. 169 p.

Reviews recent political and ideological history of Paraguay focusing on topics such as democracy, development, freedom of expression, states of siege, and violations of basic rights.

1024
Münzel, Mark. *The Manhunts: Aché Indians in Paraguay.* In Veenhoven, William A., et. al., eds. *Case studies on human rights and fundamental freedoms: a world survey.* v. 4. The Hague, Martinus Nijhoff, 1976. p. 351-403.

Ethnographic study of Indian enslavement in eastern Paraguay based on interviews, newspaper articles, and Indian poetry. Concludes with the story of one official's brief efforts to curb abuses.

1025
Organization of American States. Inter-American Commission on Human Rights. *Report on the situation of human rights in Paraguay.* Washington, Organization of American States, General Secretariat, 1978. 89 p. (Organiza-tion of American States. Official records. OEA/Ser. L/V/II.43 doc. 13 corr. 1)

Report of an investigation conducted by the Inter-American Commission which concludes that basic human rights are still being violated in Paraguay.

1026
[Paraguay and native Americans]. *American Indian journal,* v. 3, July 1977: 2-15.

Collection of articles on the Indians of Paraguay, focusing on the violation of the human rights of the Aché and on the Project Marandú, a plan for establishing a system of Indian self management and community development programs.

1027
Paraguay repression escalates. *LADOC,* v. 7, Sept./Oct. 1976: 11-13.

Describes political repression and economic problems in Paraguay.

1028
Paraguayan atrocities condoned by the United States government. *Computers and automation,* v. 22, Dec. 1973: 30-33.

Reports evidence of genocide perpetrated on the Aché Indians of Paraguay.

1029
Roa Bastos, Augusto. *Los exilios del escritor en el Paraguay.* Nueva sociedad (San Jose, Costa Rica), marzo/abr. 1978: 29-35.

Major Paraguayan novelist considers the effects of underdevelopment and political repression on Paraguayan intellectuals.

1030
Schatz, Barbara A., and Dorothy J. Samuels. *Challenging the iron fist.* Juris doctor, v. 8, June/July 1978: 43, 46-47.

Among other issues, discusses slavery in Paraguay.

1031

Shankman, Paul. *The denouement of the South American Indians. Journal of ethnic studies, v. 7, fall 1979: 87-94.*

Review article of books dealing with the destruction of native American culture and possible genocide in Brazil and Paraguay.

1032

Stephansky, Ben S., and David M. Helfield. *Denial of human rights in Paraguay; report of the Second Commission of Inquiry of the International League for Human Rights. New York, International League for Human Rights, 1977. 76, [24] p.*

Sequel to the 1976 report; covers the International League's mission to Paraguay during 1977. Discusses Paraguayan politics, constitutional law, and judicial process. Includes recommendations and appendixes describing specific cases of rights violations.

1033

Stephansky, Ben S., and Robert J. Alexander. *Report of the First Commission of Inquiry into Human Rights in Paraguay. New York, International League for Human Rights, 1976. 58 p.*

Recapitulates background material on the Stroessner regime. Details political repression and human rights violations of political opponents and indigenous people. Contains conclusions and recommendations concerning political prisoners.

1034

Symposium on Inter-ethnic Conflict in South America, Bridgetown, Barbados, 1971. *La situación del indígena en América del Sur: aportes al estudio de la fricción inter-étnica en los Indios no-andinos. Geneva, World Council of Churches, 1972. 453 p. (Publications of the Department of Ethnology, University of Berne, no. 3)*

"Organized by the Department of Ethnology of the University of Berne"

Collection of papers by social anthropologists dealing with the relationship of government policies to the extermination of indigenous American groups in Venezuela, Colombia, Ecuador, Peru, Bolivia, Paraguay, Argentina, Brazil and the Guianas.

Peru

1035

Amnesty International. *Peru.* *[New York]*, 1979. *[15] p.* *(Briefing paper, no. 15)*

Report on an Amnesty International investigation of human rights violations during April 1978. Includes statistics on political prisoners in Peru.

1036

Comisión Episcopal de Acción Social. *Justicia: un clamor en la selva.* Lima *[197?]*. *74 p.* *(Cuadernos de documentación, no. 2)*

Articles describing violations of the basic rights of Indians of the Peruvian Amazon region.

1037

Comisión Evangélica Latino-americana de Educación Cristiana. *D.S. 010: una respuesta represiva; análisis económico y político.* Lima, CELADEC, 1978. *28 p.* *(Serie cuadernos, no. 1)*

Entire first issue devoted to a statute authorizing the dismissal of workers who participate in strikes.

1038

Comisión Evangélica Latino-americana de Educación Cristiana. *Perú y los derechos humanos.* Lima, CELADEC, 1977. *76 p.*

Describes popular protest against emergency economic measures in Peru.

1039

Cussianovich, Alejandro. *Llamados a ser libres.* Lima, Centro de Estudios y Publicaciones (CEP), Equipo JOC, Empleadas de Hogar, 1974. *209 p. illus.* *(CEP, no. 9)*

Discusses the exploitation of domestic employees in Peru and throughout Latin America. Presents the Catholic Church's response to the situation.

1040

Dammert Bellido, José. *The rights of man in Peru: the status of human rights in Peru twenty years after the United Nations Declaration of Human Rights. In Between honesty and hope.* Maryknoll, N.Y., *[197?]*. *p. 63-66.* *(Maryknoll documentation series, no. 4)*

Pastoral letter issued by the Bishop of Cajamarca examining the issue of human rights in Peru.

1041

Davis, Shelton H., and Robert O. Mathews. *The geological imperative; anthropology and development in the Amazon Basin of South America.* Cambridge, Mass., Anthropology Resource Center, 1976. *103 p. illus.*

Analysis of national and international resource policies that uproot native peoples of the Amazon Basin. Includes essays on the Yanamamö, the role of multinational corporations in the area, and an article on eastern Peru.

1042

Espinosa, Juan Antonio. *La tierra grita.* Lima, Centro de Estudios y Publicaciones, 1975. *127 p.* *(Centro de Estudios y Publicaciones, no. 14)*

Songs and lyrics describing the struggles and desires of the Peruvian campesino, many of which are included on a phonorecord by the same name.

1043

Harding, Colin. *Press censorship in Peru. Index on censorship,* v. 7, July/Aug. 1978: 50-57.

Describes strictures placed on the press throughout ten years of military rule in Peru.

1044

International Commission of Jurists. *Human rights in the world: Peru. In its Review,* Dec. 1974: 19-25.

Discusses the human rights situation after the establishment of the National Council of Justice and the enactment of the new Press Law that placed strictures on the print media.

1045

La lucha de los despedidos (julio 1977-enero 1978); testimonios. *Lima, Centro de Estudios y Publicaciones, 1978. 38 p. illus.*

Polemic against the Peruvian government's dismissal of workers who participate in strikes. Denounces police brutality as a response to worker unrest.

1046

Menchaca, A. A. *La recepción de la Declaración Universal de Derechos Humanos en el derecho peruano y sus efectos internacionales. Foro (Peru), v. 53, 1966: 92-120.*

Examines Peruvian law in light of the Universal Declaration of Human Rights.

1047

Pease García, Henry, and Olga Verme Insúa. *Perú 1968-[1976]: cronología política. Lima, Centro de Estudios y Promoción del Desarrollo, 1974-77. 4 v.*

Contains information on struggles for human rights, agrarian reform, and efforts to secure greater freedom of the press.

1048

Peruvians stress right to a dignified life. *Latinamerica press, Feb. 15, 1979: 1.*

Open letter signed by 61 Peruvian labor union and church leaders and other professionals, announcing the creation of a National Human Rights Commission that would call attention to human rights violations.

1049

La represión en el Perú. *Lima, Ediciones Represión en el Perú, 1978. 80 p. illus.*

Contains articles on miners, strikes, and political prisoners, as well as a statement of international solidarity among repressed peoples.

1050

Symposium on Inter-ethnic Conflict in South America, Bridgetown, Barbados, 1971. *La situación del indígena en América del Sur: aportes al estudio de la fricción inter-étnica en los Indios no-andinos. Geneva, World Council of Churches, 1972. 453 p. (Publications of the Department of Ethnology, University of Berne, no. 3)*

"Organized by the Ethnology Department of the University of Berne."

Collection of papers by social anthropologists, dealing with the relationship of government policies to the extermination of indigenous American groups in Venezuela, Colombia, Ecuador, Peru, Bolivia, Paraguay, Argentina, Brazil and the Guianas.

Uruguay

1051

Amnesty International. *Evidence of torture: studies of the Amnesty International Danish Medical Group.* London, Amnesty International Publications, 1977. *39 p. illus.*

Description of medical research on torture. Includes case studies from Chile, Argentina and Uruguay.

1052

Amnesty International. *Muertos en la tortura en Uruguay: 22 casos conocidos.* London, Amnestía Internacional, Secretariado Internacional, 1976. *8 p. illus.*

Pamphlet describing 22 cases of death due to torture.

1053

Amnesty International. *Uruguay; deaths under torture, 1975-77.* London, Amnesty International Publications, 1978. *12 p.*

Describes 12 cases of death and disappearance attributed to government action or negligence.

1054

Arismendi, Rodney. *Uruguay y América Latina en los años setenta; experiencias y balance de una revolución. 3 ed.* Montevideo, Ediciones Pueblos Unidos [1973]. *114 p.*

Political treatise by the leader of the communist opposition in Uruguay that includes a critique of the Tupamaros and brief references to political repression.

1055

Basso, Lelio, ed. *Atti della prima sessione del Tribunale Russell II.* Venice, Italy, Marsilio Editore, 1975. *376 p.*

Charges and testimony from the Bertrand Russell Tribunal on human rights violations in Chile, Uruguay, and Bolivia.

1056

Bayardo Bengoa, Fernando. *Los derechos del hombre y la defensa de la nación.* Montevideo, Ediciones Jurídicas, Amalio M. Fernández, 1977. *177 p.*

Study of Uruguayan laws and legal institutions within the context of universal human rights law. Contains a chapter on abuses of the law in the name of freedom.

1057

Brewin, Andrew, Louis Duclos, and David MacDonald. *One gigantic prison: the report of the fact-finding mission to Chile, Argentina and Uruguay.* Toronto, Inter-Church Committee on Chile, 1976. *69 p.*

Report by three members of the Canadian Parliament concerning their 1976 visit to Chile, Argentina, and Uruguay. Concludes that "a grave situation exists in regard to human rights" in the three countries. Includes appendixes.

1058

Camaño Rosas, Antonio. *Delitos contra la libertad. La justicia uruguaya, v. 42, 1960/61: 95-112.*

Brief historical, theoretical discussion of violations of laws protecting freedoms in Uruguay.

1059

Comité de Solidaridad con los Pueblos Latinoamericanos. *Testimonios de lucha; Chile, Brasil, Uruguay.* Buenos Aires, 1974. *39 p. (Its Boletín, no. 2)*

Presents an account of the activities of the popular resistance movements in Brazil and Uruguay. Describes U.S. involvement in Brazil and Chile. Includes a transcript of Allende's last words.

1060

Council on Hemispheric Affairs. *Human rights in Uruguay.* Washington, 1978. *2 p.*

Concludes that most of the Uruguayan government's troubles can be attributed to the use of repression and its inflexible stand against internal opposition.

1061

Derechos humanos en el Uruguay. *Montevideo, 1977. 183 p. (Serie de temas nacionales, no. 2)*

At head of title: "Realización de la División Publicaciones de la Biblioteca del Poder Legislativo. Selección, textos y compilación: Federico Fernández Prando."

Defense of the human rights record of Uruguay. Compares the rights guaranteed in the Uruguayan Constitution with those outlined in the Universal Declaration of Human Rights and the American Declaration of the Rights and Duties of Man.

1062

Echegoyen, Maruja. *The Onetti affair. Index on censorship, v. 3, winter 1974: 3-7.*

Brief account of the arrest and detention of Uruguay's well- known novelist, Juan Carlos Onetti. Others imprisoned at that time included Jorge Rufinelli, the then literary editor of the journal Marcha of Montevideo, Mercedes Rein, and Nelson Marra. Onetti and Rein were subsequently transferred to a psychiatric clinic.

1063

El enfrentamiento iglesia-militares. *Cuadernos de marcha, no. 38, jun. 1979: 3-20.*

Describes the role of the Catholic Church in taking a stand against violations of civil rights.

1064

Federación de Estudiantes Universitarios de Uruguay. *"El Infierno": un centro especializado de tortura en Uruguay. OCLAE, (Organización Continental Latinoamericana de Estudiantes), v. 11, no. 3, 1977: 28-35. illus.*

Not available for annotation.

1065

Ferreira, Juan. *Derechos humanos en Uruguay: denuncia presentada ante la Comisión Inter-Americana de Derechos Humanos de la OEA. Washington, 1977. 15 p.*

Describes human rights violations in Uruguay.

1066

Fialho, A. Veiga. *Uruguai: um campo de concentração. Textos especiais de Eduardo Galeano e Jorge Amado. Rio de Janeiro, Civilização Brasileira, 1979. 257 p.*

Describes the violation of the human rights of intellectuals and professionals in Uruguay. Contains articles by writers Jorge Amado and Eduardo Galeano expressing solidarity with those persecuted in Uruguay.

1067

Fyra latinamerikanska militärdiktaturer. *Stockholm, Amnesty International, Svenska Sektionen, 1974. 2 v. in one.*

Two slim volumes that examine violations of human rights. Volume 1 deals with Brazil and Chile, while volume 2 examines Bolivia and Uruguay. Both contain lists of intellectuals who have been jailed or exiled, based on information provided by Amnesty International.

1068

Goldman, Robert K. *The Uruguayan regime as it relates to international law. In Secretariat International de Juristes pour l'Amnistie en Uruguay, ed. Amnesty: symposium on the state of emergency and human rights in Uruguay; appeal for amnesty; 15-16 Dec. 1978. Paris, 1979. p. 81-101.*

Analyzes Uruguay's legal and government structure since 1973 and the compatibility of these institutions with the international human rights law. Discusses cases of persons who have disappeared and other violations of basic rights.

1069

Goldman, Robert K., Joaquín Martínez Bjorkman, and Jean-Louis Weil. *Memorandum on laws and decrees of the government of Uruguay which violate U.N. conventions and declarations in the human rights area, March 1, 1978. [London, Amnesty International, 1978]. 9 leaves.*

Report of a mission of inquiry to Uruguay in 1977, supported by Mouvement International des Juristes Catholiques, Pax Romana, Fédération Internationale, and the National Council of Churches of Christ. Evaluates legal measures enacted in Uruguay since 1973 that violate U.N. conventions in the field of human rights.

1070

Goytisolo, Juan. *Uruguay's withering culture. Index on censorship, v. 8, Mar./Apr. 1979: 36-37.*

The case of Julio Castro, journalist and editor of Marcha, who vanished from Uruguay without a trace, is used by the Spanish writer Juan Goytisolo to expose growing repression and deteriorating human rights conditions in Uruguay.

1071

Handelman, Howard. *Uruguayan journal. Worldview (New York), v. 20, Oct. 1977: 16-24.*

Political scientist's personal account of the emotional effects of stories about torture on his Uruguayan acquaintances, 1975 to 1976.

1072

El infierno: la tortura en el Uruguay. *Montevideo, 1976. 39 p.*

Contains descriptions of the different types of torture used in Uruguay.

1073

International Commission of Jurists. *Dr. Héctor Gross Espiell's reply for the Uruguay government. In its Review, Dec. 1972: 1-4.*

Letter to the Commission by the representative of Uruguay to the U.N. in Geneva, dated July 23, 1972. Concerns an article on Uruguay which appeared in the I.C.J. Review, no. 8, 1972.

1074

International Commission of Jurists. *Human rights in the world: Chile and Uruguay, contrasts and comparisons. In its Review, June 1974: 5-7.*

Article by the Secretary General of the International Commission of Jurists based upon the report of an I.C.J. mission to Chile and a joint I.C.J. and Amnesty International mission to Uruguay in April and May, 1974.

1075

International Commission of Jurists. *Human rights in the world: Uruguay. In its Review, June 1972: 15-16.*

Expresses concern for the increasing use of violence as a political tool in Uruguay. Article produced heated debate.

1076

International Commission of Jurists. *Notes and comments: Uruguay. In its Review, June 1973: 8-9.*

Discusses the deterioration of the rule of law in Uruguay.

1077

International Commission of Jurists. *Report of mission to Uruguay, 1974. New York, 1975. 1 v. (unpaged)*

Included in the joint I.C.J.-Amnesty International report are such matters as the legal basis for the arrest and detention of political suspects; the absence of notification concerning arrest; and torture and ill treatment. Supplements were published in 1975 and 1976.

1078

Jackson, Sir Geoffrey. *Surviving the long night: an autobiographical account of a political kidnapping. New York, Vanguard Press, 1974. 226 p. plates.*

Personal testimony of the former British ambassador to Uruguay who was abducted and held prisoner for 9 months by the Tupamaro guerrillas.

1079

Jornadas de la cultura uruguaya en el exilio. *Mexico, 1977. 2 v.*

Collection of reports, declarations, and descriptions of cultural activities emerging from a solidarity meeting of Latin American and European artists and intellectuals held in August, 1977.

1080

Lernoux, Penny. *Church cowed by Uruguayan military. New York, Alicia Patterson Foundation, 1977. 8 p.*

Criticizes the Uruguayan church hierarchy for its failure to speak out more vehemently against repression by the military.

1081

López, Braulio. *Singing in exile. Index on censorship, v. 7, July/ Aug. 1978: 44-49.*

Account of the work of this Uruguayan singer and of his life in exile, based on an interview by Gerónimo de Sierra and Cristina Torres, two Uruguayan social scientists also living in exile.

1082

Martínez Moreno, Carlos. *Los días que vivimos; dieciséis ensayos inmediatos. Montevideo, Editorial Girón, 1973. 155 p. (Col. Los uruguayos, no. 4)*

Collection of newspaper essays that examines the misuse of laws by the Uruguayan government in its efforts to maintain order.

1083

Martínez Moreno, Carlos. *La "muerte civil" del escritor uruguayo; persecución y destierro. Nueva sociedad (San José, Costa Rica), marzo/abr. 1978: 68-73.*

Historical analysis of the persecution and exile of Uruguayan writers from the 1930's to the present.

1084

McDonald, Ronald H. *The rise of military politics in Uruguay. Inter-American economic affairs, v. 28, spring 1975: 25-43.*

Describes the transfer of power from civilian to military rule in 1973. Comments on the military's disregard for Uruguay's traditional constitutional safeguards of civil liberties.

1085

Moura, Ernesto. *Political kidnappings in Brazil. Third world, v. 1, May 1979: 47-48.*

Discusses the implications of cooperation between repressive regimes in light of the abduction of two Uruguayans and their children living in exile in Brazil.

1086

National Academy of Sciences. *National Academy of Sciences Committee on Human Rights: results of a visit to Argentina and Uruguay. Washington, 1978. 16 p.*

Three person task force report on the effects of the repression of the Argentine scientific community by the military regime. Describes the task force's efforts to secure the release of a mathematician and his wife who were imprisoned in Uruguay.

1087

North American Congress on Latin America. *Uruguay police agent exposes U.S. advisors. NACLA's Latin America & empire report, v. 6, July/Aug. 1972: 20-25.*

Deals with the events denounced by a Uruguayan senator who alleged that U.S.A.I.D. operatives played a role in creating and supplying the intelligence apparatus for Uruguay's police.

1088

Organization of American States. Inter-American Commission on Human Rights. *Report on the situation of human rights in Uruguay. Washington, Organization of American States, General Secretariat, 1978. 70 p. (Organization of American States. Official records. OEA/Ser. L/V/II.43 doc. 19 corr. 1)*

Assessment of the status of human rights in Uruguay, using as a base the American Declaration of the Rights and Duties of Man. Commission found violations and made various recommendations.

1089

Otero, Mario. *Oppression in Uruguay. Bulletin of the atomic scientists, v. 37, Feb. 1981: 29-31.*

Argues that the economic crisis, coupled with political repression, has produced an almost total paralysis of scientific and cultural activity in Uruguay.

1090

Primakc, Joel. *Human rights in the Southern Cone. Bulletin of the atomic scientists, v. 37, Feb. 1981: 24-29.*

Claims that repression in Uruguay and Argentina has had disastrous effects on education and science.

1091

Quigley, Thomas. *Uruguay: a torture state. Sojourners,* July/Aug. 1976: 5-6.

Article in the journal of the People's Christian Coalition that discusses the torturing of political dissidents in Uruguay.

1092

Real, Alberto Ramón. *Garantía internacional de los derechos humanos. Justicia uruguaya, v. 46, 1962/1963:* 37-45.

Speech delivered to the National Commission of U.N.E.S.C.O. in Uruguay on the development of international and inter-American human rights organizations, advocating unity of purpose.

1093

Saxlund, Ricardo. *Relying on bayonets. New times (Moscow), no. 13, Apr. 1974: 12-13.*

Describes the anti-communist movement and general political conditions in Uruguay.

1094

Secrétariat International de Juristes pour L'Amnistie en Uruguay, ed. *Amnesty: symposium on the state of emergency and human rights in Uruguay; appeal for amnesty,* 15-16 Dec. 1978. Paris, 1979. 155 p.

Contains papers delivered at the symposium, plus syntheses and conclusions. Topics include Uruguayan military and civil law, political prisoners, and international law and the Uruguayan regime.

1095

Sierra, Gerónimo de. *Migrantes uruguayos hacia la Argentina. Mexico, Instituto de Investigaciones Sociales, 1977.* 31 p.

At head of title: "Documento preparado para la VI Reunión del Grupo de Trabajo sobre Migraciones Internas de la Comisión de Población y Desarrollo de CLASCO."

Not available for annotation.

1096

Situación de los derechos humanos en Uruguay. *[s.l., s.n., 1976?]* 55 p.

Cover title: Violaciones de los derechos humanos.

Anonymous pamphlet on the relation between internal security needs and human rights violations under a military government.

1097

Styron, Rose. *Uruguay: the Oriental republic. Nation, v. 223, Aug. 14, 1976: 107-111.*

Reports on the torture of political prisoners in Uruguay.

1098

Tarigo, Enrique E. *Temas de nuestro tiempo. Montevideo, Fundación de Cultura Universitaria, 1979. 2 v.*

Compilation of newspaper editorials that the author wrote for El Día from 1974 to 1978. Volume 1 includes sections on liberalism, human rights, and legal practices. Volume 2 includes sections on democracy, freedom of the press, and economics. Focuses on the current political situation in Uruguay.

1099

Torrents, Nissa. *Uruguay; getting rid of critics. Index on censorship, v. 6, May/June 1977: 9-11.*

Points out that a number of valuable professionals and intellectuals have left Uruguay because of increasing repression since 1973.

1100

Torturas. *Cuadernos de marcha. dic. 1970: 1-80.*

Examines torture in Brazil, Uruguay and Argentina. Includes the "black book" of torture.

1101

Uruguay. Junta de Comandantes en Jefe. *Las fuerzas armadas al pueblo oriental; la subversión. v. 1. Montevideo, Fuerzas Armadas Uruguayas, 1976. 370 p.*

Discusses international communism, the special role of Cuba, guerrilla tactics, and the subversive groups in Uruguay, with special attention to the Tupamaros.

1102

Uruguay. Junta de Comandantes en Jefe. *Las fuerzas armadas al pueblo oriental; la subversión. v. 2. Montevideo, Fuerzas Armadas Uruguayas, 1976. [409] p.*

Discusses the structure and organization of the various far left movements, their strategies, and urban and rural warfare.

1103

Uruguay. Junta de Comandantes en Jefe. *Las fuerzas armadas al pueblo oriental; el proceso político. Montevideo, Fuerzas Armadas Uruguayas, 1978. 746 p.*

Describes the disruption produced in Uruguay by activities of guerrilla groups. Includes a detailed justification for political developments after 1973.

1104

Uruguay. *Organización Continental Latinoamericana de Estudiantes, v. 10, no. 6, 1976: whole issue.*

Includes sections on the suppression of human rights and the future of education in Uruguay.

1105

Uruguay: bajo el fascismo. *La Habana, Casa de las Américas, 1976. 120 p. (Instituto Cubano del Libro, no. 97)*

Items included range from an interview with Rodney Arismendi, Secretary General of the Communist Party of Uruguay, to a college professor's account of repression in the university. Also presents a 1974 report by Amnesty International.

1106

Violations of human rights in Uruguay 1972-1976. *Update to 1978 provided by the Inter-Church Committee on Human Rights in Latin America. Translated by Chris Rosene and Sheila Katz. Toronto, 1978. 145 p. illus.*

A chronological history prepared inside Uruguay. Describes the different stages of the process of social deterioration and human rights violations during this period. Includes bibliographic references.

1107

Washington Office on Latin America. *Special update: Uruguay; five years of military rule. Washington, 1978. 8 p.*

At head of title: Latin America.

Describes the policies of the military regime, government expenditures, and the cost of repression. Discusses the Carter administration's position concerning Uruguay.

Venezuela

1108

Arraiz, Rafael Clemente. *Contenido y defensa de los derechos humanos en el sistema interamericano. Academia de Ciencias Políticas y Sociales. Boletín (Caracas), v. 36, oct./dic. 1977: 117-127.*

Speech on the Venezuelan Constitution's human rights provisions, their application, and their place in the changed political context of the Americas in the 1970's. Discusses human rights protection in the hemisphere.

1109

Davis, Shelton H., and Robert O. Mathews. *The geological imperative; anthropology and development in the Amazon Basin of South America. Cambridge, Mass., Anthropology Resource Center, 1976. 103 p. illus.*

Analysis of national and international resource policies that uproot native peoples of the Amazon Basin. Includes essays on the Yanamamö, the role of multinational corporations in the area, and an article on eastern Peru.

1110

Pérez, R. *Derecho y libertad en la sociedad actual. Caracas, Universidad Simón Bolívar, 1971. 70 p.*

Discusses specific safeguards to protect basic rights in democratic societies with special emphasis on Venezuela.

1111

Prieto, F. L. B. *Declaración universal de los derechos humanos y el pensamiento venezolano. La justicia (Mexico), v. 20, feb. 1960: 31.*

Not available for annotation.

1112

Ruiz Carrillo, Rafael. *Análisis y proyección del derecho laboral venezolano. Caracas, Editorial Salto Angel, 1975. 178 p. (Col. Anri, v. 19)*

Not available for annotation.

1113

Symposium on Inter-ethnic Conflict in South America, Bridgetown, Barbados, 1971. *La situación del indígena en América del Sur: aportes al estudio de la fricción inter-étnica en los Indios no- andinos. Geneva, World Council of Churches, 1972. 453 p. (Publications of the Department of Ethnology, University of Berne, no. 3)*

"Organized by the Ethnology Department of the University of Berne."

Collection of papers by social anthropologists dealing with the relationship of government policies to the extermination of indigenous American groups in Venezuela, Colombia, Ecuador, Peru, Bolivia, Paraguay, Argentina, Brazil, and the Guianas.

Amnesty International

1114

Amnesty International. *Amnesty International publications, 1962-1979. Zug, Switzerland, Inter Documentation Co., 1980. 1 v. (microfiche in a binder)*

Includes, in microfiche format, the following materials: Amnesty International newsletter, 1971-1979; Amnesty International report, 1961-1979; Briefings, 1976-1979; Country report; International reports on topics; and a collection entitled "Amnesty International general information."

1115

Amnesty International. *Annual report. 1976 + London, Amnesty International, International Secretariat.*

Provides country-by-country survey of human rights violations. Report year ends May 31.

1116

Amnesty International. *Country dossiers, 1975-1979. Zug, Switzerland, Inter Documentation Co., 1980. 1 v. (microfiche in a binder)*

Presents a comprehensive record on 105 individual countries, including reports from official Amnesty International missions and unpublished background information. A printed catalog is supplied with the microfiche collection.

1117

Amnesty International. *The death penalty; an Amnesty International report. London, Amnesty International Publications, 1979. 209 p.*

Examination of death penalty legislation and practice in 110 countries including various ones in Latin America. Based on the 1978 Stockholm Conference on the Campaign for the Abolition of the Death Penalty.

1118

Amnesty International. *Derechos humanos en América Latina. London, Amnesty International Publications, 1978. 11 p.*

Amnesty International's message to the second General Conference of Latin American Bishops held at Puebla, Mexico, 1978.

1119

Amnesty International. *Disappearances: a workbook. New York, Amnesty International Publications, 1981. 168 p.*

A book based on papers presented at a seminar on disappearances, with participants from Amnesty International and other nongovernmental and inter-governmental organizations. Contains country studies and essays on aspects of the general problem of disappearances as an international human rights violation.

1120

Amnesty International. *The "disappeared" of Argentina. List of cases reported to Amnesty International March 1976-February 1979. London, Amnesty International Publications, 1979.*

Computer printout providing data on thousands of cases of "disappeared" persons in Argentina. Categories include identity card number, nationality, age, family/children, profession, and date and place of disappearance.

1121

Amnesty International. *Disappeared prisoners in Chile. Dossier on political prisoners held in secret detention camps in Chile. [London?] Amnesty International Publications, 1977. 1 v.*

Reports on 219 political prisoners held in secret detention in Chile. Includes case histories and appeals from relatives of the prisoners.

1122

Amnesty International. *Impartiality and the defence of human rights. New York, Amnesty International Publications, 1978. [5] p.*

Outlines the procedures Amnesty International follows in order to maintain its policy of independence, universality and impartiality.

1123

Amnesty International. *Informe de una misión de Amnistía Internacional a la República de Colombia: 15-31 de enero de*

1980. London, Amnesty International, International Secretariat, 1980. 248 p.

A comprehensive report on the current human rights situation in the Republic of Colombia based on an official Amnesty International mission during 1980.

1124

Amnesty International. *Lawyers against torture. International Commission of Jurists. Review, June 1976: 29-41.*

Prepared in September 1975 as part of Amnesty International's Campaign for the Abolition of Torture. Discusses the need for professional law associations to assist lawyers around the world who are persecuted for representing political dissidents. Reviews global examples, including cases in Brazil, Argentina, Chile and Uruguay. Contains conclusions, recommendations, and draft principles for a lawyers' code of ethics regarding torture.

1125

Amnesty International. *Political imprisonment in Uruguay. London, Amnesty International, International Secretariat, 1979.*

An information packet on political imprisonment in Uruguay. Includes documents on the cases of 14 prisoners of conscience and on torture and conditions of detention.

1126

Amnesty International. *Report: 1979. London, Amnesty International Publications, 1979. 219 p.*

Provides country-by-country survey of human rights in over 100 nations during a one year period ending May 1, 1979. Reports about human rights violations in Latin American countries can be found in the chapter entitled "The Americas." Volumes for previous years are also available.

1127

Amnesty International. *Report of allegations of torture in Brazil. 3d ed. London, Amnesty International Publications, 1976. 104 p.*

Reprint of 1972 report on military repression during a period of rapid economic development.

1128

Amnesty International. *Report of an Amnesty International mission to Argentina. London, Amnesty International Publications, 1976.*

Overview of the human rights situation in Argentina based on a 1976 mission to that country. Includes presentations on legislation, prison conditions, "disappearance," and torture and gives conclusions and recommendations.

1129

Amnesty International. *Report on torture. New York, Farrar, Strauss, and Giroux, 1975. 285 p.*

Report prepared as part of Amnesty's Campaign Pro Abolition of Torture. Contains informative essays on the historical, medical, psychological, and legal aspects of torture, as well as a survey concerning the use of torture during the previous decade in over 60 countries. Includes a special report on Chile and an appendix by Rose Styron. Provides bibliography.

1130

Amnesty International. *The Republic of Nicaragua: an international report including the findings of a mission to Nicaragua, May 1976. New York, Amnesty International Publications, 1977. 75 p.*

Comprehensive report of an investigative mission to Nicaragua. The focus of the report is on due process of law, use of torture, and political executions. The evidence cited comes from prisoners, ex-prisoners, testimonies of the relatives of prisoners, their lawyers, and observers, as well as from government documents, published news accounts, and news reports officially censored from the press.

1131

Amnesty International. *Results of examinations of 14 Argentinian torture victims by the Danish Medical Group Amnesty International. Copenhagen, Amnesty International, Danish Medical Group, 1980. 56 p.*

Individual reports of 14 Argentinian torture victims complete with country background information, short presentations of each case, and conclusions of each examination including psychological and physical forms of torture. Findings summarized in tables.

1132

Amnesty International. *Testimony on secret detention camps in Argentina. New York, Amnesty International Publications, 1980. 1 v.*

This report spans a period of 15 months in the lives of two prisoners in secret camps in Buenos Aires, Argentina, where they were held from November 1977 until February 1979. Also provides detailed information on 330 of an estimated 800 prisoners who passed through these camps during the period.

1133

Amnesty International. *Uruguay: the cases of fourteen prisoners of conscience. London, Amnesty International, 1979. 21 p.*

Case by case presentation of fourteen prisoners of conscience in Uruguay.

1134

Amnesty International. Queensland Section. *Writers and journalists in prison. Moorvale, Queensland, Australia, 1974. 16 p.*

Provides a directory and describes conditions for writers and journalists imprisoned throughout the world.

1135

Ehrman, Robert. *The doggedness of conscience. Foreign service journal, v. 54, June 1977: 14-17.*

Reports on the work of Amnesty International on behalf of human rights around the world including efforts for the release of political prisoners and the cessation of torture.

1136

Hanson, Christopher. *Amnesty International: prisoner of success. Progressive, v. 42, Apr. 1978: 38-40.*

Author fears that the newly acquired prestige of Amnesty International could impair its effectiveness.

1137

Hill, Christopher R., ed. *Rights and wrongs: some essays on human rights. Edited for Amnesty International by Christopher R. Hill. Harmondsworth, United Kingdom, Penguin Books, 1969. 189 p.*

Not available for annotation.

1138

International Conference for the Abolition of Torture, Paris, 1973. *Conference for the abolition of torture: final report. London, Amnesty International Publications, 1974. 32 p.*

Sponsored by Amnesty International, the conference surveyed cases of torture in Brazil, Argentina, Chile, and Uruguay. Case studies are followed by recommendations and an appendix of draft principles for a lawyers' code of ethics in dealing with torture cases.

1139

Nash, George H. *Ordeal of Amnesty International. National review, v. 26, Dec. 6, 1974: 1407-1411.*

Article critical of the organization, challenging its political objectivity.

1140

Scoble, Harry M., and Laurie S. Wiseberg. *Human rights and Amnesty International. Annals of the American Academy of Political and Social Science, v. 1974: 11-26.*

Analyzes Amnesty International's role in protecting human rights.

The Churches and Human Rights

1141

Adjali, Mia, ed. *Of life and hope: toward effective witness in human rights.* Cincinnati, Ohio, National Council of Churches, Friendship Press, 1979. 96 p.

Fourteen authors focus on the Christian response in working for the protection of human rights. Volume provides the international covenants of human rights.

1142

Amidst persecutions and consolations; Latin American bishops discuss human rights. *LADOC, no. 15, 1977: 6-15.*

Statement issued by the entire Catholic episcopal conference on June 12, 1976, in response to increasing government repression of the Church and other groups in Paraguay.

1143

Arrupe, Pedro. *Witnessing to justice.* Vatican City, Pontifical Commission Justice and Peace, 1972. 62 p. (*Justice in the World, no. 2*)

At head of title: "Commentary on the document 'Justice in the world' of the Synod of Bishops."

This handbook suggests how Catholics should work to preserve human rights. Includes bibliographic references.

1144

Arzobispado de Santiago, Chile. Vicaría de la Solidaridad. *Declaración Universal de los Derechos Humanos.* Santiago, Chile, 1978. [37] p. (*Reflexión, no. 6*)

Prepared in collaboration with the Coordinadora Ecuménica de Servicios de Brasil in commemoration of the 30th anniversary of the Universal Declaration of Human Rights. Relates the Declaration to the Bible and the principles of the Christian churches.

1145

Arzobispado de Santiago, Chile. Vicaría de la Solidaridad. *El derecho de los pobres; planteamiento de la Iglesia brasileña.* Santiago, Chile, 1976. 23 p. (*Formación, no. 6*)

Summarizes the message delivered at the meeting of the Representative Commission of the Brazilian National Bishops Conference, Rio de Janeiro, October 19 to 25, 1976, reaffirming the Catholic Church's dedication to human rights. Among the subjects treated are political repression, violence, and the needy.

1146

Arzobispado de Santiago, Chile. Vicaría de la Solidaridad. *Derechos humanos.* Santiago, Chile, 1978. 114 p. (*Estudios, no. 1*)

Presents articles on the ideological, religious, historical, social, and current political implications of human rights. Includes a document entitled, "La Iglesia y los derechos del hombre," that was presented by the President of the Comisión Pontificia Justitia et Pax to the National Commission of Justice and Peace, as well as the text of the report on human rights by the General Assembly of the World Council of Churches.

1147

Arzobispado de Santiago, Chile. Vicaría de la Solidaridad. *Estudios: problemas actuales del recurso de protección. Cuadernos jurídicos, v. 4, nov. 1977: 6-62.*

Studies the problems of protecting individual constitutional rights during states of emergency. Includes a sample case before a military court.

1148

Arzobispado de Santiago, Chile. Vicaría de la Solidaridad. *Una experiencia de Iglesia.* Santiago, Chile, 1978. 51 p.

Discussion of the implications of the Puebla conference for the Church's position on human rights, addressed to the Cardinal of Santiago and the Episcopal Conference of Chile.

1149

Arzobispado de Santiago, Chile. Vicaría de la Solidaridad. *No basta con decir "Señor, Señor...." derechos humanos; misión de Iglesia. Santiago, Chile, 1978. 1 v. (unpaged) (Reflexión, no. 10)*

José Comblin, the Cardinal of Santiago, and Ronaldo Muñoz elaborate on the Church's responsibility to work for the human rights of workers, indigenous peoples, the marginated and the politically abused.

1150

Arzobispado de Santiago, Chile. Vicaría de la Solidaridad. *La no violencia evangélica, fuerza de liberación. Santiago, Chile, 1978. 59 p. (Reflexión, no. 5)*

Discussion of the meeting of Latin American bishops held in Bogotá, Nov. 29 through Dec. 4, 1977, at the invitation of the Movimiento Internacional de Reconciliación, Pax Christi, the Secretariado Latinoamericano de Cáritas, and the Servicio Paz y Justicia. Examines the political, social, and economic violence that exists throughout Latin America.

1151

Bergman, Gregory. *Puebla: negligible liberation for women. Christian century, v. 96, May 9, 1979: 529-530, 532.*

Review of proceedings of "Mujeres Para el Diálogo," a meeting of Latin American women religious held in Puebla, Mexico, concurrent with but independent of the CELAM bishops conference. The bishops are criticized for failing to speak effectively to the condition of women in Latin America.

1152

Billings, Peggy. *Paradox and promise in human rights. Cincinnati, Ohio, National Council of Churches, Friendship Press, 1979. 128 p.*

Assesses the thoughts and events of the late 1960's and early 1970's and raises questions about the implementation of the Universal Declaration and the Covenant on Human Rights. Draws on historical case histories for comparison with the present promise of change coming from the U.N. One chapter discusses theological foundations of a human rights ethic.

1153

Blazquez Carmona, Feliciano. *Hélder Câmara: el grito del pobre. Madrid, Ediciones Sígueme, 1972. 162 p. illus. (Testigos del hombre, no. 10)*

Discusses the noted Brazilian archbishop's non-violent philosophy as a means of achieving social change and justice. Includes samples of his writings.

1154

Bono, Agostino. *Catholic bishops and human rights in Latin America. Worldview (New York), v. 21, Mar. 1978: 4-7.*

Analyzes current tensions between the Church and military regimes of Latin America. Argues that, rather than the Church becoming more leftist, the governments of Latin America have moved farther to the right.

1155

Bouchaud, Joseph. *El fuego: de feu qui nous vient d'Amérique Latine. Paris, Editions Ouvrières, 1973. 109 p. (Col. a pleine vie)*

This French publication discusses the activist role of the Catholic Church on behalf of social justice and human rights in Latin America.

1156

Câmara, Dom Hélder. *Church and colonialism. London, Sheed and Ward, 1969. 181 p.*

Contains addresses by the noted Brazilian archbishop and human rights activist, relating Christianity and social justice to development.

1157

Câmara, Dom Hélder. *Spiral of violence. London, Sheed and Ward, 1971. 82 p.*

Translation of volume in French about social injustice and violence, suggesting means for the alleviation of inhuman conditions in the Third World.

1158

Catholic Church. Pontificius Coetus Studiosorum Iustitia et Pax. *La Iglesia y los derechos del hombre. [Santiago de Chile?] Instituto Chileno de Estudios Humanísticos [1976] 85 p.*

Emphasizes the Catholic Church's dedication to human rights, its historical pastoral and doctrinal positions, specific pastoral orientations in its defense of human rights, and certain concrete national and international initiatives that may be taken. Includes bibliographical references.

1159

Centro de Estudios y Publicaciones. *Signos de lucha y esperanza; testimonios de la Iglesia en América Latina, 1973-1978. Lima, 1978. 400 p. (Centro de Estudios y Publicaciones, no. 25)*

Using church documents, this book reports on the Church and the struggles of the poor and oppressed.

1160

Centro de Estudios y Publicaciones. *Signos de liberación: testimonios de la Iglesia en América Latina, 1969-1973. Lima, 1973. 296 p.*

Contains post-Medellin Catholic Church documents concerning the search for a new society and human liberation.

1161

Church, state and human rights. *Christianity and crisis, v. 36, Dec. 1976: 1-15.*

Presents addresses made at the Human Rights Conference held on Nov. 5, 1975, in honor of the 35th anniversary of the journal, Christianity and crisis. Former U.S. Congressman Donald Fraser, a leading human rights advocate, emphasizes U.S. responsibility for defending rights in his speech entitled, "The U.S. and Human Rights."

1162

Clark, James A. *The Church and the crisis in the Dominican Republic. Westminster, Md., Newman Press, 1967. 254 p.*

Describes church efforts to alleviate physical suffering in the Dominican Republic during the 1965 revolt.

1163

Claver, Francisco F. *The stones will cry out: pastorals. Maryknoll, N.Y., Orbis Books, 1978. 196 p.*

Includes radio addresses by a Jesuit human rights advocate.

1164

Clergy and Laity Concerned. Human Rights Coordinating Center. *DINA, SAVAK, KCIA: our allies' secret agents have come to the United States. Washington, 1977. 6 p.*

Summarizes the activities in the U.S. of these foreign intelligence agencies, the "complicity of the U.S. government," and what the public can do.

1165

Colonnese, Louis M., ed. *Conscientization for liberation. Washington, United States Catholic Conference, Division for Latin America, 1971. 305 p.*

Papers presented at the 1970 Catholic Inter-American Cooperation Program, held in Washington, dealing with the Latin American Catholic Church since Medellin, the theology of liberation, and the Church's increasingly active role in defending basic rights.

1166

Comisión Evangélica Latinoamericana de Educación Cristiana. *Declaración sobre la tortura. In Documentos Docet. Lima, Centro de Documentación y Editorial, Programas de Comunicación y Documentación, CELADEC, 1978. p. 13-18. (Documento, no. 32 A)*

"Texto final votado por el Comité Central del Consejo Mundial de Iglesias."

Provides final text of the Commission's unequivocal condemnation of torture.

1167

Comisión Evangélica Latinoamericana de Educación Cristiana. *Derechos humanos; el derecho a una vida digna. Lima, CELADEC, 1978. 36 p. (Cuadernos, no. 2)*

Posits ideological questions on fundamental human rights, analyzes political, economic, and social rights in underdeveloped Latin America, and reviews historical and current means of enforcing human rights policies.

1168

Comisión Evangélica Latinoamericana de Educación Cristiana, ed. *Derechos humanos; derechos de Dios. Lima, CELADEC, Centro de Documentación y Editorial [197?]. 27 p. (DOCET, Serie D, no. 2)*

Deals with the responsibility of churches to promote and defend human rights. Includes "La Iglesia y los derechos humanos" by Argymiro Pereira, "La Iglesia frente a las dictaduras militares en América Latina" by Michel Leclerq, and "declaración Cristiana sobre derechos humanos" by Jurgen Moltman.

1169

Comisión Evangélica Latinoamericana de Educación Cristiana. *Derechos humanos; D.S. 010-77 TR: una respuesta represiva; análisis económico y político. Lima, CELADEC, 1978. 28 p. (Cuadernos, no. 1)*

Scrutinizes the antecedents, application of, and responses to the Peruvian government's decree D.S. 010-77 TR which resulted in the dismissal of thousands of workers. Concludes with the implication that this was a political and economic response on the part of the Peruvian military government to the organizing popular sectors and to the nation's economic crisis. Appendixes contain general information and the actual text of this controversial decree.

1170

Comisión Evangélica Latinoamericana de Educación Cristiana. *Evangelio y derechos humanos. Lima, CELADEC, Centro de Documentación y Editorial, 1978. 19 p. (DOCET, Serie G, no. 6)*

Contains two articles which treat the Catholic Church's role in human rights and evangelism: "Los Derechos Humanos ¿de quienes?" by José Miguez Bonino and "Derechos Humanos, Evangelización e Ideología" by Juan Luis Segundo.

1171

Comité Pro Libertad de los Presos Políticos de El Salvador. *Casos de desaparecidos. San Salvador, 1978. [17] p.*

In response to a request made to Archbishop Oscar A. Romero by relatives of detained and disappeared persons, the Committee for the

Liberation of All Political Prisoners in El Salvador published this list of 99 cases, providing the name, age, profession, civil status, place of residence, and the circumstances of detention of each person on the list.

1172

Conferencia General del Episcopado Latinoamericano, 2d, Bogotá and Medellin, 1968. *The Church in the present-day transformation of Latin America in the light of the Council. v. 2. 3d. ed. Washington, National Conference of Catholic Bishops, Secretariat for Latin America, 1979. 221 p.*

Discusses the human condition in Latin America, with reference to rights violations and international tensions. Comments on the role of the Catholic Church.

1173

Conferencia General del Episcopado Latinoamericano, 2d, Bogotá and Medellín, Colombia, 1968. *The Church in the present-day transformation of Latin America in the light of the Council. v. 1. Washington, United States Catholic Conference, Division for Latin America, 1973. 239 p. illus.*

Includes statements by Pope Paul VI, and discussions on human rights and the role of the Catholic Church in promoting them.

1174

Conferencia General del Episcopado Latinoamericano, 3d, Puebla, Mexico, 1979. *Evangelization at present and in the future of Latin America: conclusions. Washington, National Conference of Catholic Bishops, Secretariat, Committee for the Church in Latin America, 1979. 220 p.*

Discusses topics such as evangelization, human rights, social conditions, and political ends in Latin America.

1175

Consejo Episcopal Latinoamericano. Encuentro Latinamericano sobre Desarrollo en América Latina, Panamá, 1975. *Desarrollo integral de América Latina. Bogota, CELAM, Secretariado General, 1976. 2 v. (Documento CELAM, no. 24)*

Minutes of the discussion at a 1975 meeting that focused on the Catholic Church's response to

Latin America's development needs, the episcopacy's responsibility to work for the protection of human rights, and the economic and social improvement of the disadvantaged.

1176
Consulta Latinoamericana de Iglesia y Sociedad, 2d , El Tabo, Chile, 1966. *Social justice and the Latin churches. Translated by Jorge Lara-Braud. Richmond, Va., John Knox Press [1969]. 137 p.*

Summarizes the discussions and reports presented at the second Latin American Conference on Church and Society, held in 1966 to address issues on human rights and social justice.

1177
Crahan, Margaret. *Salvation through Christ or Marx; religion in revolutionary Cuba. Journal of inter-American studies and world affairs, v. 21, Feb. 1979: 156-184.*

Based on a survey of some 40 Cuban church leaders, both clerical and lay, and of several in-depth studies, the author deftly evaluates general trends among Cuban church members. Unlike other Latin American churches, those in Cuba are said not to have been liberalized. The author predicts increased ideological pressure on Christians, as well as on those holding Afro-Cuban beliefs.

1178
Cussianovich, Alejandro. *Llamados a ser libres. Lima, Centro de Estudios y Publicaciones, Equipo JOC, Empleadas de Hogar, 1974. 209 p. illus. (CEP, no. 9)*

Discusses the exploitation of domestic employees in Peru and throughout Latin America. Demands response from the Catholic Church to their situation.

1179
Davies, John Gordon. *Christians, politics and violent revolution. London, SCM Press, 1976. 216 p.*

Examines the role of the Christian in seeking a revolutionary solution to the problems of political and economic inequalities. Includes references, an index, and an extensive bibliography.

1180
De Medellín a Puebla; los derechos humanos hoy en Latinoamérica. *Las declaraciones y documentos de las iglesias, de la Iglesia Universal y de las Naciones Unidas. 2d ed. completamente renovada. Lima, Centro de Proyección Cristiana, 1979. 228 p. (Cuadernos de teología actual, ciencias sociales y realidad nacional, 2)*

Contains documents on human rights by several churches, including the Roman Catholic, as well as U.N. materials on the subject. The focus, however, is on stands taken by segments of the Catholic Church.

1181
Declaración Universal de los Derechos Humanos. *Acción (Asuncion), v. 8, no. 33, 1977: 1-32.*

Catholic religious exhortation to uphold human rights principles advocated by the Vatican Council and in the Universal Declaration of Human Rights. Includes references to current human rights activities by the Church in American nations.

1182
Della Cava, Ralph. *Fontes para o estudo de catolicismo e sociedade no Brasil. Religão e sociedade, no. 5, 1980: 211-240.*

The first of three contributions which comprise a selective inventory of sources for the study of the Catholic Church and society in Brazil for the 1964 to 1978 period.

1183
Della Cava, Ralph. *A vision of short-term politics and long-term religion: the Roman Catholic Church in Brazil in April 1978. LARU working paper (Toronto), no. 24, June 1978: 10-38.*

Discusses the debate on Catholic Church activities and politics in Brazil in light of the presidential election.

1184
Los derechos humanos, las abuelas y el Papa. *Paz y justicia: boletín informativo del Servicio Paz y Justicia en América Latina, no. 78, agosto/set. 1980: 9-10.*

A letter from the "Abuelas de Plaza de Mayo" of Argentina, appealing on behalf of their grandchildren who have disappeared, to Pope John Paul II during his trip to Brazil. The letter includes dossiers of individual cases.

1185

Dodson, Michael. *The Christian left in Latin American politics. Journal of inter-American studies and world affairs, v. 21, Feb. 1979: 45-68.*

Analyzes diverse points of view about the Catholic Church's potential for promoting social change and human rights. Enumerates several strategies of political action, using Chile and Argentina as specific examples.

1186

Duclerq, Michel. *La Iglesia frente a las dictaduras militares en América Latina. Lima, Comisión Evangélica Latinoamericana de Educación Cristiana, Centro de Documentación y Editorial, 1978. 1 v. (various pagings) (Serie D, no. 2)*

Examines the often antagonistic position of the Catholic Church when confronting military dictatorships in Latin America.

1187

Eldridge, Joseph, and Cressida McKean. *Uncivil strife in El Salvador: landless peasants, official terror, and prophetic witness. Sojourners, v. 6, July 1977: 26-28.*

Report on rights violations in rural El Salvador and on church activity on behalf of peasants.

1188

Exigencias cristãs de uma ordem política. *2a ed. [São Paulo] Edições Paulinas, 1977. 22 p. (Documentos da CNBB, no. 10)*

"Documento aprovado pela XV Assembléia Geral da CNBB, Itaici, 8 a 17 de fevereiro de 1977."

Examination of Christian ethics by Brazilian Catholic bishops. Discusses both the rights and duties of the state and individual freedom and security.

1189

Falconer, Alan D. *Ecumenical notes and documentation: the churches and human rights. One in Christ, v. 13, no. 4, 1977: 321-350.*

Compact reference guide to church thought and activity on human rights from 1967 to 1977. Describes various church organizations, studies, and conferences.

1190

Frenz, Helmut. *Human rights: a Christian viewpoint. Christianity and crisis, v. 36, June 21, 1976: 146-151.*

Portions of an address about the Christian commitment to human rights, delivered by a Lutheran bishop whom the military junta expelled for his activities on behalf of refugees.

1191

Gerety, Peter L. *Examination of human rights and U.S. foreign policy by the Archbishop of Newark, N.J. Maryknoll, v. 71, Nov. 1977: 3-9.*

Not available for annotation.

1192

Geyer, Alan. *A faith for human rights. Circuit rider, v. 2, Apr. 1978: 1, 7-8.*

Criticizes "belated" church interest in human rights. Calls for the U.S. government to lead the search for an international, biblically based consensus defining human rights. The journal is published by the United Methodist Church.

1193

Geyer, Georgie Ann. *From here to eternity: how a priest-congressman and the president of Georgetown University have tried to stop murder, but not necessarily revolution in tiny El Salvador. Washington post magazine, Sept. 10, 1978: 8-15.*

Describes the efforts by the Revs. Timothy Healy and Robert Drinan to focus Washington's attention on the violation of human rights by the Humberto Romero government in El Salvador.

1194

Gheerbrant, Alain. *The rebel church in Latin America. Translated [from French] by Rosemary Sheed; with an introd. by Richard Gott. Harmondsworth, Baltimore, Penguin, 1974. 357 p. (The Pelican Latin America library)*

Translation of L'Église rebelle d'Amérique latine. Describes Pope Paul VI's visit to Bogotá and the impact it had on progressive clergymen in Latin America. Many of these later became actively engaged in promoting the protection of human rights.

1195

Gilfeather, Katherine Anne. *Women religious, the poor, and the institutional church in Chile. Journal of inter-American studies and world affairs, v. 21, Feb. 1979: 129-153.*

A Maryknoll nun examines the tensions and frustrations of religious women within the Catholic Church. Cites documents reflecting the secondary position of women in Latin American society and within the Church and urges attention to these problems.

1196

Gottardi, José, Aux., et al. *La condenación del comunismo y del marxismo por la Iglesia Católica: actualidad y vigencia de la encíclica Divini Redemptoris, ratificada por el Concilio Vaticano II. Montevideo, Barreiro y Ramos [1977 or 1978]. 70 p.*

Papers concerning human rights presented by several prominent religious leaders at a meeting of the Club Católico of Montevideo on March 17, 1977.

1197

Goulet, Denis. Prolegomenon to a policy: thinking about human rights. *Christianity and crisis, v. 37, May 16, 1977: 100-104.*

Describes the ecumenical nature and ethical base of human rights, suggesting that the U.S. formulate a coherent policy with a single standard of judgment for human rights' performance.

1198

Gutierrez, Gustavo. *A theology of liberation: history, politics and salvation. Translated and edited by Sister Caridad Inda*

and John Eagleson. Maryknoll, N.Y., Orbis Books, 1973. 323 p.

Describes Catholic political and social activism and its philosophical underpinnings. Includes Church's concern with human rights. Provides bibliographic references.

1199

Hehir, J. Bryan. *Religious organizations and international affairs. Network quarterly, v. 4, summer 1976: 1-6.*

States that the universal moral character of human rights makes their protection and promotion a logical concern for religious organizations.

1200

Howell, Bruce F. *Toward international freedom of religion: a proposal for change in FCN treaty practice. Journal of law reform, v. 7, spring 1974: 553-574.*

Advocates the establishment of religious freedom as a fundamental human right in international law because current bilateral treaties of Friendship, Commerce and Navigation are limited in their effect.

1201

[Human rights in Latin America]. *Lucha (New York), Oct./Nov. 1978: 1-23.*

Describes the religious response to military repression in Latin America. Concentrates on Argentina and Chile. Journal published by Christians Concerned for Chile and the Latin American Information Service.

1202

La Iglesia y América Latina: aportes pastorales desde el CELAM, conclusiones de los principales encuentros organizados por el CELAM en los diez últimos años. *Bogotá, Consejo Espiscopal Latinoamericano, Secretariado General del CELAM, 1978. v. 1. (various pagings) (Auxiliar para la III Conferencia General del Episcopado Latinoamericano, 2)*

Features the conclusions reached by the second Latin American Bishops Conference.

1203

Instituto de Estudios Políticos para América Latina y África. *Iglesia y seguridad nacional en América Latina.* Madrid, IDOC - España, 1977. 95 p.

Examines human rights issues within the context of the Catholic Church in Latin America with emphasis on the gap that exists between theory and practice. Includes a bibliography.

1204

Intelectuales: apoyo a la Iglesia. *Brasil. Paz y justica: boletín informativo del Servicio de Paz y Justicia en América Latina, no. 78, agosto/set. 1980: 3-8.*

Contains a letter to Pope John Paul II, signed by 3,000 prominent Brazilian intellectuals, expressing support of the Catholic Church in Brazil and its work towards social justice and human rights. Also includes information about comunidades de base in Brazil.

1205

International Movement of Catholic Students. *They will suffer persecution for my cause: 10 years of church-state conflict in Latin America.* Lima, 1979. 320 p.

Chronology of events and Catholic Church statements from 1968 to 1978, regarding injustice and human rights issues in Latin America.

1206

Iriarte, José Joaquín. *La fuerza de la fé: Juan Pablo II en América.* Madrid, Mundo Cristiano, 1979. 161 p.

Chronicles Pope John Paul II's first trip to Latin America in January 1979. Includes photographs and the Pope's speeches and homilies. Points out the human rights import of his message at the opening of the Third General Conference of the Latin American Episcopate at Puebla, Mexico, where the Pope said, "The Church painfully sees the massive increase, at times, of human rights violations in many parts of the world," and then deplored "the materialism that makes the rich richer and the poor each time poorer."

1207

Izquierda Cristiana de Chile. *La voz del pueblo cristiano, marginada de Puebla. Izquierda cristiana (Mexico), v. 5, no. 43: 13-26.*

Guatemalan peasants, Mexican workers from Veracruz, and clandestine Chilean groups describe their plight and problems in their respective countries.

1208

John XXIII, Pope. *Encíclica pacem in terris: sobre la paz mundial. Fundada sobre un orden basado en la verdad y la justicia; la caridad y la libertad.* Santiago, Chile, Arzobispado de Santiago, Vicaría de la Solidaridad [1978] 1 v. (unpaged) (Formación, no. 10)

"Edición conmemorativa del XV aniversario; 11 de abril de 1963 - 11 de abril de 1978."

Describes the moral order of the universe, the necessary rights of man within this order, political power and its relations to society, and family relations. Concludes with specific pastoral recommendations.

1209

John Paul II, Pope. *Pastor universal habló al corazón de América. Separata solidaridad (Chile), feb. 1979: 1-8.*

Official text of Pope John Paul II's inaugural address at the Third Conference of Latin American Bishops in Puebla, Mexico, given on January 28, 1979. Addresses human rights as a central issue.

1210

Latin American bishops discuss human rights. *Washington, Latin American Documentation [1977?] 2 v. (LADOC Keyhole series, no. 15 and no. 16)*

Pastoral letters that include specific accounts of the suppression of political freedoms and human rights in Argentina, Brazil, Chile, El Salvador, Nicaragua, and Paraguay.

1211

The Latin American Church; from Medellín to Puebla. *Documentation and Research Center Chile-America (Rome), no. 43-45, June/July 1978: 1-278.*

Dossier pertaining to the recent preparatory debate of the Third General Conference of the Latin American Episcopate held in Puebla, Mexico in October 1978. The human rights section includes articles on the assassination of Orlando Letelier and the situation of detained and disappeared persons in Chile.

1212

Lepargneur, Hubert. *A Igreja e o reconhecimento dos direitos humanos na história. São Paulo, Brazil, Cortez e Morães, 1977. 139 p.*

Cover title: Declaracão Universal dos Direitos Humanos.

Assesses the historical human rights positions of the Catholic Church from the French Revolution to modern times. Discusses doctrines promoting human rights and ecclesiastical practice, the Church and democracy, the effects of Christianity throughout history, and the Church's actual activities and gains in human rights. The Universal Declaration of Human Rights of the U.N. is included as an appendix.

1213

Lepargneur, Hubert. *Uma Igreja que luta pelos direitos humanos. Convergência, v. 11, mço. 1978: 105-115.*

States that the Church must seek to reduce the gap separating the theory from the practice of human rights.

1214

Lernoux, Penny. *Cry of the people: United States involvement in the rise of fascism, torture, and murder and the persecution of the Catholic Church in Latin America. Garden City, N.Y., Doubleday, 1980. 535 p. maps.*

Describes the opposition of the Catholic Church to the repression and violence of the military regimes in Latin America. Analyzes the role of the U.S. Defense Department, the C.I.A., and corporations in giving rise to these regimes. Includes documentation from the U.S. Congress, Amnesty International, and the Catholic Church.

1215

Lernoux, Penny. *Religious cold war heats up in Latin America. New York, Alicia Patterson Foundation, 1976. 11 p.*

Examines the proposition that the Latin American military regimes, in exchange for Catholic Church support in the war against communism, guarantee the Church's security and provide financial assistance.

1216

Luce, Don. *Oh, freedom! A human rights liturgy. Washington, Clergy and Laity Concerned, Human Rights Coordinating Center [1977?] 12 p.*

Collage of poems, religious scripture, and information on worldwide human rights conditions.

1217

Moltman, Jurgen. *La imagen de Dios y los derechos humanos. Traducción de Raúl López. Cristianismo y sociedad, v. 16, no. 55, 1978: 39-51.*

Presents theological arguments in support of his proposition that the Catholic Church has a special mission to accomplish with regard to the achievement of respect for human rights.

1218

[La nacionalidad]. *Cuadernos jurídicos (Santiago de Chile), dic. 1977: 1-135.*

Unsigned polemic from the Archdiocese of Santiago challenging the military junta's right to expatriate Chilean citizens, who are protected by international legal norms. Includes case studies and a statement of support for the U.N. resolution against torture.

1219

National Assembly of Women Religious. *[Third General Conference of Latin American Bishops]. Probe, v. 8, Apr. 1979: 1-8.*

Observation and commentary on the Third General Conference of Latin American Bishops (CELAM) at Puebla, Mexico. Also discusses the role of nuns and the need for greater social justice. Includes an interview with human rights advocate Bishop Leónidas Proaño of Ecuador.

1220

National Conference of Brazilian Bishops. *Comunicação pastoral o povo de Deus. Sao Paulo, Brazil, Edições Paulinas, 1976. 22 p.*

Pastoral letter written in response to the assassination of two priests and the kidnapping of a bishop in Brazil.

1221

National Conference of Catholic Bishops. *To live in Jesus Christ; a pastoral reflection on the moral life. Washington, United States Catholic Conference, 1976. 48 p.*

Speaks of moral life in the family, the nation, and the community of nations, touching on such topics as employment, women in society, the development of peoples, peace, and human rights.

1222

National Council of Churches, Division of Overseas Ministries, Human Rights Office. *Sounds in struggle: experiences in human rights. [Cincinnati, Ohio, National Council of Churches, Friendship Press, 197?] Phonotape. 30 min.*

This cassette and accompanying booklet relate the experiences of persons and groups who have actively engaged in the struggle for human rights. Such issues as working for political change, solidarity, and encountering human rights violations are poignantly told.

1223

North American Congress on Latin America. *Latin American Christians in the liberation struggle. NACLA's Latin America & empire report, v. 6, Feb. 1972: 11-23.*

Describes some of the diverse tendencies inside the Catholic Church and reproduces documents, including a report on the Dominican Camilista Movement, an interview with a Chilean priest, and a letter from the Peronist Armed Forces (FAP) to the priests of the Third World.

1224

Nute, Betty Richardson. *Hélder Câmara's Latin America. London, Friends Peace and International Relations Committee, 1974. 26 p. illus. (Non-violence in action series)*

Pamphlet biography of a non-violent activist for human rights, who was proposed by British and American Quakers for the 1973 Nobel Peace prize.

1225

Parilla-Bonilla, Antulio. *La Iglesia y los derechos humanos. Nueva sociedad, mayo/jun. 1978: 45-52.*

Not available for annotation.

1226

Paul VI, Pope. *Los derechos humanos: discurso del Papa al cuerpo diplomático acreditado ante La Santa Sede, el 14 de enero. Revista del centro de investigación y acción social (Buenos Aires), v. 27, marzo 1978: 42-45.*

Discusses religious liberty, human dignity and equality.

1227

Paul VI, Pope. *Octogesima adveniens. In Iglesia latinoamericana; política y socialismo. Caracas, Universidad Andrés Bello, 1977. p.9-44. (Col. Manoa, no.2)*

On the 80th anniversary of the papal encyclical Rerum novarum, Pope Paul VI wrote an apostolic letter stressing that Christians should work towards a just society.

1228

Paul VI, Pope. *Octogesima adveniens; apostolic letter. A.A.S., v. 63, 1971: 401-441.*

On the 80th anniversary of the papal encyclical Rerum novarum, Pope Paul VI spoke about its applicability to the twentieth century, especially in the realm of human rights.

1229

Peerman, Dean. *CELAM III; measured steps forward. Christian century, v. 96, Apr. 1979: 373-378.*

Critical but generally laudatory assessment of the final document of the third hemispheric conference of Latin America's Catholic bishops. Sees the document as constituting a clear and unequivocal commitment to the poor and the oppressed.

1230

Poblete, Renato. *From Medellín to Puebla; notes for reflection. Journal of inter-American studies and world affairs,* v. 21, Feb. 1979: 31-44.

Assessment of tension within the Catholic Church, before the meeting at Puebla. Differences over its temporal role have resulted in the development of three trends: Catholic integralism on the right, progressivism inspired by papal and hierarchical documents in the center, and a movement called theology of liberation on the left.

1231

Puebla: moment of decision for the Latin American Church. *Cross country,* v. 28, spring 1978: whole issue.

Deals with the current problems facing the Catholic Church in Latin America. Emphasis is on rights.

1232

Quigley, Thomas. *Brazil: new generals vs. renewal bishops. Christianity and crisis,* v. 34, Apr. 1, 1974: 61-64.

Discusses the schism in the Brazilian Catholic Church between the traditional wing and the Brazilian bishops who fight for human rights, and who sometimes come into conflict with the ruling military.

1233

Rausch, James S. *Human rights: reflections on a twin anniversary. Address to the National Council of Catholic Laity, New Orleans, Oct. 17, 1973. Washington, United States Catholic Conference, National Conference of Catholic Bishops, Publications Office, 1973. [14] p.*

Examines the relationship between the Universal Declaration of Human Rights and the encyclical, Pacem in Terris, of Pope John XXIII.

1234

Roma, J. A. de. *Paz del pueblo: Hélder Câmara. Barcelona, Ediciones Don Bosco [1974?] 63 p. illus. (Cuadernos Edebé, no. 11)*

Study of Brazilian church leader's philosophy of non-violence as a means of reforming the eco-

nomic, political, and social structures of the Third World. Emphasis is on Brazil. Includes a substantial bibliography.

1235

Ruíz García, Samuel. *Los cristianos y la justicia en América Latina. Chiapas, Mexico, CELAM, Secretariado Latinoàmericano, Departamento de Misiones [1975]. 28 p. (Movimiento Internacional de Estudiantes Católicos, Juventud Estudiantil Católica Internacional, no. 4)*

Analysis of current repression, torture, and economic dependency in Latin America in light of the Catholic Church's pledge at the Bishops Conference of Medellín (1968) to social and distributive justice.

1236

Santibáñez, Abraham. *Nueva institucionalidad: el proyecto de los obispos. Hoy (Santiago de Chile),* v. 2, nov. 29/dic. 5, 1978: 8-10.

Deals with the role of the Catholic Church hierarchy in human rights advocacy, particularly after a recent conference of bishops on the same subject.

1237

Schall, James V. *Culture and human rights. America (New York),* v. 138, Jan. 14, 1978: 14-17.

Brief refutation of the cultural relativity of definitions of human rights, in which the author advocates a universal standard of definition similar to that expressed traditionally in Catholic social values. Published in Jesuit journal.

1238

Schilling, Paulo R. *Hélder Câmara. Translation into English by Aida Castagno. Montevideo, Biblioteca de Marcha, 1969. 108 p.*

Not available for annotation.

1239

Segundo, Juan Luis. *Direitos humanos, evangelização e ideologia. Revista eclesiástica brasileira,* v. 37, mço. 1977: 91-105.

Jesuit author explores the arguments in the New Testament for the Catholic Church's defense of human rights in Latin America.

1240

Shelton, D. *Human rights within churches: a survey concerning discrimination within religious organizations. Droits de l'homme: human rights journal, v. 6, 1973: 487-563.*

Not available for annotation.

1241

Silva, Hernando. *¿A donde va el cambio en América Latina? Bogotá, Ediciones Paulinas, 1976. 94 p. (Col. Iglesia liberadora, no. 13)*

Analysis of the Latin American episcopacy's response to the injustices in Latin America, as expressed at the second meeting of Latin American bishops in Medellín. Discusses "comunidades de base." Includes a bibliography.

1242

Simmons, Marlise. *El Arzobispo de El Salvador: la solución es el diálogo, pero la represión lo imposibilita. Proceso (Mexico), enero 15, 1979: 24-25.*

Spanish version of an interview, by a Washington Post correspondent, with Archbishop Oscar Arnulfo Romero about his persecution.

1243

Simposio Internacional sobre Derechos Humanos, Santiago de Chile, 1978. *La Iglesia y la dignidad del hombre. Santiago, Chile, Arzobispado de Santiago, Vicaría de la Solidaridad, 1978. 1 v. (various pagings) (Estudios, no. 4)*

Includes major addresses delivered at the 1978 International Symposium on Human Rights in Santiago, concerning church activities protecting basic rights.

1244

Sinclair, John H., ed. *Protestantism in Latin America: a bibliographical guide. South Pasadena, Calif., William Carey Library [1976]. 414 p.*

Guide to the study of Protestant churches in Latin America. The annotated bibliography provides references in English, Spanish, and Portuguese, as well as useful suggestions concerning basic resources and materials.

1245

Smith, Brian H. *Churches and human rights in Latin America; recent trends in the subcontinent. Journal of inter-American studies and world affairs, v. 21, Feb. 1979: 89-127.*

Examines church programs for human rights in Argentina, Bolivia, Brazil, Chile, and Paraguay. Three issues are analyzed: how and why churches have become involved in human rights, the scope and extent of their work, and the impact of new structures both on society and on the churches themselves.

1246

Theological perspectives on human rights; report on a Lutheran World Federation consultation on human rights. *Geneva, Department of Studies, Lutheran World Federation, 1976. 42 p.*

Presents theological foundations enforcing the observation of human rights in the world and justification for active participation by the churches in the human rights field.

1247

The theology of liberation. *Washington, U.S. Catholic Conference, Division for Latin America [1972?]. 60 p. (LADOC Keyhole series, no. 2)*

Surveys Catholic Church activities in furthering a social reform and the protection of human rights. Asserts the obligation of Christians to bring about needed changes in order to create a just society.

1248

Unitarian Universalist Service Committee. *Investigations in El Salvador. Boston, 1977. 5 p.*

Report on human rights violations, specifically the murder of unarmed civilians, arbitrary arrests, electoral fraud, and religious persecution.

1249

United Presbyterian Church in the U.S.A. *Christian social witness in repressive societies and United States responsibility. New York, United Presbyterian Church in the U.S.A., Unit on Church and Society [1974?] 47 p.*

Background paper and policy statement adopted at the 186th General Assembly of the United Presbyterian Church U.S.A. in 1974. Includes reports on Brazil.

1250

U.S. Catholic Conference. *Resolution of the United States Catholic Conference on the twenty-fifth anniversary of the Universal Declaration of Human Rights. Washington, United States Catholic Conference, Publications Office, 1973. [3] p.*

Informational pamphlet on human rights which includes references to the encyclical, Pacem in Terris, of Pope John XXIII.

1251

U.S. Catholic Conference. *U.S. bishops on human rights in Brazil. LADOC, v. 5, Jan. 1975: 10-12.*

Statements of solidarity with the Brazilian Catholic Church concerning human rights violations in Brazil.

1252

U.S. Catholic Conference. Division of Justice and Peace. *Human rights: a question of conscience. Washington, D.C., 1974. 41 p. (Primer, no. 2)*

General world survey of human rights from a Catholic perspective. Provides case studies of current conditions in various countries including Brazil.

1253

U.S. Catholic Conference. Latin America Documentation. *Latin American bishops discuss human rights. Washington, Latin American Documentation U.S.C.C., 1977. 67 p. (LADOC keyhole series, no. 15 and no. 16)*

Contains pastoral statements that emphasize the need for Christian involvement in combating the political and economic injustices in Argentina, Brazil, Chile, Cuba, El Salvador, and Peru.

1254

U.S. Catholic Conference. Office of International Justice and Peace. *Human rights: human needs; an unfinished agenda. Washington, 1978. 32 p. illus.*

Defines the Catholic Church's perspective on human rights and its commmitment to defend and uphold human rights principles as part of its ministry.

1255

Violence and fraud in El Salvador: a report on current political events in El Salvador. *London, Latin American Bureau, 1977. 37 p.*

Includes sections on political fraud and the persecution of the Catholic Church.

1256

La voz de los pastores latinoamericanos. *Iglesia y política. Paz y justicia: boletín informativo del Servicio Paz y Justicia en América Latina, no. 76, mayo/jun. 1980: 2-8.*

A special section of the bulletin deals with the duty of churches to work towards human rights and social justice goals. The special section will continue in subsequent issues of the newsletter.

1257

When all else fails; Christian arguments on violent revolution. *Edited by IDO-C. Philadelphia, Pilgrim Press, 1970. 230 p. (IDO-C international series)*

Collection of essays on religion and revolution. Among other topics, discusses human liberation and Marxism. Based on the book published originally in Milan as Vangelo violenza rivoluzione. Includes bibliographic references.

1258

Wilde, Alexander. *Ten years of change in the Church; Puebla and the future. Journal of inter-American studies and world affairs, v. 21, Aug. 1979: 299-312.*

Analysis of a ten-year period in which the Catholic Church became increasingly committed to improving the situation of the poor in Latin America and was often found in opposition to state authorities. The Church's stance is considered in light of the recommendations of the

January 1979 Puebla conference of Catholic bishops.

1259

World Council of Churches. Commission of the Churches on International Affairs. *Human rights and Christian responsibility, elements for a better understanding of the problem. Geneva, 1974. 75 p.*

> Background material related to a Consultation of the same title organized by the Commission.

1260

World Council of Churches. Commission of the Churches on International Affairs. *Human rights and Christian responsibility, further perspectives. Geneva, 1974. 79 p.*

> Describes a variety of approaches to human rights in different parts of the world, showing how different socio-economic and political circumstances lead to the establishment of different orders of priority.

1261

World Council of Churches. Commission of the Churches on International Affairs. *Human rights and Christian responsibility; 2. Geneva, 1974. 101 p.*

Second dossier of background materials that discusses the role of religion in relation to human rights. Among the articles included is "A Provisional Typology of Human Rights Violations in Latin America and Action Strategies for Combatting Repression."

1262

World Council of Churches. Commission of the Churches on International Affairs. *Human rights and Christian responsibility; report of the Consultation. Geneva, 1974. 23 p.*

> Reflects on the status of human rights throughout the world including Latin America.

1263

World Council of Churches. Commission of the Churches on International Affairs. *Religious freedom; main statements by the World Council of Churches, 1948-1975. Geneva, [1975?] 75 p.*

> Statements on the development of ecumenical thinking concerning human rights, based mainly on the 1965 publication, "Main Ecumenical Statements on Principles Concerning Religious Freedom," prepared by the World Council of Churches Secretariat on Religious Liberty.

International Commission of Jurists

1264

Dolan, Jo Ann, and Maria Laetitia van den Assum. *Torture and the 5th U.N. Congress on crime prevention. International Commission of Jurists. Review, June 1975: 55-64.*

Overview of the use of torture by law enforcement agencies, a subject discussed at the 5th U.N. Congress on the Prevention of Crime and the Treatment of Offenders, meeting in Toronto, September 1 to 12, 1975. Analyzes reasons for the use of torture, the work of Amnesty International in this field, the U.N.'s minimum standards on torture, and its Sub-Commission on the Prevention of Discrimination and Protection of Minorities.

1265

Geneva Conference on Human Rights. International Commission of Jurists. *Bulletin, Mar. 1968: 1-7.*

Discusses the broad exchange of views concerning the promotion and protection of human rights throughout the world that took place during the Conference of Non-Governmental Organizations, Geneva, January 29 to 31, 1968.

1266

Herrera, Felipe. *L'ordre social international et les droits de l'homme. International Commission of Jurists. Journal, v. 9, June 1968: 16-21.*

Discussion of the Universal Declaration of Human Rights with emphasis on its civil, political, social and cultural aspects. Notes the distance between the objectives in the document and actual global practice.

1267

International Commission of Jurists. *American Convention on Human Rights. In its Review, Mar. 1970: 1-5, 44-62.*

Includes basic text of the Convention, with commentary outlining the procedures for individual petitioning that are provided for in Part II under "Means of Protection."

1268

International Commission of Jurists. *The application in Latin America of international declarations and conventions relating to asylum: a study. Geneva, 1975. 64 p.*

Contains an analysis of asylum and extradition under international law, including background information on the refugee situation in eight countries, individual cases of offenses against refugees, and comments and conclusions. An appendix sets out the relevant provisions of various Latin American conventions and declarations on asylum.

1269

International Commission of Jurists. *Draft principles on the freedom to leave any country and return to one's own country. In its Review, Dec. 1973: 61-64.*

Discusses draft principles of the U.N.'s Economic and Social Council May 18, 1973 Resolution 1778 (LIV).

1270

International Commission of Jurists. *Le droit des personnes arretées de communiquer avec ceux qu'il leur necessaire de consulter pour assurer leur défense ou proteger leur intérêts essentiels. In its Revue, v. 5, summer 1964: 109-130.*

Report of the I.C.J. to the U.N. Division of the Rights of Man, examining the nature and exercise of the right of those accused of criminal violations to communicate with their relatives, friends and legal advisers in ordinary or emergency situations.

1271

International Commission of Jurists. *Gross violations of human rights. Geneva, 1973. 27 p.*

Practical guide to filing communications concerning human rights with the U.N. and the International Commission of Jurists.

1272

International Commission of Jurists. *Human rights in the world: South America (Chile, Argentina, Uruguay, Bolivia, Brazil, Colombia). In its Review, Dec. 1973: 11-17.*

Not available for annotation.

1273

International Commission of Jurists. *The Inter-American Convention on Human Rights. In its Review, Dec. 1978: 27-30.*

Outlines the Convention, also called the Pact of San José, enacted in 1978, which the International Commission of Jurists considers an advance over the regional instruments relating to human rights available in the hemisphere.

1274

International Commission of Jurists. *Latin America; a crisis for democracy: Brazil and Bolivia. In its Review, Dec. 1969: 15-20.*

Studies the legal provisions suspending fundamental guarantees of individual freedom established by the military regimes in Brazil and Bolivia.

1275

International Commission of Jurists. *Latin America: dangerous swing back to militarism. In its Review, Mar. 1969: 10-15.*

Presents a general overview of the political and legal situation in Latin American countries whose constitutional governments have been overthrown by military regimes, such as Brazil, Peru and Panama.

1276

International Commission of Jurists. *Latin America: expulsion, the rights to return, passports. In its Review, June 1975: 3-8.*

States that the practice of expelling both nationals and aliens, preventing them from re-entering a country, and depriving them of passports is increasing in Latin American countries such as Bolivia, Chile, Paraguay, Peru, and Uruguay.

1277

International Commission of Jurists. *Law and the prevention of torture. In its Review, Dec. 1973: 23-27.*

Based upon a report given by the Secretary General of the International Commission of Jurists to a Conference on Torture that was organized by the British Section of Amnesty International in London, October 20, 1973.

1278

International Commission of Jurists. *The legal protection of privacy: a comparative survey of ten countries. International social science bulletin, v. 24, 1972: 417-583.*

Latin American countries included in the survey are Mexico, Venezuela, Argentina, and Brazil.

1279

International Commission of Jurists. *Loss of nationality and exile. In its Review, June 1974: 22-27.*

Discusses the loss of nationality and exile as penalties and the serious consequences these entail, as well as efforts since World War II to remedy these ills.

1280

International Commission of Jurists. *Military regimes in Latin America. In its Review, Dec. 1976: 13-26.*

Examines the authoritarian and anti-juridical features of the following military regimes in the 1960's and 1970's: Paraguay, Brazil, Peru, Bolivia, Uruguay, Chile, and Argentina.

1281

International Commission of Jurists. *Minimum treatment of prisoners. In its Review, Dec. 1969: 46-59.*

Reproduces in full the Standard Minimum Rules for the Treatment of Prisoners.

1282

International Commission of Jurists. *Principles of equality in the administration of justice. In its Review, June 1973: 57-62.*

Gives in full the principles of equality in the administration of justice that were approved during the 29th session of the U.N. Commission on Human Rights, Geneva in 1973.

1283

International Commission of Jurists. *The Rule of Law and human rights. New York, 1966. 83 p.*

Presents principles and definitions as elaborated during the congresses and conferences that were held under the auspices of the International Commission of Jurists, 1955 to 1966, rearranging them according to subject matter with cross references to the principal human rights conventions. Includes index.

1284

International Commission of Jurists. *The Rule of Law in South America. In its Review, Dec. 1973: 11-17.*

Brief survey of Argentina, Uruguay, Bolivia, Brazil and Colombia during 1973.

1285

International Commission of Jurists. *Torture and other violations of human rights as international crimes. In its Review, Dec. 1976: 41-50.*

Examines a 1976 discussion by the International Law Commission concerning human rights violations as international crimes. Includes draft texts of the articles on state responsibility.

1286

International Commission of Jurists. *Torture continues. In its Review, June 1973: 10-12.*

States that one common feature of countries where torture is widely used is that there is no effective judicial control of the executive. Suggests safeguards.

1287

International Commission of Jurists. *U.N. Commission on Human Rights. In its Review, June 1978: 29-35.*

Describes the work of the Commission during its 34th session, held in 1978. Among the decisions and resolutions adopted were the creation of a voluntary trust fund to aid victims of human rights violations in Chile, and a request that member states set up national institutions dedicated to the promotion and protection of human rights.

1288

International Commission of Jurists. *The U.N. Sub-Commission on discrimination and Minorities. In its Review, Dec. 1975: 41-45.*

Includes discussions concerning human rights of the 28th session of the Sub-Commission, Geneva, 1975, with emphasis on the human rights situation in Chile.

1289

International Commission of Jurists. Secretary General. *Chile and Uruguay: contrasts and comparisons. In its Review, June 1974: 5-7.*

Reports on an International Commission of Jurists' mission to Chile and a joint Amnesty International and International Commission of Jurists visit to Uruguay in 1974.

1290

International Seminar on Human Rights, Their Protection and the Rule of Law in a One-party State, Dar-es-Salaam, Tanzania, 1978. *London, Search Press in cooperation with the International Commission of Jurists, 1978. 133 p.*

At head of title: Human rights in a one-party state.

Organized by the International Commission of Jurists in 1976, this seminar dealt with the protection of civil rights.

1291

MacDermott, Niall. *The work of the International Commission of Jurists. Index on censorship, v. 1, autumn/winter 1972: 155-159.*

Personal essay by the Commission's Secretary General about this important non-governmental organization dedicated to the promotion of human rights through legal means. Includes Commission's composition and place within the framework of international organizations.

1292

Marcic, René. *Devoirs et limitations apportées aux droits. International Commission of Jurists. Journal, v. 9, June 1968: 68-82.*

Study of the Universal Declaration of Human Rights, including Article 29, the individual and the community, and Article 30, limitations and freedom from suppression.

1293

O'Donnell, Daniel. *States of exception. International Commission of Jurists. Review, Dec. 1978: 52-60.*

Examines states of exception, including what various legal systems refer to as state of emergency, internal war, crisis, or martial law, in light of international instruments such as the International Covenant on Civil and Political Rights.

1294

Suckow, Samuel. *Conference on Humanitarian Law; phase 2. International Commission of Jurists. Review, June 1975: 42-54.*

Examines the work of the Second Session of the Diplomatic Conference on the Reaffirmation and Development of International Humanitarian Law Applicable in Armed Conflicts, Geneva, 1975.

1295

Suckow, Samuel. *The development of international humanitarian law: a case study. International Commission of Jurists. Review, June 1974: 50-57.*

Describes the work accomplished in the first session of the Diplomatic Conference on the Reaffirmation and Development of International Humanitarian Law, Geneva, February 20 to March 29, 1974. Discusses the updating of the rules of war in light of experience since the adoption of the Four Geneva Conventions in 1949.

1296

Suckow, Samuel. *The development of international humanitarian law: concluded. International Commission of Jurists. Review, Dec. 1977: 46-62.*

Examines the Final Act of the Conference on the Reaffirmation and Development of International Humanitarian Law, June 10, 1977.

1297

Suckow, Samuel. *Humanitarian Law Conference. International Commission of Jurists. Review, June 1976: 51-60.*

Progress report on the Third Session of the Diplomatic Conference on the Reaffirmation and Development of International Humanitarian Law Applicable in Armed Conflicts, Geneva, April 21 to June 11, 1976.

1298

U.N. and International Commission of Jurists. *Inter-American Convention on Human Rights. International Commission of Jurists. Review, June 1976: 23-24.*

Short commentary on the structure of the Inter-American Convention on Human Rights and its functions.

Organization of American States

1299

Inter-American Specialized Conference on Human Rights, San Jose, Costa Rica, 1969. *American Convention on Human Rights. Washington, Organization of American States, General Secretariat, 1970. [28] p. (Organization of American States. Official records. OEA/Ser. K/XVI/1.1 doc. 65 rev. 1 corr. 2)*

Discusses various basic human rights and reviews the organization and activities of the Inter-American Commission on Human Rights and the Inter-American Court of Human Rights.

1300

Inter-American Specialized Conference on Human Rights, San Jose, Costa Rica, 1969. *Final act. Washington, Organization of American States, General Secretariat, 1970. 18 p. (Organization of American States. Official records. OEA/Ser. C/VI.18.1)*

Contains background information on the Conference, resolutions and recommendations approved, and statements by various governments on human rights.

1301

Inter-American Specialized Conference on Human Rights. San Jose, Costa Rica, 1969. *Final act. Washington, Organization of American States, General Secretariat, 1970. 15 p. (Organization of American States. Official records. OEA/Ser. K/XVI/1.1 doc. 70 rev. 1 corr. 1)*

Establishes two working committees to study human rights protection and to revise various draft amendments from recent conventions on human rights submitted by the Inter-American Council of Jurists, the Inter-American Commission on Human Rights, and the governments of Chile and Uruguay.

1302

Inter-American Specialized Conference on Human Rights, San Jose, Costa Rica, 1969. *Report. Washington, Organization of American States, General Secretariat, 1978.*

534 p. (Organization of American States. Official records. OEA/Ser. K/XVI/1.2)

Not available for annotation.

1303

Organization of American States. *Human rights in the American States. Study prepared in accordance with Resolution XXVII of the Tenth Inter-American Conference. Preliminary ed. Washington, 1960. [232] p.*

A complete set of resolutions and studies on human rights prepared under O.A.S. sponsorship up to 1960. Includes bibliographical footnotes.

1304

Organization of American States. Council. *Sesión solemne del Consejo de la Organización con motivo del XX aniversario de la Declaración Universal de los Derechos Humanos, 11 de diciembre de 1968. Washington, Pan American Union, General Secretariat, 1968. 11 p.*

Contains speeches delivered by the President of the Council of the O.A.S., the President of the Inter-American Commission on Human Rights, and the Secretary of the General Secretariat of the O.A.S.

1305

Organization of American States. Council. *Transition from the present Inter-American Commission on Human Rights to the Commission provided for in the American Convention of Human Rights. Washington, 1978. 2 p. (Organization of American States. Official records. OEA/Ser.G.CP/ Res. 253/78 [343/78])*

Text of the resolution which decided that the Inter-American Commission on Human Rights shall continue to exercise its duties until a new Commission is duly installed.

1306

Organization of American States. General Secretariat. *Declaración Americana de los Derechos y Deberes del Hombre...vigésimo quinto aniversario. Washington, 1973. [9] p.*

Contains text in Spanish and English of the American Declaration of the Rights and Duties of Man as adopted at the 9th International

Conference of the O.A.S. (Final act, Resolution XXX).

1307

Organization of American States. General secretariat. *La Organización de los Estados Americanos y los derechos humanos, 1960-1967.* Washington, 1972. 657 p.

Indispensable Spanish-English volume which assembles the basic documents of the O.A.S. pertaining to human rights, from the establishment of the Inter-American Commission on Human Rights up to 1968, the U.N.'s International Year for Human Rights. Includes bibliographies.

1308

Organization of American States. Inter-American Commission on Human Rights. *Annual report; 1978.* Washington, Organization of American States, General Secretariat, 1979. 179 p. (Organization of American States. Official records. OEA/Ser. L/V/II.47 doc. 13 rev. 1)

Section 2, part 1-2 provides information given by some member states on the progress achieved in the realization of the goals set forth in the American Declaration of the Rights and Duties of Man. Discusses areas in which further steps are needed. Section 2, part 3 describes the activities of the Commission during 1978 including its "in loco" observations in El Salvador, Haiti, and Nicaragua. Section 2, part 4 examines the development of the human rights situation in Chile, Panama, Paraguay, and Uruguay.

1309

Organization of American States. *Inter-American Commission on Human Rights. Annual report; 1979-1980.* Washington, Organization of American States, General Secretariat, 1980. 153 p. (Organization of American States. Official records. OEA/Ser. L/V/II.50 doc. 13 rev. 1)

Brief summary of the Commission's origins and principal activities. Contains reports on progress towards human rights objectives provided by several governments at the Commission's request.

1310

Organization of American States. Inter-American Commission on Human Rights. *Anotación sobre el*

Proyecto de Convención Interamericana sobre Protección de Derechos Humanos. Washington, Pan American Union, General Secretariat, 1969. 57 p. (Organization of American States. Official records. OEA/Ser. L/V/II.19 doc. 53)

Reviews the project in light of the current human rights activities of the O.A.S. Includes an analysis of the Preamble and text.

1311

Organization of American States. Inter-American Commission on Human Rights. *La Comisión Interamericana de Derechos Humanos; ¿que es y como funciona?* Washington, Organization of American States, General Secretariat, 1970. [8] p.

Outlines the history, nature, organization and functions of the Commission, as well as the requirements that must be met by the petitioners in denouncing human rights violations.

1312

Organization of American States. Inter-American Commission on Human Rights. *Comparative study of the International Covenants on Human Rights together with the Optional Protocol to the International Covenant on Civil and Political Rights adopted by the United Nations (December 1966), the Draft Convention on Human Rights of the Int er-American Council of Jurists (Fourth Meeting 1959), and the text of the amendments to the IACJ draft adopted by the Inter-American Commission on Human Rights (October 196 6 and January 1967).* Washington, Pan American Union, General Secretariat, 1968. 133 p. (Organization of American States. Official records. OEA/Ser. L/V/II.19 doc. 4)

Contains the discussions of human rights in the three texts presented side by side for analysis and comparison purposes.

1313

Organization of American States. *Inter-American Commission on Human Rights. La Convención Americana sobre Derechos Humanos.* Washington, Organization of American States, General Secretariat, 1980. 248 p.

Eight papers presented at a conference on human rights held in San José, Costa Rica, in 1979. Topics include conflicts between international and national legal codes, a comparison of European and American contentions, and U.N. mechanisms for protecting human rights. Included also is a reprint of the American Convention.

1314

Organization of American States. Inter-American Commission on Human Rights. *El derecho de petición (segundo informe); documento de antecedentes. Preparado por la Secretaría de la Comisión Interamericana de Derechos Humanos con una introducción por el relator Dr. Durward V. Sandifer, Vice-Presidente de la Comisión.* Washington, Organization of American States, General Secretariat, 1970. 145 p. (Organization of American States. Official records. OEA/Ser. L/V/II.24 doc. 10)

Discusses historical aspects of and juridical observations on the right to petition in human rights violations. Includes extensive appendixes and constitutional documents.

1315

Organization of American States. *Inter-American Commission on Human Rights. Estatuto de la Comisión Inter-Americana de Derechos Humanos.* Washington, Organization of American States, General Secretariat, 1968, 1 v., various pagings. (Organization of American States. Official records. OEA/Ser. L/V/II.14 doc. 33 rev. 2)

Not available for annotation.

1316

Organization of American States. Inter-American Commission on Human Rights. *Examen comparado de los proyectos de Convención sobre Derechos Humanos del Consejo Interamericano de Jurisconsultos, aprobado durante su cuarta reunión, Santiago de Chile 1959; y de los presentados por Uruguay y por Chile a la Segunda Conferencia Interamericana Extraordinaria, Río de Janeiro 1965: derechos civiles y políticos.* Washington, Pan Pan American Union, General Secretariat, 1966. 29 p. (Organization of American States. Official records. OEA/Ser. L/V/II.14 doc. 7 corr.)

Texts of the discussions pertaining to civil and political rights in the three documents are printed side by side for analysis and comparison purposes.

1317

Organization of American States. Inter-American Commission on Human Rights. *Examen comparado de los proyectos de convención sobre derechos humanos del Consejo Interamericano de Jurisconsultos, aprobado durante su cuarta*

reunión, Santiago de Chile 1959; y de los presentados por Uruguay y por Chile a la Segunda Conferencia Interamericana Extraordinaria, Río de Janeiro 1965: derechos económicos, sociales y culturales. Washington, Pan American Union, General Secretariat, 1966. 30 p.(Organization of American States. Official records. OEA/Ser. L/V/II.15 doc. 2)

Analyzes, using a side-by-side presentation format, the treatment each of the three documents gives to basic economic, social, and cultural rights.

1318

Organization of American States. Inter-American Commission on Human Rights. *Examen comparado de los proyectos de convención sobre derechos humanos del Consejo Inter-Americano de Jurisconsultos, aprobado durante su cuarta reunión de Chile 1959; y los presentados por Uruguay y por Chile a la Segunda Conferencia Inter-American a Extraordinaria, Río de Janeiro 1965: medidas de aplicación y cláusulas.* Washington, Pan American Union, General Secretariat, 1966. 47 p.

Continuation of side-by-side comparison of the three documents.

1319

Organization of American States. Inter-American Commission on Human Rights. *First report on trade union freedom. Prepared by Dr. Justino Jiménez de Aréchaga, member of the Inter-American Commission on Human Rights.* Washington, Organization of American States, General Secretariat, 1971. 113 p. (Organization of American States. Official records. OEA/Ser. L/V/II.24 doc. 2)

Specifies the scope of trade union freedom and explains how it has been recognized and protected, especially at the international level.

1320

Organization of American States. *Inter-American Commission on Human Rights. Handbook of existing rules pertaining to human rights.* Washington, Organization of American States, General Secretariat, 1979. 74 p. (Organization of American States. Official records. OEA/Ser. L/V/II.23 doc. 21 rev. 6)

Compilation of declarations and current rules of the O.A.S. concerning the protection of human rights. Includes appendixes on statutes and regulations such as the American Declaration of the Rights and Duties of Man and the Statute of the Inter-American Commission on Human Rights. Also available in Spanish.

1321

Organization of American States. Inter-American Commission on Human Rights. *Handbook of existing rules pertaining to human rights. Updated to July 1980. Washington, Organization of American States, General Secretariat, 1980. 147 p. (Organization of American States. Official records. OEA/Ser. L/V/11.50 doc. 6)*

Contains the texts of the instruments of ratification of human rights conventions by 16 countries who are O.A.S. members. Includes the regulations of the Inter-American Commission on Human Rights and a "model complaint".

1322

Organization of American States. Inter-American Commission on Human Rights. *Human rights and representative democracy. Washington, Pan American Union, General Secretariat, 1965. 15 p. (Organization of American States. Official records. OEA/Ser. L/V/II.24)*

Short commentary on a report by Durward V. Sandifer concerning the relationship between human rights and effective representative democracy. Points out that without basic rights men are dependent on the whim of those who seize power.

1323

Organization of American States. *Inter-American Commission on Human Rights. Informe Anual de la Comisión Interamericana de Derechos Humanos, 1979-1980. Washington, Pan American Union, General Secretariat, 1980. 145 p. (Organization of American States. Official records. OEA/Ser. L/V/II.50 doc. 13, rev. 1).*

Describes the origin and juridical basis of the Commission, presents its new statutes and regulations, reviews its activities for 1979, and provides a listing of information supplied by member states.

1324

Organization of American States. Inter-American Commission on Human Rights. *Informe anual de la Comisión Interamericana de Derechos Humanos, 1978.*

Washington, Organización de los Estados Americanos, Secretaría General, 1979. 180 p. (Organization of American States. Official records. OEA/Ser. L/V/II.47 doc. 13 rev. 1)

Annual report of the Inter-American Commission on Human Rights. Includes explanation of goals and authority, reports by various countries about human rights achievements, results of the Commission's inquiries into human rights violations in El Salvador, Haiti and Nicaragua, and surveys of human rights developments in Chile, Panama, Paraguay and Uruguay. Original in Spanish.

1325

Organization of American States. Inter-American Commission on Human Rights. *Informe de la Organización de Estados Americanos a la Conferencia Internacional sobre Derechos Humanos. Washington, Organization of American States, General Secretariat, 1968. 1 v. (Organization of American States. Official records. OEA/Ser. L/V/I.5)*

Not available for annotation.

1326

Organization of American States. *Inter-American Commission on Human Rights. Informe sobre la situación de los derechos humanos en Argentina. Washington, 1980. 289 p. (Organization of American States. Official records. OEA/Ser. L/V/II.49, doc. 19)*

Report of human rights violations in Argentina from 1975 to 1979 drawn from interviews held by representatives of the Commission with former political prisoners and their relatives in the fall of 1979. Includes specific recommendations.

1327

Organization of American States. Inter-American Commission on Human Rights. *The Organization of American States and human rights, 1960-1967. Washington, Organization of American States, General Secretariat, 1972. 675 p.*

Comprehensive summary of the work done by the Inter- American Conference on Human Rights from its origins in 1960 to the designated Human Rights Year of 1968. Includes reports on individual countries, specific studies concerning

ORGANIZATION OF AMERICAN STATES 151

human rights in the Americas, and other relevant documents.

1328

Organization of American States. Inter-American Commission on Human Rights. *Program of the Inter-American Commission on Human Rights in joining in the observance in 1971 of the International Year for Action to Combat Racism and Racial Discrimination. Washington, Organization of American States, General Secretariat, 1970. 2 p. (Organization of American States. Official records. OEA/Ser. L/V/II.24 doc. 14)*

"Approved by the Inter-American Commission on Human Rights at the tenth meeting, held on October 22, 1970."

Outlines program for combating racism and racial discrimination, including a special meeting of the Commission, publication of a commemorative pamphlet, approval of a resolution and the organization of a symposium.

1329

Organization of American States. Inter-American Commission on Human Rights. *Reglamento de la Comisión Interamericana de Derechos Humanos. Washington, Organization of American States, General Secretariat, 1967. 1 v. (Organization of American States. Official records. OEA/Ser. L/V/II.17 doc. 26)*

Not available for annotation.

1330

Organization of American States. Inter-American Commission on Human Rights. *Regulations; as amended in 1961, 1962 and 1966. Washington, Pan American Union, General Secretariat, 1966. 10 p.*

These regulations were approved by the Commission during the 10th and 12th sessions, held April 26 to 27, 1966.

1331

Organization of American States. *Inter-American Commission on Human Rights. Report on the situation regarding human rights in the Dominican Republic. Washington, Pan American Union, General Secretariat, 1962. 79p. (Organization of American States. Official records. OEA/Ser. L/V/II.4, doc.32)*

Continues series of reports on the status of human rights in the Americas.

1332

Organization of American States. Inter-American Commission on Human Rights. *Report on the work accomplished by the Inter-American Commission on Human Rights during its nineteenth session (special); July 1 through July 11, 1968. Washington, Organization of American States, General Secretariat, 1969. 97 p. (Organization of American States. Official records. OEA/Ser. L/V/II.19 doc. 51)*

Provides minutes from the Commission's 19th session. Contains a review of the human rights situation in the Americas as well as background information on and a preliminary text of the Inter-American Convention on the Protection of Human Rights.

1333

Organization of American States. *Inter-American Commission on Human Rights. Report on the work accomplished by the Inter-American Commission on Human Rights during its twentieth session; December 2 through 24, 1968. Washington, Organization of American States, General Secretariat, 1969.1 v.*

Continuation of series concerning the human rights situation in the American countries.

1334

Organization of American States. Inter-American Commission on Human Rights. *Report on the work accomplished by the Inter-American Commission on Human Rights during its twenty-first session, April 7-17, 1969. Washington, Organization of American States, General Secretariat, 1970. 60 p. (Organization of American States. Official records. OEA/Ser. L/V/II.21 doc. 27)*

Reviews the Inter-American Convention on Human Rights project. Includes correspondence directed to the Commission, as well as an examination of human rights in Cuba, Haiti, and other American nations.

1335

Organization of American States. Inter-American Commission on Human Rights. *Report on the work accomplished by the Inter-American Commission on Human Rights during its twenty-second session; first and second parts;*

August 5-7 and November 7-22, 1969. Washington, Organization of American States, General Secretariat, 1970. 45 p. (Organization of American States. Official records. OEA /Ser. L/V/II.22 doc. 15 add. 1)

First part of the session was devoted to analyzing the human rights situation in El Salvador and Honduras. During the second part of the session the Commission acted as an advisor to the Inter-American Specialized Conference on Human Rights.

1336

Organization of American States. Inter-American Commission on Human Rights. *Report on the work accomplished by the Inter-American Commission on Human Rights during its twenty-third session; April 6-16, 1970. Washington, Organization of American States, General Secretariat, 1970. 50 p. (Organization of American States. Official records. OEA/Ser. L/V/II.23 doc. 27)*

Reports on human rights in El Salvador, Honduras, and Cuba. Also includes a series of provisions approved by the Commission relating to the establishment and organization of national committees on human rights for each of the member nations.

1337

Organization of American States. Inter-American Commission on Human Rights. *Report on the work by the Inter-American Commission on Human Rights during its twenty-fourth session; October 13-22, 1970. Washington, Organization of American States, General Secretariat, 1971. 59 p. (Organization of American States. Official records. OEA/Ser. L/II.24 doc. 32 rev. corr.)*

Discusses terrorism for political or ideological purposes as a violation of human rights, the first report on Trade Union Freedom (OEA/Ser. L/II.24 doc. 2, May 7, 1971), and the second report on The Right of Petition (OEA/Ser. L/II.24 doc. 10).

1338

Organization of American States. Inter-American Commission on Human Rights. *Report on the work accomplished by the Inter-American Commission on Human Rights during its twenty-fifth session; March 1-12, 1971. Washington, Organization of American States, General*

Secretariat, 1971. 50 p. (Organization of American States. Official records. OEA/Ser. L/V/II.25 doc. 41 rev.)

Contains a study of the human rights situation in the Americas and the Commission's general work program, including its position regarding the right to an education, and the implications of technological development of human rights.

1339

Organization of American States. Inter-American Commission on Human Rights. *Report on the work accomplished by the Inter-American Commission on Human Rights during its twenty-sixth session; October 27-November 4, 1971. Washington, Organization of American States, General Secretariat, 1972. 65 p. (Organization of American States. Official records. OEA/Ser. L/V/II.26 doc. 37 rev. 1)*

Continuation of series on human rights situations in the American countries.

1340

Organization of American States. Inter-American Commission on Human Rights. *Report on the work accomplished by the Inter-American Commission on Human Rights during its twenty-seventh session; February 28 through March 8, 1972. Washington, Organization of American States, General Secretariat, 1973. 70 p. (Organization of American States. Official records. OEA/Ser. L/V/II.27 doc. 42 rev. 1)*

Continuation of series concerning the human rights situation in the Americas.

1341

Organization of American States. Inter-American Commission on Human Rights. *Report on the work accomplished by the Inter-American Commission on Human Rights during its twenty-eighth session (special), May 1-5, 1972. Washington, Organization of American States, General Secretariat, 1972. 42 p. (Organization of American States. Official records. OEA/Ser. L/V/II.28 doc. 24 rev. 1)*

Considers several cases of alleged violations of human rights in the Western Hemisphere, especially in Brazil, and a report on the exhaustion of internal legal remedies.

1342

Organization of American States. Inter-American Commission on Human Rights. *Report on the work accomplished by the Inter-American Commission on Human Rights during its twenty-ninth session, October 16-27, 1972. Washington, Organization of American States, General Secretariat, 1972.69 p. (Organization of American States. Official records. OEA/Ser. L/V/II.29 doc. 40 rev. 1)*

Reviews the communications received and the cases under consideration since the 27th session and indicates the decisions that were taken. Includes revisions made on the Commission's general work program as well as a discussion of the program.

1343

Organization of American States. Inter-American Commission on Human Rights. *Report on the work accomplished by the Inter-American Commission on Human Rights at its thirtieth session; April 16-27, 1973. Washington, Organization of American States, General Secretariat, 197 3. 69 p. (Organization of American States. Official records. OEA/Ser. L/V/II.30 doc. 45 rev. 1)*

Reviews communications addressed to the Commission, especially those involving specific cases under examination, as well as the general work program of the Commission.

1344

Organization of American States. Inter-American Commission on Human Rights. *Report on the work accomplished at its thirty-first session, Bogotá and Cali, Colombia; October 15-25, 1973. Washington, Organization of American States, General Secretariat, 1974. 83 p. (Organization of American States. Official records. OEA/Ser. L/V/II.31)*

Continuation of series on human rights situations in American countries.

1345

Organization of American States. Inter-American Commission on Human Rights. *Report on the work accomplished by the Inter-American Commission on Human Rights during its thirty-second session; April 8-18, 1974. Washington, Organization of American States, General Secretariat, 1975.74 p. (Organization of American States. Official records. OEA/Ser. L/V/11.32 doc. 31 rev. 1)*

Considers communications assessing the human rights situations in various member nations directed to the Commission during 1973. Discusses the right to education and the development

of science, technology and human rights. Includes an appendix of human rights documents.

1346

Organization of American States. Inter-American Commission on Human Rights. *Report on the work accomplished by the Inter-American Commission on Human Rights during its thirty-third session; July 22-August 2, 1974. Washington, Organization of American States, General Secretariat, 1975. 28 p. (Organization of American States. Official records. OEA/Ser. L/V/II.33 doc. 15 rev. 1)*

Discusses the Commission's inquiries with Chilean government authorities and representative organizations concerning their human rights policies, meetings with lawyers and wives of detained or disappeared persons, the communications they received concerning the Chilean human rights situation, and their other activities in Chile such as visits to jails.

1347

Organization of American States. Inter-American Commission on Human Rights. *Report on the work accomplished by the Inter-American Commission on Human Rights during its thirty-fourth session; October 15-30, 1974. Washington, Organization of American States, General Secretariat, 1975.83 p. (Organization of American States. Official records. OEA/Ser. L/V/II.34 doc. 30 rev. 1)*

Report, approved unanimously, regarding the situation of human rights in Chile. Includes communications received from Colombia, Cuba, Chile, Nicaragua, Peru, and Uruguay.

1348

Organization of American States. Inter-American Commission on Human Rights. *Report on the work accomplished by the Inter-American Commission on Human Rights during its thirty-fifth session; May 20-30, 1975. Washington, Organization of American States, General Secretariat, 1976. 131 p. (Organization of American States. Official records. OEA/Ser. L/V/II.35 doc. rev. 1)*

Includes a draft report regarding the human rights situation in Cuba, a resolution approved by the O.A.S. General Assembly on human rights in Chile, as well as an analysis of human rights violation cases in a number of Latin American countries.

1349

Organization of American States. Inter-American Commission on Human Rights. *Situation of political refugees in America: information received from the government.* Washington, Pan American Union, General Secretariat, 1964. 7 p.

Not available for annotation.

1350

Organization of American States. Inter-American Commission on Human Rights. *Veinte años de evolución de los derechos humanos. Mexico, Universidad Nacional Autónoma de México, Instituto de Investigaciones Jurídicas, 1974. 603 p. (Serie G - Estudios doctrinales, Instituto de Investigaciones Jurídicas, no. 5)*

Contains essays on the general problem of the international protection of human rights and the outlook for human rights in specific countries and regions. Collected at a seminar sponsored by Mexico's foreign secretary and the Inter-American Commission on Human Rights.

1351

Organization of American States. Inter-American Commission on Women. *La acción de la CIM, las libertades sindicales y los derechos humanos. [Colaboración: Alberto Valdivia] Washington, Secretaría General de la Organización de los Estados Americanos, 1979. 59 p. illus.*

Defines and examines trade union rights and international instruments designed to protect them.

1352

Organization of American States. Inter-American Commission on Women. *Guía básica de acción sindical. Washington, Secretaría General de la Organización de los Estados Americanos, 1979. 72 p. illus.*

General discussion of trade unions and their protection. Appendixes include international instruments to safeguard workers' rights.

1353

Organization of American States. *Inter-American Court of Human Rights. Informe Anual de la Corte Inter-Americana de Derechos Humanos a la Asamblea General, 1980. Washington, Organization of American States, General Secretariat, 1980. 55 p. (Organization of American States. Official records. OEA/Ser. L/V/II.50 doc. 13 rev.1)*

A historical review of the origin, structure, competence, and activities of the court. Accompanied by appendixes that include the court's statutes and rules, speeches by the presidents of Venezuela and Costa Rica, and a country by country review of endorsements of the court's structure.

Organization of American States—Related Publications

1354

Bianchi Gundián, Manuel. *Misión cumplida: la Comisión de Derechos Humanos en la República Dominicana; relatorio y documentos, 1960-1966.* Santiago de Chile, Editorial Andrés Bello, 1967. *[129 p.]*

Summarizes the Inter-American Commission on Human Rights' monitoring activities in the Dominican Republic during a period of turbulence, concluding with the general elections of 1966.

1355

Buergenthal, Thomas. *The revised O.A.S. Charter and the protection of human rights.* American journal of international law, v. 69, Oct. 1975: 828-836.

Analyzes the transformation of the inter-American system for the protection of human rights, resulting from O.A.S Charter revisions. Traces the development of the O.A.S. Charter.

1356

Cabranes, José A. *Human rights and non-intervention in the inter- American system.* Michigan law review, v. 65, Apr. 1967: 1147-1182.

Survey of the O.A.S. changing from indifference to concern for human rights as evidenced by its establishment of the Inter-American Commission on Human Rights.

1357

Cabranes, José A. *The protection of human rights by the Organization of American States.* American journal of international law, v. 62, Oct. 1968: 889-909.

Details the efforts of the O.A.S. on behalf of human rights, and discusses the international and domestic priorities that must exist in order to ensure enforcement of these rights at an international level.

1358

Camargo, Pedro Pablo. *The American Convention on Human Rights.* Revue des droits de l'homme: human rights journal, v. 3, no. 2, 1970: 333- 356.

Review of the civil, cultural, economic, political and social rights in the American Convention on Human Rights that was signed by twelve American nations on November 22, 1969 in San José, Costa Rica.

1359

Clark, Roger S. *The Organization of American States and human rights, 1960-1967.* Washington, Organization of American States, Secretariat, 1972. 656 p.

Outlines the actions taken by the O.A.S. concerning human rights in Cuba, the Dominican Republic, and Haiti.

1360

Convención Americana sobre Derechos Humanos. *La Gaceta (Costa Rica),* v. 92, mar. 14, 1970: 1029-1033.

Provides the text of the American Convention on Human Rights.

1361

Domínguez Fermán, Serafín. *Principios constitucionales, fundamento de la actuación de México en la O.E.A.* Mexico, Universidad Nacional Autónoma de México, 1963. 158 p.

Law school thesis which traces the historical development of Mexico's constitutional protections of the rights of man and compares them with the protections outlined in the charters of the O.A.S. and the U.N.

1362

Eadie, Florence. *Synopsis of part of the Fletcher school of Law and Diplomacy Project in Observance of International Women's Year; a compilation and analysis of laws discriminating against women.* Washington, Organization of American States, Inter-American Commission on Women, 1976. 55 p. (Organization of American States. Official records. OEA/Ser. L/II.2.18 CIM/doc. 82/76)

Reports on the legal discrimination of women in the Americas.

1363

Farer, Tom J., and James P. Rowles. *The Inter-American Commission on Human Rights. In Tuttle, James C., ed. International human rights; law and practice. Chicago, American Bar Association, 1978. p. 47-81.*

Describes the organization, scope, operations, publications and impact of the Commission. Outlines steps to lodge complaints.

1364

Fox, Donald T. *The protection of human rights in the Americas. The Columbia journal of transnational law, v. 7, no. 2, 1968: 222-234.*

Discusses the slowness of the O.A.S. in providing a means for the promotion of human rights in the Americas. Analyzes the formation of the O.A.S.'s Inter-American Commission on Human Rights and its activities since 1960.

1365

Heinl, Robert Debs, and Nancy Gordon Heinl. *Written in blood: the story of the Haitian people, 1942-1971. Boston, Houghton Mifflin, 1978. 785 p. illus., plates.*

General history of modern Haiti which includes references to frustrated O.A.S. and U.N. efforts on behalf of human rights. Provides an extensive bibliography of unpublished U.S. government documents as well as student theses.

1366

Inter-American Court of Human Rights. *Proceedings of the installation. San Jose, Costa Rica, 1979. 108 p. illus.*

Description of the installation of the justices of the Inter-American Court. The Court was established in 1979 as part of the inter-American system to hear and resolve complaints involving violations of human rights. Its first meeting took place on June 29 of that year at the O.A.S. headquarters in Washington.

1367

Inter-American Specialized Conference on Human Rights, San José, Costa Rica, 1969. *Final act. Washington, General Secretariat of the Organization of American States, 1970. 18 p. facsims. (Organization of American States. Official records. OEA/Ser. C/VI.18.1)*

Recommends a study by the Inter-American Commission on Human Rights concerning the violation of political rights in Latin America. Includes comments by the representatives of Argentina El Salvador, and Mexico.

1368

International Commission of Jurists. *Haiti's denunciation of the Inter-American Convention on Asylum. In its Bulletin, Dec. 1968: 13-18.*

Editorial comment criticizing Haiti's reply to the Inter- American Commission on Human Rights' report on conditions in Haiti.

1369

LeBlanc, Lawrence J. *The O.A.S. and the promotion and protection of human rights. The Hague, M. Nijhoff, 1977. 179 p.*

Revised and expanded version of the author's thesis; discusses Inter-American obligations concerning human rights, as well as the origins, organization, and functions of the Inter-American Commission on Human Rights. Includes definitions, conclusions, bibliographic references and an index.

1370

Levi-Ruffinelli, Fernando. *Derechos humanos. Asuncion, Talleres Gráficos Orbis, 1977. 142 p.*

Lists constitutions, charters and documents guaranteeing human rights. Analyzes the protection of civil rights in Paraguayan law.

1371

Martins, Daniel Hugo. *La protección internacional de los derechos esenciales del hombre. Washington, Organization of American States, Inter-American Commission on Human Rights, 1966. 1 v. (Organization of American States. Official records. OEA/Ser. L/V/II.15 doc. 28)*

Not available for annotation.

1372

McNeill, F.J., and William D. Rogers. *U.S. discusses human rights items in O.A.S. General Assembly; tests of statements and resolutions adopted. U.S. Department of State. Department of State bulletin, v. 72, June 1975: 879-881.*

Contains speeches that were delivered before the U.N. General Assembly concerning the Inter-American Commission on Human Rights and the status of civil liberties in Chile.

1373

Orfila, Alejandro. *Human rights in the Americas. Worldview, v. 20, Oct. 1977: 25-26, 35.*

The Secretary General of the O.A.S. suggests that an Inter-American Court of Human Rights, similar to the existing European Court of Human Rights, be created.

1374

Pierre-Charles, Gerard. *El régimen de los Duvalier. America Latina: derechos humanos (Mexico), mayo 1978: 11-16.*

Denounces the Duvalier governing style. States that Haiti should still be on the O.A.S. list of human rights violators.

1375

Ricord, Humberto E. *Los derechos humanos y la Organización de los Estados Americanos. Mexico, Impresiones Modernas, 1970. 179 p.*

General discussion of human rights with emphasis on Europe and the Third World. Examines legal questions, as well as the Inter-American System.

1376

Scheman L., Ronald. *The Inter-American Commission on Human Rights. American journal of international law, v. 59, Apr. 1965: 335-344.*

Provides background information concerning the origin, powers and activities of the Inter-American Commission on Human Rights.

1377

Schreiber, Anna P. *The Inter-American Commission on Human Rights. Leyden, Netherlands, A.W. Sijthoff, 1970. 187 p.*

Important exposition of the organization and membership of the Commission, as well as of its work in various Latin American countries, including Cuba, Haiti, Guatemala and the Dominican Republic.

1378

Seminar on Trade Union Freedom, Caracas, 1972. *Informe del Seminario sobre Libertad Sindical, aprobado en la octava sesión celebrada el 10 de noviembre de 1972. Washington, Secretaría General de la Organización de los Estados Americanos, 1974. 32 p. (Organization of American States. Official records. OEA/Ser. L/V/IV. LS/doc. 29, rev. 1)*

Organized by the Inter-American Commission on Human Rights, under the auspices of the Government of Venezuela.

1379

Silveria, Azevedo da. *Address of Chancellor...June 15, 1977 at the VII General Assembly of the O.A.S. in Grenada on the subject of human rights. Brazil today, no. 13, June 23, 1977: 2.*

Not available for annotation.

1380

Thomas, Ann van Wynen, and A. J. Thomas. *The Inter-American Commission on Human Rights. Southwestern law journal, v. 20, June 1966: 282-309.*

Contains a useful exposition of the Commission's history and functions. Includes a detailed account of its actions in the Dominican Republic during 1965.

1381

Vance, Cyrus. *Secretary Vance attends O.A.S. General Assembly at Grenada. U.S. Dept. of State. Department of State bulletin, v. 77, July 18, 1977: 69-77.*

Provides text of Secretary Vance's speech discussing the promotion of human rights by the U.S. government. Includes the resolution adopted by the General Assembly.

1382

Vasak, Karel. *La Commission Interaméricaine des Droits de l'Homme. Avant-propos de René Cassin. Paris, Librairie*

Générale de Droit de Jurisprudence, Pichon & Durand-Auzias, 1968. 287 p. (Bibliothèque constitutionnelle et de science politique, no. 35)

At head of title: La protection internationale des droits de l'homme sur le continent américain.

Covers the origin and early history of the Inter-American Commission on Human Rights, its statutes, functions and organization, and its role in the promotion and juridical protection of human rights. Includes an introduction by René Cassin.

1383

Vasak, Karel. *La Commission Interaméricaine des Droits de l'Homme: son role e son importance pour les pays en voie de développement. Internationales Colloquium über Menschenrechte, 1968: 191-211.*

Examines the composition, activities, and areas of influence of the Inter-American Commission on Human Rights, as well as the Commission's importance for developing countries.

1384

Washington Office on Latin America. *The Organization of American States and the protection of human rights. Special update, June 1978: [7] p.*

Not available for annotation.

United Nations

1385

U.N. *Background papers: the International Bill of Human Rights. [New York] 1977. 18 p. (Its [U.N. Publication] OPI/588)*

Brief history of the development of U.N. human rights covenants. Includes General Assembly action, implementation, and limitations on rights. Lists of ratifying states are also included.

1386

U.N. *Human rights: a compilation of international instruments. New York, 1978. 132 p. (U.N. [Publication] ST/HR/1/Rev. 1)*

Latest of three comprehensive editions of U.N. human rights instruments. Contains the texts of the sixteen instruments, dates of ratification, and a chronology of documents from 1962 forward.

1387

U.N. *Human rights; a compilation of international instruments of the United Nations. [Prepared by the Division of Human Rights of the U.N. Secretariat. Rev. ed.] New York, 1973. [112] p. (U.N. [Document] ST/HR/1)*

At head of title: Twenty-fifth anniversary of the Universal Declaration of Human Rights, 1948-1973.

Includes instruments adopted up to December 31, 1972, among which are the International Bill of Human Rights; Prevention of Discrimination; Freedom of Association; Marriage and the Family; Childhood and Youth; and Nationality, Statelessness, Asylum, and Refugees.

1388

U.N. *Human rights bulletin. New York, Division of Human Rights, no. 1, July, 1969-*

Semi-annual bulletin, also published in French and Spanish, dealing with human rights issues.

1389

U.N. *Human rights international instruments; signatures, ratifications, accessions...1 Jan. 1979. New York, 1979. (U.N. [Document] ST/HR/4/ Rev. 1)*

Information in chart is gleaned from the publication Multilateral treaties in respect of which the Secretary-General performs depository functions (U.N. [Document] ST/LEG/SER. D/11).

1390

U.N. *Human rights seminar on the effective realization of civil and political rights at the national level. Kingston, Jamaica, 1967. Organized by the United Nations, Division of Human Rights, in cooperation with the Government of Jamaica. New York, 1967. (U.N. [Document] ST/TAO/HR/29)*

Review of existing arrangements and specific national institutions for the safeguarding of political and civil rights, as well as an examination of emergency situations affecting their protection.

1391

U.N. *International Conference on Human Rights. Teheran, 1968. [New York, 1968] 19 p. (U.N. [Document] A/CONF. 32/41)*

Discusses the obligations of U.N. member states to the Human Rights Conventions.

1392

U.N. *The International covenants on human rights and Optional Protocol. New York, U.N. Office of Public Information, 1979. 34 p. (U.N. [Publication] OPI/627)*

Texts of human rights covenants and the Optional Protocol.

1393

U.N. *International year for human rights, 1968: newsletter. New York, U.N. Office of Public Information, 1967-*

Features information on human rights. A supplement appeared in 1969. Ceased publication.

1394

U.N. *Seminar on freedom of association. London, June-July 1968. Organized by the United Nations, Divison of Human*

Rights, in cooperation with the Government of the United Kingdom. New York, 1968. [32] p. (U.N. [Document] ST/TAO/HR/32)

General discussion of the purpose and role of association, the exercise of freedom of association and other rights essential to its enjoyment, and other national and international policies to protect this freedom.

1395

U.N. Seminar on human rights in developing countries. Kabul, Afghanistan, May 1964. Organized by the United Nations in cooperation with the Government of Afghanistan. New York, 1964. [54] p.(U.N. [Document] ST/TAO/HR/21)

At head of title: Secretariat.

General discussion of human rights in the developing countries. Concludes that all or most of the civil rights in these countries should be guaranteed immediately, and that the need for economic planning does not in general justify any curtailment of those rights.

1396

U.N. Seminar on special problems relating to human rights in developing countries. Nicosia, Cyprus, 1969. New York, United Nations, 1970. [53] p. (U.N. [Document] ST/TAO/HR/36)

Seminar organized by the U.N. Division of Human Rights. Concentrates on specific human rights problems in the Third World.

1397

U.N. Seminar on the civic and political education of women. Accra, Ghana, Nov.-Dec. 1968. Organized by the United Nations, Division of Human Rights, in cooperation with the Government of Ghana. New York, 1969. [50] p. (U.N. [Document] ST/TAO/HR/35)

Examines the factors which influence the exercise of the civic and political rights of women. Recommends techniques and methods for encouraging women to make the fullest use of these rights.

1398

U.N. Seminar on the effects of scientific and technological developments on the status of women. Iasi, Rumania, 1969. Organized by the United Nations, Division of Human Rights, in cooperation with the Government of Rumania. New York, 1976. [47] p. (U.N. [Document] ST/TAO/HR/37)

Seminar emphasizing problems in education and employment.

1399

U.N. Seminar on the promotion and protection of the human rights of national, ethnic and other minorities. Obrid, Yugoslavia, 1974. Organized by the United Nations, Division of Human Rights. New York, 1974. 41 p. (U.N. [Document] ST/TAO/HR/49)

Not available for annotation.

1400

U.N. Seminar on the role of youth in the promotion and protection of human rights. Belgrade, 1970. Organized by the United Nations, Division of Human Rights. New York, 1970. [42] p. (U.N. [Document] ST/T AO/HR] 39 [text])

Examines the aspirations of youth concerning the standards that should prevail in the field of protecting basic rights.

1401

U.N. Status of the International Covenant on Civil and Political Rights and of International Optional Protocol to the International Covenant on Civil and Political Rights. Note by the Secretary-General. New York, 1979. [5] p. (U.N. [Document] A/33/149)

At head of title: General Assembly.

Includes appendices giving status, date of signature, and dates of ratification or accession of basic human rights documents.

1402

U.N. United Nations action in the field of human rights. New York, 1974. 212 p. (U.N. Publication ST/HR/2)

At head of title: 1948-1973; twenty-fifth anniversary of the Universal Declaration of Human Rights.

Chronicles U.N. activities in the area of human rights. Part one traces the development of human rights concern expressed in the U.N. Charter. The second part describes implementation, structure, and procedure. The report is based on two studies submitted by the Secretary General to the International Conference on Human Rights (Teheran, 1968): measures taken within the U.N. in the field of human rights (U.N. [Document] A/CONF. 32/5 and Add. 1) and methods used by the U.N. in the field of human rights (U.N. [Document] A/CONF. 32/6 and Add. 1).

1403

U.N. Commission on Human Rights. *Further promotion and encouragement of human rights and fundamental freedoms, including the question of the programme and methods of work of the Commission. New York, United Nations, 1978. (17 p. U.N. [Document] E/CN. 4/1273/Add. 1)*

At head of title: Economic and Social Council. Agenda item 11 of the provisional agenda.

Report prepared by the Secretary General pursuant to Decision 4 (XXXIII) of the Commission on Human Rights.

1404

U.N. Commission on Human Rights. *Information submitted in accordance with Economic and Social Council Resolution 1159 (XLI) regarding cooperation with regional intergovernmental bodies concerned with human rights. Note by the Secretary General. New York, United Nations, 1972. 15 p.(U.N. [Document] E/CN. 4/1089/Add. 3)*

At head of title: Economic and Social Council.

Addendum containing communication dated February 14, 1972, from the Organization of American States on "...work accomplished... [by the O.A.S.]...in the field of human rights."

1405

U.N. Commission on Human Rights. *Information submitted in accordance with Economic and Social Council Resolution 1159 (XLI) regarding cooperation with regional intergovernmental bodies. Note by the Secretary General. New York, United Nations, 1973. 19 p. (U.N. [Document] E/CN. 4/1120] Add. 1)*

At head of title: Economic and Social Council. Twenty-ninth session.

Report to the General Assembly of the O.A.S.'s Inter-American Commission on Human Rights. Includes constitutional provisions and court decisions handed down in the Americas, a listing of measures which should be taken on behalf of human rights, a summary of the communications received by the Commission in 1971, and the request of the Commission to the General Assembly.

1406

U.N. Commission on Human Rights. *Information submitted in accordance with Economic and Social Council Resolution 1159 (XLI) regarding cooperation with regional intergovernmental bodies concerned with human rights. Note by the Secretary General. New York, United Nations, 1974. 21 p. (U.N. [Document] E/CN. 4/1139/Add. 1)*

At head of title: Economic and Social Council. Thirtieth session.

Communications from the Inter-American Commission on Human rights to the Secretary General concerning the work accomplished by the O.A.S. in the field of human rights during 1973. Includes sections devoted to the Inter-American Commission of Women, the Inter-American Children's Institute, and the Inter-American Indigenous Institute.

1407

U.N. Commission on Human Rights. *Report, v. 1+ Jan./Feb. 1947+ New York, United Nations. (U.N. [Document] E, E/CN.4)*

Issued as supplements of the official records of the Economic and Social Council.

1408

U.N. Economic and Social Council. *Report of the Economic and Social Council. Jan. 23/Oct. 3, 1946+New York, United Nations.*

At head of title: General Assembly. Title varies slightly.

Not available for annotation.

1409

U.N. Educational, Scientific and Cultural Organization. *Further promotion and encouragement of human rights and fundamental freedoms, including the question of a long-*

term programme of work of the commission. New York, United Nations, 1976. 40 p.

Not available for annotation.

1410

U.N. Educational, Scientific and Cultural Organization. *Human rights; comments and interpretations: a symposium edited by U.N.E.S.C.O., with an introduction by Jacques Maritain. Westport, Conn., Greenwood Press [1973]. 287 p.*

Reprint of 1949 edition. Includes bibliographic references.

1411

U.N. Educational, Scientific and Cultural Organization. *Human rights in the administration of justice. New York, United Nations, 1976. 22 p.*

Booklet outlining standards of the U.N. with regard to those human rights most directly involved with the treatment of offenders.

1412

U.N. Educational, Scientific and Cultural Organization. *Illiteracy and human rights. Published on the occasion of the International Year for Human Rights, 1968. [Paris, 1968]. 15 p. illus.*

Includes extracts from an address by Pene Maheu, the text of a paper by the U.N.E.S.C.O. Secretariat, and the text of a resolution presented at various international meetings held during the International Year for Human Rights, 1968.

1413

U.N. Educational, Scientific and Cultural Organization. *Recommendations concerning education for international understanding, cooperation and peace; and education relating to human rights and fundamental freedom. New York, United Nations, 1974. 1 v. (various pagings)*

Not available for annotation.

1414

U.N. General Assembly. *Declaración universal de los derechos humanos. 1948-1978, treinta aniversario de los derechos humanos. Lima, CELADEC y ULAJE, 1978. 1 v.*

The Comisión Evangélica de Educación Cristiana and the Unión Latinoamericana de Juventudes Ecuménicas present an annotated edition of the Universal Declaration of Human Rights. The publication was sponsored by the Vicaría de la Solidaridad of the Archdiocese of Santiago, Chile.

1415

U.N. General Assembly. *Equal rights for women—a call for action: the United Nations Declaration on the Elimination of Discrimination Against Women. New York, United Nations, 1973. [34] p. (U.N. [Document] OPI/494)*

Emphasizes obtaining universal recognition and observance of women's equal rights in law, and exploring means by which all women can be given an equal opportunity to exercise these rights.

1416

U.N. General Assembly. *Informe del Consejo Económico y Social: protección de los derechos humanos. New York, U.N. General Secretariat, 1976. 234 p.*

Report on the protection of human rights issued by the Economic and Social Council.

1417

U.N. General Assembly. *Report of the Human Rights Committee. New York, 1977. 72 p. (U.N. [Document] A/32/44)*

At head of title: Official records, thirty-second session, supplement no. 44.

Proceedings of the thirty-second session of the U.N. General Assembly's Human Rights Committee. Report describes the organization and operations of the committee.

1418

U.N. General Assembly. *Social, Humanitarian and Cultural Committee. Report of the Commission on Human Rights. Advisory services in the field of human rights, report of the Social Committee. [New York] United Nations, 1969. 36 p. (U.N. [Document] E/4693)*

At head of title: United Nations. Economic and Social Council.

Not available for annotation.

1419

U.N. Library, Geneva. *League of Nations and United Nations monthly list of selected articles; cumulative, 1920-1970: economic questions.* Edited by Norman S. Field. Dobbs Ferry, N.Y., Oceana Publications, 1973/1975. 6 v.

A compilation arranged by subject and country in chronological order from the card file used to issue the library's Liste mensuelle d'articles selectionnés. Includes bibliographies.

1420

U.N. Library, Geneva. *League of Nations and United Nations monthly list of selected articles; cumulative, 1920-1970: legal questions.* Edited by Norman S. Field. Dobbs Ferry, N.Y., Oceana Publications, 1972. 2 v.

A compilation arranged by subject and country in chronological order from the card file used to issue the Library's Liste mensuelle d'articles selectionnés. Volume 1 is a discussion of public international law.

1421

U.N. Library, Geneva. *League of Nations and United Nations monthly list of selected articles; cumulative, 1920-1970: political questions.* Edited by Norman S. Field. Dobbs Ferry, N.Y., Oceana Publications, 1971/1973. 6 v.

A compilation arranged by subject and country in chronological order from the card file used to issue the Library's Liste mensuelle d'articles selectionnés.

1422

U.N. Office of Public Information. *The International Covenants on Human Rights and Optional Protocol.* [New York] 1976. (Its U.N. [Publication] OPI/562)

Texts of the legal instruments binding signatories to protect economic, social, cultural, civil, and political rights. Includes the Optional Protocol.

1423

U.N. Office of Public Information. *Questions and answers on human rights.* [New York] 1973. 20 p. (Its [U.N. publication] OPI/493)

Booklet of answers to basic questions about human rights. Briefly states U.N. human rights

goals. Commemorates the 25th anniversary of the Universal Declaration of Human Rights.

1424

U.N. Office of Public Information. *The United Nations and human rights.* New York, United Nations, 1968. 93 p. (Its [U.N. Publication] E 67.I.29)

Describes human rights activities sponsored or initiated by the United Nations.

1425

U.N. Office of Public Information. *The United Nations and human rights.* New York, United Nations, 1973. 87 p.

A survey of the services and procedures in U.N. human rights activities.

1426

U.N. Office of Public Information. *The United Nations and human rights.* New York, 1978. 166 p. (Its [U.N. publication] OPI/ 621)

Significant current account of human rights achievements. Identifies the broad range of U.N. committees, conventions, programs, and human rights approaches.

1427

U.N. Office of Public Information. *The United Nations and the human person; questions and answers on human rights.* [New York, 1967] 21 p.

"Prepared to mark the 20th anniversary of the adoption of the Universal Declaration of Human Rights and 1968 as the International Year for Human Rights."

1428

U.N. Office of Public Information. *United Nations programme of advisory services in the field of human rights.* [New York, 1970]. 15 p. (Its [U.N. publication] OPI/403)

General discussion of the U.N.'s "action programme," which includes periodic reports on human rights, studies of specific human rights, and advisory services in the field of human rights.

1429

U.N. Office of Public Information. *United Nations work for human rights. New York, 1965. 47 p.*

Digest of the human rights activities of the General Assembly, the Economic and Social Council, and the Trusteeship Council. Provides background information on the Commission on Human Rights from its establishment in 1946 to 1965.

1430

U.N. Secretariat. *Yearbook on human rights. New York, United Nations, 1946+ (U.N. [Document] E/75/XIV/1)*

Yearly publication up to 1972, thereafter published biannually. Contains material from governments, government-appointed correspondents, and research work produced by the U.N. Secretariat. Describes constitutional, legislative, and judicial developments in many states, reports on developments in trust and non-self-governing territories, and reproduces complete texts or selections from international agreements and instruments on human rights.

1431

U.N. Secretary General. *Alternative approaches and ways and means within the United Nations system for improving the effective enjoyment of human rights and fundamental freedoms; report. [New York] United Nations, 1977. 32 p. (U.N. [Document] A/32/178)*

At head of title: General Assembly. Thirty-second session, item 76 of the provisional agenda.

Examines the ratification of the International Covenants on Human Rights and suggests the adoption of such measures as periodic reports, fact-finding procedures, and the establishment of a U.N. High Commissioner of Human Rights.

1432

U.N. Secretary General. *Annual report on freedom of information. 1960/61+[New York?].(U.N. [Document] E/CN.4)*

Reports submitted to the Commission on Human Rights. Report year ends June 30; first report covers period from Jan. 1960-June 1961. Addenda accompany some of the reports.

1433

U.N. Secretary General. *Elimination of all forms of religious intolerance; note. [New York] United Nations, 1976. 5 p. (U.N. [Document] A/31/158)*

At head of title: General Assembly. Thirty-first session, item 77 of the provisional agenda.

Includes draft of the declaration and draft of the International Convention on the Elimination of All Forms of Intolerance and of Discrimination Based on Religion or Belief.

1434

U.N. Secretary General. *Human rights in the administration of justice: memorandum. New York, United Nations, 1972. 17 p. (U.N. [Document] E/AC. 57/5)*

At head of title: Economic and Social Council. Committee on Crime Prevention and Control. First session, item 8 of the provisional agenda.

Description of the principal aspects of the protection of human rights in the administration of justice considered by U.N. organs and, in particular, by the Commission on Human Rights.

1435

U.N. Secretary General. *Report of the Secretary-General on the work of the organization, June 1969-June 1970. New York, United Nations, 1970. 255 p. (U.N. [Document] A/8001)*

At head of title: General Assembly. Official records. Twenty- fifth session, Suppl. no. 1.

Covers political and security questions; decolonization; economic, social, and humanitarian activities; legal questions; and other matters such as public information activities and administrative and financial questions.

1436

U.N. Secretary General. *Respect for human rights in armed conflicts: fourth session of the Diplomatic Conference on the Reaffirmation and Development of International Humanitarian Law Applicable in Armed Conflicts; report. New York, United Nations, 1977. [145] p. (U.N. [Document] A/32/144)*

At head of title: General Assembly. Thirty-second session, item 115 of the provisional agenda.

Account of proceedings and results on relevant developments concerning human rights in armed conflicts. Annex 1 contains text of Protocol Additional to the Geneva Conventions of August 1949 relating to the protection of victims of international armed conflicts; Annex 2 contains text of Protocol Additional to the Geneva Conventions of August 1949 relating to the protection of victims of non-international armed conflicts.

1437

U.N. Secretary General. *Torture and other cruel, inhuman or degrading treatment or punishment. Draft code of conduct for law enforcement officials; report. [New York] United Nations, 1978. [20] p. (U.N. [Document] A/33/215)*

At head of title: General Assembly. Thirty-third session, item 83 of the provisional agenda.

The Code deals with the rights and duties of law enforcement officials in the performance of their work, stressing the obligation to respect and to protect human dignity and rights, and the prohibition of torture. Includes three annexes: the draft resolution by the Economic and Social Council, the Declaration of the Hague, and an excerpt on medical services from the Standard Minimum Rules for the Treatment of Prisoners and Related Recommendations.

1438

U.N. Secretary General. *Torture and other cruel, inhuman or degrading treatment or punishment in relation to detention and imprisonment: analytical summary. [New York] United Nations, 1975. 41 p. (U.N. [Document] A/10158—*

At head of title: General Assembly.

Includes discussions on political prisoners and detention of persons.

1439

U.N. Secretary General. *Torture and other cruel, inhuman or degrading treatment or punishment in relation to detention and imprisonment; note. New York, United Nations, 1976. [16] p. (U.N.[Document] A/31/234)*

At head of title: General Assembly. Thirty-first session, agenda item 74.

Chronological review of relevant developments in the U.N. and in the World Health Organization since the adoption by the General Assembly of Resolutions 3452 (XXX) and 3453 (XXX). Annex 1 is a resolution adopted by W.H.O. concerning the coordination with the U.N. of the development of codes of medical ethics. Annex 2 is the Declaration of Tokyo, guidelines for medical doctors adopted by the 29th World Medical Assembly in Tokyo during October 1975.

1440

U.N. Sub-Commission on Prevention of Discrimination and Protection of Minorities. *Human rights and scientific and technological developments: written statement submitted by the International Commission of Jurists. New York, United Nations, 1978. 2 p. (U.N. [Document/78 E/CN. 4/Sub. 2/NGO/78)*

At head of title: Economic and Social Council. Commission of Human Rights.

Contains text of document ensuring protection of human rights along with scientific developments. The International Commission of Jurists is a non-governmental organization in consultative status.

1441

U.N. Sub-Commission on Prevention of Discrimination and Protection of Minorities. *Question of the human rights of persons subjected to any form of detention or imprisonment: draft body of principles for the protection of all persons under any form of detention or imprisonment. New York, United Nations, 1978. 9 p. (U.N. [Document] E/CN.4/Sub. 2/L. 688)*

At head of title: Economic and Social Council. Commission on Human Rights.

Contains draft of principles as acopted by the Sub-Commission at its 807th through 810th meetings.

1442

U.N. Sub-Commission on the Prevention of Discrimination and the Protection of Minorities. *Study of discrimination in respect of the rights of everyone to leave any country, including his own and to return to his country. New York, United Nations, 1963. 115 p. (U.N. [Document] E/CN. 4/Sub. 2/229/Rev. 1)*

Not available for annotation.

1443

U.N. Sub-Commission on the Prevention of Discrimination and the Protection of Minorities. *Study of discrimination in the matter of political rights. New York, United Nations, 1962. 105 p. (U.N. [Document] E/CN.4/Sub. 2/213/Rev. 1)*

Third in a series of discrimination studies on education and religion, this report defines political discrimination, and U.N. and national protections, and suggests additional safegaurds.

1444

U.N. Third Committee. *United Nations decade for women: equality, development and peace. Draft Convention on the Elimination of Discrimination against Women. New York,* *United Nations, 1978. 17 p. (U.N. [Document] A/C. 3/33 /WG. 1/CRP. 1)*

At head of title: General Assembly.

Contains text of draft convention aimed at eliminating discrimination against women.

1445

U.N. and International Commission of Jurists. *Inter-American Convention on Human Rights. In International Commission of Jurists, Review, June 1978: 23-24.*

Short commentary on the structure of the Inter-American Convention of Human Rights and its functions.

United Nations—Related Authors

1446

Abram, Morris B. *The United Nations and human rights. Foreign affairs, v. 47, Jan. 1969: 363-374.*

Examines some of the reasons why the U.N. has not been able to make the crucial transition from an agency engaged in defining principles of human rights to an effective instrument for implementing those rights. Questions assumptions that human rights are a common concern of the international community.

1447

Asamblea Permanente de Derechos Humanos de Bolivia. *Declaración Universal de Derechos Humanos. La Paz, 1978. 1 v. (unpaged)*

Discusses human rights violations in Bolivia. Written in commemoration of the 30th anniversary of the Universal Declaration of Human Rights.

1448

Asamblea Permanente de Derechos Humanos de Bolivia. *El fascismo en Bolivia; la Declaración de los Derechos Humanos y la represión en Bolivia. La Paz, 1977. 19 p.*

Examines government repression of human rights in Bolivia.

1449

Assembly for Human Rights. *Montreal statement of the Assembly for Human Rights. [New York] The Assembly [1968?] [17] p. illus.*

Proposes that the U.N. rededicate itself to the implementation of the Universal Declaration of Human Rights and the adoption of an International Convention on the Elimination of All Forms of Intolerance and of Discrimination Based on Religion or Belief. Suggests methods for achieving these goals at national levels.

1450

Beerits, Henry C. *The United Nations and human survival. Philadelphia, Information Services, American Friends Service Committee, 1976. 85 p.*

Studies human rights through an analysis of the subjects discussed in the U.N.-sponsored world conferences on the human environment (Stockholm, 1972), food shortages (Rome, 1974), and the population explosion (Vancouver, 1976).

1451

Carazo Odio, Rodrigo. *Discurso pronunciado por el Presidente de Costa Rica Lic. Rodrigo Carazo ante la XXXIII Asamblea General de las Naciones Unidas. New York [s.n.] 1978. [21] p.*

Speech presented by President Carazo before the U.N. General Assembly. Analyzes the human rights policy of Costa Rica.

1452

Carey, John. *U.N. protection of civil and political rights. Syracuse, N.Y., Syracuse University Press, 1970. 205 p.*

Detailed analysis and critique of human rights enforcement, including a systematic approach to how individuals, given the realities of international politics, can be protected from their own governments.

1453

Carta de Derechos y Deberes Económicos de los Estados. *Revista de la Asociación Guatemalteca de Derecho Internacional, v. 2, 1976: 276-289.*

Contains the text of the Charter of Economic Rights and Duties of the States as adopted by the U.N. General Assembly on Dec. 12, 1974. Article 16 of the Charter sets forth the right and the duty of all states, individually and collectively, to eliminate colonialism, apartheid, racial discrimination, neocolonialism, and all forms of aggression, including occupation and foreign domination.

1454

Cassese, Antonio. *Two United Nations procedures for the implementation of human rights; the role that lawyers can play therein. In Tuttle, James C., ed. International human rights;*

law and practice. Chicago, American Bar Association, 1978. p. 39-46.

Survey of the U.N.'s public discussion procedure in the Sub- Commission of Gross and Large-Scale Violations of Human Rights (1967), and the U.N.'s procedure entitled Confidential Consideration of Communications Relating to Gross Violations of Human Rights (1970).

1455

Clark, Roger Stenson. *A United Nations High Commissioner for Human Rights.* The Hague, Martinus Nijhoff, 1972. 186 p.

Explores the history and future prospects of the High Commissioner's proposal for more effective enforcement of U.N. human rights policies, suggesting approaches such as fact-finding, publicity, and persuasion. Includes bibliography.

1456

Commission to Study the Organization of Peace. *The United Nations and human rights.* Dobbs Ferry, N.Y., Oceana Publications, 1968. 239 p.

Covers significant human rights declarations, conventions, issues, and future programs. Includes a supplementary paper by Louis B. Sohn that relates the history of various international instruments with an emphasis on certain human rights covenants. Annexes contain the texts of five major human rights declarations and covenants.

1457

Dammert Bellido, José. *The rights of man in Peru: the status of human rights in Peru twenty years after the United Nations Declaration of Human Rights.* In Between honesty and hope. New York, Maryknoll [197?] p. 63-66. (Maryknoll documentation series, no. 4)

Pastoral letter issued by the Bishop of Cajamarca examining human rights in Peru.

1458

Declaração Universal dos Direitos Humanos. *Brasília, Ministério da Justiça, 1978. 33 p.*

Pamphlet containing a Portuguese translation of the Universal Declaration of Human Rights. Also includes brief descriptions of each article.

1459

Declaración de la Conferencia de las Naciones Unidas Sobre el Medio Humano. *Revista de la Asociación Guatemalteca de Derecho Internacional, v. 2, 1976: 263-275.*

Contains the text of the Declaration as approved by the U.N. Conference on Human Environment (Stockholm, 1972) which establishes the rights and duties of men in relation to their environment, and condemns the policies which promote or perpetuate apartheid, discrimination, colonialism, and all forms of foreign domination.

1460

Declaración Sobre la Eliminación de la Discriminación Contra la Mujer. *Revista de la Asociación Guatemalteca de Derecho Internacional, v. 2, no.2, 1976: 271-275.*

Text of the Declaration banning discrimination against women. Promotes the adoption of appropriate means to assure equal rights.

1461

Declaración Universal de los Derechos Humanos. *Acción (Asuncion), v. 8, no.33, 1977: 1-32.*

Catholic religious exhortation to uphold human rights principles advocated by the Vatican Council and in the Universal Declaration of Human Rights. Includes references to current human rights activities by the Church in American nations.

1462

Los derechos humanos; como hacerlos realidad. *Bogotá, CODECAL, Corporación Integral para el Desarrollo Cultural y Social, 1979. 146 p. illus.*

A human rights manual which outlines procedures for conducting meetings and group discussions. In addition, defines the human rights guaranteed in the Universal Declaration of Human Rights. Includes a listing of international organizations.

1463

Los derechos humanos y la escuela. *Santiago de Chile, Centro de Investigación y Desarrollo de la Educación, 1978. [31] p. illus. (Cuadernos de educación, v. 10, oct. 1978)*

At head of title: Todo hombre tiene derecho a ser persona.

Teaching aid which explains the provisions of the U.N. Declaration of Human Rights.

1464
Ecumenical Service Commission. *The Universal Declaration of Human Rights. Washington, Latin American Documentation - USCC, Office of International Justice & Peace, 1973. [16] p. illus.*

English reprint of an ecumenical edition of the Universal Declaration of Human Rights. Prepared in commemoration of the Declaration's 25th anniversary. Contains biblical quotes and statements from Christian churches.

1465
Fowler, D. B. *The developing jurisdiction of the United Nations High Commissioner for Refugees. Human rights journal, v. 7, 1974: 119-144.*

Noting that human rights violations produce refugees, the author argues that the U.N.'s refugee commissioner's jurisdiction should be expanded to include more categories of refugees. Includes historical survey of the Commissioner's legal powers.

1466
Frances, Frank. *Libraries and human rights. U.N.E.S.C.O. Bulletin for libraries, v. 22, Sept./Oct. 1968: 225-228.*

Explores the role of the librarian in fostering the right to education set forth in the Universal Declaration of Human Rights.

1467
Fraser, Donald M. *Double standard: human rights at the United Nations. Nation, v. 219, no. 8, Sept. 1974: 230-232.*

Despite the declaration in the U.N. Charter to promote human rights as one of the organization's basic purposes, there is little evidence of a sustained effort by member countries to review alleged cases of torture, violence, and political repression.

1468
Goolby, Richard Hays. *Progress report on the United Nations human rights activities to protect prisoners. Georgia journal of international and comparative law, v. 7, summer 1977: 467-476.*

Author suggests that U.N. organs will be more effective in combating violations of prisoners' human rights only when states are willing to support a stronger U.N.

1469
Green, James Frederick. *Changing approaches to human rights: the United Nations, 1954 and 1974. Texas international law journal, v. 12, spring/summer 1977: 223-238.*

Describes the dramatic changes in substantive issues in the field of human rights and in the procedures in the U.N. for handling them that have occurred during the last 20 years. Compares and contrasts activities in two U.N. organs, the Commission on Human Rights and the General Assembly, in 1954 and 1974.

1470
Guggenheim, Malvina H. *The implementation of human rights by the U.N. Commission on the Status of Women; a brief comment. Texas international law journal, v. 12, spring/summer 1977: 239-249.*

The Commission has compiled an impressive record of resolutions and conventions of women's rights, thus contributing significantly to the development of international law in this area. The author contends that it should now devote its efforts to the implementation of these rights.

1471
Guggenheim, Malvina H. *Key provisions of the new United Nations rules dealing with human rights petitions. New York University journal of international law and politics, v. 6, winter 1973: 427-454.*

Examines the rules for admissibility of petitions before the U.N. Human Rights Commission.

1472
Guyomar, G. *Nations Unies et organisations regionales dans la protection des droits de l'homme. Revue général de droit international public, v. 68, 1964: 687-707.*

Analysis of the present situation of human rights protection. Discusses the determination and guarantee of man's basic rights.

1473

Heinl, Robert Debs, and Nancy Gordon Heinl. *Written in blood: the story of the Haitian people, 1942-1971. Boston, Houghton Mifflin, 1978. 785 p. illus.*

General history of modern Haiti which includes references to frustrated O.A.S. and U.N. efforts on behalf of human rights. Extensive bibliography and notes include unpublished material from U.S. government agencies and archives, as well as student theses.

1474

Humphrey, John. *The right of petition in the United Nations. Droits de l'homme: human rights journal, v. 4, no. 2/3, 1971: 463-475.*

Overview of the right to petition, and the unsuccessful efforts to incorporate this right into the United Nations Universal Declaration of Human Rights.

1475

Ingles, José D. *Study of discrimination in respect of the right of everyone to leave any country, including his own, and to return to his country. New York, United Nations, 1963. 115 p. (U.N. [Document] E/CN.4/Sub. 2/229/Rev. 1)*

Fourth of a series of studies which include A study of discrimination in education (1957), Study of discrimination in the matter of religious rights and practices (1960), and Study of discrimination in the matter of political rights (1963).

1476

International Labour Office. *Trade union rights and their relation to civil liberties. Seventh item on the agenda. Geneva, 1969. 70 p.*

At head of title: Report VII, International Labour Conference, 54th session, Geneva, 1970.

Conference report comparing rights protections listed in the International Declaration of Human Rights with trade union experiences at the international and national levels.

1477

International NGO Conference on Human Rights, UNESCO, Paris, 16-20 September, 1968. *International Commission of Jurists, Bulletin, no. 36, Dec. 1968: 35-45.*

Brief report on a conference which reviewed the Human Rights Year in light of the U.N.'s Teheran Conference and established future work priorities.

1478

Joyce, James Avery. *Human rights: international documents. Dobbs Ferry, N.Y., Oceana Publications, Co-published with Sijthoff & Noordhoff, Alphen aan den Rijn, Netherlands, 1979. 3 v.*

Compilation of human rights documents issued in the 30 years since the U.N. Declaration on Human rights, covering the U.N., national, and inter-governmental as well as non-governmental documentation and action.

1479

Kizilbash, Hamid H. *United Nations and human rights: a failure report. Pakistan horizon, v. 27, spring 1974: 50-60.*

Brief examination of the protection of human rights in the light of international covenants.

1480

Korey, William. *United Nations human rights: illusion and reality. Freedom at issue, Sept./Oct. 1977: 27-34.*

Examination of the performance and the promise of the "disaster area of the world organization."

1481

Leary, Virginia. *When does the implementation of international human rights constitute interference into the essentially domestic affairs of a state? The interactions of Articles 2(7), 55 and 56 of the U.N. Charter. In Tuttle, James C., ed. International human rights; law and practice. Chicago, American Bar Association, 1978. p. 15-21.*

States that "gross violations of human rights can no longer be considered a matter essentially within the domestic jurisdiction of the offending state under the U.N. Charter."

1482

Levi Ruffinelli, Fernando. *Derechos humanos. Asuncion, Talleres Gráficos Orbis, 1977. 142 p.*

Lists constitutions, charters and documents guaranteeing human rights. Analyzes the protection of civil rights in Paraguayan law.

1483

Liskofsky, Sidney. *Human rights minus liberty? Worldview, July/Aug. 1978: 26, 35-36.*

"The intrusion of essentially political issues into the U.N. human rights program is bound, by a kind of Gresham's law, to depreciate the currency of clearly established, traditional principles of human rights, especially the individual freedoms."

1484

MacDonald, R. St. J. *A United Nations High Commissioner for Human Rights: the decline and fall of an initiative. Canadian yearbook of international law, v. 10, 1972: 40-54.*

Review of developments in the 25th and 26th sessions of the General Assembly dealing with the proposed High Commissioner for Human Rights. Puts forth differences of opinion about the merits of the proposal and the failure of the initiative.

1485

Marcic, René. *Devoirs et limitations apportées aux droits. International Commission of Jurists, Revue, v. 9, June 1968: 68-82.*

A study of the 29th and 30th articles of the Universal Declaration of Human Rights, concerning the individual and the community and the limitations on freedom from suppression.

1486

Marks, Stephen. *UNESCO and human rights: the implementation of rights relating to education, science, culture, and communication. Texas international law journal, v. 13, winter, 1977: 35-68.*

Description of rights relating to education, science, culture, and communication which fall within U.N.E.S.C.O.'s fields of competence.

1487

Melady, Thomas Patrick. *Selective outrage. America (New York), v. 132, Feb. 8, 1975: 88-91.*

"Published by the Jesuits of the United States and Canada."

Author suggests that the U.N. not concentrate on a particular country violating human rights but speak out against violations as they occur throughout the world.

1488

Menchaca, A. A. *La recepción de la Declaración Universal de Derechos Humanos en el derecho peruano y sus efectos internacionales. El Foro (Peru), v. 53, 1966: 92-120.*

Not available for annotation.

1489

Mower, A. Glenn. *The implementation of the U.N. Covenant on Civil and Political Rights. Revue des droits de l'homme: human rights journal, v. 10, no. 2, 1977: 271-295.*

Examines the decision to include measures of implementation for the U.N. Covenant, some objections to this, and factors likely to influence the effectiveness of the implementation.

1490

Ortiz Martín, Gonzalo. *Análisis de los articulados de la Declaración Universal de los Derechos Humanos emitida por la Asamblea de las Naciones Unidas y correspondientes de la Constitución política de Costa Rica. Revista de ciencias jurídicas (Costa Rica), mayo 1964: 59-88.*

Compares the human rights provisions that are outlined in the Costa Rican Constitution with the provisions that are included in the Universal Declaration of Human Rights.

1491

Quadri, Ricardo Pedro. *La cuestión de la coordinación de los instrumentos internacionales sobre derechos humanos. [Buenos Aires] Zeta Duplicador, 1970. 14 p.*

Discussion concerning the coordination of the international instruments of the U.N. relating to human rights.

1492

Ramcharan, B. G. *Inter-governmental organizations: the United Nations Division on Human Rights. Human Rights Internet newsletter, v. 3, Aug. 1978: 23-27.*

Description of the history, function, internal structure, and programs of the Division, and an assessment of its contributions to the U.N.'s work in the area of human rights.

1493

Real, Alberto Ramón. *Garantía internacional de los derechos humanos. Justicia uruguaya, v. 46, 1962/1963: 37-45. (Irregular pagination)*

Speech delivered to the National Commission of U.N.E.S.C.O. in Uruguay on the development of international and inter-American human rights organizations, advocating unity of purpose.

1494

Rolz-Bennett, José. *Human rights, 1945-1970. [New York] United Nations, 1970. 11 p. (U.N. Office of Public Information OPI/407)*

General discussion of the Universal Declaration, the Covenants, the Optional Protocol, and the international instruments designed to promote and protect the enjoyment of various rights and freedoms.

1495

Saario, V. Voitto, and Rosemary Higgins Cass. *United Nations and the international protection of human rights: a legal analysis and interpretation. California Western international law journal, v. 7, summer 1977: 591-614.*

Survey of the modern origins of international protection of human rights. Traces its development through the history of the U.N., reviews its implementation, and suggests future directions.

1496

Santa Cruz, Hernán. *Study of discrimination in the matter of political rights. New York, United Nations, 1962. 105 p. (U.N.[Document] E/CN.4/Sub. 2/213/Rev. 1)*

"Third of a series of studies undertaken by the Sub-Commission on Prevention of Discrimina-

tion and Protection of Minorities with the authorization of the Commission on Human Rights and the Economic and Social Council. A study of discriminition in education, the first in the series, was published in 1957, and the Study of discrimination in the matter of religious rights and practices, the second of the series, was published in 1960."

1497

Tardu, Max E. *Human rights: the international petition system, a repertoire of practice. Dobbs Ferry, N.Y., Oceana Publications, 1978.v. 1 (various pagings)*

First volume of a projected series of three volumes consisting of a comparative legal essay on the petition that was accepted by the 1976 U.N. Covenant. Different petition procedures, types of petition systems and strategies are discussed. Volumes 2 and 3 will include a repertoire of law and practice regarding the petition procedures of various international organizations concerned with human rights.

1498

Tardu, Max E. *The protocol to the United Nations Covenant on Civil and Political Rights and the Inter-American System: a study of co-existing petition procedures. American journal of international law, v. 70, Oct. 1976: 778-800.*

Examines the main legal question that arises from the co-existence of two sets of international procedures for handling individual petitions: the system established by the Optional Protocol to the U.N. Covenant and the regional procedures within the framework of the O.A.S.

1499

U.S. Department of State. Office of Media Services. *Human rights. Washington, U.S. Government Printing Office, 1975. 29 p. (Selected documents, no. 5)*

At head of title: Seven selected documents on human rights.

Collection of excerpts from significant human rights documents of the United Nations.

1500

Van Boven, Theo C. *Human Rights forums at the United Nations. How to select and to approach the most appropriate forum. What procedural rules govern?* In Tuttle, James C., ed. *International human rights; law and practice.* Chicago, American Bar Association, 1978. *p. 83-92.*

The author, director of the U.N. Division of Human Rights, examines the principal human rights forums in the U.N. and the guiding factors in the selection of the most appropriate forum.

1501

Vasak, Karel. *National, regional and universal institutions for the promotion and protection of human rights. Droits de l'homme: human rights, v. 1, no. 2, 1968: 165-179.*

Comparative analysis of the scope and functions of existing institutions for the protection of human rights. Includes those sponsored by individual countries, those of countries grouped by geographic region, and those of universal orientation, such as the U.N.

1502

World Conference to Combat Racism and Racial Discrimination, Geneva, 1978. *Report. New York, United Nations, 1979. 141 p. (U.N. [Document] A/CONF.92/40)*

Proceedings of a U.N. conference about implementation of U.N. resolutions designed to eliminate racial discrimination and apartheid. Suggests the adoption of measures to promote decolonization, self-determination, and human rights enforcement.

1503

Young, Andrew. *The challenge to the Economic and Social Council: advancing the quality of life in all its aspects. U.S. Department of State. Department of State bulletin, v. 76, May 16, 1977: 494-502.*

Statement by the U.S. representative to the U.N. made before the U.N. Economic and Social Council (ECOSOC) in New York on April 19, 1977. Discusses the inseparable nature of human freedoms, combating world hunger and famine, the problem of torture, U.N. human rights machinery, and racism and racial discrimination.

U.S. Congress and Government Documents

1504

Four treaties pertaining to human rights. *Message from the President of the United States...Washington, U.S. Govt. Print. Off., 1978. 64 p. (95th Congress, 2d session. Senate. Executive, C-F)*

Message transmitting the International Convention on the Elimination of all Forms of Racial Discrimination (1966), the International Covenant on Civil and Political Rights (1977), and the American Convention on Human Rights (1977) as well as other instruments.

1505

U.S. Congress. House. Committee on Foreign Affairs. *Report of the special study mission to the Dominican Republic, Guyana, Brazil, and Paraguay, comprising Armistead I. Selden [and] William S. Mailliard. Pursuant to the provisions of H. Res. 84, 89th Congress. Washington, U.S. Govt. Print. Off., 1967. 61 p.*

At head of title: 90th Congress, 1st session.

Not available for annotation.

1506

U.S. Congress. House. Committee on Foreign Affairs. *Subcommittee on Inter-American Affairs. Cuba and the Caribbean. Hearings, 91st Congress, 2d session. Washington, U.S. Govt. Print. Off., 1970. 247 p.*

Hearings held July 8 to August 3, 1970, examining the political situation in the Caribbean and the role of Cuba in the region.

1507

U.S. Congress. House. Committee on Foreign Affairs. Subcommittee on Inter-American Affairs. *Human rights in Chile. Hearings before the Subcommittees on Inter-American Affairs and on International Organizations and Movements of the Committee on Foreign Affairs, House of Representatives, 93d Congress, 2d session, December 7, 1973, May 7, 13, and*

June 11, 12, 18, 1974. *Washington, U.S. Govt. Print. Off., 1974-75. 2 v.*

Joint hearings about human rights violations and mistreatment of political suspects by the military regime in Chile. Appendixes include submitted statements, correspondence, reports, press releases, articles, and reports by the International Commission of Jurists on legal systems and the protection of human rights in Uruguay and Chile, as well as responses by the Chilean government.

1508

U.S. Congress. House. Committee on Foreign Affairs. Subcommittee on Inter-American Affairs. *New directions for the 1970's: toward a strategy of inter-American development. Hearings...91st Congress, 1st session [and 92d Congress, 1st session], March 11-May 1, 1969, and February 18-August 4, 1971. Washington, U.S. Govt. Print. Off., 1969-71. 2 v. maps.*

Discusses general policy of the U.S. toward Latin America. Includes a list of documents on economic development and military assistance. Volume 2 has the subtitle: Development assistance options for Latin America.

1509

U.S. Congress. House. Committee on Foreign Affairs. Subcommittee on Inter-American Affairs. *United States relations with Panama. Hearing...93d Congress, 1st session, February 20, 1973. Washington, U.S. Govt. Print. Off., 1973. 53 p.*

Hearing to discuss U.S.-Panamanian relations and issues in negotiating a new Panama Canal treaty.

1510

U.S. Congress. House. Committee on Foreign Affairs. *Subcommittee on Inter-American Affairs. U.S. and Chile during the Allende years: 1970-1973. Hearings...July 1, and October 15, 1971; September 11, 1972; March 6, September 20 and 25, October 11 and 31, and December 7, 1973; August 5, and September 17 and 18, 1974. Washington, U.S. Govt. Print. Off., 1975. 677 p.*

Transcript of hearings that discuss developments in U.S.- Chilean relations and examine the role of U.S. foreign policy in events which occurred before and after the September 11, 1973 military coup. Considered are allegations concerning possible U.S. engagement in economic reprisals against Chile in response to Allende expropriations of American-owned business properties, and charges of C.I.A. covert interference in the Chilean political process. Includes bibliographic references.

1511

U.S. Congress. House. Committee on Foreign Affairs. Subcommittee on Inter-American Affairs. *United States-Chilean relations. Hearing...93d Congress, 1st session, March 6, 1973. Washington, U.S. Govt. Print. Off., 1973. 97 p.*

Includes testimony concerning U.S. companies operating in Chile and a chronology of events since the election of Salvador Allende.

1512

U.S. Congress. House. Committee on Foreign Affairs. Subcommittee on International Organizations and Movements. *The American Convention on Human Rights. Hearing...93d Congress, 1st session, August 1-December 7, 1973. Washington, U.S. Govt. Print. Off., 1974. 681 p.*

Documents tracing the development of the American Convention on Human Rights and other materials presented by the American Society of International Law.

1513

U.S. Congress. House. Committee on Foreign Affairs. Subcommittee on International Organizations and Movements. *Human rights and the phenomenon of disappearances. Hearings...96th Congress, 1st session, September 20, 25, and October 18, 1979. Washington, U.S. Govt. Print. Off., 1980. 636 p.*

Hearings addressing the international problem of missing and disappeared persons, with testimony from U.S. officials, representatives of nongovernmental and inter-governmental organizations, and statements from Latin Americans who temporarily disappeared. Disappearances in Latin America, and especially in Argentina, Chile, and El Salvador, are frequently cited.

1514

U.S. Congress. House. Committee on Foreign Affairs. Subcommittee on International Organizations and Movements. *Human rights in the world community: a call for U.S. leadership; report. Hearings... 93d Congress, 2d session, March 27, 1974. Washington, U.S. Govt. Print. Off., 1974. 54 p. (International human rights. Committee print)*

Report based on public testimony and correspondence during 1973 hearings. Examines U.S. relations with governments that violate human rights. Discusses human rights protection through international, regional, and nongovernmental organizations, and problems, such as massacre and torture, deemed deserving of U.N. action. Includes disclaimers and opposing views.

1515

U.S. Congress. House. Committee on Foreign Affairs. Subcommittee on International Organizations and Movements. *International protection of human rights; the work of international organizations and the role of U.S. foreign policy. Hearings...93d Congress, 1st session, August 1; September 13, 19, 20, 27; October 3, 4, 10, 11, 16, 18, 24, 25; November 1; December 7, 1973. Washington, U.S. Govt. Print. Off., 1974. 987 p. illus. (International human rights)*

Account of hearings held to examine U.S., U.N., and international non-governmental organizations' responses to human rights violations in relation to determining U.S. foreign policy. Includes reports on "The Evolution of the American Convention on Human Rights and Prospects for its Ratification by the U.S.," "Report in Support of the Treaty-Making Power of the U.S. in Human Rights Matters," and recommendations for strengthening the U.N. in the human rights field.

1516

U.S. Congress. House. Committee on Foreign Affairs. Subcommittee on International Organizations and Movements. *Report in support of the treaty-making power of the United States in human rights matters. Prepared by the Special Committee of Lawyers of the President's Commission for the Observance of Human Rights Year 1968. 93d Congress, 1st session, August 1-December 7, 1973. Washington, U.S. Govt. Print. Off., 1974. 987 p.*

Documentation and testimony to support the treaty-making power of the U.S. to further the protection of human rights.

1517

U.S. Congress. House. Committee on Foreign Affairs. Subcommittee on International Organizations and Movements. *Review of the U.N. Commission on Human Rights. Hearings...93d Congress, 2d session, June 18 and 20, 1974. Washington, U.S. Govt. Print. Off., 1974. 92 p. (International human rights)*

Hearing to review the U.N.'s methods of handling human rights violations, the U.S. position on U.N. resolutions relating to human rights, and the U.S. role in increasing U.N. effectiveness to prevent human rights violations. Appendixes include submitted correspondence and statements and U.N. resolutions on human rights violations.

1518

U.S. Congress. House. Committee on Foreign Affairs. Subcommittee on International Organizations and Movements. *Torture and oppression in Brazil. Hearing...93d Congress, 2d session, December 11, 1974. Washington, U.S. Govt. Print. Off., 1975. 51 p. (International human rights)*

Record of testimony from a former missionary-journalist about his subjection to torture in Brazil and from a member of the U.S. Catholic Conference's delegation to Brazil in support of the human rights efforts of Brazilian clerics. Appendix includes newspaper articles on torture.

1519

U.S. Congress. House. Committee on Foreign Affairs. Subcommittee on International Organizations and Movements. *U.S. observance of International Human Rights Year 1968. Hearings...89th Congress, 2d session, August 11, 17, 1966. Washington, U.S. Govt. Print. Off., 1966. 50 p.*

Contains documents relating to human rights, as well as texts of testimonies.

1520

U.S. Congress. House. Committee on Internal Security. *The theory and practice of communism. Part 5: Marxism imposed on Chile-- Allende regime. Hearings...93d Congress, 1st session, November 15, 1973 and March 7 and 13, 1974. Washington, U.S. Govt. Print. Off., 1974. 1 v. illus. (various pagings)*

Hearings on conditions in Chile before and after the military coup of September 1973, containing testimony on the political and economic philosophy of Allende and the impact of international communist and socialist influences in Chile and other Latin American countries. Appendixes present photographs, statements, and articles on conditions in Chile, including "Three Years of Destruction," by the Chilean Printer's Association.

1521

U.S. Congress. House. Committee on International Relations. *Renewed concern for democracy and human rights, special bicentennial program, Washington, 1976; report, December 1976. Washington, U.S. Govt. Print. Off., 1977. 72 p.*

Report of the U.S. delegates to the tenth meeting between members of the House and the European Parliament, held in Washington, D.C. in 1976. Summarizes sessions and contains texts of papers dealing with common concerns such as human rights and the development of democratic institutions.

1522

U.S. Congress. House. Committee on International Relations. Subcommittee on Inter-American Affairs. *United States policy toward the Caribbean. Hearings...95th Congress, 1st session, June 28 and 30, 1977. Washington, U.S. Govt. Print. Off., 1977. 87 p.*

Report of hearings called to identify major economic and social problems and trends in Caribbean nations, and to explore their implications for U.S. foreign policy. Appendixes contain witnesses' responses and statements by scholars regarding the Caribbean.

1523

U.S. Congress. House. Committee on International Relations. *Subcommittee on International Organizations. Chile: the status of human rights and its relationship to U.S. economic assistance programs. Hearings...94th Congress, 2d session, April 29, May 5, 1976. Washington, U.S. Govt. Print. Off., 1976. 198 p.*

Hearings include testimony from witnesses from the U.S. Agency for International Development, the National Council of Churches, the Overseas Private Investment Corporation, and the U.S. Department of State. Document ends with appendixes on legal interpretations and texts provided by private human rights organizations.

1524

U.S. Congress. House. Committee on International Relations. *Subcommittee on International Organizations. Foreign assistance legislation for fiscal year 1979 (part 4): U.S. policy on human rights and military assistance Thailand, and Iran; U.S. voluntary contributions to international organizations and programs. Hearings...95th Congress, 2d session, February 15, 16, 28 and March 7 and 8, 1978. Washington, U.S. Govt. Print. Off., 1978. 787 p.*

Hearings to consider foreign economic and social assistance for fiscal year 1979. The portions dealing with Nicaragua include O.A.S. reports and testimony by Miguel D'Escoto urging the U.S. Congress to terminate U.S. military assistance to President Somoza's government.

1525

U.S. Congress. House. Committee on International Relations. *Subcommittee on International Organizations. Foreign assistance legislation for fiscal year 1980-81 (part 7): human rights reports and U.S. policy; U.S. voluntary contributions to international organizations and programs. Hearings...96th Congress, 1st session, February 28 and March 1 and 2, 1979. Washington, U.S. Govt. Print. Off., 1979. 278 p.*

Contains hearings regarding the withholding of foreign assistance from governments which persist in violating human rights and U.S. contributions to international organizations. Included also are testimonies, correspondence, and other documentation.

1526

U.S. Congress. House. Committee on International Relations. Subcommittee on International Organizations. *Human rights and United States foreign policy: a review of the Administration's record. Hearing...95th Congress, 1st session, October 25, 1977. Washington, U.S. Govt. Print. Off., 1978. 74 p.*

Hearing to review the Carter administration's human rights policy and its role in foreign affairs. Appendix includes State Department written responses to questions, an issue brief analyzing the role of human rights concerns in U.S. foreign policy formulation, and a 1974 to 1977 list of Congressional hearings, reports, and documents on human rights.

1527

U.S. Congress. House. Committee on International Relations. *Subcommittee on International Organizations. Human rights in Argentina. Hearings, 94th Congress, 2d session, September 28 and 29, 1976. Washington, U.S. Govt. Print. Off., 1976. 67 p. (International human rights)*

Report of hearings that dealt with political refugees leaving Latin America, the U.S. immigration law affecting them, and anti-Semitism, political prisoners, and torture in Argentina.

1528

U.S. Congress. House. Committee on International Relations. *Subcommittee on International Organizations. Human rights in Chile. Hearing...94th Congress, 1st session, December 9, 1975. Washington, U.S. Govt. Print. Off., 1976. 36 p.*

Eyewitness accounts of human rights conditions in Chile by two Catholic priests.

1529

U.S. Congress. House. Committee on International Relations. *Subcommittee on International Organizations. Human rights in Haiti. Hearing...94th Congress, 1st session, November 18, 1975. Washington, U.S. Govt. Print. Off., 1975. 137 p.*

Hearing to consider the implications of the human rights situation in Haiti for U.S. policy. Appendix includes submitted statements, correspondence, affidavits, and reports on human rights violations in Haiti, including Senator Edward Brooke's Congressional study mission report, "U.S. Foreign Assistance in Haiti," and the National Council of Churches of Christ in the U.S.A. 1974 resolution in support of Haitian refugees.

1530

U.S. Congress. House. Committee on International Relations. *Subcommittee on International Organizations. Human rights in Nicaragua, Guatemala, and El Salvador; implications for U.S. policy. Hearings...94th Congress, 2d session, June 8-9, 1976. Washington, U.S. Govt. Print. Off., 1976. 253 p.*

Report of hearings that considered alleged violations of human and political rights in several Central American countries, including the extent to which U.S. economic and military assistance may have contributed to such violations as well as the possible impact of termination of U.S. foreign aid in accordance with Foreign Assistance Act human rights provisions. Appendix includes statements by Central American political figures, academics, members of the U.S. Congress, and North American human rights experts.

1531

U.S. Congress. House. Committee on International Relations. *Subcommittee on International Organizations. Human rights in the Dominican Republic; the 1978 presidential elections. Hearing...95th Congress, 2d session, May 23, 1978. Washington, U.S. Govt. Print. Off., 1978. 27 p.*

Report of hearing that examined the implications for continued U.S. aid in light of the intervention by the Dominican Republic military in the May 16, 1978 presidential election. Appendix contains correspondence and testimonies.

1532

U.S. Congress. House. Committee on International Relations. *Subcommittee on International Organizations. Human rights in Uruguay and Paraguay. Hearings...94th Congress, 2d session, June 17, July 27 and 28, and August 4, 1976. Washington, U.S. Govt. Print. Off., 1976. 228 p.*

Report of hearings that examined the human rights situation in Uruguay and Paraguay. Considers application of the International Security Assistance and Arms Control Act of 1976, the possibility of amending the human rights provisions of the Foreign Assistance Act of 1961, and the proscription of U.S. security assistance to countries engaged in a consistent pattern of gross violation of human rights.

1533

U.S. Congress. House. Committee on International Relations. *Subcommittee on International Organizations. Human rights issues at the seventh regular session of the Organization of American States General Assembly. Hearing...95th Congress, 1st session, September 15, 1977. Washington, U.S. Govt. Print. Off., 1977. 30 p.*

Hearing to review the June 1977 session of the O.A.S. General Assembly concerning its consid-

erations of human rights issues. U.S. Representative to the O.A.S., Gale McGee, describes the O.A.S. debate on hemispheric human rights issues, and Tom Farer, Jr., member of the Inter-American Commission on Human Rights, discusses the structure and operation of the O.A.S. Human Rights Commission.

1534

U.S. Congress. House. Committee on International Relations. *Subcommittee on International Organizations. Human rights issues at the sixth regular session of the Organization of American States General Assembly. Hearing...94th Congress, 2d session, August 10, 19, 1976. Washington, U.S. Govt. Print. Off., 1976. 32 p. (International human rights)*

Hearing to review human rights issues discussed at the Sixth Regular Session of the O.A.S. General Assembly, Santiago, Chile, June 1976, focusing on the Inter-American Human Rights Commission investigation of the Chilean government's violation of internationally recognized human rights. Appendixes include replies to subcommittee written questions, texts of the resolutions that were adopted during the session, press releases, correspondence, Henry A. Kissinger's June 8, 1976 O.A.S. General Assembly address on human rights, and a Chilean government draft proposal on human rights.

1535

U.S. Congress. House. Committee on International Relations. *Subcommittee on International Organizations. The recent presidential elections in El Salvador: implications for U.S. foreign policy. Hearings...95th Congress, 1st session, March 9 and 17, 1977. Washington, U.S. Govt. Print. Off., 1977. 93 p.*

Hearings to consider the implications for continued U.S. aid of alleged fraud associated with the 1977 election of General Carlos H. Romero as President of El Salvador and of alleged subsequent political repression. Appendixes contain submitted statements, correspondence, written responses to subcommittee questions, and documentation supporting allegations of election fraud in El Salvador.

1536

U.S. Congress. House. Committee on International Relations. *Subcommittee on International Organizations.*

Religious persecution in El Salvador. Hearings...95th Congress, 1st session, July 21 and 29, 1977. Washington, U.S. Govt. Print. Off., 1977. 85 p. (International human rights)

Hearings to investigate allegations of religious persecution by the government of El Salvador, including incidents of torture, assassination, and imprisonment of Catholic priests, and the relationship between the government and the White Warriors Union. Appendixes include submitted statements and press releases, and an analysis of the Catholic Church's role in El Salvador with a list of incidents of persecution of Catholic priests.

1537

U.S. Congress. House. Committee on International Relations. Subcommittee on International Organizations. *Review of the United Nations 33d Commission on Human Rights. Hearing...95th Congress, 1st session, May 19, 1977. Washington, U.S. Govt. Print. Off., 1977. 35 p. (International human rights)*

Hearing to consider the U.S. delegation's report on the U.N. Commission on Human Rights, presented to a session held in Geneva in 1977. A statement by U.S. Representative to the U.N., Allard Lowenstein, is also included.

1538

U.S. Congress. House. Committee on International Relations. *Subcommittee on International Political and Military Affairs. U.S. citizens imprisoned in Mexico. Hearings...94th Congress, 1st session, April 29 and 30, 1975, October 22, 1975, January 27, 1976, and June 29, 1976. Washington, U.S. Govt. Print. Off., 1975-1976. 3 v.*

Reports from three sets of hearings that were held to investigate charges of mistreatment of U.S. citizens arrested and imprisoned on drug charges by Mexican authorities. Included are texts of the President's message on drug abuse (1976), statements by the U.S. Department of State describing its own investigations and efforts on behalf of U.S. citizens detained in Mexico, as well as statements by the U.S. Drug Enforcement Administration and a description of its functions.

1539

U.S. Congress. *House. Committee on International Relations. Subcommittee on International Trade and Commerce. U.S. trade embargo of Cuba. Hearings...94th Congress, 1st session,*

on H.R. 6382... Washington, U.S. Govt. Print. Off., 1976. 653 p.

Report of hearings held May 8 to September 23, 1975, presenting various views on the U.S. trade embargo of Cuba. Includes ample documentation.

1540

U.S. Congress. Senate. Ad Hoc Subcommittee on Human Rights Conventions. *Human rights conventions. Hearings...90th Congress, 1st session. Washington, U.S. Govt. Print. Off., 1967. 2 v.*

Hearings on international conventions dealing with the protection of human rights. Lists countries that have ratified certain treaties protecting basic rights.

1541

U.S. Congress. Senate. Committee on Foreign Relations. *Subcommittee on Foreign Assistance. Human rights. Hearings...95th Congress, 1st session, March 4 and 7, 1977. Washington, U.S. Govt. Print. Off., 1977. 104 p.*

Hearings focusing on possible cutoff or reduction of military and economic aid under the Foreign Assistance Act and Foreign Military Sales Act to countries found guilty of violating internationally recognized human rights. Includes recommendations for congressional measures to promote rights observance abroad, and summarizes the previous administration's rights attitudes and policies, and the potential effects of aid withdrawal.

1542

U.S. Congress. Senate. Committee on Foreign Relations. Subcommittee on Foreign Assistance. *Human rights reports. 95th Congress, 1st session, March 1977. Washington, U.S. Govt. Print. Off., 1977. 143 p.*

Annual report to Congress by the U.S. Department of State reviewing human rights practices in those countries proposed as security assistance recipients for fiscal year 1978. Contains individual summaries reviewing political and legal situations affecting civil liberties and the observance of internationally recognized human rights in each of 82 countries, as of December 1976.

1543

U.S. Congress. Senate. Committee on Government Operations. Permanent Subcommittee on Investigations. *International human rights: selected declarations and agreements. 94th Congress, 2d session. Washington, U.S. Govt. Print. Off., 1976. 69 p. (Committee print)*

Annotated collection of human rights documents drawn from publications of the U.N., the O.A.S., and the European Community.

1544

U.S. Congress. Senate. Committee on Government Operations. *Permanent Subcommittee on Investigations. International human rights; selected statements and initiatives. 95th Congress, 1st session. Washington, U.S. Govt. Print. Off., 1977. 46 p. (Committee print)*

Comments by international human rights advocates regarding freedom of the press, security assistance, political prisoners, and refugees. Included are a brief chronology of events in Chile during 1973 to 1974 and a human rights report from Paraguay.

1545

U.S. Congress. Senate. Committee on the Judiciary. Subcommittee on Criminal Laws and Procedures. *The terrorist and his victim. Hearings...95th Congress, 1st session, July 21, 1977. Washington, U.S. Govt. Print. Off., 1977. 33 p.*

Report of a hearing in which were discussed causes and effects of terrorism and possible countermeasures for combating terrorist activities. Testimony emphasizes the importance of terrorists' personality traits over political motivation, and the emotional repercussions for terrorists' hostages. It suggests countermeasures of expanded domestic intelligence efforts and changes in news media coverage of terrorist actions. Includes bibliographic references.

1546

U.S. Congress. Senate. Committee on the Judiciary. Subcommittee to Investigate Problems Connected with Refugees and Escapees. *Refugee and humanitarian problems in Chile. Part 1. Hearing... 93d Congress, 1st session, September 28, 1973. Washington, U.S. Govt. Print. Off., 1973. 117 p.*

Hearing examining the extent of the violation of human rights following the overthrow of the Allende government in Chile, and U.S. policy toward and relations with the new government. Appendixes contain submitted statements, articles, and the Kennedy Amendment to the Foreign Assistance Authorization on Human Rights in Chile, from the Congressional Record of October 2, 1973 and the Kennedy-Fraser Resolution on Chile, September 20, 1973. Classified information has been deleted.

1547

U.S. Congress. Senate. Committee on the Judiciary. Subcommittee to Investigate Problems Connected with Refugees and Escapees. Refugee and humanitarian problems in Chile. *Part 2. Hearing... 93d Congress, 2d session, July 23, 1974. Washington, U.S. Govt. Print. Off., 1974. 304 p. illus.*

Report of continued hearings on the extent of violation of human rights in Chile and on U.S. policy toward and relations with the Pinochet government. Appendixes include correspondence between General Pinochet and U.S. government officials regarding the status and treatment of persons associated with the Allende government, as well as a "Memorandum on the Application of the Penal Law in Cases under Prosecution for Political Motives in Chile."

1548

U.S. Congress. Senate. Committee on the Judiciary. Subcommittee to Investigate Problems Connected with Refugees and Escapees. Refugee and humanitarian problems in Chile. *Part 3: Chile parole program. Hearing...94th Congress, 1st session, October 2, 1975. Washington, U.S. Govt. Print. Off., 1976. 221 p. illus.*

Continuation of hearings to investigate humanitarian problems resulting from the 1973 coup in Chile. This hearing focuses on the apparent lack of urgency within Federal agencies to assist in resettlement of Chilean political refugees. Appendixes include correspondence, articles, submitted statements, and the General Accounting Office's 1975 "Assessment of Selected U.S. Embassy Consular Efforts to Assist and Protect Americans Overseas During Crises and Emergencies."

1549

U.S. Department of State. *Country reports on human rights practices. Report submitted to the Committee on International Relations, U.S. House of Representatives, and the Committee on Foreign Relations, U.S. Senate. 95th Congress, 2d session. Washington, U.S. Govt. Print. Off., 1978. 426 p. (Joint committee print)*

Contains a section on Latin America. Concise summary format analyzing each country's human rights situation in terms of torture, degrading punishment, arbitrary arrest or imprisonment, denial of fair public trial, invasion of the home, government policies, respect for civil and political liberties, and government investigations of human rights violations.

1550

U.S. Department of State. *Human rights and U.S. policy: Argentina, Haiti, Indonesia, Iran, Peru, and the Philippines. Reports submitted to the Committee on International Relations, U.S. House of Representatives by the Department of State, pursuant to Section 502 B(c) of the International Security Assistance and Arms Export Control Act of 1976. Washington, U.S. Govt. Print. Off., 1976. 37 p.*

Declassified reports by the State Department on the differential observance of internationally recognized human rights and the implications of such uneven observance for U.S. foreign policy in Argentina, Haiti, Indonesia, Iran, Peru, and the Philippines.

1551

U.S. Department of State. *Human rights practices in countries receiving U.S. aid. Report submitted to the Committee on Foreign Relations, U.S. Senate, and Committee on Foreign Affairs, U.S. House of Representatives, by the Department of State in accordance with Sections 116(d) and 502B(b) of the Foreign Assistance Act of 1961, as amended February 8, 1979. 96th Congress, 1st session. Washington, U.S. Govt. Print. Off., 1979. 706 p.*

Brief reports comparing constitutional protections of human rights with actual conditions in 20 Central and South American countries.

1552

U.S. Department of State. *Human rights practices in countries receiving U.S. security assistance. Report submitted to the Committee on International Relations, House of Repre-*

sentatives, April 15, 1977. 95th Congress, 1st session. Washington, U.S. Govt. Print. Off., 1977. 137 p. (Committee print)

Annual report to Congress by the Department of State, reviewing human rights in those countries proposed as security assistance recipients for fiscal year 1978. Contains individual summaries of political and legal situations affecting civil liberties and the observance of internationally recognized human rights in each of 82 countries as of December 1976.

1553

U.S. Department of State. Bureau of Public Affairs. *Human rights, unfolding of the American tradition. Washington, U.S. Govt. Print. Off., 1968. 127 p.*

A selection of significant documents and statements relating to human rights, compiled by the Department of State's Historical Office for the President's Commission for the Observance of Human Rights Year 1968.

1554

U.S. Library of Congress. Foreign Affairs and National Defense Division. *Human rights conditions in selected countries and the U.S. response. Prepared for the Subcommittee on International Organizations of the Committee on International Relations, U.S. House of Representatives, by the Foreign Affairs and National Defense Division, Congressional Research Service, Library of Congress. Washington, U.S. Govt. Print. Off., 1978. 372 p.*

At head of title: 95th Congress, 2d session. Committee print.

After a brief discussion of the criteria used in its human rights evaluations, each country chosen is analyzed succinctly, and U.S. policy recommendations are given. Argentina, Brazil, Chile, Cuba, and El Salvador are the Latin American nations considered. Includes bibliographic references.

1555

U.S. Library of Congress. Foreign Affairs and National Defense Division. *Human rights in the international community and in U.S. foreign policy, 1945-1976. Prepared for the Subcommittee on International Organizations of the Committee on International Relations, House of Representatives, by the Foreign Affairs and National Defense*

Division, Congressional Research Service, Library of Congress. Washington, U.S. Govt. Print. Off., 1977. 58 p.

At head of title: 95th Congress, 1st session. Committee print.

Discusses human rights traditions, international community action to protect human rights, and human rights and U.S. foreign policy. Appendixes include charts of international human rights documents concluded under the auspices of the U.N. and its agencies as well as current and other legislation enacted on human rights.

1556

U.S. President, 1974-1977 (Ford). *Bill of Rights Day, Human Rights Day and Week, 1976: a proclamation. U.S. Department of State. Department of State bulletin, v. 76, Jan. 10, 1977: 29.*

Bicentennial Presidential proclamation setting December 10, 1976 as Human Rights Day and December 15, 1976 as Bill of Rights Day, and calling on the American people to observe the week of December 10, 1976 as Human Rights Week. All Americans are also urged to bring about the full realization of the ideals and aspirations expressed in the Bill of Rights and the U.N. Declaration of Human Rights.

1557

U.S. President, 1977-1981 (Carter). *Memorandum of February 15, 1978. Determination pursuant to Section 2(c)(1) of the Migration and Refugee Assistance Act of 1962, as amended, (the "Act") authorizing the use of $300,000 of funds made available from the United States Emergency Refugee and Migration Assistance Fund. Federal register, v. 43, Mar. 1, 1978: 8249.*

Statement of President Carter's determination to authorize financial assistance to political refugees from Latin America.

U.S. Policy Regarding Human Rights in Latin America

1558
Ackerman, David M. *Human rights conditions on foreign aid statutes.* [Washington, D.C., Library of Congress, Congressional Research Service] 1976. 8 p.

Not available for annotation.

1559
Arnson, Cynthia, and Michael Klare. *Law or no law; the arms flow. Nation, v. 226, Apr. 29, 1978: 502-505.*

Argues that if the Carter administration's human rights policy is to be taken seriously, there must be strict enforcement of the ban on arms sales to Chile as stipulated in the Arms Export Control Act of 1976.

1560
Astiz, Carlos A. *U.S. policy and Latin American reaction. Current history, v. 74, Feb. 1978: 49-52, 89.*

Analyzes the effects of U.S. policies toward Latin America and concludes that: "As the violations are toned down (or are covered up more efficiently), no major controversies appear on the horizon [and that] considering the demands placed on the U.S. by other parts of the world, the continuation of its policy of 'benign neglect' is not only prudent but perhaps even in the best interest of all concerned."

1561
Balmer, Thomas. *The use of conditions in foreign relations legislation. Denver journal of international law and policy, v. 7, spring 1978: 197-238.*

Considers possible conflict in foreign policy over human rights between the Congress and the President and suggests that Congress should supervise and the President should shape policy. Describes the use by Congress of "condition clauses" to link foreign aid to human rights.

1562
Behuniak, Thomas E. *The law of unilateral humanitarian intervention by armed forces: a legal survey. Military law review, v. 79, winter 1978: 157-191.*

U.S. Army Staff Judge Advocate reviews laws and customs governing the use of force by one country to protect inhabitants of other countries from mistreatment. Drawing on examples from Latin America, the Middle East, and Africa, the author concludes that U.S. treaties of mutual defense should uphold the principle of limited intervention.

1563
Bender, Lynn Darrell. *Selective morality: U.S. foreign policy and human rights in Latin America. Review/Revista Interamericana, v. 7, summer 1977: 161-162.*

Not available for annotation.

1564
Bennet, Douglas J. *Letters of October 13, 1977 and October 21, 1977 to Edward M. Kennedy. Extension of remarks of the Hon. Edward M. Kennedy, of Massachusetts, December 15, 1977. Congressional record, 95th Congress, 1st session, v. 123, no. 197: S 19525-S 19526.*

Reply to Senator Kennedy from the Assistant Secretary for Congressional Relations, U.S. Department of State, about the plight of Jesuits in El Salvador.

1565
Bilder, Richard B. *Human rights and U.S. foreign policy: short term prospects. Virginia journal of international law, v. 14, summer 1974: 597-609.*

Discusses the role of human rights in U.S. foreign policy. Attempts to provide conceptual, empirical, and humanistic reasons for the low priority traditionally given to human rights policy objectives.

1566
Boersner, Demetrio. *Carter, los derechos humanos, y América Latina. Nueva sociedad, no. 31-32, jul./oct. 1977: 61-75.*

Surveys President Carter's human rights policy in Latin America.

1567

Brockman, James R. *Our man in Managua. America (New York), v. 136, Mar. 26, 1977: 268-269.*

Brief statement of concern about U.S. military and human rights policies in the Carter administration during President Somoza's state of siege in Nicaragua.

1568

Brown, Peter G., and Douglas MacLean, eds. *Human rights and U.S. foreign policy: principles and applications. Lexington, Mass., Lexington Books, 1979. 310 p.*

Discusses the Carter administration's human rights policy in several parts of the world, including Latin America. Includes bibliographic references and index.

1569

Buergenthal, Thomas. *International human rights: U.S. policy and priorities. Virginia journal of international law, v. 14, summer 1974: 611-621.*

Argues that the role of the U.S. is diminishing in influencing international human rights programs. Offers explanation of legislative obstacles to the development of more effective policies and proposes measures by which the U.S. could regain some of its former influence in the creation of international human rights law.

1570

Buncher, Judith F., ed. *Facts on file: human rights and American diplomacy; 1975-1977. New York [s.n.] 1977. 271 p.*

Reports on the Carter administration's activities in the field of human rights and on specific countries. Contributing authors are Joseph Fickes, Alexander Grant, Christopher Hunt, Hal Kosut, Chris Larson, and Melinda Maidens.

1571

Carliner, David. *The implementation of human rights under U.S. immigration law. In Tuttle, James C., ed. International human rights; law and practice. Chicago, American Bar Association, 1978. p. 127-134.*

Examines U.S. laws and programs regulating aliens and refugees, taking into account the effects of the 1967 U.N. Protocol on Refugees' rights.

1572

Carter, Jimmy. *Remarks before the Venezuelan Congress, March 29, 1978. In U.S. President. Public papers of the President of the United States; Jimmy Carter. 1978, v. 1. Washington, U.S. Govt. Print. Off., 1979. p. 619-626.*

Text of President Carter's speech. Discusses Venezuela's significant contribution to the American Convention on Human Rights, the Inter-American Human Rights Commission, and the promotion of democracy in Latin America.

1573

Carter y la lógica del imperialismo. *Hugo Assman, ed., colaboran Noam Chomsky...[et al]. Ciudad Universitaria Rodrigo Facio, Costa Rica, Editorial Universitaria Centroamericana, 1978. 475 p. (Col. Dei)*

Articles and essays devoted to analyzing the Carter administration's human rights policy. Examines critically Carter's conception of "pax americana," inter-American relations, and U.S. Latin American policy.

1574

Carter y los derechos humanos. *Estudios centroamericanos, v. 32, abr./mayo 1977: 311-312.*

Very brief statement about President Carter's foreign policy and human rights.

1575

Center for International Policy. *Human rights and the U.S. foreign assistance program. Washington, Center for International Policy, 1977/78 +*

Report for 1977/78 issued in 2 vols.

Concerned with U.S. military and economic aid programs and their effect on human rights in Chile, Brazil, Nicaragua, and Argentina. Presents a brief history of each country and summarizes current conditions of juridical, political, social, and economic rights. Includes graphs, charts, and maps.

1576

Center for National Security Studies. *CIA's covert operations vs. human rights. Washington, 1978. 23 p.*

Criticizes C.I.A. operations in the Third World and calls for an active citizens' campaign in the U.S. to end the C.I.A.'s covert activities abroad.

1577

Chomsky, Noam. *"Human rights" and American foreign policy.Nottingham, United Kingdom, Spokesman Books, 1978. 90 p.*

Critical assessment of U.S. human rights policies, arguing that they are a camouflage for traditional national interests.

1578

Chomsky, Noam, and Edward S. Herman. *The United States versus human rights in the Third World. Monthly review, v. 29, July/Aug. 1977: 22-45.*

Strongly criticizes U.S. human rights policies for their inconsistencies, using the Dominican Republic, Argentina, Brazil, Chile, Cuba, Guatemala, and Uruguay as examples.

1579

Christopher, Luella Sue. *Pro and con arguments relating to the proposed human rights amendment (sec. 502b) to S. 2662, the Senate substitute to the administration bill, "International Security Assistance and Arms Export Control Act of 1976." [Washington, Library of Congress, Congressional Research Service] 1976. 7 p.*

Presents both sides of the argument of tying international security assistance to human rights issues.

1580

Christopher, Warren. *The diplomacy of the first year. U.S. Department of State. Department of State bulletin, v. 78, no. 2012, Mar. 1978: 30-33.*

Briefly outlines U.S. foreign policy during the first year of the Carter administration.

1581

Christopher, Warren. *Human rights: principle and realism.Current world leaders; speeches and reports, v. 6, Dec. 1977: 1-9.*

The U.S. Deputy Secretary of State clearly enunciates President Carter's policy for the promotion of human rights in the hemisphere. Defends the compatibility of economic development with political and civil rights and praises the Inter-American Commission of Human Rights.

1582

Coalition for a new foreign and military policy. *Human rights action guide, 1978. Washington [1978?]. 15 p.*

Analyzes President Carter's human rights policy. Recommends Congressional lobbying procedures and a timetable for human rights action. Lists human rights covenants and discusses legal terrorism in the U.S.

1583

Comblin, Joseph. *A ideologia da segurança nacional: o poder militar na América Latina. Rio de Janeiro, Civilizaçao Brasileira, 1978. 251 p.*

Reviews the doctrine of national security in the U.S. and Latin America. Among the Latin American countries discussed are Argentina, Bolivia, Brazil, Chile, Ecuador, Peru, and Uruguay.

1584

Comment: the international human rights treaties: some problems of policy and interpretation. *University of Pennsylvania law review, v. 126, Apr. 1978: 886-929.*

Editorial comment on President Carter's U.S. human rights policies and U.S. government powers to enter into treaties having human rights content. Includes summary of treaties, covenants, and conventions on human rights. Concludes advising U.S. ratification of four treaties then under consideration.

1585

Commission on United States-Latin American Relations. *The Americans in a changing world: a report of the*

Commission on United States-Latin American Relations. With a pref. by Sol M. Linowitz; selected papers by Kalman H. Silvert...[et al.] New York, Quadrangle, New York Times Book Co. [1975]. 248 p.

Commission report that includes several opinions about human rights policy objectives of the U.S. and suggestions for policy changes by the chairman, Sol M. Linowitz and other scholars.

1586
Commission on United States-Latin American Relations. *The United States and Latin America, next steps: a second report. New York, Center for Inter-American Relations, 1976. 26 p.*

General discussion of what are termed disturbing developments in the area of human rights throughout Latin America.

1587
Conference on Implementing a Human Rights Commitment in United States Foreign Policy, Carnegie Endowment for International Peace, 1977. *Report. New York, International League for Human Rights, 1977. [85] leaves.*

Reaffirms the commitment to human rights as an integral part of the foreign policy of the U.S. Includes recommendations to the Carter administration and the world monetary agencies.

1588
Conference Report on Human Rights 9214, I.M.F. Supplementary Financing Facility. *Congressional record, 95th Congress, 2d session, v. 124, Sept. 8, 1978: H11037-H11046.*

Discussion concerning the reinstatement of the human rights amendment to the Bretton Woods Agreement Act, which allowed the U.S. to participate in the Supplementary Financing Facility of the International Monetary Fund.

1589
[Congressional Colloquy on Capitol Hill] Washington, 1977. *United States policy toward refugees; special focus on Latin America. New York, Fund for New Priorities in America, 1977. 20 p.*

Reviews briefly current U.S. policy regarding refugees from Latin America.

1590
Costello, Mary. *Political prisoners. Editorial research reports (Washington), v. 2, no. 13, 1976: 723-744.*

Reviews the plight of political prisoners around the world and the North American response to international violations of human rights.

1591
Los derechos humanos en América Latina. *Organización Continental Latinoamericana de Estudiantes (OCLAE), v. 13, no. 5, 1979: 5-21.*

Critical of the Carter administration's human rights policies toward Latin America.

1592
Derian, Patricia M. *The Carter administration and human rights, pt. 2: a commitment sustained. Worldview, v. 21, July/Aug. 1978: 11-12.*

Not available for annotation.

1593
Derian, Patricia M. *Human rights and American foreign policy. Universal human rights, v. 1, Jan./Mar. 1979: 3-9.*

Assesses recent U.S. human rights policy, its focus, characteristics, and diplomatic efforts. Concludes with observations supporting increased promotion and incorporation of human rights.

1594
Derian, Patricia M. *Human rights and United States foreign relations: an overview. Case Western Reserve journal of international law, v. 10, spring 1978: 243-249.*

Synopsis of the Carter administration's human rights policy objectives and recent reorganization efforts, prepared by the Assistant Secretary of State for Human Rights.

1595
Derian, Patricia M. *Human rights in Latin America. Washington, U.S. Department of State, Bureau of Public Affairs, 1979. 3 p. (Current policy, no. 68)*

The Assistant Secretary for Human Rights and Humanitarian Affairs briefly describes U.S. human rights policy and reviews the present human rights situation in Argentina, Cuba, Nicaragua, El Salvador, Guatemala, Uruguay, and other American nations. Speech presented at Florida International University, Miami, May 18, 1979.

1596

Derian, Patricia M. *Human rights in United States foreign policy; the executive perspective. In Tuttle, James C., ed. International human rights; law and practice. Chicago, American Bar Association, 1978. p. 177-181.*

Examines the U.S. human rights concern and the foreign policy initiatives taken by the Carter administration.

1597

Development Coordination Committee. *Development issues: U.S. actions affecting the development of low-income countries. The first annual report of the Chairman of the Development Coordination Committee transmitted to the Congress February 1, 1979. Washington, U.S. Department of State, Agency for International Development, 1979. 204 p. illus.*

Focuses on the role of developing countries in the world economy and the relationship between human rights and basic human needs. Discusses U.S. foreign assistance programs and international instruments for building human resources.

1598

Drew, Elizabeth. *Human rights; a reporter at large. New Yorker, July 18, 1977: 36-38, 40-42, 44, 46, 51-52, 54-62.*

Holds that a human rights policy will be hard to implement because the advocacy of human rights as a foreign policy can interfere with other legitimate foreign policy goals.

1599

Drinan, Robert, John J. McAward, and Thomas P. Anderson. *El Salvador-1978; report of findings of an investigatory mission. Boston Unitarian Universalist Service Committee, 1978. 87 p.*

Report of an inquiry conducted by U.S. Congressman Robert Drinan, John J. McAward, and

Thomas P. Anderson, exposing human rights violations. Includes useful appendixes.

1600

Early, Tracy. *The Carter administration and human rights, part 1: a crusade quickly cancelled. Worldview, v. 21, July/Aug. 1978: 10, 12.*

Not available for annotation.

1601

Fagen, Patricia Weiss. *U.S. foreign policy and human rights: the role of Congress. In Cassese, Antonio, ed. Parliamentary control over foreign policy. Leyden, Netherlands, Sijthoff and Noordhoff, 1980.*

Reviews human rights policies and positions taken by the U.S. Congress from 1973 to 1979.

1602

Fagen, Richard R., ed. *Capitalism and the state in U.S.-Latin American relations. Contributors, Cynthia Arnson...[et al.] Stanford, Calif., Stanford University Press, 1979. 446 p.*

Three chapters deal with the human rights consequences of U.S. economic and political policies. Other chapters include information relevant to human rights concerns in U.S.-Latin American relations.

1603

Farer, Tom L. *United States foreign policy and the protection of human rights: observations and proposals. Virginia journal of international law, v. 14, summer 1974: 623-651.*

Examines the nature and impact of human rights considerations on U.S. foreign policy. Suggests that Congress might encourage support for the human rights cause through the organized educational system, mass media, committee hearings, and legislation.

1604

Fontaine, Roger W. *The end of a beautiful relationship. Foreign policy, no. 28, fall 1977: 166-174.*

Argues that a century of close ties between the U.S. and Brazil has ended on two issues: human rights and nonproliferation of nuclear weapons.

1605

Frankel, Charles. *Human rights and foreign policy. New York, Foreign Policy Association, 1978. 64 p. (Headline series, 241)*

Holds that the association of the U.S. with the idea of fundamental human rights has made the country a place of special hope.

1606

Fraser, Donald M. *Freedom and foreign policy. Foreign policy, no. 14, spring 1977: 140-156.*

Makes suggestions concerning the formulation of a less ambiguous U.S. human rights policy which will take into account the need to protect internationally recognized freedoms.

1607

Fraser, Donald M. *Human rights and United States foreign policy; the Congressional perspective. In Tuttle, James C., ed. International human rights; law and practice. Chicago, American Bar Association, 1978. p. 167-181.*

Analyzes the Carter administration policy in the human rights field, the use of human rights as an ideological weapon, military and economic aid, and the administration's support for ratification of several important human rights treaties.

1608

Fraser, Donald M. *The U.S. and human rights. Christianity and crisis, v. 36, Dec. 27, 1976: 314-316.*

Examines the role of the U.S. government in the promotion of human rights.

1609

Fraser, Donald M., and John P. Salzberg. *Foreign policy and effective strategies for human rights. Universal human rights, v. 1, Jan./Mar. 1979: 11-18.*

Finds evidence of a general weakening in the commitment to human rights on the part of the U.S. Congress and the Carter administration. Some problems in the international promotion of human rights are discussed and strategies for more effective realization of human rights suggested.

1610

Fund for New Priorities in America. *United States policy toward refugees: special focus on Latin America. New York, 1977. 20 p.*

Edited transcript of a Congressional colloquy dealing with the present U.S. policy toward refugees, with special attention to Latin America and the Southern Cone.

1611

Hanson, Christopher. *Behind the paper curtain: asylum policy versus asylum practice. An article from the New York University Review of Law and Social Change of Winter 1978. Extension of remarks of the Hon. Edward Kennedy, of Massachusetts, in the Senate, Sept. 15, 1978. Congressional record, 95th Congress, 2d session, v. 124: S 15247-S 15258.*

Examines the need for the U.S. to establish a national refugee policy. Includes a discussion of the plight of Chilean and Haitian refugees.

1612

Henkin, Louis. *The Constitution, treaties, and international human rights. University of Pennsylvania law review, v. 116, Apr. 1968: 1012-1032.*

Discusses the general refusal of the U.S. to adhere to international efforts to establish common minimum standards for individual human rights, the limitations that treaties are subject to under the Constitution, and U.S. involvement with international human rights covenants.

1613

Henkin, Louis. *The United States and the crisis in human rights. Virginia journal of international law, v. 14, summer 1974: 653-671.*

Identifies the "crisis" in human rights and the responsibility of the U.S. in promoting leadership to alleviate that crisis. Also discusses the origins of human rights in U.S. foreign policy, and the problems generated by their inclusion.

1614

Holland, Max, and Kai Bird. *Siracusa, our man in Uruguay. Nation, v. 224, Mar. 19, 1977: 334-337.*

Argues that the U.S. Ambassador to Uruguay caters to the sensitivities of Uruguayan officialdom at the expense of human rights, in spite of changes in official American foreign policy.

1615

Human rights abroad: reality or illusion for U.S. policy? Great decisions (New York), no. 240, 1978: 4-15. *Holds that President Carter's proclamation of human rights as a fundamental tenet of U.S. foreign policy has pleased some leaders and worried others. Argues that, within the U.S., the stance was welcomed as reflecting the U.S. heritage of freedom and its desire to be a moral force in the world.*

1616

Human rights and humanitarian affairs. *United States government manual. Washington, U.S. Govt. Print. Off., 1980. p. 433.*

Explains that the Bureau of Human Rights and Humanitarian Affairs of the U.S. Department of State has responsibility for the formulation and development and, in cooperation with other bureaus, the implementation of U.S. policy relating to the observance of human rights in the world. The Bureau maintains liaison with nongovernmental organizations active in the human rights field. It is responsible for the preparation of the annual report on human rights practices in countries that are members of the U.N.

1617

Humphrey, Hubert H. *The Senate Foreign Relations Committee and the issue of international human rights. In Tuttle, James C., ed. International human rights; law and practice. Chicago, American Bar Association, 1978. p. 183-188.*

The late Senator Humphrey examines the issues of international human rights with which the U.S. Senate Foreign Relations Committee has been grappling. Describes four legislative initiatives in the area of human rights.

1618

International Commission of Jurists. *Report on the events in Panama, January 9-12, 1964. Geneva [1964]. 46 p.*

Commission report that exonerates U.S. Canal Zone police of alleged violations of human rights during civil disturbances, but that suggests a change in attitude among U.S. residents of the Zone.

1619

International League for Human Rights. *Implementing a human rights commitment in United States foreign policy. [New York] 1977. 83 p.*

A wide-ranging report with many specific suggestions concerning how the President, Congress, the U.N. and nongovernmental agencies could further the human rights cause.

1620

Iriarte, Gregorio, and Arturo Sist. *De la seguridad nacional al trilateralismo. Estudios centroamericanos (ECA), v. 33, enero/feb. 1978: 28-36.*

Analyzes the Carter administration's human rights stance and the changes it has made in U.S. foreign policy toward military regimes.

1621

Johnson, Donald C. *Congress, the executives and human rights legislation. Foreign service journal, v. 53, Dec. 1976: 18- 20, 28.*

Argues that recent U.S. Congressional legislation making economic and security assistance to developing countries contingent on each country's level of civil liberties is poorly conceived.

1622

Karnow, Stanley. *Carter and human rights. Saturday review, v. 4, Apr. 2, 1977: 7-11.*

Asks whether the President's bold initiatives can improve the plight of millions of people oppressed by tyranny.

1623

Kennedy, Edward M. *Human rights in El Salvador. Remarks in the Senate of the United States, Dec. 15, 1977. Congressional record, 95th Congress, 1st session, v. 123, no. 197: S 19524-S 19525.*

Presents Senator Kennedy's correspondence with the U.S. Department of State concerning the safety of Jesuits in El Salvador.

1624

Kennedy, Edward M. *Human rights in Nicaragua. Remarks in the Senate of the United States, Dec. 15, 1977.*

Congressional record, 95th Congress, 1st session, v. 123, no. 197 - part 2: S 19787-S 19788.

Statement on human rights in Nicaragua, suggesting that no military assistance be provided by the U.S. to the Somoza government.

1625
Kennedy, Edward M. *Our hemisphere's mission. Speech to the Inter-American Press Association, Miami, Fla., Oct. 13, 1978. Congressional record, 95th Congress, 2d session, v. 12 4, no. 168 - part 5, Oct. 14, 1978: S 19428-S 19432.*

Summarizes the outstanding issues between the U.S. and its neighbors in the Western Hemisphere. Includes a discussion of the human rights record in the Dominican Republic, Brazil, and Chile.

1626
Kennedy, Edward M. *U.S. policy toward Argentina. Remarks and extension of remarks in the Senate of the United States, Oct. 14, 1978. Congressional record, 95th Congress, 2d session, v. 124, no. 168 - part 5: S 19433-S 19452.*

Correspondence with the U.S. Department of State about human rights violations in Argentina. Introduced to show the basis for the senator's objections to continued U.S. assistance to Argentina.

1627
Kinzer, Stephen. *Nicaragua: a wholly-owned subsidiary. New republic, v. 176, Apr. 9, 1977: 14-17.*

Summarizes past U.S. policy toward Nicaragua and compares it to the new emphasis of the Carter administration on human rights.

1628
Klare, Michael T. *Supplying repression: U.S. support for authoritarian regimes abroad. Washington, Institute for Policy Studies, 1978. 72 p.*

Discusses the U.S. role in supplying Third World governments with the weaponry and "the know-how of repression."

1629
Klare, Michael T., and Max Holland. *Conventional arms restraint: an unfulfilled promise. Washington, Institute for Policy Studies, 1978. 8 p.*

Analysis of the recent U.S. arms export policy, with suggestions that it reflect more closely the human rights concerns of the Carter administration.

1630
Klare, Michael T., and Nancy Stein. *Exporting the tools of repression: handcuffs, mace and armored cars. Nation, v. 223, Oct. 16, 1976: 365-370.*

Discussion of U.S. military sales to civil security forces abroad, based on documents obtained under the U.S. Freedom of Information Act. Includes examples drawn from several Latin American countries.

1631
Kommers, Donald P., and Gilbert D. Loescher, eds. *Human rights and American foreign policy. Notre Dame, Ind., University of Notre Dame Press, 1979. 333 p.*

General work that includes essays on individual and group rights and American foreign policy.

1632
Lefever, Ernest W. *Prospects for United States-Chilean relations. Statement. In U.S. Congress. House. Committee on Foreign Affairs. Subcommittee on Inter-American Affairs. United States and Chile during the Allende years, 1970-1973. Hearing...August 5, 1974. Washington, U.S. Govt. Print. Off., 1975. p. 181-205. illus.*

Testimony by a senior fellow at the Brookings Institution concerning the prospects for U.S.-Chilean relations.

1633
Lefever, Ernest W. *The trivialization of human rights. Policy review, no. 3, winter 1978: 11-26.*

Examines six alleged flaws in the human rights crusade of the Carter administration.

1634

Lillich, Richard B. *Humanitarian intervention and the United Nations. Charlottesville, University Press of Virginia [1973]. 240 p. (Virginia legal studies)*

Proceedings of a conference sponsored by the International Law Institute and the Carnegie Endowment for International Peace, held in Charlottesville, Va., in March 1972.

1635

Lockwood, Theodore D., Duane Shank, and Phillip Wheaton. *Jimmy Carter's foreign policy: human rights and the Trilateral Commission. Washington, American Christians Toward Socialism, 1977. 73 p.*

Critical assessment of President Carter's foreign policy.

1636

Loescher, G. D. *U.S. human rights policy and international financial institutions. World today (London), v. 33, Dec. 1977: 453-463.*

Praises President Carter's policies as superior to those of either Presidents Nixon or Ford. Criticizes Congress for continuing to provide financial assistance to countries that violate human rights.

1637

Martin, William M. *Human rights and foreign policy: the relationship of theory and action. Parameters, v. 8, Sept. 1978: 30-40.*

Analyzes the implications of President Carter's human rights policies for East-West relations, answering critics of those policies. Includes bibliographic references.

1638

Martz, John D., and Lars Schoultz, eds. *Latin America, the United States, and the inter-American system. Boulder, Colo., Westview Press, 1980. 271 p. illus. (Westview special studies on Latin America and the Caribbean)*

Analyzes the perspectives with which policymakers and policy analysts orient the theory and practice of contemporary inter-American relations. Explains the prominence of these per-spectives in terms of major societal values. Discusses human rights and policy toward Latin America. Includes index.

1639

Members of Congress for Peace through Law. *Education Fund and Human Rights Internet, eds. Human rights directory, 1979. Washington, Human Rights Internet, 1979. 155 p.*

Comprehensive directory of international human rights organizations, prepared as a reference for members of the U.S. Congress and their staff, government officials, human rights activists, and students. Includes subject and topical index.

1640

Mondale, Walter F. *Human rights in America. Catholic lawyer, v. 23, winter 1977: 25-32.*

Address to the American Bar Association by the U.S. Vice President, former member of the U.S. Senate Select Intelligence Committee. Discusses investigations of governmental abuse of power.

1641

Moral policemen of the world? *U.S. news and world report, v. 82, Mar. 14, 1977: 17-21. Asserts that worldwide implementation of President Carter's human rights doctrine could lead to difficult and dangerous situations.*

1642

Morell, Jim. *A human rights success story: the Harkin Amendment on the international bank. Memo of the Center for International Extension of the remarks of the Honorable Tom Harkin, of Iowa, in the House of Representatives, Sept.7, 1978. Congressional record, 95th Congress, 2d session, v. 124: E 4847-E 4848.*

Assesses the effectiveness of human rights language in the International Financial Institutions Act of 1977.

1643

Moynihan, Daniel P. *The politics of human rights. Commentary, v. 64, Aug. 1977: 19-26.*

Argues that human rights constitute the most important weapon for the defense of liberty.

1644

Nathan, James A. *Human rights and international order. Foreign service journal, v. 55, Feb. 1978: 9-12, 33-36.*

Discusses the Carter administration's human rights policy. Examines historical antecedents and differentiates between a human rights policy based on moral principles and one based on national interests.

1645

Nicaragua: an ally under siege. *Washington, Council on American Affairs, 1978. 148 p.*

Historical examination of U.S.-Nicaraguan relations. Discusses the relevance of the human rights doctrine for the Nicaraguan revolution.

1646

Nóbrega, Vandick Londres da. *1964 (i.e. Mil novecentos e sessenta e quatro): segurança e defensa do Brasil. Rio de Janeiro, Livraria Freitas Bastos, 1977. 597 p., 39 leaves of plates, illus.*

"149 conclusões em portugues, frances, ingles e alemão a partir da página 293."

Analyzes the military's role in Brazil. Refers to the U.S. human rights policy and to the Brazilian government's reaction to that policy. Includes summaries of conclusions in French, English, and German.

1647

North American Congress on Latin America. *Uruguay police agent exposes U.S. advisors. NACLA's Latin America & empire report, v. 6, July/Aug. 1072: 20-25.*

Deals with the role of U.S.A.I.D. operatives in creating, supplying, and coordinating the intelligence apparatus for Uruguay's police.

1648

On U.S. relations with El Salvador: the Koch-State Department correspondence. *Inter-American economic affairs, v. 30, summer 1976: 79-83.*

Congressman Edward Koch's inquiry about specific human rights violations in El Salvador and U.S. military assistance. Reprinted from the Congressional record.

1649

Orrego Vicuña, Claudio. *La administración Carter y los derechos humanos; seminario sobre derechos humanos. Santiago, Instituto de Formación Demócrata Cristiana, 1977. 27 p.*

Unpublished booklet that chronologically reviews and analyzes the human rights policy and actions taken during the first year of the Carter administration.

1650

Orrego Vicuña, Claudio. *La era tecnotrónica y los derechos humanos: la Administración Carter y América Latina. Santiago, Ediciones Aconcagua, 1977. 192 p. (Col. Lautaro)*

Essays on the significance of President Carter's policy on human rights for Latin American in 1977 and on the thought of his national security adviser, Zbigniew Brzezinski.

1651

Petras, James. *President Carter and the "new morality." Monthly review, v. 29, June 1977: 42-50.*

Maintains that the apparent pursuit of high moral values is the work of consummate politicians whose purpose is to legitimize an expansive foreign policy.

1652

Pike, David Wingate. *Human rights: the conscience of the individual. Latin American yearly review (Paris), v. 3, 1975: 4-11.*

Pleads for the U.S. to support democracy and denounce political repression in Latin America. Criticizes the Nixon-Kissinger record in support of human rights up to 1975.

1653

President Carter signs American Convention on Human Rights. *U.S. Department of State. Department of State bulletin, v. 77, July 1977: 28-40.*

Contains remarks made by President Carter upon signing the American Convention on Human Rights at the Pan American Union on June 1, 1977, together with the text of the convention.

1654

Ravenal, C. Earl. *Carter's fear of human rights. Inquiry,* Jan. 23, 1978: 8-12.

Accuses the Carter administration of "hypocrisy" and inflexibility, and alleges "retrenchment in its human rights policies."

1655

Ray, Philip L., and J. Sherrod Taylor. *The role of nongovernmental organizations in implementing human rights in Latin America. Georgia journal of international and comparative law, v. 7, summer 1977: 477-506.*

Describes the principal nongovernmental organizations involved in human rights and their attempts to influence the U.S. Congress, the Department of State, and the Inter-American Commission on Human Rights. Lists only those organizations believed by the authors to be the most active and the most effective.

1656

Redington, Robert J., and Walter J. Landry. *Report of the United States Delegation to the Inter-American Conference on Protection of Human Rights, San José, Costa Rica, November 9-22, 1969. Washington, U.S. Department of State, 1970. 1 v.(various pagings)*

Report of the U.S. delegation to the 1969 Inter-American Conference on Protection of Human Rights. Provides background information on negotiations leading to the American Convention on Human Rights.

1657

Regional approaches to human rights: the inter-American experience. *American Society of International Law. Proceedings of its meeting. 72d; 1978. Washington. p. 197-223.*

Presents a panel discussion among law professors and representatives from the U.S. Department of State. Assesses the effects of the American Convention on Human Rights on the activities of the Inter-American Commission on Human Rights and evaluates U.S. human rights policies as these affect Western Hemisphere countries.

1658

Riesman, David. *Human rights: conflicts among our ideals. Commonweal, v. 104, Nov. 11, 1977: 711-715.*

Discusses the orientation of President Carter's human rights policy with some reference to Latin America.

1659

Riesman, Michael. *The pragmatism of human rights diplomacy of the possible. Nation, v. 224, May 7, 1977: 554-558.*

Skeptical view of past and present U.S. human rights policies.

1660

Robertson, A. H. *Human rights: a global assessment. In Kommers, Donald P., ed. Human rights and American foreign policy. Notre Dame, Ind., University of Notre Dame Press, 1979. p. 5-28.*

Includes brief section on the O.A.S. and the American Convention on Human Rights.

1661

Rogers, William D., and F. J. McNeil. *U.S. discusses human rights items in O.A.S. General Assembly. U.S. Dept. of State. Department of State bulletin, v. 72, June 23, 1975: 879-883.*

Contains the texts of statements by the U.S. secretary of state and by the alternate representative to the O.A.S., praising the Inter-American Commission on Human Rights for its report on Chile.

1662

Ronfeldt, David, and Caesar Sereseres. *U.S. arms transfers, diplomacy, and security in Latin America and beyond. Santa Monica, Calif., Rand Corp., 1977. 62 p. (Rand paper series)*

The human rights issue is discussed as it relates to internal political and military development in Latin America. Includes bibliographic references.

1663

Rubin, Barry M., and Elizabeth Peterson Spiro, eds. *Human rights and U.S. foreign policy. With a foreword by Muriel S. Humphrey. Boulder, Colo., Westview Press, 1979. 283 p.*

Presents a collection of opinions from prominent U.S. professors and policy makers. Includes essays by Peter Berger, David Riesman, Secretary of State Cyrus Vance, current and former U.N. ambassadors, President Jimmy Carter, former U.S. congressmen, and researchers for the U.S. Congress.

1664

Salzberg, John, and Donald D. Young. *The parliamentary role in implementing international human rights: a U.S. example. Texas international law journal, v. 12, spring/summer 1977: 251-278.*

Examines the role that the U.S. Congress, particularly the House of Representatives, has played since 1973 in the formulation of governmental policy and public attitudes toward international human rights issues.

1665

Schmidhauser, John R., and Larry L. Berg. *The American Bar Association and human rights conventions: the political significance of private professional associations. Social research, v. 38, summer 1971: 362-410.*

Examines the extent of the American Bar Association's influence in the debate over ratification of the U.N. Covenant on Human Rights from the 1940's to the 1960's.

1666

Schneider, Mark L. *A new priority in the foreign policy of the United States. In Inter-American Bar Foundation. The legal protection of human rights in the Western Hemisphere. Washington, Inter-American Bar Foundation, 1978. p. 14-21.*

Examines the Carter administration's human rights position and its implications for U.S. foreign policy.

1667

Schoultz, Lars. *Human rights and United States policy toward Latin America. New scholar, v. 7, no. 1/2, 1979: 87-104.*

Praises recent changes in U.S. foreign policy toward human rights in Latin America by contrasting it with traditional diplomacy. Places current Chilean rights violations in the context of the militarism of the 1970's.

1668

Sereseres, Caesar D. *Inter-American security relations: the future of U.S. military diplomacy in the Hemisphere. Parameters, v. 7, no. 3, 1977: 46-56.*

Examines perceptions, conditions, and government policies that have contributed to the strain in security and military relations between the U.S. and Latin America.

1669

Sewell, John. *The United States and world development: agenda for action, 1977. John Sewell and the staff of the Overseas Development Council. New York, Published for the Overseas Development Council [by] Praeger, 1977. 250 p. illus. (Praeger special studies in international economics and development)*

Includes a discussion of the basic needs approach to equity and human rights.

1670

Shestack, Jerome J., and Roberta Cohen. *International human rights: a role for the United States. Virginia journal of international law, v. 14, summer 1974: 673-701.*

Describes the present role of the U.S. in international human rights preservation and provides justification for U.S. involvement within the framework of ideological commitment and national interest. Offers insightful propositions for an expanded U.S. human rights agenda.

1671

Shue, Henry. *Basic rights: subsistence, affluence, and U.S. foreign policy. Princeton, N.J., Princeton University Press, 1980. 231 p.*

A philosopher examines the moral questions inherent in government policies affecting human lives, with examples drawn from Latin America, Asia, and Africa.

1672

Sist, Arturo, and Gregorio Iriarte. *De la seguridad nacional al trilateralismo; razones por las que el gobierno de Carter defiende la vigencia de los derechos humanos. La Paz, Asamblea Permanente de los Derechos Humanos de Bolivia, 1977. 13 p.*

Criticizes the motives of the change in U.S. policy toward military regimes in Latin America.

1673

Slater, Jerome. *The United States and Latin America: premises for the new administration. Yale review, v. 64, Oct. 1974: 1-10.*

Argues that although the U.S. is not fully aware of it, Latin America is important in terms of economic and strategic considerations.

1674

Snyder, Edward F. *The role of the private bar and public interest lawyers in human rights matters before Congress; a lobbyist's view.In Tuttle, James C., ed. International human rights; law and practice. Chicago, American Bar Association, 1978. p. 189-205.*

Anticipates human rights issues for 1978. An appendix lists members of U.S. Congressional committees who deal with human rights, and another lists participants in the Human Rights Working Group of the Coalition for a New Foreign Military Policy.

1675

Spiro, Elizabeth Peterson. *A paradigm shift in American foreign policy. Worldview (New York), v. 20, Jan./Feb. 1977: 42-47.*

Considers the problems involved in the shift from a foreign policy in support of economic gain to one in support of human rights.

1676

Toward a humanitarian diplomacy: a primer for policy. *Tom J. Farer, ed. New York, New York University Press, 1980. 229 p.*

General treatment of the subject of human rights, with special focus on the relationship between human rights and U.S. foreign policy. A major book on the subject.

1677

Toward improved United States-Cuba relations: report of a special study mission to Cuba, February 10-15, 1977. *Washington, U.S.Govt. Print. Off., 1977. 73 p. (Committee print)*

At head of title: 95th Congress, 1st session. "Submitted to the Committee on International Relations."

Report of a mission to Cuba led by Congressman Jonathan B. Bingham and aimed at assessing views of Cuban leaders regarding improvement and eventual normalization of relations with the United States. Includes observations on Cuban education, quality of life, and the human rights of political prisoners.

1678

United States policy on human rights in Latin America (Southern Cone). *[Congressional Colloquy on Capitol Hill] Washington, 1977. New York, Fund for New Priorities in America, 1978. 195 p.*

Provides an assessment of Carter administration human rights policies in light of the "rapidly deteriorating situation in the Southern Cone countries of South America." Participants included members of Congress Mike Gravel, Robert Drinan, Alan Cranston, and Donald Fraser.

1679

United States; report of the delegation to the Inter-American Specialized Conference on Human Rights, April 22, 1970: American Convention on Human Rights. *International legal materials, v. 9, July 1970: 710-757.*

Text of an international treaty for the protection of human rights. The first part contains the substantive material of the treaty and latter two parts present procedural clauses. Includes resolutions proposed for adoption by the O.A.S.

1680

U.S. Department of State. *Human rights and international organizations. Its Bulletin, v. 78, Sept. 1978: 52.*

Based on an address given on April 6, 1978, at Grinnell College, Grinnell, Iowa, by Edward M. Mezvinsky, Representative to the U.N. Commission on Human Rights.

1681

U.S. Department of State. *Sixth General Assembly of the Organization of American States, Santiago, Chile, 1976. Secretary Kissinger [on] human rights, cooperation for development, [and] O.A.S. reform; joint report, U.S. and Panama; and Secretary Kissinger's statement at the U.N. Economic Commission for Latin America.* [Washington] Department of State, 1976. 19 p.(Inter-American series, 111. Dept. of State publication, 8866)

Topics covered by Kissinger include the challenges that human rights considerations pose to the American nations, the need for greater cooperation among the Latin American countries, and proposals for improved representation and financing of the O.A.S.

1682

U.S. President, 1977-1981 (Carter) Arms, economic prosperity, and human rights. *President Jimmy Carter before the Permanent Representatives of the United Nations. Washington, Department of State, Bureau of Public Affairs, Office of Media Services, 1977. 4 p. (News release, March 17, 1977)*

The President discusses his human rights and foreign policy objectives, stressing peace and the reduction of the arms race, building a cooperative international economic system, and working with adversaries as well as friends to advance the human rights cause.

1683

U.S. President, 1977-1981 (Carter) International transfer of technology. *Report of the President to the Congress, together with assessment of the report by the Congressional Research Service, Library of Congress. Prepared for the Subcommittee on International Security and Scientific Affairs of the Committee on International Relations, U.S. House of Representatives. Washington, U.S. Govt. Print. Off., 1979. 55 p.*

At head of title: 95th Congress, 2d session. Committee print.

Presents reports on questions relating to exchange of technology and inter-American scientific affairs.

1684

U.S. President's Commission for the Observance of Human Rights Year 1968. *To continue action for human rights; Human Rights Year, 1968. [Washington, U.S. Govt. Print. Off., 1969] 69 p. ports.*

Reports on the Commission's activities during 1968.

1685

Utley, T. E. *A reappraisal of the human rights doctrine. Policy review, winter 1978: 27-34.*

Examines the proposition that the defense of human rights should be among the chief objectives of foreign policy. Argues that this stance could become dangerous.

1686

Vance, Cyrus. *Human rights and foreign policy. Georgia journal of international and comparative law, v. 7, summer 1977: 223-229.*

Address by Secretary of State Vance at Law Day ceremonies at the University of Georgia School of Law, April 30, 1977. Enunciates the resolve of the Carter administration to make the advancement of human rights a central part of U.S. foreign policy.

1687

Vance, Cyrus, et al. *Secretary Vance attends O.A.S. General Assembly at Grenada. U.S. Dept. of State. Department of State bulletin, v. 77, July 18, 1977: 69-77.*

Contains text of Secretary of State Cyrus Vance's first speech before the General Assembly of the O.A.S., meeting at St. George's, Grenada, June 14 to 24, 1977, which placed emphasis on human rights as a special concern of the U.S. government. A text of the resolution adopted by the Assembly is included.

1688

Van Dyke, Vernon. *Human rights, the United States, and world community. New York, Oxford University Press, 1970. 292 p.*

Discusses U.S. policy in the U.N. and the O.A.S. with the intention of informing U.S. citizens about international human rights obligations and associated problems of implementation.

1689

Vogelsang, Sandra. *What price principle? U.S. policy on human rights. Foreign affairs, v. 56, July 1978: 819-841.*

Assesses briefly the Carter administration's human rights policies. Suggests changes in executive and legislative branch management of human rights issues. Advocates the possible restriction of private sector involvement in countries violating human rights.

1690

Washington Office on Latin America. *The Carter administration and human rights. Update, v. 5, Oct. 1980: 1-2.*

States that during President Carter's administration the U.S. government "came out demonstratively in favor of the transition from authoritarian to democratic rule," leaning heavily on groundwork laid by the U.S. Congress. Sees the human rights component as an important part of U.S. foreign policy.

1691

Washington Office on Latin America. *Congress, legislation, human rights: the year in review. Update Latin America, Nov./Dec. 1978: 1-2.*

Calling the U.S. Senate ratification of the two Panama Canal treaties the most significant Congressional action, this concise review also discusses U.S. economic and military aid policies and trade legislation.

1692

Weeks, Albert L. *Morality in the affairs of nations. Freedom at issue, May/June 1977: 12-15.*

Examines the implications of President Carter's new moral posture. Asks whether such a stance can work in the present world "non-community," whether it might entail risk for the U.S. alliances and security, and how the U.S. can avoid danger while yet pursuing the moral purpose implicit in democracy.

1693

Weiss, Peter. *Human rights and vital needs. Washington, Institute for Policy Studies, 1977. 5 p.*

Concludes that the U.S. human rights policy must consider economic, social, and cultural rights as well as political and civil rights.

1694

Weissbrodt, David. *Human rights legislation and U.S. foreign policy. Georgia journal of international and comparative law, v. 7, no. 1, supplement 1977: 231-287.*

Cogent analysis of President Carter's human rights policy. Includes discussion of the effect of foreign aid legislation on selected Latin American countries.

1695

Wiarda, Howard J. *Democracy and human rights in Latin America: toward a new conceptualization. Orbis, v. 22, spring 1978: 137- 160.*

Deals with the issues of human rights and U.S. relations with authoritarian regimes of Latin America. Asks whether democracy and human rights are everywhere the same and universal and whether they are relevant in the same sense to all societies and in all time frames.

1696

Woito, Robert, ed. *Human rights: United States foreign policy at issue in Illinois; an introductory kit, pt. 2. Chicago, World without War Publications, 1978. 22 p.*

One of four parts, the kit is intended to aid citizens in participating in foreign policy formulation. Includes policy statements of the World Without War Council, a discussion of the principal human rights issues, a statement by Secretary of State Cyrus Vance, and a select bibliography.

1697

Yale Task Force on Population Ethics. *Moral claims, human rights, and population policies. Theological studies, v. 35, Mar. 1974: 83-113.*

For the field of human rights and population control, compares traditional U.S., Marxist, and Catholic policies with those of the United Nations.

1698

Young, Andrew. *The challenge to the Economic and Social Council: advancing the quality of life in all its aspects. U.S.*

Dept. of State. Department of State bulletin, v. 76, May 16, 1977: 494-502.

Statement by the U.S. Representative to the U.N. before the U.N. Economic and Social Council (ECOSOC) in New York on April 19, 1977. Discusses the inseparability of questions dealing with human freedoms, world hunger, torture, racism, and racial discrimination and describes the human rights machinery of the U.N.

Newsletters

1699

ALAI. Agence latine-américaine d'information. *1977 + 1224 Ste. Catherine 0.403, Montreal, Quebec H3G-1P2 Canada.*

Weekly bulletin providing information about Latin America. Published in Spanish and French. Regularly includes information on human rights in Latin America.

1700

Amauta. Semanario de los pueblos jóvenes y los trabajadores. *SAGSA, Cuzco 440, 7 Piso, Lima, Perú, and Avda. J.C. Mariátegui 820, Lima, Perú.*

Deals with human rights violations, provides information on current legislation, and analyzes the consequences of its application in Peru.

1701

América Latina; derechos humanos. *1977 + Comisión Evangélica Latinoamericana de Educación Cristiana y Centro Nacional de Comunicación Social, Apartado Postal 74-307, México, D.F., México.*

A monthly exposé of human rights violations in Latin America.

1702

American-Chilean Council report. *1978 + American-Chilean Council, Suite 808, 95 Madison Ave., New York, N.Y. 10016.*

Newsletter aimed at counteracting a perceived communist economic and propaganda offensive in Chile.

1703

Análisis. *1978 + Academia de Humanismo Cristiano, Crescente Errázuriz 1711, Santiago, Chile.*

Contains articles on Latin American social, political, and economic issues and human rights. The focus is on applying Christian principles to solving problems in contemporary society.

1704

Anistia. *1978 + Comité Brasileiro pela Anistia, and Movimento Feminino pela Anistia, São Paulo, Brasil.*

Works for the release of political prisoners.

1705

Annual report on freedom of information. *1960/61 + U.N. Secretary General. [New York] (U.N. [Document] E/CN.4)*

Reports submitted to the Commission on Human Rights. Addenda accompany some reports.

1706

Argentina outreach. *1978 + Argentine Information Service Center, 2700 Bancroft, Berkeley, Calif. 94704. Regional office: 156 5th Ave., No. 1008, New York, N.Y. 10010.*

Covers news analysis and action in Argentina by a national organization with chapters in New York and San Francisco. Bimonthly.

1707

Argentina today. *Argentine Information Service Center, 2700 Bancroft, Berkeley, Calif. 94704. Regional office: 156 5th Ave., No. 1008, New York, N.Y. 10010.*

Dedicated to the defense of human rights and political prisoners in Argentina. Irregular.

1708

Argentine bulletin. *1979? + Committee of Solidarity with the Argentine People, México D.F., México*

A monthly publication in Spanish which includes testimonies from Argentine exiles on various aspects of the human rights situation. Among topics covered are prison conditions and methods of torture.

1709

Argentine independent review. *Argentina Society, Inc., P. O. Box 614, Lenox Hill Station, New York, N.Y. 10021.*

Objective is to stimulate a wider understanding of Argentina and her way of life as a nation. Monthly publication.

1710

Background. *1978 + Center for International Policy, 120 Maryland Ave., N.E., Washington, D.C. 20002.*

Covers foreign policy, the Third World, and human rights.

1711

Boletín bibliográfico mexicano. *1970 + Librería de Porrúa Hermanos y Cia., S.A., Argentina y Justo Sierra, México 1, D.F., México.*

Bimonthly newsletter which is devoted to Latin American issues.

1712

Boletín de derechos humanos. *1978 + Asamblea Permanente de Derechos Humanos en Bolivia, Casilla 3077, La Paz, Bolivia.*

Deals with human rights theory and human rights violations in Bolivia.

1713

Boletín informativo del Centro de Residentes Argentinos. *1978 + San José, Costa Rica.*

Published by an Argentine group living in Costa Rica. Critical of alleged human rights violations on the part of the Argentine government.

1714

Boletín informativo Mapuche. *1978 + Indigenous Minorities Research Council, 20-22 Hepburn Road, St. Paul's, Bristol 2, Great Britain.*

Provides information on the situation of the Mapuche people both inside Chile and in exile. Irregular.

1715

Boletín la cruz de los pueblos. *1976 + Centro Episcopal Universitario, Calle Mariana Bracetti No. 16 oeste, Rio Piedras, Puerto Rico 00925.*

Provides information on the current situation in Argentina. Irregular.

1716

Boletín noticias ecuménicas. *1975 + Centro de Planificación y Acción Ecuménica, CEPAE, Benito Monción, No. 204, Apto. 252-2, Santo Domingo, D.N., Dominican Republic.*

News bulletin of the Caribbean regional office of the Unión Evangélica Latino-Americana (UNELAM).

1717

Boletines bibliográficos. *1979 + CRIE, Centro Regional de Informaciones Ecuménicas, Centro de Estudios Ecuménicos, Ocotepec 39, San Jerónimo, México 20, D.F., México.*

A bibliographic guide to articles, documents, clippings, books, and conference addresses covering important CRIE concerns.

1718

Bulletin. *1976 + Argentine Commission for Human Rights, P.O. Box 2635, Washington, D.C. 20013.*

Concerns rights violations in Argentina.

1719

Bulletin. *1978 + Centre for the Independence of Judges and Lawyers, International Commission of Jurists, B.P. 120, 1224 Chêne-Bougeries, Geneva, Switzerland.*

Devoted to legal issues in protecting basic rights.

1720

Bulletin. *1978 + Commission Argentine des Droits de l'Homme. [Paris]*

Concerns the protection of human rights in Argentina. Irregular.

1721

Bulletin. *1954 + International Commission of Jurists, 109 Route de Chêne, 1224 Chêne-Bougeries, Geneva, Switzerland.*

Merged in 1969 with the Journal of the International Commission of Jurists. Published in French and English.

1722

Canada/Argentina bulletin. *1978 + Group for the Defense of Civil Rights in Argentina, No Candu for Argentina Committee, and the Emergency Committee for Argentine Political Prisoners and Refugees, 175 Carlton St., Toronto, Ontario, Canada.*

Concerned with human rights violations in Argentina.

1723

Carta-CEPAE. *1977 + Centro de Planificación y Acción Ecuménica; CEPAE, Benito Monción, No. 204, Apto. 252-2, Santo Domingo, D.N., Dominican Republic.*

Newsletter of the Caribbean regional office of the Unión Evangélica Latino-Americana (UNELAM).

1724

CEAL Informations. *Comité Belge Europe Amérique Latine, Rue du Conseil 39, 1050 Bruxelles, Belgium.*

Bimonthly bulletin.

1725

Central America report. *1978 + Inforpress Centroamericana, 9 Calle 3-19, Zona 1, Guatemala City, Guatemala.*

Devoted to human rights in Central America.

1726

Chile; action bulletin on political prisoners and human rights. *1978 + Non-Intervention in Chile (NICH), Box 800, Berkeley, Calif. 94701.*

Bimonthly bulletin concerning liberation causes in all of Latin America but with special emphasis on Chile. Promotes a letter-writing campaign on behalf of political prisoners.

1727

Chile-America. *1979 + Centro Studi e Documentazione, Viale Trastevere, 00153 Rome, Italy.*

Oriented to assisting Chilean refugees in Europe.

1728

Chile lucha, Chile monitor. *1978 + Chile Lucha and Chile Solidarity Campaign, 129 Seven Sisters Road, London N7, Great Britain.*

Quarterly dealing with political and cultural articles on all Latin America with special focus on the promotion of human rights and the integration of Chileans into the British Labor movement.

1729

Chile solidaritet; pressebulletin. *1978 + Komiteen Salvador Allende, Blagardsgadell, 2200 Kobenhavn K, Denmark.*

Irregularly published newsletter about human rights in Chile.

1730

Chile solidarity report: Chile informativo. *1977 + Committee for Defense of Human Rights in Chile, c/o CALC, 1322 18th St., N.W., 3rd Floor, Washington, D.C.20009.*

Serial reports, published in both English and Spanish, about rights violations.

1731

Chile: summary of recent events. *1977 + Embassy of Chile, Press Office, 1736 Massachusetts Ave., N.W., Washington, D.C. 20036.*

Bimonthly newsletter representing the official position of the Chilean government.

1732

Chile today. *Office for Political Prisoners and Human Rights in Chile, 156 5th Ave., Room 521, New York, N.Y. 10010.*

Monthly newsletter calling sympathizers to action against the Pinochet regime, through various campaigns and statements.

1733

CIMADE-Information. *CIMADE, Bureau de Defense des Droits de l'Homme, Section Amérique Latine, 176 Rue de Grenelle, 75007 Paris, France. CCP 4088.87.*

Deals with infractions of human rights in Haiti. Bimonthly, plus four "dossiers" yearly.

1734

Clamor. *Committee for the Defense of Human Rights in Southern Cone Nations of São Paulo's Archdiocesan Commission for Human Rights and the Marginalized. Avenida Higienópolis 890, sala 12, 01238 São Paulo, Brazil.*

Monthly publication in English relating to human rights violations in the Southern Cone nations.

1735

Comité cristiano mexicano de apoyo a los perseguidos en América Latina. *Apartado Postal 85-13, México 20, D.F., México.*

Provides information on the human rights situation in Latin America and efforts made by Christians in the promotion and defense of human rights. Irregular.

1736

Comunicaciones CENCOS. *Centro Nacional de Comunicación Social, Medellín No. 33, Col. Roma, México 7, D.F., México.*

Weekly political, social, and economic analyses of direct and indirect human rights violations in Latin America and other parts of the world.

1737

Cuadernos de cristianismo y sociedad. *1962 + Editorial Tierra Nueva S.R.L., San José 28, 1076 Buenos Aires, Argentina.*

An Argentine journal containing articles on human rights, published monthly except January and February.

1738

Cuadernos jurídicos. *1978 + Arzobispado de Santiago, Vicaría de la Solidaridad, Plaza de Armas 444, Casilla 30 D, Santiago, Chile.*

Important monthly publication on the legal aspects of human rights. Contains general studies and discusses specific problems in Chile.

1739

Denuncia. *1980 + CONADE, Comité Nacional de Defensa de la Democracia en Bolivia, P. O. Box 32024, Washington, D.C. 20007.*

Bilingual newsletter publicizing human rights violations and the political situation in Bolivia since the military coup of July 1980. Published biweekly.

1740

Derechos humanos; bulletin. *1978 + Asociación Colombiana de Derechos Humanos, Ministerio de Justicia, Apartado Aéreo 16985, Bogotá, D.E., Colombia.*

Deals with human rights in Colombia and other parts of Latin America.

1741

Derechos humanos; revista mensual. *1973 + Comité Pro Defensa Derechos Humanos en la República Dominicana. [Santo Domingo, D.N., Dominican Republic]*

Monthly publication dealing with human rights conditions in the Dominican Republic.

1742

Dialogando. *1977 + Arzobispado de Santiago, Vicaría de Pastoral Obrera, Santiago, Chile.*

Newsletter relating to human rights in Chile and Latin America generally.

1743

Diálogo. *23 Av. 00-61, Zona 7, Apartado 174, Guatemala City, Guatemala.*

Articles, editorials, and documents concerning the Christian struggle for human rights in Latin America. Irregular.

1744

Documento de fundación. *1976 + Movimiento Ecuménico por los Derechos Humanos, Buenos Aires, Argentina.*

Published irregularly.

1745

El Salvador reports. *Committee against Violations of Human Rights in El Salvador, Box 759, Old Chelsea Station, New York, N.Y. 10011.*

Bilingual newsletter dealing with human rights issues in El Salvador. Bimonthly.

1746

Envío CRIE. *1979 + CRIE, Centro Regional de Informaciones Ecuménicas, Centro de Estudios Ecuménicos, Ocotepec 39, San Jerónimo, México 20, D.F., México.*

Biweekly listing of relevant magazine articles, documents, and newspaper clippings classified according to the major themes of CRIE, human rights being a central issue.

1747

Gacetilla. *International Commission of Jurists, Geneva, Switzerland.*

Newsletter regarding legal issues of rights enforcement.

1748

Gesamtbericht, Referate, Protokolle. *1952 + International Commission of Jurists, The Hague, Netherlands.*

Reports on legal aspects of human rights throughout the world.

1749

Gist. *1977 + U.S. Department of State, Bureau of Public Affairs, Washington, D.C.*

Provides information on Latin American political and social affairs, and human rights.

1750

Guatemala report. *American Friends of Guatemala, P. O. Box 2283, Station A, Berkeley, Calif. 94702.*

Irregular publication devoted to current information and documentation about the situation in Guatemala, focusing on policies of repression.

1751

Human rights. *Southern Methodist University, School of Law, Dallas, Tex. 75275.*

Not available for annotation.

1752

Human Rights Internet newsletter. *1976 + Human Rights Internet, 1502 Ogden St., N.W., Washington, D.C. 20010.*

An important resource in the human rights field; published nine times a year. Covers rights issues on a worldwide basis. The size of the newsletter has been steadily growing. Contains bibliographies.

1753

Human rights news. *1976 + Ontario Human Rights Commission, Toronto, Canada.*

Concerned with human rights in the Third World.

1754

Human rights perspectives. *Human Rights Office, Division of Overseas Ministries, National Council of Churches/U.S.A., 475 Riverside Drive, Room 634, New York, N.Y. 10027.*

Newsletter providing theological reflection on international human rights issues. Ample coverage of Latin America, as well as an updated list of resource materials.

1755

Human rights watch. *Panamanian Committee for Human Rights, 607 G Street, S.W., Washington, D.C. 20024.*

Quarterly report on human rights violations in Panama and other Central American nations.

1756

Infor-act bulletin. *New York Circus, P. O. Box 37, Times Square Station, New York, N.Y. 10036.*

Reports on the activities of the Center for the Interchange of Religious Concerns in the U.S. (Circus), which works with the Latin American community in New York City. Provides information to a wider audience on the churches in Latin America. Bimonthly.

1757

Informaciones. *1976? + GRISUR, Grupo de Información y Solidaridad Uruguay, Case postale 92, 1211 Geneva 4. Switzerland.*

Provides current information on the political, economic, and human rights situation in Uruguay and on the resolutions approved by the international organizations concerning these rights.

1758

Informativo. *1978 + Centro de Documentación e Información sobre Derechos Humanos en Argentina, CEDIHA, Casilla de Correo, 1000 Correo Central, Buenos Aires, Argentina.*

Provides discussion and information regarding the major human rights questions in Argentina. Includes analysis of related declarations by the junta, as well as coverage of the work of international human rights organizations in Argentina.

1759

Informativo CLAT; vocero del Movimiento de los Trabajadores Comprometidos con la Liberación de los Pueblos de América Latina. *1975 + Buró CLAT, Apartado 6681, Caracas 101, Venezuela.*

Newsletter devoted to labor issues which regularly denounces human rights violations. Issued nine times a year.

1760

Informativo CODEH. *1978 + Comité de Defensa de los Derechos Humanos de Chile, Ricardo Santa Cruz 630, Santiago, Chile.*

Monthly publication on the human rights situation in Chile, including analyses of legal procedures applied by the military regime. Reproduces the texts of many significant documents in the human rights field.

1761

Informativo "CODES." Organo Oficial del Comité de Defensa de los Derechos Sindicales, Ricardo Santa Cruz No. 630, Santiago, Chile. *Official voice of an organization devoted to defending the rights of labor unions.*

1762

Informedh; boletín informativo del Movimiento Ecuménico por los Derechos Humanos. *1976 + Movimiento Ecuménico por los Derechos Humanos, Cerrito 466, Of. 76, Cap. 1010, Buenos Aires, Argentina.*

Bimonthly includes conference addresses and programs, related articles by different Christian denominations, and excerpts from newspapers and other journals.

1763

Informes. *1978 + Arzobispado de Santiago, Vicaría de la Solidaridad, Secretaría de Comunicaciones, Plaza de Armas 444, Casilla 30 D, Santiago, Chile.*

Dedicated to describing the actions and positions of the Vicaría de la Solidaridad in its struggle against oppression and poverty. Irregular.

1764

Izquierda cristiana. *Izquierda Cristiana en Chile en el Exterior, Apartado Postal 74-007, México 13, D.F., México.*

Maintains that socialism and Christian solidarity are desirable means of achieving equality and justice. Publishes articles, interviews, documents, addresses, and poems. Official organ of Izquierda Cristiana.

1765

Journal. *1969 + International Commission of Jurists. Geneva, Switzerland.*

Contains articles on international and comparative aspects of the rule of law and human rights, as well as a digest of judicial decisions of the superior courts of the world on those topics. Published twice a year, in four languages: English, French German, and Spanish. Merged with I.C.J. Bulletin in March 1969 to form the I.C.J. Review.

1766

Justicia y paz; boletín de las Comunidades Rurales Cristianas. *San Salvador. 1978 + [San Salvador]*

Articles about Catholic priests expelled, tortured, or killed in El Salvador. Irregular.

1767

Latin America calls. *Latin America Bureau, Latin American Division of the U.S. Catholic Conference, 1430 K Street, N.W., Washington, D.C. 20005.*

Monthly newspaper devoted to political and social issues.

1768

Latin America: liberation and Christianity. *Chicago Area Group on Latin America (CAGLA), The CAGLA Collective, 800 W. Belden, Chicago, Ill. 60614.*

Publication of the Chicago Area Group on Latin America, a research and action group of students, artists, clergy, and social scientists seeking solidarity with movements for liberation in Latin America.

1769

Latinamerica press; the English language publication of Noticias Aliadas. *1969 + Latinamerica Press, Apartado 5594, Lima 1, Perú, and Francisco del Castillo 178, Lima 18, Perú.*

Documents Latin American affairs and regularly covers news concerning human rights violations. Issued weekly.

1770

Liaisons internationales. *Centre Oecuménique de Liaisons Internationales, 68, Rue de Babylone, 75007 Paris, France.*

Quarterly which contains articles, news notices, document texts, and bibliographies concerning political, social, and economic liberation.

1771

Lucha; Christian response to military repression in Latin America. *Christians Concerned for Chile, 300 East 4th Street, New York, N.Y. 10009.*

Bimonthly intended to inform North Americans of the struggles of oppressed peoples in Latin America, and of the role that Christians have taken in these struggles.

1772

Maria Quiteria: boletim do Movimento Feminino pela Anistia. *1977 + São Paulo, Brasil.*

Concerned with the wider participation of women in the economic, political, and social life of Brazil and with obtaining amnesty for political prisoners in Brazil.

1773

Movimento. *1976 + Edição S.A., Rua Dr. Virgilio de Carvalho Pinto 625, Pinheiros, São Paulo, Brazil.*

A weekly based in São Paulo with a socialist orientation, owned by the journalists who write for it. Provides critical commentary and analysis published in Brazil.

1774

News notes. *Maryknoll Justice and Peace Office, Maryknoll, New York 10545.*

Bimonthly newsletter following international human rights issues and conferences, plus relevant U.S. policy.

1775

News release. *Latin America Bureau, Latin American Division of the U.S. Catholic Conference, 1430 K Street, N.W., Washington, D.C. 20005.*

Bimonthly news coverage from Latin America, emphasizing refugee and human rights problems.

1776

News; the Republic of Haiti. *1979 + Edelman International Corporation, 1730 Pennsylvania Ave., N.W., Suite 460, Washington, D.C. 20006.*

The organization issuing this irregular newsletter represents the government of Haiti.

1777

Newsletter. *1976 + Chile Committee for Human Rights.*

Quarterly publication containing information on conditions in Chile, including reports on DINA, missing prisoners, the ruling junta, the Church, and labor conditions.

1778

Newsletter. *1975 + International Commission of Jurists, 777 United Nations Plaza, New York, N.Y. 10017.*

Deals with legal issues regarding basic rights. Also issued in French.

1779

Newsletter. *Tucson Committee for Human Rights in Latin America. P. O. Box 6.341, Tucson, Arizona 85733.*

Monthly publication aimed at promoting the observance of human rights in Latin America.

1780

Nicaragua news. *1974 + Nicaragua Government Information Service, 1266 National Press Building, Washington, D.C. 20045.*

Official news service of the government of Nicaragua until the fall of Somoza.

1781

Noticias aliadas. *Apartado 5594, Lima 1, Perú.*

Comprehensive news service on the cultural and social concerns of the Church in Latin America. English edition is titled Latin America Press. Issued weekly.

1782

Noticias del Caribe. *Estudios y Documentación del Caribe (EDOC), Apartado Postal 290-2, Santo Domingo, Dominican Republic.*

Covers human rights and economic and political issues in the Caribbean and countries of the Western Hemisphere. Includes reprints from other periodicals as well as original articles. Monthly.

1783

Nueva sociedad. Noticias, datos, informes. *Editorial Nueva Sociedad Ltda., Edificio Plaza Artillería, Apartado 874, San José, Costa Rica.*

Dedicated to the idea of political, economic, and social democracy.

1784

Pan y agua. *1979 + Twin Cities Chile Resistance Committee, P. O. Box 14248, Minneapolis, Minn. 55414.*

Denounces the Pinochet military government and other allegedly dictatorial regimes in Latin America. Irregular.

1785

Paraguay watch. *P. O. Box 21061, Washington, D.C. 20009.*

Monthly newsletter focusing on political repression in Paraguay and containing news about international human rights support.

1786

Paz y justicia; boletín informativo del Servicio Paz y Justicia de América Latina. *1975 + Servicio Paz y Justicia, México 479, 1097 Buenos Aires, Argentina.*

Founded by Adolfo Pérez Esquivel, 1980 Nobel Peace prize winner, this monthly bulletin is devoted to the promotion of human rights, peace, and justice in Latin America.

1787

Press release. *Council on Hemispheric Affairs. 30 5th Ave., New York, N.Y. 10011, and 1125 15th Street, N.W., Suite 600, Washington, D.C. 20005.*

Provides information on the situation of human rights in Latin America. Irregular.

1788

Proceso. *1976 + Fresas 13, México, D.F., México.*

Weekly news magazine frequently critical of basic rights violations in Mexico and other Latin American countries.

1789

Report. *International Commission of Jurists. 777 United Nations Plaza, New York, N.Y. 10017.*

Reports on the status of human rights, especially the legal aspects. Irregular.

1790

Review. *1969 + International Commission of Jurists. Geneva, Switzerland.*

Presents laws protecting human rights. Formed by the union of the Commission's Bulletin and the Commission's Journal. English, French, German, and Spanish editions are also published.

1791

Revista de cultura contemporânea. *1978 + Centro de Estudos de Cultura Contemporânea (CEDEC), Rio de Janeiro, Brasil.*

Seeks to promote debate and diversity of thought about urgent issues that confront Latin American society. Articles deal with such topics as censorship, problems of trade unions, and political crises in Latin America.

1792

SAGO. Monthly information bulletin. *Information Center Bolivia, Peter Verbiststraat 29, 2610 Wilrijk, Belgium.*

Each issue contains material relating to human rights. Monthly.

1793

Servicio de Información y Documentación (SID). *1977 + Jesuitas de Bosques de Altamira, Apartado C-14, Managua, Nicaragua.*

Deals with Nicaraguan civil rights issues.

1794

Servicio de Informaciones Religiosas (SIR). *1977 + Centro de Estudios Cristianos y el Departamento de Comunicaciones, Facultad de Teología, Camacuá 282, Buenos Aires, Argentina.*

Covers human rights concerns and the role of the churches in that respect. Monthly.

1795

Servicio social. *Escuela de Servicio Social de la Junta de Beneficencia.1927 + Santiago de Chile.*

Magazine of the Chilean Catholic Church. Published three times a year.

1796

Tricontinental magazine. *North American edition. Peoples Press, P. O. Box 40176, San Francisco, Calif. 94140.*

Contains information and articles by Third World leaders, listing of books from and on Third World nations, and new materials on national liberation movements. Organ of the Organization of Solidarity of the People of Africa, Asia and Latin America (OSPAAL).

1797

Trinidad and Tobago review. *1977 + Tapia House Publishing Company, 22 Cipriani Blvd., Port of Spain, Trinidad & Tobago, West Indies.*

Focuses on social and cultural issues in Latin America, including human rights. Also contains poetry, fiction, and some bibliographic references. Monthly publication.

1798

Update Latin America. *Washington Office on Latin America (WOLA), 110 Maryland Ave., Washington, D.C. 20002.*

Reviews the status of human rights in the Western Hemisphere. Gives information on Latin American and U.S. policies. Bimonthly.

1799

Uruguay Information Project newsletter. *1977 +*

Provides information on the political and human rights situation in Uruguay. Biweekly.

1800

Uruguay newsletter. *1979 + Committee in Solidarity with the Uruguayan People, Box 234, Wycoff Station, Brooklyn, N.Y. 11237*

Provides information and discussion on Uruguayan political prisoners, Uruguayans fighting for democracy, exiles, and the human rights situation of the country in general.

Bibliographies and Directories

1801

Arzobispado de Santiago, Chile. *Vicaría de la Solidaridad. Estudio bibliográfico: seguridad nacional; fuerzas armadas; la guerra; geopolítica y geoestrategia; nacionalismo. [Santiago] Arzobispado de Santiago, Vicaría de la Solidaridad, 1977. [76] leaves.*

Cover title: Estudio bibliográfico sobre seguridad nacional.

Includes 525 entries, some with brief annotations, relating to the national security doctrine in Latin American countries and the United States; to the armed forces in those countries; to the concepts of war, rebellion, violence, subversion, and authority; to articles on American geopolitics and geo-strategy; and to nationalism in Latin America. The first part of the work provides a bibliography of 29 significant bibliographies on the subject.

1802

Arzobispado de Santiago, Chile. *Vicaría de la Solidaridad. Estudio bibliográfico sobre derechos humanos. Santiago, Chile, 1978. 80 leaves.*

Includes 399 annotated entries relating to historical aspects of human rights, individual rights, specific rights of unionized workers, human rights in the international context, Chile, and women's rights, as well as items relating to freedom of religion.

1803

Ballantyne, Lygia Maria F. C. *Haitian publications: an acquisition guide and bibliography. [Washington] Library of Congress, Processing Services, Hispanic Acquisitions Project, 1979. 53 p.*

Report prepared for internal use by the Library of Congress and for limited outside distribution, discussing the book trade, non-commercial publishing, and library and documentation services in Haiti. Includes appendices on bookstores and publishing houses, institutional publishers, serials,

and monographs published between 1970 and 1979, a number of which touch on human rights issues.

1804

Bibliography. *In Organization of American States. The Organization of American States and human rights. Washington, Organization of American States, General Secretariat, 1972. p. 643-650.*

Lists 130 selected publications in the field of human rights that were published between 1960 and 1967.

1805

Casa de Chile en México. *Catálogo. 1977/78 + Mexico, D. F., Casa de Chile en México, Centro de Documentación y Biblioteca. 111 leaves.*

Contains over 1,000 entries on Chile discussing art, international relations, law, politics, education, health, and economics. Included are a significant number of selected publications in the field of human rights, such as testimonies of prisoners, documents and declarations of Chilean solidarity groups, and conference reports.

1806

Claude, Richard Pierre. *Reliable information: the threshold problem for human rights research. Human rights, v. 6, winter 1977: 169-187.*

Explores the reasons why the study of human rights and civil liberties has remained academically underdeveloped. Concludes with a bibliography on human rights, with listings by country.

1807

Cooperation in Documentation and Communication. *Bibliographical notes for understanding the military coup in Chile. [Edited by Mary Tiesch and Harry Strharsky] Washington, CoDoc International Secretariat, 1974. 96 p. (Its Common catalogue, no. 1)*

Bibliography concerning the military coup in Chile, drawn from the publications of the member organizations of CoDoc in Latin America and the United States.

1808

Cooperation in Documentation and Communication. *Bibliographical notes for understanding the Brazilian model: political repression & economic expansion. [Edited by Mary Riesch and Harry Strharsky]* Washington, CoDoC International Secretariat, 1974. [78] p. (Its Common catalogue, no. 2)

Lists Brazilian documents on both politics and economics. Comprises one volume of a series devoted to Third World issues.

1809

Deal, Carl W., ed. *Latin America and the Caribbean; a dissertation bibliography.* Ann Arbor, Mich., University Microfilms International [1978?] 164 p.

List of 7,200 dissertations assembled through 1977 by University Microfilms International. Includes titles relevant to human rights and supersedes the listing issued in 1974.

1810

Garling, Marguerite, ed. *The human rights handbook: a guide to British and American international human rights organizations.* London, Macmillan Press, 1979. 299 p.

Guide to human rights organizations, including those concerned with Latin America on a general or individual country basis. Provides addresses, officers, and a brief statement of purpose for each organization.

1811

Garling, Marguerite, ed. *Human rights research guide: library holdings in London on human rights; censorship and freedom of expression with select bibliography.* London, Writers and Scholars Educational Trust, 1978. 77 p.

Gives information on the types and locations of human rights materials available within the major library collections in London, including many difficult to find, non-official materials.

1812

Grech, Anthony P. *Selected bibliography on international protection of human rights. In Carey, John, ed. International protection of human rights; background paper and proceedings of the Twelfth Hammarskjöld Forum.* Dobbs Ferry, N.Y., Oceana Publications, 1968. p. 71-90.

At bottom of title: Published for the Association of the Bar of the City of New York.

Covers general authors, United Nations, International Labour Organization, European Commission on Human Rights, and Inter-American Commission on Human Rights.

1813

Harding, Colin, and Christopher Roper, eds. *Latin America review 1 of books. Foreword by Richard R. Fagen.* Palo Alto, Calif., Ramparts Press [1974] 222 p.

Comprehensive review and listing of books published between 1971 and 1973 that are available on Latin American economic, political and social issues, including human rights.

1814

International human rights bibliography. *Chicago, World Without War Council, 1978. 29 p.*

Not available for annotation.

1815

International Institute of Human Rights. *Bibliothèque minimum dans le domaine des droits de l'homme: a basic library of books on human rights.* Strasbourg, France, [1972] 10 p.

"Préparée à l'occasion du Festival International du Livre, Nice 19-25 mai 1972."

Pamphlet intended as a purchasing aid for university librarians that lists French, English, and German books on human rights. Although it covers history, international law, and international, regional, and national organizations, inadequate references impair its usefulness.

1816

La Mura, Enzo, ed. *Militar und Politik in Lateinamerika, Auswahlbibliographie. Fuerzas armadas y política, bibliografía selecta.* Hamburg, German Federal Republic, Instituto de Estudios Iberoamericanos, Centro de Documentación Latinoamericana, 1976. 80 p. (Serie A)

Excellent bilingual reference work containing a listing by subject and country of publications on the armed forces and politics, the libraries in which these may be obtained, and the journals in which they may be found.

1817

Mark, S., ed. *Selected bibliography on the international and comparative law of human rights. In Human rights studies in universities. Strasbourg, France, International Institute of Human Rights, 1973. p. 1-12.*

Listings of documents and periodicals from international and regional organizations involved with human rights.

1818

Miller, William, ed. *International human rights: bibliography, 1970-1976. Donald P. Kommers, project director. Notre Dame, Ind., Center for Civil Rights, University of Notre Dame Law School, 1976. 118 p.*

Continuing international human rights bibliographical service begun in 1965 which includes author and subject indexes, a section on monographs and documents, and appendixes on general bibliographical materials, periodicals and indexes. Includes only entries published in English or with a summary of contents in English.

1819

North American Congress on Latin America. *NACLA's bibliography on Latin America. New York, 1973. 50 p. illus. (NACLA's Latin America & empire report, v. 7, Mar. 1973)*

Entire issue devoted to bibliographic references, with breakdowns by subject and country. Includes a listing of articles appearing in the NACLA newletter and the NACLA report. A number of entries deal with human rights.

1820

Reynolds, Thomas H. *Highest aspirations or barbarous acts: the explosion in human rights documentation; a bibliographic survey. Law library journal, v. 71, Feb. 1978: 1-48.*

Designed primarily as an aid to librarians for the purchase of human rights materials, this is a valuable tool for researchers interested in the nature and availability of publications from the U.N. and regional organizations active in human rights documentation.

1821

Said, Abdul Aziz. *Bibliography of supplementary works on human rights. Washington, New TransCentury Foundation, 1977. 23 p.*

Section VI (p. 18-20), entitled "Human Rights in the Inter-American System," contains 29 items spanning the years 1958 to 1975.

1822

Sinclair, John H., ed. *Protestantism in Latin America: a bibliographical guide. South Pasadena, Calif., William Carey Library, 1976. 414 p.*

Compilation of bibliographies, monographs, reports of conferences, and periodicals, dealing with Protestantism in Latin America. Also included are selected items on Roman Catholicism and religious and political movements. Many entries deal with human rights.

1823

Thomas, Sandra. *Bibliography. In her Women of the Americas: political participants emerging in an era of change; ways to promote broader political participation among women. Washington, Inter-American Commission on Women, 1977. p. 77-88.*

Lists public documents, books, articles, periodicals, and unpublished materials relating to women's roles in the Americas.

1824

U.N. Secretariat. *Bibliography on the protection of human rights of works published after December 1939. [New York, United Nations, 1951] 248 p. (U.N. [Document] E/CN.4/540)*

At head of title: United Nations Economic and Social Council.

Not available for annotation.

1825

U.S. Department of State. Library. *Human rights [selected bibliography, 1976-77]. [Washington] 1977. 4 p.*

Unannotated list of periodical articles about human rights, available at the U.S. Department of State library. The arrangement is chronological.

1826

Wiseberg, Laurie S., and Harry M. Scoble, eds. *1980 North American human rights directory. Washington, Human Rights Internet, 1980. 190 p.*

Lists nearly 500 U.S. and Canadian based organizations active in the human rights field. There are plans to revise this useful guide every year.

1827

Wright, Robert Ernest Middleton. *Human rights: a booklist. [Worthing, Sussex] Worthing College of Further Education, College Library, 1968. 10 p.*

Guide to human rights literature available in the Worthing College library. Publications are predominately from the United Kingdom.

Author Index

Appendix
Human Rights Organizations

ACADEMIA DE HUMANISMO CRISTIANO
Ismael V. Vergara 348 Of. 102
Santiago, Chile

Church organization that publishes material pertaining to human rights in Chile and Latin America.

ACTION LATIN AMERICA
105 Memorial Hall
c/o Cambridge Ministries in Higher Education
Cambridge, Mass. 02138

Research and information center.

AD HOC COMMITTEE AGAINST REPRESSION IN HAITI
333 Lincoln Place
Brooklyn, N.Y. 11238

Gathers information about violations of human rights in Haiti.

AD HOC COMMITTEE ON THE HUMAN RIGHTS AND GENOCIDE TREATIES
25 East 78th St.
New York, N.Y. 10021

Supports efforts to advance the United Nations Charter, advocating the prompt ratification of the international human rights conventions and the development of a body of international law in the field.

ALBUQUERQUE CHILE SOLIDARITY COMMITTEE
Box 6888
Albuquerque, N.M.87107

Focuses on Chilean issues.

AMERICAN ASSOCIATION FOR THE ADVANCEMENT OF SCIENCE
1515 Massachusetts Ave., NW.
Washington, D.C. 20005

Furthers the work of scientists fostering scientific freedom and responsibility and improving the effectiveness of science in the promotion of human welfare. Publishes Science (weekly journal), symposium volumes, and reports.

AMERICAN BAR ASSOCIATION. SECTION ON INTERNATIONAL LAW. COMMITTEE *OF INTERNATIONAL HUMAN RIGHTS*
1155 East 60th St.
Chicago, Ill. 60637

Prepares reports on international human rights. Makes recommendations to the ABA House of Delegates in support of human rights treaties. Publishes the quarterly, Human Rights.

AMERICAN-CHILEAN COUNCIL
95 Madison Ave., Suite 808
New York, N.Y. 10016

Established by private citizens of both countries to counter Communist propaganda in Chile. Publishes the newsletter American-Chilean Council Report.

AMERICAN ENTERPRISE INSTITUTE FOR PUBLIC POLICY RESEARCH
1150 17th St., NW.
Washington, D.C. 20036

Nonprofit, privately supported organization that fosters innovative research, identifies and presents varying points of view on issues, formulates practical options, and analyzes public policy proposals. Areas of interest include factual analyses of current national and international public policy issues. Has a social sciences library of approximately 10,000 titles. Library holdings include technical reports, pamphlets, reprints, and clippings. Among its publications is the quarterly newsletter AEI Memorandum.

AMERICAN FEDERATION OF LABOR-CONGRESS OF INDUSTRIAL ORGANIZATIONS
815 16th St., NW.
Washington, D.C. 20006

Focuses on labor issues primarily. Gathers information about the status of human rights in the United States and abroad.

AMERICAN FRIENDS OF BRAZIL
Box 2279
Station A
Berkeley, Calif. 94702

Publishes the Brazilian Information Bulletin, a quarterly containing up-to-date information on political and economic developments in Brazil.

AMERICAN FRIENDS OF GUATEMALA
Box 2283
Station A
Berkeley, Calif. 94702

AMERICAN FRIENDS SERVICE COMMITTEE
1501 Cherry St.
Philadelphia, Pa. 19102

Nonprofit organization, supported by gifts and contributions, that seeks to create a resistance to war through training in non-violence. Provides aid to refugees and technical training to developing countries. Publishes pamphlets and the Quaker Service Bulletin. Distributes films.

AMERICAN JEWISH COMMITTEE AND JACOB BLAUSTEIN INSTITUTE FOR THE ADVANCEMENT OF HUMAN RIGHTS. INSTITUTE OF HUMAN RELATIONS
165 East 56th St.
New York, N.Y. 10022

Interested in fostering a respect for civil and human rights.

AMERICAN MATHEMATICAL SOCIETY. HUMAN RIGHTS COMMITTEE
c/o Professor Lipman Bers
City University
Dept. of Mathematics
New York, N.Y. 10027

AMERICAN PHYSICAL SOCIETY. COMMITTEE ON INTERNATIONAL FREEDOM OF SCIENTISTS
335 East 45th St.
New York, N.Y. 10017

AMERICAN PSYCHOLOGICAL ASSOCIATION. COMMITTEE ON INTERNATIONAL RELATIONS
1200 17th St., NW.
Washington, D.C. 20036

AMERICAN PUBLIC HEALTH ASSOCIATION
1015 18th St., NW.
Washington, D.C. 20003

Professional association, the interests of which include the analysis of human rights issues.

AMERICAN SOCIETY OF INTERNATIONAL LAW
2223 Massachusetts Ave., NW.
Washington, D.C. 20008

Generates research about the implementation of human rights in the Inter-American system. Interested in providing legal services to deprived groups in Latin America and the Caribbean.

AMERICANS FOR DEMOCRATIC ACTION
1411 K St., NW.
Washington, D.C. 20005

Independent center that promotes human rights in the Americas from the perspective of the social sciences. Publishes a semi-monthly legislative newsletter when Congress is in session.

AMNESTY INTERNATIONAL. INTERNATIONAL SECRETARIAT
10 Southampton St.
London WC2E 7HF, United Kingdom

Worldwide non governmental organization concerned for the welfare of prisoners. Seeks the release of conscientious objectors, fair trials for political prisoners, and the abolition of the death penalty, torture, and other degrading punishments. Publishes regular bulletins as well as individual reports and analyses.

AMNESTY INTERNATIONAL. UNITED STATES SECTION
2112 Broadway
New York, N.Y. 10023

ANN ARBOR COMMITTEE FOR HUMAN RIGHTS IN LATIN AMERICA
Box 7426
Ann Arbor, Mich. 48107

Nongovernmental organization that publishes human rights materials and provides relief services to Latin Americans.

ANTI-SLAVERY SOCIETY FOR THE PROTECTION OF HUMAN RIGHTS
60 Weymouth St.
London WIN 4D, United Kingdom

APPEAL OF CONSCIENCE FOUNDATION
119 West 57 St.
New York, N.Y. 10019

ARGENTINA COALITION OF BOSTON
Box 304
Astor St.
Boston, Mass. 02123

Concentrates on human rights issues in Argentina and assists political exiles.

ARGENTINE COMMISSION FOR HUMAN RIGHTS
Box 2635
Washington, D.C. 20013

Private institution involved in research, the provision of relief services, and the coordination of efforts pertaining to labor rights.

ARGENTINE INFORMATION AND SOLIDARITY COMMITTEE
339 Lafayette St.
New York, N.Y. 11794

ARGENTINE INFORMATION SERVICE CENTER
c/o Unitas House
2700 Bancroft Way
Berkeley, Calif. 94704

Nonprofit organization that works on behalf of human rights and political prisoners in Argentina. Publications include Argentine Outreach and Argentina Today.

ARGENTINE SUPPORT MOVEMENT
1 Cambridge Terrace
London NWIP 2DQ, United Kingdom

Nongovernmental organization involved in relief work. Disseminates information concering labor and political rights in Argentina.

ARZOBISPADO DE SANTIAGO. VICARÍA DE LA SOLIDARIDAD
Plaza de Armas 444
Casilla 30-D, 2º Piso
Santiago, Chile

Organization of the Archdiocese of Santiago, Chile. Publishes pamphlets and monographs on human rights. Included among its publications is the biweekly Solidaridad.

ASAMBLEA PERMANENTE DE DERECHOS HUMANOS. BOLIVIA
Casilla 1361
La Paz, Bolivia

Nongovernmental organization that publishes Boletín de Derechos Humanos.

ASAMBLEA PERMANENTE POR LA DEFENSA DE LOS DERECHOS HUMANOS. PERÚ
Avenida Uruguay 335
Lima, Perú

ASAMBLEA PERMANENTE POR LOS DERE-
CHOS HUMANOS. ARGENTINA
Paraná 638, 2⁰ Piso
Domicilio Postal: Caja Correo 52, Sucursal 2
1089 Buenos Aires, Argentina

Supports the implementation of the Universal
Declaration of Human Rights in Argentina.
Appeals for an end to terrorism there.

ASOCIACION COLOMBIANA PRO-DERE-
CHOS HUMANOS
Ministerio de Justicia
Apdo. Aereo 16985
Bogotá, D.E., Colombia

Disseminates information concerning cultural,
civil, and political rights.

ASPEN INSTITUTE FOR HUMANISTIC STUD-
IES. PROGRAM ON JUSTICE, SOCIETY AND
THE INDIVIDUAL
36 West 44th St.
New York, N.Y. 10036

ASSOCIATION OF AMERICAN PUBLISHERS.
INTERNATIONAL FREEDOM TO PUBLISH
COMMITTEE
1 Park Ave.
New York, N.Y. 10016

Concerned with fostering freedom of expression
and ending censorship.

ASSOCIATION OF THE BAR OF CHICAGO.
INTERNATIONAL COMMITTEE ON HUMAN
RIGHTS
29 South La Salle St.
Chicago, Ill. 60603

ASSOCIATION OF THE BAR OF THE CITY OF
NEW YORK. COMMITTEE ON INTERNA-
TIONAL HUMAN RIGHTS
42 West 44th St.
New York, N.Y. 10036

AUSTIN COMMITTEE FOR HUMAN RIGHTS
IN CHILE
2204 San Gabriel
Austin, Tex. 78705

BALTIMORE CHILE SOLIDARITY GROUP
Box 1194
Baltimore, Md. 21203

BAPTIST JOINT COMMITTEE ON PUBLIC
AFFAIRS
200 Maryland Ave., NE.
Washington, D.C. 20002

BATTELE MEMORIAL INSTITUTE. LIBRARY
Columbus Laboratories
505 King Ave.
Columbus, Ohio 43201

Research institution interested in international
human rights.

BAY AREA HUMAN RIGHTS WORKING COM-
MITTEE
Box 1313
Oakland, Calif. 94604

BERKELEY INTERNATIONAL HUMAN
RIGHTS GROUP
Joan Pomerlau
c/o Boalt Hall
Berkeley, Calif. 94720

BLOQUE POPULAR REVOLUCIONARIO
Box 31424
San Francisco, Calif. 94131

Publishes Boletín El Salvador.

B'NAI BRITH INTERNATIONAL
1640 Rhode Island Ave., NW.
Washington, D.C. 20036

Nongovernmental religious organization that promotes human rights at the international level. Activities include teaching, training, research, dissemination of materials, relief work, and funding.

BOLIVIA COMMITTEE FOR HUMAN RIGHTS
c/o 5 Jolley Way
Cambridge, United Kingdom

BRAZILIAN STUDIES
Box 673
Adelaide St.
Toronto, Ont., Canada

BREAD FOR THE WORLD
207 East 16th St.
New York, N.Y. 10003

Concerned with meeting basic needs at the international level. Activities include dissemination of materials and funding.

BRITISH ARGENTINA CAMPAIGN
c/o 1 Cambridge Terrace
London NW1 4JL, United Kingdom

Organization in solidarity with Argentine dissidents. Interested in human rights issues.

BROOKINGS INSTITUTION
1775 Massachusetts Ave., NW.
Washington, D.C. 20036

Private, nonprofit research and educational organization interested in policy oriented research, education, and publication in the fields of economics, government, and foreign policy. Publishes 20 to 25 books and monographs annually, the thrice yearly journal Brookings Papers on Economic Activity, the quarterly Brookings Bulletin, an annual report, and reprints of scholarly articles by Brookings authors.

BUFFALO LATIN AMERICA SOLIDARITY COMMITTEE
Box 40
SUNY at Buffalo
Norton Union
Buffalo, N.Y. 14214

BUREAU DE DEFENSE DES DROITS DE L'HOMME. SECTION AMERIQUE LATINE
CCP 4088 87
Paris, France

Publishes the bimonthly Cimade-Information and various dossiers on human rights.

CAMPAIGN FOR POLITICAL RIGHTS
201 Massachusetts Ave., NE., 112
Washington, D.C. 20002

CANADIAN COMMITTEE FOR JUSTICE TO LATIN AMERICAN POLITICAL PRISONERS
Box 128
Station O
Toronto 16, Ont., Canada

CARIBBEAN CONFERENCE OF CHURCHES
Box 876
154 Charlotte St.
Port of Spain, Trinidad

Involved in relief work. Disseminates materials.

CARIBBEAN HUMAN RIGHTS AND LEGAL AID CO.
Box 2978
Paramaribo, Surinam

CARIBBEAN LABOUR SOLIDARITY
10 Leigh Road
London N5 1AH, United Kingdom

CATHOLIC COMMISSION FOR INTERNATIONAL JUSTICE AND PEACE
38-40 Ecclesion Square
London SW1V 1PD, United Kingdom

CATHOLIC FUND FOR OVERSEAS DEVEL-
OPMENT
21a Soho Square
London W1V 6NR, United Kingdom

CATHOLIC INSTITUTE FOR INTERNATION-
AL RELATIONS
1 Cambridge Terrace
London NW1 4JL, United Kingdom

Nongovernmental organization involved in research, the dissemination of information, and the
coordination of human rights groups at the
international level. Focuses on social and minority rights.

CENTER FOR CONCERN
3700 13th St., NE.
Washington, D.C. 20017

CENTER FOR INFORMATION ON LATIN
AMERICA
Box 576
Station N
Montreal 129, Que., Canada

Publishes the newsletter Grito y Fusil.

CENTER FOR INTER-AMERICAN RELA-
TIONS. COMMISSION ON U.S. LATIN RELA-
TIONS
680 Park Ave.
New York, N.Y. 10021

Nonprofit membership corporation financed by
foundation grants, dues, and gifts. Provides a
forum for those concerned with political, social,
and economic activity in the Americas. Attempts
to deepen the appreciation in the United States
of the cultural achievements of Latin American
and Caribbean authors and artists. Sponsors
translations and art exhibitions. Publishes the
Review, books on the visual arts, and seminar
and conference reports and papers.

CENTER FOR INTERCULTURAL DOCUMEN-
TATION
Apdo. 479
Cuernavaca, México

Church related organization of scholars engaged
in research. Issues publications that discuss
current socio-cultural issues in Latin America.

CENTER FOR INTERNATIONAL POLICY
120 Maryland Ave., NE.
Washington, D.C. 20002

Research group interested in human rights from
an economic perspective. Publishes annual in
depth studies on human rights as well as reports
analyzing U.S. foreign policy toward the developing countries.

CENTER FOR LAW AND SOCIAL POLICY
1751 N St., NW.
Washington, D. C. 20036

Indepndent center that promotes civil rights at
the international level. Involved in relief work.

CENTER FOR NATIONAL SECURITY STUD-
IES
122 Maryland Ave., NE.
Washington, D.C. 20002

Monitors the work of U.S. and foreign intelligence services throughout the world. Provides
information about the repressive activities of
these services.

CENTRAL AMERICA HUMAN RIGHTS COM-
MITTEE
c/o 59a Church St.
Old Isleworth
Middlesex TW7 6BE, United Kingdom

CENTRAL AMERICAN REPORT. INFORPRESS CENTROAMERICANA
9 Calle 3-19
Zona 1
Ciudad de Guatemala, Guatemala

Independent research center that focuses on Central America.

CENTRAL LATINOAMERICANA DE TRABA-JADORES
CLAT Apdo. 6681
Caracas 101, Venezuela

Central labor union office for Venezuela.

CENTRE OECUMENIQUE DE LIAISONS IN-TERNATIONALES
68 Rue de Babylone
75007 Paris, France

Christian group interested in political, economic, and social liberation in Latin America. Publishes the quarterly bulletin Liaisons Internationales in Spanish, English, and French.

CENTRO BOLIVIANO DE INVESTIGACION Y ACCION EDUCATIVA
Casilla 1479
La Paz, Bolivia

Ecumenical organization that works on behalf of human rights in Bolivia. Bases its work on the social sciences. Activities include teaching, training, and research.

CENTRO DE DOCUMENTACION E INFOR-MACION SOBRE DERECHOS HUMANOS EN ARGENTINA
Casilla de Correo, Correo Central, 1000
Buenos Aires, Argentina

Publishes the bulletin Informativo.

CENTRO DE DOCUMENTACION LATINO AMERICANA
14 Rue du Val de Grace
75005 Paris, France

CENTRO DE ESTADISTICA RELIGIOSA E INVESTIGAÇÕES SOCIAIS
Rua Dr. Julio Ottoni 571
3 S., Santa Teresa
ZC 45, 20000
Rio de Janeiro, Brazil

CENTRO DE ESTUDIOS URUGUAY-AMERICA LATINA
Apdo. 19-131
México 19, D.F., México

Nonprofit publishing house that issues Cuadernos de Marcha, a bimonthly similar in orientation to the Uruguayan newspaper Marcha. Marcha, founded in 1939, was shut down by the Uruguayan government in 1974.

CENTRO DE ESTUDIOS Y ACCION SOCIAL
Apdo. 6-133
El Dorado, Panamá

Focuses on human rights in Central America. Uses analytical techniques of the social sciences. Involved in research, the publicizing of violations, and relief work.

CENTRO DE ESTUDIOS Y PROMOCION DEL DESARROLLO
Avenida Salaverry 1945
Lima 14, Perú

Independent research center that focuses on human rights in Latin America from the perspective of the social sciences.

CENTRO DE ESTUDIOS Y PUBLICACIONES
Apdo. 6118
Lima 1, Perú

Publishes articles on civil and political rights in Latin America.

CENTRO DE INFORMACION DE LAS NA-CIONES UNIDAS PARA COLOMBIA, ECUA-DOR Y VENEZUELA
Calle 10, No. 3-61
Bogotá, Colombia

CENTRO DE INFORMACION ONU
Pte. Masaryk 29, 7° Piso
México 5, D.F., México

CENTRO DE INVESTIGACION Y ACCION SOCIAL
C.C. 95 (Sucursal 26)
O'Higgins 1331
1426 Buenos Aires, Argentina

Research center concerned with human rights from the point of view of the social sciences. Involved in relief work.

CENTRO DE INVESTIGACION Y DOCENCIAS ECONOMICAS
Carretera México-Toluca Km. 16.5
Apdo. 10-883
México 10, D.F., México

Governmental organization interested in the international economic order and human rights. The perspective is that of the social sciences. Involved in teaching and research. Publishes—Cuadernos Semestrales semi-annually.

CENTRO DE PLANIFICACION Y ACCION ECUMENICA
Apto. 252-2
Benito Monción, No. 204
Santo Domingo, D.N., Dominican Republic

Caribbean office of the Unión Evangélica Latino-Americana. Publishes Carta-CEPAE and Boletín/Noticias Ecuménicas.

CENTRO DE PROYECCION CRISTIANA
Avenida Horacio Urteaga 452
Lima, Perú

CENTRO ECUMENICO DE DOCUMENTAÇÃO E INFORMAÇÃO
Rua Cosme Velho
98 Fundos--Cosme Velho
Rio de Janeiro, Brasil

CENTRO GUMILLA
Apdo. 40225
Caracas 104, Venezuela

CENTRO NACIONAL DE COMUNICACION SOCIAL
Medellín 33
México 7, D.F., México

Independent center interested in human, economic, and social rights. Involved in research and relief work throughout Latin America.

CENTRO PARAGUAYO DE EDUCACION CIVICA
Iturbe 936
Asunción, Paraguay

Nongovernmental organization that promotes civil rights in Paraguay.

CENTRO REGIONAL DE INFORMACIONES ECUMENICAS
Centro de Estudios Ecuménicos
Ocotepec 39-San Jerónimo
México 20, D.F., México

Religious group that promotes human rights in the Caribbean region. Publishes Envio CRIE, a biweekly listing of relevant magazine articles, documents, and newspaper clippings, Boletines Bibliográficos, and various other documents and studies.

CHASQUI-AEL-BOLIVIA
34 Göttingen
Nikolansbergerweg 9
West Germany

CHICAGO AREA GROUP ON LATIN AMERICA *2546 N. Halsted*
Chicago, Ill. 60614

Expresses solidarity with liberation movements in Latin America. Involved in research. Publishes Latin America: Liberation and Christianity.

CHICAGO COMMITTEE FOR HUMAN RIGHTS IN ARGENTINA
22 E. Van Buren, 5th Floor
Chicago, Ill. 60605

Involved in relief work.

CHILE COMMITTEE FOR HUMAN RIGHTS. ENGLAND
1 Cambridge Terrace
London NW1 4JL, United Kingdom

Nongovernmental organization that works to defend and promote civil and political rights in Chile.

CHILE COMMITTEE FOR HUMAN RIGHTS. UNITED STATES
1901 Q St., NW.
Washington, D.C. 20009

Concerned with the plight of disappeared prisoners and the rights of exiled artists. Distributes films, sponsors seminars, holds concerts and receptions, and issues literary publications. The London and Washington offices issue separate editions of the Chile Committee for Human Rights Newsletter.

CHILE DEMOCRATICO
777 United Nations Plaza, 8th Floor
New York, N.Y. 10017

International association involved in disseminating information to the U.S. public concerning repression in Chile. Serves as a liaison to the United Nations, with offices in New York, Rome, and Mexico. Publishes a newsletter and issues press releases.

CHILE LEGISLATIVE CENTER
201 Massachusetts Ave., NE.
Washington, D.C. 20002

Nongovernmental organization, the purpose of which is to inform the Congress about the human rights situation in Chile in the hope of persuading the U.S. government to end its support of the Pinochet regime. Issues updates and memoranda on current U.S. legislation affecting Chile.

CHILE RESISTANCE COMMITTEE
Box 14348
Minneapolis, Minn. 55414

Group in solidarity with the Chilean working class in particular and with Latin American workers in general. Speaks in defense of political prisoners, campaigns against U.S. corporate and government programs to aid the military junta, and helps support the underground Chilean press.

CHILE SOLIDARITY CAMPAIGN
129 Seven Sisters Road
London N7 7QG, United Kingdom

Nongovernmental organization involved in promoting and defending civil and political rights in Chile. Publishes a newsletter.

CHILE SOLIDARITY COMMITTEE
Box 1466
SUNY at Binghamton
Binghamton, N.Y. 13901

CHRISTIAN ACTION FOR DEVELOPMENT IN THE CARIBBEAN
Box 616
Bridgetown, Barbados

Ecumenical church organization interested in human, economic, and social rights. Activities include teaching, the dissemination of information, and legal work.

CHRISTIAN AID
Box No. 1
240/250 Ferndale Road
London SW9 8BH, United Kingdom

Church organization that funds activities to meet basic needs and to protect civil, political, and religious rights at the international level.

CHRISTIAN CHURCH. DIVISION OF OVER-
SEAS MINISTRIES
Box 1986
Indianapolis, Ind. 46206

Church organization with missions in Latin
America.

CHRISTIAN CHURCH. INTERNATIONAL HU-
MAN RIGHTS PROGRAM
Box 1986
Indianapolis, Ind. 46206

CHRISTIAN RESPONSE TO MILITARY RE-
PRESSION IN LATIN AMERICA
1618 N. French St.
Santa Ana, Calif. 92701

Church organization concerned with relief work
and the promotion of economic, civil, cultural,
political, and social rights.

CHRISTIANS CONCERNED FOR CHILE
300 East 4th St.
New York, N.Y. 10009

CHURCH WOMEN UNITED
475 Riverside Dr., Rm. 812
New York, N.Y. 10027

CIDOS
Casilla 8738
La Paz, Bolivia

Independent center that promotes human rights
in Bolivia. Publishes Coyuntura.

CIRCULO DE PERIODISTAS URUGUAYOS
ANTIFACISTAS
Nuevo Léon 144, Of. 101
México 11, D.F., México

CLERGY AND LAITY CONCERNED
198 Broadway
New York, N.Y. 10038

Church organization involved in the promotion
of human rights at the international level.
Publishes the monthly CALC Report.

COALITION FOR A NEW FOREIGN AND MIL-
ITARY POLICY. HUMAN RIGHTS WORKING
GROUP
120 Maryland Ave., NE.
Washington, D.C. 20002

Promotes human rights at the international level.
The perspective is that of the political sciences.

COLORADO COALITION OF GLOBAL HU-
MAN RIGHTS
1995 S. Washington
Denver, Colo. 80210

COLORADO COORDINATING COMMITTEE
FOR A FREE CHILE
2239 East Colfax, Rm. 202
Denver, Colo. 80206

COLORADO LATIN AMERICAN SOLIDARITY
GROUP
2239 East Colfax, Rm. 202
Denver, Colo. 80206

COLUMBIA UNIVERSITY. CENTER FOR THE
STUDY OF HUMAN RIGHTS
704 International Affairs Bldg.
New York, N.Y. 10027

COLUMBIA UNIVERSITY. INTERNATIONAL INSTITUTE FOR THE STUDY OF HUMAN REPRODUCTION. CENTER FOR POPULATION AND FAMILY HEALTH
60 Haven Ave.
New York, N.Y. 10032

Conducts applied research, teaching, and training. Concerned with developing and evaluating population and family health programs. Sponsored by the Pan American Health Agency, the National Institutes of Health, the U.S. Dept. of Health and Human Services, the Rockefeller Foundation, the Commonwealth Fund, the U.S. Agency for International Development, and the Ford Foundation. Library holdings include a specialized collection of over 9,000 documents on family planning and program development and evaluation. Publishes a series of manuals, books, a bibliography, and a thesaurus.

COMISION ARGENTINA DE SOLIDARIDAD
Apdo. 20234-Administración Correo 20
México, D.F., México

Nongovernmental organization concerned with civil and political rights in Argentina.

COMISION ARGENTINA POR LOS DERECHOS HUMANOS
61 Rue Meslay
75003 Paris, France

Nonprofit, nongovernmental international organization that works for the preservation of human rights in Argentina. Formed by a group of Argentine lawyers who, through the practice of their profession, became increasingly aware of the need for a permanent national and international organization to defend human rights in their country. Has permanent representatives in Paris, Geneva, Rome, Mexico City, and Washington, D.C. Publishes Boletín CADHU.

COMISION CENTROAMERICANA PARA LA DEFENSA DE LOS DERECHOS HUMANOS
Apdo. No. 49
Guadalupe Gocicochea, Costa Rica

Nongovernmental organization involved in the dissemination of information and in relief services pertaining to basic human needs and cultural, civil, and political rights in Central America.

COMISION COORDINADORA PARA LA DEFENSA DE DERECHOS HUMANOS
Avenida 25c No. 420
Bogotá, Colombia

COMISION DE DERECHOS HUMANOS
17a Calle Oriente
112 San Salvador, El Salvador

COMISION DE ESTUDIOS DE HISTORIA DE LA IGLESIA EN LATINOAMERICA
Apdo. 20439
Bogotá, Colombia

Independent research and teaching center concerned with human rights from the points of view of theology and history.

COMISION DE FAMILIARES DE DESAPARECIDOS POR RAZONES POLITICAS
Corrientes 1785, 5° Piso "J"
1042 Buenos Aires, Argentina

COMISION DE JUSTICIA Y PAZ
Apdo. 1112
San Salvador, El Salvador

COMISION DE SOLIDARIDAD CON LOS FAMILIARES DE LOS DETENIDOS Y DESAPARECIDOS
76 Rue de la Verrerie
75004 Paris, France

COMISION EPISCOPAL DE ACCION SOCIAL
Apdo. 59
Chimbote, Perú

COMISION EVANGELICA LATINOAMERI-CANA DE EDUCACION CRISTIANA
Apdo. 3994
General Garzón 2267, Jesús María
Lima, Perú

Church organization that works to uphold human rights in Latin America. Interested primarily in education.

COMISION PERMANENTE DE DERECHOS HUMANOS DE NICARAGUA
4 cuadras al sur de Cine Cabrera
20 varas abajo, casa no. 608
Apdo. 4234
Managua, Nicaragua

Nongovernmental organization involved in relief work. Interested both in civil and political rights and in satisfying basic human needs in Nicaragua.

COMISSÃO PONTIFICIA JUSTIÇA E PAZ. COMISSÃO ARQUIDIOCESANA DOS DIREITOS HUMANOS E DOS MARGINALIZADOS. SECRETARIADO JUSTIÇA E NÃO-VIOLENCIA
a/c Mitra Arquidiocesana
C.P. 30405
01238 São Paulo, Brasil

Church organization involved in research. Seeks to meet basic human needs. Promotes civil, cultural, and political rights in Brazil.

COMISSÃO PONTIFICIA JUSTIÇA E PAZ. SECÃO BRASILEIRA
Praça XV de Novembro 101
Rio de Janeiro G.B., Brasil

COMITE CRISTIANO MEXICANO
Apdo. 85-13
México 20, D.F., México

Aids the persecuted in Latin America.

COMITE DE DEFENSA DE LOS DERECHOS HUMANOS DE CHILE
Ricardo Santa Cruz 630
Santiago, Chile

Publishes the monthly Informativo CODEH.

COMITE DE IGLESIAS PARA AYUDAS DE EMERGENCIA
Gral. Díaz 429
Asunción, Paraguay

Ecumenical religious organization concerned both with basic human needs and with cultural, civil, and political rights in Paraguay. Activities include relief work and the dissemination of information.

COMITE DE PRESOS POLITICOS
Apdo. 9105
Bogotá, Colombia

COMITE INFORMATIVO PRO PERÚ
Box 2491
Village Station
Los Angeles, Calif. 90024

COMITE INTERNACIONAL DE LA CRUZ ROJA
7 Avenue de la Paix
Geneva, Switzerland 33 30 60

COMITE LATINOAMERICANO DE LA FE
Coronel Bogado 166
Casilla 1190
Asunción, Paraguay

COMITE PARAGUAYO PARA LA DEFENSA DE LOS DERECHOS HUMANOS
Nuestra Señora de Asunción 870
Asunción, Paraguay

Nongovernmental organization.

COMMISSION FOR INTERNATIONAL DUE PROCESS OF LAW AND WORLD HABEAS CORPUS
105 W. Adams St.
Chicago, Ill. 60603

COMMISSION TO STUDY THE ORGANIZATION OF PEACE
866 United Nations Plaza
New York, N.Y. 10017

COMMITTEE AGAINST REPRESSION IN BRAZIL
Box 426
Hyattsville, Md. 20782

COMMITTEE AGAINST VIOLATIONS OF HUMAN RIGHTS IN EL SALVADOR
Box 759
Old Chelsea Station
New York, N.Y. 10011

Nongovernmental organization founded in June 1977 to call attention to the abuses of the human rights of workers, peasants, students, and church leaders in El Salvador. Works to mobilize support for changes in the human rights policies of the governments of El Salvador and the United States. Publishes the bimonthly El Salvador Report as well as periodic special reports and bulletins.

COMMITTEE FOR HUMAN RIGHTS IN ARGENTINA
1 Cambridge Terrace
London NW1 4JL, United Kingdom

COMMITTEE FOR HUMAN RIGHTS IN PARAGUAY
c/o Box 82
London E2 9DS, United Kingdom

COMMITTEE FOR HUMAN RIGHTS IN URUGUAY
c/o 1 Cambridge Terrace
London NW1 4JL, England

Private organization dedicated to disseminating information concerning civil, cultural, and political rights in Uruguay. Provides legal services.

COMMITTEE FOR PROGRESSIVE SALVADOREANS
Box 12355
San Francisco, Calif. 94112

Nongovernmental organization involved in defending and promoting cultural, civil, and political rights in El Salvador. Publishes the bimonthly newsletter El Pulgarcito.

COMMITTEE FOR THE DEFENSE OF HUMAN RIGHTS IN ARGENTINA
Box 335
Port Credit Station, L5G 4L8, Ont., Canada

Nonprofit group of Canadians and Argentinians opposed to the repression of civil rights in Argentina.

COMMITTEE FOR THE DEFENSE OF HUMAN RIGHTS IN THE SOUTHERN CONE
Avenida Higienopolis 890
01238 São Paulo, S.P., Brasil

Agency of the Archdiocesan Pastoral Commission for Human Rights and Marginal People in São Paulo. Involved principally in the dissemination of information concerning basic human needs and cultural, civil, and political rights.

COMMITTEE IN SOLIDARITY WITH THE URUGUAYAN PEOPLE
Box 234
Wyckoff Station
Brooklyn, N.Y. 11237

Opposes the Uruguayan dictatorship. Seeks an end to repression and proposes a return to democracy. Publishes the Uruguay Newsletter.

COMMITTEE OF CONCERNED SCIENTISTS
9 East 40th St.
New York, N.Y. 10017

COMMITTEE OF SOLIDARITY WITH THE PEOPLE OF NICARAGUA
Box 40885
San Francisco, Calif. 94140

Promotes support for the people of Nicaragua. Sponsors rallies, lectures, and slide shows. Publishes the newsletter Gaceta Sandinista.

COMMITTEE ON HUMAN RIGHTS FOR NICARAGUA
1934-3 Rosemary Hills Drive
Silver Spring, Md. 20910

Nongovernmental organization that reports on the violations of civil and political rights in Nicaragua.

COMMON FRONT FOR LATIN AMERICA
Box 426
Hyattsville, Md. 20782

COMMUNITY ACTION ON LATIN AMERICA
731 State St.
Madison, Wis. 53703

Independent center interested in human rights in the Americas from the perspective of the political sciences. Publishes the CALA Newsletter and occasional reports.

COMMUNITY OF THE PEACE PEOPLE, INC.
Castle Station
New Rochelle, N.Y. 10801

CONFEDERACION INTERAMERICANA DE EDUCACION CATOLICA
Calle 78 No. 12-16, Of. 101
Bogotá, Colombia

CONFERENCE OF NON-GOVERNMENTAL ORGANIZATIONS IN CONSULTATION WITH THE U.N. ECONOMIC AND SOCIAL COUNCIL. NON-GOVERNMENTAL ORGANIZATIONS COMMITTEE ON HUMAN RIGHTS
35 East 84th St.
New York, N.Y. 10028

CONFERENCE ON LATIN AMERICAN HISTORY
Department of History
Duke University
Durham, N.C. 27706

Association of university professors who study Latin American history. Human rights is one of the topics of interest.

CONFERÊNCIA NACIONAL DOS BISPOS DO BRASIL. SECRETARIADO GERAL
C.P. 13-2067
70000 Brasilia, D.F., Brasil

CONSEJO EPISCOPAL LATINOAMERICANO. SECRETARIA GENERAL
Apdo. 5278
Bogotá, Colombia

Involved in the struggle for human rights in Latin America since the mid 1960's.

CONSEJO LATINOAMERICANO DE CIENCIAS SOCIALES
Calle 875, 3⁰ Piso
E. Buenos Aires, Argentina

Independent research center that focuses on issues in the social sciences in the Americas. Human rights is one of the topics of study.

CONTEMPORARY ARCHIVE ON LATIN AMERICA
1 Cambridge Terrace
London NW1 4JL, United Kingdom

Researches human rights issues in Latin America. Publishes the CALA Fact Sheet. Its London library is open to the public.

COORDINADORA DE ENTIDADES Y ORGANI-
ZACIONES CRISTIANAS
Perú 630, 5° Piso
Dpto. 19
Buenos Aires, Argentina

COORDINADORA ECUMENICA DE SERVICIO
C.P. 1596
01000 São Paulo, S.P., Brasil

Ecumenical organization interested in the social
sciences. Researches issues on human rights in
Latin America.

COORDINATING COMMITTEE OF MAPUCHE
LIVING IN EXILE
29 Islington Park St.
London N1 10B, United Kingdom

CORPORACION DE INVESTIGACIONES
ECONOMICAS PARA LATINOAMERICA
Avenida Colón No. 3494
Casilla 16496-Correo 9
Santiago, Chile

CORPORACION INTEGRAL PARA EL
DESARROLLO CULTURAL Y SOCIAL
Carrera 21 No. 56-33
Apdo. 20439
Bogotá, Colombia

COUNCIL ON HEMISPHERIC AFFAIRS
1735 New Hampshire Ave., NW.
Washington, D.C. 20009

Private, nonprofit research organization that
monitors United States-Latin American relations.

COUNCIL ON RELIGION AND INTERNA-
TIONAL AFFAIRS
170 East 64th St.
New York, N.Y. 10021

CUBA RESOURCE CENTER
Box 206
Cathedral Station
New York, N.Y. 10025

Funded by Protestant and Roman Catholic
Church groups. Provides religious communities
with information on Cuba. Publishes the newsletter Cuba Review.

CULTURAL SURVIVAL
11 Divinity Ave.
Cambridge, Mass. 02138

Independent research center concerned with
minority rights at the international level. Publications include the Newsletter of the Democratic Left.

DEMOCRATIC SOCIALIST ORGANIZING
COMMITTEE
853 Broadway, Rm. 617
New York, N.Y. 10003

DIAL
170 Boulevard de Mont Parnasse
75104 Paris, France

ECUMENICAL PROGRAM FOR INTER-AMER-
ICAN COMMUNICATION AND ACTION
1740 Irving St., NW.
Washington, D.C. 20010

Group in solidarity with the peoples of Central
America and the Caribbean. Interested in
human, cultural, and political rights in the
region. Involved in research, the dissemination of
information, and relief services. Publications
include several short monographs and a newsletter.

8th [i.e., EIGHTH] DAY CENTER FOR JUSTICE
22 East Van Buren St.
Chicago, Ill. 60605

FACULTAD LATINOAMERICANA DE CIENCIAS SOCIALES
José M. Infante 51
Casilla 3213 Correo Central
Santiago, Chile

Independent research center concerned with human rights in Latin America from juridical, political, and historical points of view.

FEDERATION INTERNATIONAL DES DROITS DE L'HOMME
27 Rue Jean Dolent
75014 Paris 14, France

FEDERATION OF AMERICAN SCIENTISTS
307 Massachusetts Ave., NW.
Washington, D.C. 20002

FOREIGN POLICY ASSOCIATION
345 East 46th St.
New York, N.Y. 10017

Private, nonprofit organization that works to develop an informed public opinion on major issues in U.S. foreign policy. Cooperates with national and local organizations. Prepares a number of publications, including the Great Decisions annual, the Headline Series, and several booklets on the Panama Canal treaties.

FORO POR EL RESPETO DE LOS DERECHOS HUMANOS EN ARGENTINA
29 Rue Descartes
75005 Paris, France

FOUNDATION FOR LEGAL AID IN CHILE
Ianskerkhof 16
Utrecht, Netherlands

FOUNDATION FOR THE ESTABLISHMENT OF AN INTERNATIONAL CRIMINAL COURT
Box 12
Auburndale, Mass. 02166

FREEDOM HOUSE
Willkie Memorial Bldg.
20 West 40th St.
New York, N.Y. 10018

FREEDOM OF FAITH
170 East 64th St.
New York, N.Y. 10021

FRENTE SOLIDARIO SALVADOREÑO
Box 748
Old Chelsea Station
New York, N.Y. 10011

FRIENDS COMMITTEE ON NATIONAL LEGISLATION
245 Second St., NE.
Washington, D.C. 20002

Areas of interest include congressional action on U.S. foreign policy issues, economic policy, and human and civil rights. Library holdings include Congressional Record clippings, transcripts of congressional hearings, reports, current newspaper clippings, 250 books, and over 100 periodical titles. Publishes the Washington Newsletter, the FCNL Memo, reports, statements of legistative policy, and background papers.

FRIENDS OF HAITI
Box 348
New York, N.Y. 10956

Provides political and economic support of the Haitian struggle for liberation. Its activities include broadcasting, publishing the quarterly Haiti Report, and distributing films.

FUND FOR FREE EXPRESSION
205 East 42nd St., Rm. 1305
New York, N.Y. 10017

FUND FOR HUMAN RIGHTS, INC.
112 East 19th St.
New York, N.Y. 10003

FUND FOR NEW PRIORITIES IN AMERICA
122 East 42nd St.
New York, N.Y. 10017

Sponsors colloquia on Capitol Hill that focus on human rights violations in Latin America. Publishes transcripts of the colloquia.

FUND FOR PEACE
1995 Broadway
New York, N.Y. 10023

Researches global problems that threaten human survival, such as the extreme contrast in levels of health, education, economic security, and social welfare between the rich and poor countries and the systematic attacks on basic human rights by governments. Issues the monthly Defense Monitor, the International Policy Report, the monthly First Principles, and various publications authored or edited by persons in the Fund's fellowship program for doctoral and post-doctoral candidates.

GEORGETOWN UNIVERSITY. CENTRO DE IMMIGRACION
Georgetown University Law Center
600 New Jersey Ave., NW.
Washington, D.C. 20001

GEORGETOWN UNIVERSITY. WOODSTOCK THEOLOGICAL CENTER
1322 36th St., NW.
Washington, D.C. 20057

Institute for research and reflection established by the Maryland and New York Provinces of the Society of Jesus in 1975. Attempts to elaborate a treaty of human rights that will relate human rights to human needs in the context of the different cultural traditions of the Americas.

GUATEMALA NEWS AND INFORMATION BUREAU
Box 4126
Berkeley, Calif. 94704

Information and support organization that publishes the monthly Guatemala Update and the quarterly Guatemala!.

HABEAS
Apdo. 27-041
México 7, D.F., México

Established under the direction of the writer Gabriel García Márquez, this organization of political, religious, and literary leaders attempts to promote respect for human rights throughout Latin America.

HAITIAN REFUGEE PROJECT
110 Maryland Ave., NE., Rm. 108
Washington, D.C. 20002

Independent research center involved in the defense of civil rights in Haiti. Issues the periodical Fact Sheet as well as in depth reports.

HARVARD INTERNATIONAL LAW SOCIETY. INTERNATIONAL HUMAN RIGHTS PROJECT
Harvard Law School
Cambridge, Mass. 02138

HELSINKI WATCH COMMITTEE FOR THE UNITED STATES
c/o Professor Morton Sklar
Center for National Policy Review
Catholic University Law School
Washington, D.C. 20064

HUDSON INSTITUTE
Quaker Ridge Road
Croton-on-Hudson, N.Y. 10520

Private, nonprofit research organization that seeks to provide independent analyses of major issues in public policy. Areas of interest include national security, educational policy, and domestic and international economic policy. Publishes technical reports.

HUMAN RIGHTS INTERNET
1502 Ogden St., NW.
Washington, D.C. 20010

Nongovernmental organization that provides human rights groups with information concerning civil, economic, political, and social rights. Publishes the newsletter Human Rights Internet and the annual Human Rights Directory.

HUMAN RIGHTS RESOURCE CENTER
10 Lindfield Gardens
London NW3, United Kingdom

Publishes a catalog of human rights publications. Distributes publications from many organizations such as Amnesty International, Human Rights Internet, International Commission of Jurists, Index on Censorship, and others.

HUMAN RIGHTS WORKING GROUP OF THE COALITION FOR A NEW FOREIGN AND MILITARY POLICY
120 Maryland Ave., NE.
Washington, D.C. 20002

Composed of over fifty organizations. Actively engages in the promotion of human rights. Issues periodic action alerts.

HUMAN RIGHTS WORKING GROUP OF THE TWIN CITIES
1920 Girard Ave., S.
Minneapolis, Min. 55403

HUMANITARIAN AID FOR NICARAGUAN DEMOCRACY
c/o National Network in Solidarity with the Nicaraguan People
1322 18th St., NW.
Washington, D.C. 20036

Provides economic aid to the poor of Nicaragua and to Nicaraguan exiles.

IGLESIA Y SOCIEDAD EN AMERICA LATINA
Latin American Dept.
NCCC, Rm. 656
475 Riverside Drive
New York, N.Y. 10027

Promotes an awareness of contemporary Latin American issues. Publishes ISAL Abstracts, a monthly documentation service in both Spanish and English.

IN THE PUBLIC INTEREST
122 Maryland Ave., NE.
Washington, D.C. 20002

INDIAN LAW RESOURCE CENTER
1101 Vermont Ave., NW.
Washington, D.C. 20005

Independent teaching, research, and counseling center interested in human rights from a juridical perspective.

INDÍGENA
Box 4073
Berkeley, Calif. 94704

Independent dissemination center that promotes minority rights throughout Latin America. Publishes Indígena.

INDIGENOUS MINORITIES RESEARCH COUNCIL
2-22 Hepburn Road
St. Paul's, Bristol 2, United Kingdom

INFOR-ACT
Box 37 Times Square Station
New York, N.Y. 10036

Bimonthly information project of the New York Circus, a Center for the Interchange of Religious Concerns in the United States. Works with the Latin American community in New York City. Provides educational materials to Latin America.

INSTITUT D'ACTION CULTURELLE
27 Chemin des Crêts
CH 1218 Grand-Saconnex
Geneva, Switzerland

> Nonprofit organization involved in publishing materials and organizing conferences. Interested in education and political rights issues.

INSTITUTE FOR POLICY STUDIES
1901 Q St., NW.
Washington, D.C. 20009

> Research institution that analyzes international human rights issues. Sponsors the Letelier-Moffit Memorial Fund for Human Rights. Issues a catalog of its publications and films.

INSTITUTE FOR THE DEVELOPMENT OF INDIAN LAW
927 15th St., NW.
Washington, D.C. 20005

> Independent center concerned with teaching, research, and the dissemination of information. Focuses on human and minority rights in the Americas.

INSTITUTE FOR THE STUDY OF HUMAN ISSUES
3401 Market St., Suite 252
Philadelphia, Pa. 19104

> Nonprofit organization that conducts research in the social sciences, the natural sciences, and the humanities. Areas of interest include anthropology, politics, nutrition, sociology, trade, and narcotics. Has developed a data bank on attitudes in Chile. Publishes books, technical reports, and reprints.

INSTITUTE FOR WORLD ORDER
1140 Avenue of the Americas
New York, N.Y. 10036

> Private, nonprofit educational and research organization that seeks to develop an awareness of the need for new social, political, and economic institutions based on humane values. Areas of interest include world order, peace, and research on the future. Publishes the quarterly Alternatives: a Journal of World Peace, the Bulletin of Peace Proposals, monographs, occasional papers, bibliographies, and reprints.

INSTITUTE OF CARIBBEAN STUDIES
University of Puerto Rico
Rio Piedras, P.R. 00931

> Research center concerned with human rights in the Caribbean from the perspective of the social sciences. Publishes Caribbean Monthly Bulletin.

INSTITUTE OF INTERNATIONAL LAW AND ECONOMIC DEVELOPMENT
1511 K St., NW.
Washington, D.C. 20005

> Independent research center that focuses on human rights and on the economic situation in the Caribbean and the small island areas of the Pacific. Its point of view is juridical. Publishes the series—Small Area Studies.

INSTITUTO BRASILEIRO DE DESENVOLVIMENTO
Rua Bambina 115
Botafogo, ZC 02
20000 Rio de Janeiro, R.J., Brasil

INSTITUTO LATINOAMERICANO DE DOCTRINA Y ESTUDIOS SOCIALES
Casilla 14446
Correo 21
Santiago, Chile

INSTITUTO LATINOAMERICANO DE ESTUDIOS TRANSNACIONALES
Apdo. 85-025
México 20, D.F., México

INSTITUTO LATINOAMERICANO DE INVESTIGACIONES SOCIALES
Plaza La Castellana
Edificio PARSA, 1º Piso
Apdo. 61712, Chacao
Caracas, Venezuela

Publishes information concerning social development, politics, and economics in Latin America.

INTER-AMERICAN ASSOCIATION FOR DEMOCRACY AND FREEDOM
20 West 40th St.
New York, N.Y. 10018

Independent center interested in human rights from juridical and historical points of view. Involved in research, the dissemination of information, and relief work. Publishes the monthly Hemispherica, occasional press releases, and reports.

INTER-AMERICAN BAR FOUNDATION
1819 H St., NW.
Washington, D.C. 20006

Professional association interested in human rights in the Americas. Involved in teaching and the dissemination of information. Publications include the Legal Protection of Human Rights in the Western Hemisphere (1977).

INTER-AMERICAN DEVELOPMENT BANK. OFFICE OF THE U.S. EXECUTIVE DIRECTOR
808 17th St.
Washington, D.C. 20006

INTER-AMERICAN FOUNDATION
1515 Wilson Blvd.
Rosslyn, Va. 22209

Experimental agency for foreign assistance created by Congress to address the problems of the poor in Latin America.

INTER-CHURCH COMMITTEE ON HUMAN RIGHTS IN LATIN AMERICA
201-40 St. Clair Ave., E.
Toronto, Ont., Can. M4T 1M9

Works to satisfy basic human needs and to promote civil rights in Latin America. Involved in research, the publicizing of violations of civil rights, funding, and the coordination of human rights groups.

INTER-COMMUNITY CENTER FOR JUSTICE AND PEACE
20 Washington Square
New York, N.Y. 10011

INTERFAITH CENTER ON CORPORATE RESPONSIBILITY
475 Riverside Dr., Rm. 566
New York, N.Y. 10027

Church organization involved in teaching, research, and the dissemination of human rights materials at the international level.

INTERNATIONAL ASSOCIATION OF MACHINISTS AND AEROSPACE WORKERS
1300 Connecticut Ave., NW.
Washington, D.C. 20036

INTERNATIONAL BANK FOR RECONSTRUCTION AND DEVELOPMENT. OFFICE OF *THE U.S. EXECUTIVE DIRECTOR*
1818 H St., NW.
Washington, D.C. 20433

INTERNATIONAL CHRISTIAN SERVICE FOR PEACE
D 533 Konigswinter 1
Romlinghoven, Malteserhof, West Germany

INTERNATIONAL COMMISSION OF ENQUIRY INTO THE CRIMES OF THE MILITARY JUNTA IN CHILE
Secretariat
Bulevardi 13A
SF-00120 Helsinki 12, Finland

INTERNATIONAL COMMISSION OF JURISTS. CENTRE FOR THE INDEPENDENCE OF JUDGES AND LAWYERS

B.P. 120
1224 Chêne-Bougeries
Geneva, Switzerland

Publishes the Bulletin of the Centre for the Independence of Judges and Lawyers.

INTERNATIONAL COMMISSION OF JURISTS. EUROPE

109 Route de Chêne
1224 Chêne
Geneva, Switzerland

Nongovernmental organization that promotes the rule of law and the protection of human rights internationally. Has consultative status with the United Nations, UNESCO, and the Council of Europe.

INTERNATIONAL COMMISSION OF JURISTS. UNITED STATES

777 United Nations Plaza
New York, N.Y. 10017

Nongovernmental organization concerned with human, civil, and political rights at the international level. Activities include research, the dissemination of materials, and relief work. Publishes a biannual report and occasional monographs.

INTERNATIONAL CONFEDERATION FOR DISARMAMENT AND PEACE

ICDP & CELT-6 Endslengh St.
London WCIH ODX, United Kingdom

INTERNATIONAL FELLOWSHIP OF RECONCILIATION

35 Rue Van Elewyck
1050 Brussels, Belgium

International lobbying group that actively promotes peace and respect for human rights.

INTERNATIONAL HUMAN RIGHTS LAW GROUP

1700 K St., NW., Suite 801
Washington, D.C. 20006

Nongovernmental organization concerned with the promotion of human rights and the coordination of human rights groups at the international level.

INTERNATIONAL INDIAN TREATY COUNCIL

777 United Nations Plaza, Rm. 10-F
New York, N.Y. 10017

Nongovernmental group that focuses on treaty disputes between U.S. Indian tribes and the federal government. Involved in some international work.

INTERNATIONAL INSTITUTES OF HUMAN RIGHTS

6 Place de Bordeaux
67000 Strasbourg, France

Nongovernmental organization founded in 1969 by René Cassin. Involved in teaching, research, and the dissemination of information concerning human rights. Publishes the Human Rights Journal.

INTERNATIONAL LADIES GARMENT WORKERS UNION

1710 Broadway
New York, N.Y. 10015

INTERNATIONAL LAW ASSOCIATION

3 Paper Buildings
Temple, London EC4, United Kingdom

Issues an annual conference report which includes records from the association's sessions on human rights. Publishes some human rights related materials.

INTERNATIONAL LEAGUE FOR HUMAN RIGHTS
236 East 46th St.
New York, N.Y. 10017

Nongovernmental organization involved in relief services, the dissemination of information, and the coordination of human rights groups. Publishes the Human Rights Bulletin and special reports on human rights issues presented before the United Nations.

INTERNATIONAL LONGSHOREMEN'S AND WAREHOUSEMEN'S UNION
1188 Franklin St.
San Francisco, Calif. 94109

INTERNATIONAL MONETARY FUND. OFFICE OF THE U.S. EXECUTIVE DIRECTOR
700 19th St., NW.
Washington, D.C. 20006

INTERNATIONAL PEACE ACADEMY
777 United Nations Plaza
New York, N.Y. 10017

INTERNATIONAL PEACE BUREAU
Rue de Zurich 41
Geneva, Switzerland

INTERNATIONAL PEACE RESEARCH ASSOCIATION
c/o PR 10
Box 5052
Oslo 3, Norway

INTERNATIONAL SOCIAL SERVICE. UNITED STATES
345 East 46th St.
New York, N.Y. 10017

INTERNATIONAL UNIVERSITY EXCHANGE FUND. INTERNATIONAL DEVELOPMENT CENTRE
Parnell House
25 Wilton Road
London SW1V 1JS, United Kingdom

Involved in teaching, research, funding, and relief work. Concerned primarily with civil and minority rights at the international level. Its field office for Latin America is in Costa Rica.

INTERNATIONAL WORKING GROUP FOR INDIGENOUS AFFAIRS
Copenhagen, Denmark

Publishes a series of monographic studies on the plight of Latin American Indian groups.

JAMAICA COUNCIL FOR HUMAN RIGHTS
Box 395
Kingston, Jamaica

Nongovernmental organization that promotes cultural, civil, and political rights in the Caribbean area.

JESUIT OFFICE OF SOCIAL MINISTRIES
1717 Massachusetts Ave., NW., Rm. 402
Washington, D.C. 20036

JOINT WORKING GROUP FOR REFUGEES FROM LATIN AMERICA
21 Star St.
London W2 1QB, United Kingdom

JUSTICIA Y NO-VIOLENCIA. SECRETARIADO
Avenida Ipiranga 1267, 9º Andar
São Paulo, Brasil

LATIN AMERICA BUREAU
Box 134
London NW1 4JY, United Kingdom

Established in 1977 with the help of voluntary development agencies and church organizations. Attempts to raise public awareness concerning social, economic, political, and human rights issues in Latin America. Involved in research, the documentation of information, and the publicizing of human rights violations. Publishes the Annual Review of British-Latin American Relations as well as some occasional reports and research papers. Organizes seminars.

LATIN AMERICA RESEARCH UNIT
Box 673 Adelaine St.,
Toronto 1, Ont., Canada

Research center that focuses on human rights in Latin America from the point of view of the social sciences.

LATIN AMERICAN DOCUMENTATION CENTER
1312 Massachusetts Ave., NW.
Washington, D.C. 20005

Independent center that disseminates information on social rights in Latin America. Publishes the bimonthly LADOC and the monthly Latin America Calls.

LATIN AMERICAN REFUGEE SUPPORT COMMITTEE
107 West Indiana
Wheaton, Ill. 60187

LATIN AMERICAN SOLIDARITY COMMITTEE
Box 52115
Houston, Tex. 77052

LATIN AMERICAN SOLIDARITY FRONT
107 Harehill Ave.
Leeds 8, England

LATIN AMERICAN STUDIES ASSOCIATION
Institute of Latin American Studies
University of Texas
Austin, Tex. 78712

Promotes a better understanding of Latin America through the development of more effective teaching, training, and research methods. Publications include the Latin American Research Review issued thrice yearly, the quarterly LASA Newsletter, monographs, state-of-the-art reviews, abstracts, indexes, directories, bibliographies, data compilations, and reprints.

LATIN AMERICAN STUDIES ASSOCIATION. COMMITTEE ON ACADEMIC FREEDOM AND HUMAN RIGHTS
Institute of Latin American Studies
University of Texas
Austin, Tex. 78712

Supplies information to the LASA membership on academic freedom and human rights in Latin America. Sponsors resolutions concerning human rights at LASA meetings. Publishes reports on academic freedom in Argentina and Chile.

LATIN AMERICAN WOMEN'S GROUP
c/o Latin American Centre
16/17 Hoxton Square
London N1 6NT, United Kingdom

LATIN AMERICAN WORKING GROUP
Box 2207
Station P
M5S Toronto, Ont., Canada 2T2

Church organization interested in basic human needs and cultural, civil, and political rights. Involved in the dissemination of information and relief work.

LAWYERS COMMITTEE FOR INTERNATIONAL HUMAN RIGHTS
236 East 46th St.
New York, N.Y. 10017

Law resource center that provides services to human rights organizations. International in scope. Publishes the newsletter Lawyers Committee News.

LEADERSHIP CONFERENCE OF WOMEN RELIGIOUS OF THE USA
1302 18th St., NW., Suite 701
Washington, D.C. 20036

LETELIER-MOFFIT FUND FOR HUMAN RIGHTS
1901 Q St., NW.
Washington, D.C. 20009

Educational program funded by the Institute for Policy Studies. Examines violations of human rights in Latin America in general and in Chile in particular. Publishes a series of pamphlets on the human rights of indigenous people in the Americas. Distributes films. Maintains a speakers bureau.

LIBERATION
313315 Caledonian Road
London N1, United Kingdom

LIBERATION BRAZIL COMMITTEE
10 Rodrick Road
London NW3 2NL, United Kingdom

LIBERTY TO THE CAPTIVES
325 West Logan St.
Philadelphia, Pa. 19144

LOS ANGELES COMMITTEE FOR ACADEMICS IN PERIL
Chautauqua Blvd.
Pacific Palisades, Calif. 90272

Works closely with the Los Angeles Group for Latin American Solidarity.

LOS ANGELES GROUP FOR LATIN AMERICAN SOLIDARITY
c/o United Ministries of Higher Education
Box 32305
Los Angeles, Calif. 90032

Nongovernmental organization involved in legal work and in the promotion of cultural, civil, and political rights in Latin America.

LUTHERAN WORLD FEDERATION
Box 66
150 Route de Ferney
1211 Geneva 20, Switzerland

Church organization concerned with procedures pertaining to human rights. International in scope. Activities include research and—promotion. Works with other human rights groups.

LUTHERAN WORLD MINISTRIES
360 Park Ave., S.
New York, N.Y. 10010

Church organization involved in funding, relief work, and the coordination of human rights groups. Concerned primarily with religious freedom and with economic, social, cultural, civil, and political rights. International in scope.

MARYKNOLL CENTER FOR JUSTICE CONCERNS
110 Charles St.
Hingham, Mass. 02043

MEMBERS OF CONGRESS FOR PEACE THROUGH LAW. THE MCPL EDUCATION FUND
201 Massachusetts Ave., NE., Suite 318
Washington, D.C. 20002

Nonpartisan, nonprofit charitable and educational corporation governed by a Board of Directors. Dedicated to substituting law for war in human society, advancing human rights and equal justice under law for all people, and developing a global economy in which every person will be provided the material necessities of life and a reasonable opportunity for the pursuit of happiness. Interests include food, population, human rights, and international development. Has published New Directions in United States Foreign Policy, the Directory of Human Rights Organizations, and The United States and the Panama Canal: a New Beginning?

MINORITY RIGHTS GROUP
Benjamin Franklin House
36 Craven St.
London WC2N 5NG, United Kingdom

Nongovernmental organization interested in minority rights at the international level. Involved in research. Extends services to human rights groups.

MOVIMIENTO CRISTIANO POR LA PAZ
Falkenhoheweg 8
Box 1274
CH-3001 Berne, Switzerland

MOVIMIENTO ECUMENICO POR LOS DERECHOS HUMANOS
Yerbal 2451
Buenos Aires, Argentina

Interested in meeting basic human needs and in promoting cultural, civil, and political rights in Argentina. Publishes the bimonthly Informedh; Boletín Informativo del Movimiento Ecuménico por los Derechos Humanos.

MUJERES PARA EL DIALOGO/WOMEN IN DIALOGUE
Apdo. 579
Cuernavaca, Morelos, México

International group of Catholic women formed prior to the Third Conference of Latin American Bishops (Puebla, México, 1979). Provides a feminist perspective on such issues as birth control, human rights, and the ordination of women.

NATIONAL ACADEMY OF SCIENCES. COMMITTEE ON HUMAN RIGHTS
2101 Constitution Ave., NW.
Washington, D.C. 20418

NATIONAL ASSOCIATION OF HUMAN RIGHTS WORKERS
Box 1435
Durham, N.C. 27702

NATIONAL ASSOCIATION OF SOCIAL WORKERS
1425 H St.
Washington, D.C. 20005

NATIONAL CHILE CENTER
156 Fifth Ave.
New York, N.Y. 10010

Distributes materials and organizes support on behalf of a democratic Chile. Publishes informational pamphlets.

NATIONAL CONFERENCE OF BLACK LAWYERS
126 West 119th St.
New York, N.Y. 10026

NATIONAL COUNCIL OF CHURCHES. UNITED STATES. DIVISION OF OVERSEAS MINISTRIES. HUMAN RIGHTS OFFICE
475 Riverside Dr., Rm. 634
New York, N.Y. 10027

Church organization actively involved with human rights and religious freedom at the international level. Activities include research, dissemination of information, relief work, funding, and coordination of human rights groups.

NATIONAL ECUMENICAL COALITION, INC. OFFICE OF PUBLIC INFORMATION
Box 3554
Georgetown Station
Washington, D.C. 20007

Coalition of national and international religious organizations. Seeks to guarantee civil and constitutional rights globally. Goals include strengthening the United Nations and other international institutions, developing a world economy where each individual enjoys the material necessities of life, reducing world armaments, and defending human and civil rights secured by law. Publications include the newsletter NEC Today, monographs, technical reports, abstracts, indexes, bibliographies, directories, and reprints.

NATIONAL EDUCATION ASSOCIATION
1201 16th St., NW.
Washington, D.C. 20036

NATIONAL LAWYERS GUILD
853 Broadway, 17th Floor
New York, N.Y. 10003

NATIONAL LAWYERS GUILD. SUBCOMMITTEE ON ASYLUM AND REFUGEES OF THE IMMIGRATION PROJECT
c/o National Immigration Project
712 S. Grandview
Los Angeles, Calif. 90057

NATIONAL NETWORK IN SOLIDARITY WITH THE NICARAGUAN PEOPLE
1470 Irving St., NW.
Washington, D.C. 20010

Provides information concerning United States-Nicaraguan relations. Emphasis is on economic issues. Organizes the Week of Solidarity with Nicaragua.

NETWORK
1029 Vermont Ave., NW.
Washington, D.C. 20005

Religious organization of women that works on behalf of legislation for the poor. Publicizes human rights abuses in Nicaragua and El Salvador. Publishes the monthly Network Newsletter.

NEW DIRECTIONS
305 Massachusetts Ave., NE.
Washington, D.C. 20002

NEW ENGLAND HUMAN RIGHTS NETWORK
2161 Massachusetts Ave.
Cambridge, Mass. 02140

Quaker organization involved with human rights at the national and international level. Maintains a resource file. Publishes a monthly bulletin.

NEW TRANSCENTURY FOUNDATION. SECRETARIAT FOR WOMEN IN DEVELOPMENT
1789 Columbia Road, NW.
Washington, D.C. 20009

Sponsored partially by the U.S. Agency for International Development. Seeks to enhance the capacity of private and voluntary agencies to integrate women more fully and efficiently into their overseas programming. Maintains a collection of over 1,000 research studies on the status of women in the Third World. Publications include Development as if Women Mattered and An Annotated Bibliography with Third World Focus.

NEW YORK CIRCUS
Box 37
Times Square Station
New York, N.Y. 10036

Known also as the Center for the Interchange of Religious Concerns in the USA. Provides information to the Hispanic population of New York City concerning the Catholic Church in Latin America. Publishes the bimonthly Infor-Act Bulletin.

NEW YORK UNIVERSITY. CENTER FOR INTERNATIONAL STUDIES
40 Washington Square, S., Rm. 334
New York, N.Y. 10012

Center for international legal studies. Topics studied vary from year to year. Maintains a small collection of books, periodicals, and reports.

NEWSPAPER GUILD
1200 15th St., NW.
Washington, D.C. 20005

NICARAGUA SUPPORT FUND
c/o 20-21 Comton Terrace
London N1 2UN, United Kingdom

NON-INTERVENTION IN CHILE
Box 800
Berkeley, Calif. 94701

Supports Chilean resistance to the military junta. Publishes the bimonthly Chile Action Bulletin on Political Prisoners and Human Rights and the quarterly Chile Newsletter.

NORTH AMERICAN CONGRESS ON LATIN AMERICA
Box 57
Cathedral Station
New York, N.Y. 10025

Involved in the promotion of economic, social, civil, political, and minority rights in Latin America. Publishes the bimonthly newsletter NACLA Report on the Americas.

NOTICIAS ALIADAS
Apdo. 5594
Lima, Perú

Ecumenical information service.

NOVID
Amaliastraat 7
The Hague, Netherlands

Independent center concerned with human rights from the perspective of the social sciences. Involved in funding and promotion. International in scope.

OFFICE FOR POLITICAL PRISONERS AND HUMAN RIGHTS IN CHILE
Box 40605
San Francisco, Calif. 94140

Group in solidarity with political dissidents in Chile. Provides timely information on the human rights situation in Chile, helps coordinate the defense of political prisoners, and assists refugees. Publishes the monthly newsletter Chile Today.

ORGANIZACION CATHOLIQUE CANADIENNE. DEVELOPPEMENT ET LA PAIX
1452 Rue Drummond
Montreal, Que. H3G 1W2, Canada

ORGANIZATION FOR CHRISTIAN ACTION IN ARGENTINA
60 East 42nd St., Rm. 411
New York, N.Y. 10017

ORGANIZATION OF AMERICAN STATES. COLUMBUS MEMORIAL LIBRARY
17th St. and Constitution Ave., NW.
Washington, D.C. 20006

Areas of interest include history, culture, and the development of the OAS and the Inter-American system. Library holdings include 225,000 monographs, 2,500 periodicals, and approximately 150,000 OAS documents and publications. Library is open to the public.

ORGANIZATION OF AMERICAN STATES. IN-
TER-AMERICAN CHILDREN'S INSTITUTE
Avenida 8 de Octubre 2904
Montevideo, Uruguay

Areas of interest include children's rights, education, and family life. Maintains computer-
based information systems and data banks.
Publications include a quarterly bulletin, monographs, bibliographies, data compilations, and
reprints.

ORGANIZATION OF AMERICAN STATES. IN-
TER-AMERICAN COMMISSION ON HUMAN
RIGHTS
17th St. and Constitution Ave., NW.
Washington, D.C. 20006

Advises the OAS on human rights issues. Publications include an annual report to the General
Assembly and periodic reports on the situation of
human rights in individual countries.

ORGANIZATION OF AMERICAN STATES. IN-
TER-AMERICAN INDIGENOUS INSTITUTE
Niños Héroes No. 139
México 7, D.F., México

Represents 17 member countries. Requests,
collects, and distributes information on scientific
and legal issues concerning native American
populations. Initiates, directs, and coordinates
studies applicable to the solution of Indian
problems. Library has a collection of approximately 25,000 volumes and 30 journal subscrip-
tions. Publications include the quarterly América Indígena and its annual supplement Anuario
Indigenista as well as two series of books, the
Special Editions Series and the Social Anthropology Series.

OVERSEAS DEVELOPMENT COUNCIL
1717 Massachusetts Ave., NW.
Suite 501
Washington, D.C. 20036

Privately funded group that seeks to increase U.S.
understanding of the problems faced by developing countries and of the importance of these
countries to the United States. Areas of interest
include international development, new international economic order issues, and the inter-
dependence and dependency of basic human
needs. Publishes various series including the
Agenda for Action Series, the Development
Papers Series, the Communiques Series, the
Occasional Paper Series, and the Monograph
Series.

OVERSEAS PRESS CLUB. HUMAN RIGHTS
SUBCOMMITTEE OF THE FREEDOM OF THE
PRESS COMMITTEE
Hotel Biltmore
Madison Ave. and 43rd St.
New York, N.Y. 10017

OXFAM
274 Banbury Road
Oxford OX2 7DZ, United Kingdom

PANAMANIAN COMMITTEE FOR HUMAN
RIGHTS
607 G St., SW.
Washington, D.C. 20024

Nongovernmental organization concerned with
cultural, civil, and political rights in Panama.
Publishes Human Rights Watch approximately 4
times a year.

PARAGUAY COMMITTEE FOR HUMAN
RIGHTS
15 Burford Gardens
London N13 4LR, United Kingdom

PARAGUAY WATCH
Box 21061
Washington, D.C. 20009

Membership consists of ecumenical groups, human rights organizations, and interested American, European, and Latin American individuals. Involved in publicizing the status of human rights in Paraguay.

PARLIAMENTARY HUMAN RIGHTS GROUP
c/o Phillip Whitehead
House of Commons
London SW1A OAA, United Kingdom

PAX ROMANA
1 Route du Jura
BP 1062
1701 Fribourg, Switzerland

PEACE NEW
160 North 15th St.
Philadelphia, Pa. 19102

PEACE RESEARCH INSTITUTE
25 Dundana Ave.
Toronto, Ont., Canada

Independent research center that promotes the peaceful coexistence of nations.

P.E.N.
American Center
47 Fifth Ave.
New York, N.Y. 10003

International association of professional writers interested in the censorship, imprisonment, torture, and disappearance of artists. Maintains offices in Argentina, Brazil, Chile, Honduras, and Paraguay. Activities include the sponsorship of international writers' conferences on freedom of expression. Publishes P.E.N. Newsletter, P.E.N. in Exile, and special country reports.

PEOPLE'S TRANSLATION SERVICE
2490 Channing Way
Berkeley, Calif. 94704

Attempts to inform the U.S. public concerning Third World issues. Provides timely translations of articles from the foreign press. Publishes an illustrated packet each week.

PERMANENT ASSEMBLY FOR HUMAN RIGHTS IN ARGENTINA
Paraná 638, 2º Piso
Buenos Aires, Argentina

Nongovernmental organization involved in the promotion and the defense of cultural, civil, and political rights in Argentina.

PLANETARY CITIZENS
777 United Nations Plaza
New York, N.Y. 10017

POLITICAL SCIENTIST'S COMMITTEE FOR HUMAN RIGHTS
c/o Professor Harry M. Scoble
1502 Ogden St., NW.
Washington, D.C. 20010

PONTIFICIA COMISION JUSTICIA PAZ
Palazzo San Calisto
Vatican City State

Precursor to the Commissions on Justice and Peace established by the Catholic Church. Publishes voluminously.

QUAKER OFFICE OF THE UNITED NATIONS
345 East 46th St.
New York, N.Y. 10017

Nongovernmental organization engaged in relief services. Disseminates information concerning human rights procedures. International in scope.

RAND CORPORATION. LIBRARY
1700 Main St.
Santa Monica, Calif. 90406

Nonprofit research organization specializing in policy analysis, human resources, and communications policy. Library holdings include approximately 63,000 books, 225,000 reports, and 15,000 periodicals. Maintains a computerized data base on books and reports. Publications include bibliographies, accessions lists, and special subject catalogs.

RECHTSHULP CHILI
Europa Institut
Janskerkhof 16
Utrecht, Netherlands

Nongovernmental research and funding organization that focuses on human rights from the points of view of politics, law, and the social sciences. Chilean in scope.

RETAIL CLERKS INTERNATIONAL UNION
Suffrage Bldg.
1775 K St., NW.
Washington, D.C. 20006

SAN DIEGO FRIENDS OF NON-INTERVENTION IN CHILE
Box 3
3564
San Diego, Calif. 92103

SECRETARIADO LATINOAMERICANO DE DERECHOS HUMANOS
Apdo. 8066
Caracas 104, Venezuela

Private research center that promotes economic, social, cultural, civil, and political rights in Latin America.

SECRETARIAT INTERNATIONAL DE JURISTES POUR L'AMNISTIE EN URUGUAY
11 Rue Jean de Beauvais
75005 Paris, France

Supported by 100 jurists in 25 countries. Works to promote an international concern for the protection of human rights in Uruguay.

SERVAS INTERNATIONAL
268 W. 12th St.
New York, N.Y. 10014

SERVICIO DE INFORMACIONES RELIGIOSAS
Camacuá 282-1406
Buenos Aires, Argentina

Information service located in Argentina's principal Protestant seminary.

SERVICIO PARA LA ACCIÓN LIBERADORA EN AMERICA LATINA-ORIENTACION NO-VIOLENTA
México 479
1097
Buenos Aires, Argentina

SERVICIO PAZ Y JUSTICIA EN AMERICA LATINA
México 479
1097
Buenos Aires, Argentina

Promotes human rights in Latin America. Publishes the monthly information bulletin Paz y Justicia. The director was awarded the Nobel Peace Prize in 1980.

SOJOURNERS FELLOWSHIP
1343 Euclid St., NW.
Washington, D.C. 20009

SOLIDARIDAD LATINOAMERICA
Laan van Meerdervort 148
The Hague, Netherlands

Nongovernmental organization that focuses on basic needs and cultural, civil, and political rights in Latin America. Involved in research, relief services, and funding.

SOLIDARITY COMMISSION OF RELATIVES OF THE KILLED, DISAPPEARED, AND IMPRISONED IN ARGENTINA
c/o Rev. Maurice Keane
St. Aloysius Church
Phoenix Road
London NW1 1TA, United Kingdom

SOLIDARITY COMMITTEE WITH POLITICAL PRISONERS IN MEXICO
c/o Centro Ibérico
421 Harrow Rd.
London W9, United Kingdom

SOLIDARITY WITH CHILE COMMITTEE
c/o Community Action on Latin America
731 State St.
Madison, Wis. 53703

National network supporting dissidents in Chile. Involved in community education.

STATE UNIVERSITY OF NEW YORK AT BINGHAMTON. CENTER FOR SOCIAL ANALYSIS
Binghamton, N.Y. 13901

Facilitates, coordinates, and supports cross national and comparative policy research in the social sciences and related disciplines. Library holdings consist of a computerized (magnetic tape and disk) data archive of longitudinal aggregate data embracing some 200 variables for virtually all independent nation-states for the period 1815-1978. Data provide quantitative information on a variety of phenomena such as population, social welfare, and politics. Publishes handbooks and reports.

STICHTUNG X-Y
Amaliastraat 7
The Hague, Netherlands

Nongovernmental organization involved with funding basic human needs at the international level.

STUDY CENTER OF DEVELOPMENT IN LATIN AMERICA
B.P. 124
75663 Paris Cedex 12, France

Independent research center that focuses on human rights in Latin America from the perspective of history the social sciences.

SURVIVAL INTERNATIONAL
36 Craven St.
London WC2N 5NG, United Kingdom

TRADE UNION COMMITTEE FOR INTERNATIONAL COOPERATION AND DEVELOPMENT
Link International
WDM Bedford Chambers
London WC2, United Kingdom

TRANSNATIONAL INSTITUTE
1901 Q St., NW.
Washington, D.C. 20009

Founded in 1973 as the international arm of the Institute for Policy Studies. Topics of study include international economics and human rights.

TRIBUNAL BERTRAND RUSSELL
Via Della Dogana Vecchia
5-00186 Rome, Italy

TROCAIRE
169 Booterston Ave.
Dublin, Ireland

Church organization concerned with basic human needs at the international level. Principal activity is funding.

TUCSON COMMITTE FOR HUMAN RIGHTS IN LATIN AMERICA
Box 42621
Tucson, Ariz. 85733

Analyzes Latin American political issues and U.S. involvement in the domestic politics of its southern neighbors. Activities include the sponsorship of cultural events and the resettlement of political prisoners.

TWIN CITIES CHILE RESISTANCE COMMITTEE
Box 14248
Minneapolis, Minn. 55414

Works for an end to political repression in Chile. Publishes the bulletin Pan y Agua.

UNION DOMINICANA PARA LA DEFENSA DE LOS DERECHOS HUMANOS
30 de Marzo No. 57
Santo Domingo, Dominican Republic

Concerned with Haitian migration as well as human rights violations in the Dominican Republic.

UNITARIAN UNIVERSALIST ASSOCIATION. UNITED NATIONS OFFICE
777 United Nations Plaza, Rm. 7D
New York, N.Y. 10017

UNITARIAN UNIVERSALIST SERVICE COMMISSION
78 Beacon St.
Boston, Mass. 02108

Has focused since 1977 on human rights violations in El Salvador and Guatemala. Activities include dissemination of information and relief efforts.

UNITED AUTO WORKERS.INTERNATIONAL AFFAIRS DEPT.
1125 15th St., NW.
Washington, D.C. 20005

UNITED CHURCH OF CANADA
85 St. Clair Ave., E.
Toronto, Ont., Canada M4T IM8

Church organization that promotes basic human needs in the Americas. Disseminates information and provides funding and relief services.

UNITED METHODIST CHURCH. WOMEN'S DIVISION. BOARD OF GLOBAL MINISTRIES
475 Riverside Dr., 15th Floor
New York, N.Y. 10027

U.N. DAG HAMMARSKJOLD LIBRARY
New York, N.Y. 10017

Areas of interest include international law, area studies, human ecology and the environment, political institutions and organizations, social welfare, and economics. Geographic coverage is worldwide. Library holdings consist of 380,000 monographs, 15,000 serials, 160,000 microforms, 70,000 maps, 250 newspapers, a complete collection of U.N. documents and publications, and a selective collection of publications from other organizations within the U.N. system. All library holdings were issued after 1918.

U.N. DEPT. OF PUBLIC INFORMATION. UNITED NATIONS INFORMATION CENTRE
2101 L St., NW., Suite 209
Washington, D.C. 20037

Attempts to improve the understanding of the work of the U.N. Library collection includes publications and documents issued by the U.N. and its subsidiary bodies, but does not include the documents of the specialized U.N. agencies.Serves as a liaison to the U.S. government and cooperates with nongovernmental organizations in the dissemination of information concerning U.N. related issues.

U.N. DIVISION OF HUMAN RIGHTS
Palais des Nations
CH-1211 Geneva 10, Switzerland

Interested primarily in the impact of modern scientific and technological developments on human rights. Publishes documents.

U.N. STATISTICAL OFFICE OF THE UNITED NATIONS
New York, N.Y. 10017

Develops systems in selected fields of statistics. Provides technical cooperation to developing countries and coordinates the statistical activities of the U.N. Maintains computerized statistical data bases from which several of the Statistical Office's publications are produced.

U.N.E.S.C.O. GENERAL INFORMATION PROGRAMME DIVISION. SCIENTIFIC AND TECHNOLOGICAL DOCUMENTATION AND INFORMATION
7 Place de Fontenoy
75700 Paris, France

Promotes worldwide cooperation concerning scientific and technological information. Areas of interest include the development and coordination of information systems and services at the national, regional, and international levels. Publications include the UNISIST Newsletter four times a year, guidelines, reports, and directories.

U.N.E.S.C.O. DIVISION FOR THE INTERNATIONAL DEVELOPMENT OF THE SOCIAL SCIENCES.SOCIAL SCIENCES DOCUMENTATION CENTRE AND "DARE" DATA BANK
7 Place de Fontenoy
75700 Paris, France

Organizes the processing and handling of data pertaining to U.N.E.S.C.O. Serves as a source for the development of social science reference works. Developed DARE, a system which surveys the social science resources and skills of U.N. member states.

UNITED NATIONS ASSOCIATION, ENGLAND
3 Whitehall Court
London SW1A 2EL, United Kingdom

UNITED NATIONS ASSOCIATION, U.S.A.
300 E. 42nd St.
New York, N.Y. 10017

UNITED PRESBYTERIAN CHURCH. UNITED STATES
Unit on Church and Society
475 Riverside Dr., Rm. 1244K
New York, N.Y. 10027

U.S. AGENCY FOR INTERNATIONAL DEVELOPMENT. OFFICE FOR POLICY DEVELOPMENT AND PROGRAM REVIEW. DIVISION OF THE BUREAU FOR PROGRAM AND POLICY COORDINATION
Washington, D.C. 20523

U.S. DEPT. OF STATE. OFFICE OF HUMAN RIGHTS. BUREAU OF HUMAN RIGHTS AND HUMANITARIAN AFFAIRS
Washington, D.C. 20520

U.S. DEPT. OF STATE. OFFICE OF HUMAN RIGHTS. BUREAU OF INTERNATIONAL ORGANIZATION AFFAIRS
Washington, D.C. 20520

U.S. DEPT. OF THE TREASURY. OFFICE OF INTERNATIONAL AFFAIRS. INTERNATIONAL DEVELOPMENT BANKS
Washington, D.C. 20220

U.S. NATIONAL COMMISSION FOR U.N.E.S.C.O.
U.S. Dept. of State
Washington, D.C. 20520

U.S. SMITHSONIAN INSTITUTION
Washington, D.C. 20560

Joint public and private undertaking, the interests of which include foreign policy and historical studies. Maintains a collections of approximately 10,000 books and reports, and 500 periodicals and newspapers.

UNITED STATES CATHOLIC CONFERENCE. DIVISION FOR LATIN AMERICA
1430 K St., NW.
Washington, D.C. 20005

Disseminates news from Latin America related to human rights.

UNITED STATES CATHOLIC CONFERENCE. OFFICE OF INTERNATIONAL JUSTICE AND PEACE
1312 Massachusetts Ave., NW.
Washington, D.C. 20005

Promotes human rights in the Americas. Involved in teaching, research, and relief activities. Publications include several booklets.

UNITED STATES COMMITTEE ON LATIN AMERICA
853 Broadway, Suite 414
New York, N.Y. 10003

Civil liberties organization that defends victims of political repression in Latin America. Seeks to mobilize public opinion against U.S. involvement with totalitarian regimes. Publishes the quarterly USLA Reporter.

UNITED STATES INSTITUTE OF HUMAN RIGHTS, INC.
200 Park Ave., 13th Floor
New York, N.Y. 10017

Nonprofit organization that jointly sponsors seminars with the American Society of International Law. Assists persons to participate in the annual teaching sessions of the International Institute of Human Rights in Strasbourg, France. Interested primarily in research and education regarding human rights.

UNITED STATES MISSION TO THE UNITED NATIONS
799 United Nations Plaza
New York, N.Y. 10017

UNIVERSAL HUMAN RIGHTS
875 Avenue of the Americas
New York, N.Y. 10001

Nongovernmental organization that disseminates human rights information at the international level. Publishes the quarterly journal Universal Human Rights.

UNIVERSITY OF AKRON. CENTER FOR PEACE STUDIES
Akron, Ohio 44325

UNIVERSITY OF MARYLAND. CENTER FOR PHILOSOPHY AND PUBLIC POLICY
Woods Hall
College Park, Md. 20742

Engages in research and curriculum development. Interested in the conceptual and ethical aspects of public policy formulation and debate. One of the areas of interest is human rights. Publications include books, journal articles, and working papers. Center answers inquiries, conducts seminars, and distributes publications.

UNIVERSITY OF MINNESOTA. INTERNATIONAL HUMAN RIGHTS INTERNSHIP PROGRAM
c/o David Weissbrodt
University of Minnesota Law School
Minneapolis, Minn. 55455

UNIVERSITY OF NOTRE DAME. LAW SCHOOL. CENTER FOR CIVIL RIGHTS
South Bend, Ind. 46556

Research institution concerned with human rights from the juridical point of view. Intends to develop a major research and documentation center on this subject. Library holdings include the Rev. Theodore M. Hesburgh Collection, books on domestic and international rights, and the card catalog of the U.S. Commission on Civil Rights. Publishes two bibliographies on international human rights.

URUGUAY INFORMATION PROJECT
110 Maryland Ave., NE.
Washington, D.C. 20002

Conducts educational campaigns on the status of political and social rights in Uruguay. Publications include a newsletter and occasional reports.

VICTOR SANABRIA CENTER. AREA OF DOCUMENTATION AND INVESTIGATION
Box 472
Centro Colón
San José, Costa Rica

Independent research center involved in studying human rights in Central America from the point of view of the social sciences.

WAR ON WANT
467 Caledonian Rd.
London N7 9BE, United Kingdom

Nongovernmental organization concerned with basic human needs at the international level. Activities include teaching, research, dissemination of materials, relief services, and funding.

WASHINGTON COMMITTEE FOR HUMAN RIGHTS IN ARGENTINA
Box 19102
Washington, D.C. 20006

WASHINGTON OFFICE ON LATIN AMERICA
110 Maryland Ave.
Washington, D.C. 20002

Established in 1974 by a broad coalition of church people and scholars interested in Latin America. Disseminates data about Latin American and United States foreign policy. Publishes the monthly Update Latin America and the irregular Special Update Latin America.

WESTERN MASSACHUSETTS CHILE SOLIDARITY COMMITTEE
Box 267
Hadley, Mass. 01035

WOMEN STRIKE FOR PEACE
145 South 13th St.
Philadelphia, Pa. 19017

WOMEN'S INTERNATIONAL INFORMATION AND COMMUNICATION SERVICE
5 Route des Acacias
1227 Geneva, Switzerland

Nongovernmental organization that provides services to human rights groups concerned with minority rights at the international level.

WOMEN'S INTERNATIONAL LEAGUE FOR PEACE AND FREEDOM
1213 Race St.
Philadelphia, Pa. 19107

WOMEN'S INTERNATIONAL NETWORK
187 Grant St.
Lexington, Mass. 02173

WORLD ALLIANCE OF REFORMED CHURCHES
150 Route de Ferney
1211 Geneva 20, Switzerland

WORLD CONFERENCE ON RELIGION AND PEACE
777 United Nations Plaza
New York, N.Y. 10017

International nongovernmental organization that has consultative status with the Economic and Social Council of the United Nations.

WORLD COUNCIL OF CHURCHES. COMMISSION OF THE CHURCHES ON INTERNATIONAL AFFAIRS
Box 66
150 Route de Ferney
1211 Geneva 20, Switzerland

Church organization that coordinates human rights groups at the international level.

WORLD COUNCIL OF CHURCHES. OFFICE ON HUMAN RIGHTS RESOURCES FOR LATIN AMERICA
777 United Nations Plaza
New York, N.Y. 10017

Ecumenical organization concerned with basic human needs, religious freedom, and minority rights in Latin America. Provides relief services and funding. Coordinates human rights groups.

WORLD FEDERALISTS ASSOCIATION
Arlington Towers, Suite W-219
1011 Arlington Blvd.
Arlington, Va. 22209

Nonprofit organization that advocates world order through world government. Publications include the World Federalist Newsletter and occasional papers.

WORLD PEACE THROUGH LAW CENTER
1000 Connecticut Ave., NW., Suite 800
Washington, D.C. 20036

Nongovernment organization devoted to the continued development of international law and to the legal maintenance of world order. Sponsors the biennial World Conference, the World Law Day, and various demonstration trials. Involved in research and publishing. Three associations are affiliated with the Center: the World Association of Judges, the World Association of Lawyers, and the World Association of Law Professors. Areas of interest include world peace through law and the use of law to resolve human rights disputes. Publishes the bimonthly World Jurist, the World Law Review, and a pamphlet series.

WORLD WITHOUT WAR COUNCIL
175 Fifth Ave.
New York, N.Y. 10010

Interested in establishing pacifism as a guiding force in American life. Involved with training public, private, and church school teachers concerning human rights. Publishes the International Human Rights Kit. Distributes human rights books and materials.